Environmental, Social and Governance Accounting and Auditing

In a rapidly evolving world where environmental, social, and governance (ESG) considerations are at the forefront of business and investment decisions, understanding the intricate interplay between ESG factors and corporate performance is paramount. This book demystifies ESG by providing empirical insights from the perspective of China, shedding light on the impact of ESG on financial performance and corporate governance. It investigates the impact of environmental expertise, social variability, and board governance model on firm performance.

The book sets the stage by introducing the reader to the significance of ESG in today's corporate world, examining empirical evidence gathered from a decade of data analysis on Chinese listed companies. It explores how ESG practices influence corporate financial performance and what role audit plays in this equation. Drawing from a wealth of data, it provides practical insights into the effects of ESG disclosure, ownership structures, corporate governance, and more on the performance of businesses. It offers a clear understanding of the empirical realities in China while addressing a global audience interested in harnessing ESG for sustainable corporate success. It provides valuable lessons and comparisons that can benefit readers beyond China's borders.

The book bridges the gap between research and practice, translating complex research findings into actionable recommendations, enhancing its appeal to both academic and professional audiences. It is a must-read for scholars, students, and researchers seeking actionable insights into the world of ESG. Furthermore, it discusses ESG practice and policy implications, offering recommendations for stakeholders, including policymakers, investors, managers, and auditors.

Tarek Rana is an associate professor of accounting at RMIT University, Melbourne, Australia.

Md Jahidur Rahman is an assistant professor of accounting at Wenzhou-Kean University, Wenzhou, China.

Peter Öhman is a professor and head of business administration at Mid Sweden University and director of the Centre for Research on Economic Relations (CER).

Routledge Studies in Accounting

54. Accounting, Accountability and Crisis Management
Lessons from Italy's Pandemic Response
Edited by Ericka Costa, Massimo Contrafatto and Lee Parker

55. Earnings Management and Corporate Finance
The Importance of Transparent Financial Reporting
Edited by Joanna Lizińska, Marzena Remlein and Leszek Czapiewski

56. Long-Term Financial Sustainability Accounting and Reporting in the Public Sector
Hassan Ouda

57. Sustainability Reporting and Blockchain Technology
Edited by Harjit Singh, Neha Puri and Nandita Mishra

58. International Financial Reporting Standards in the MENA Region
Adaptation and Application in Morocco
Issam Benhayoun

59. Accounting for Carbon Neutrality
Corporate Accountability in the Hydrogen Economy
Assunta Di Vaio and Tayyab Ali

60. Carbon Accounting for Sustainability and Environmental Management
Case Studies from China
Edited by Tarek Rana, Md Jahidur Rahman and Peter Öhman

61. Environmental, Social and Governance Accounting and Auditing
Perspectives from China
Edited by Tarek Rana, Md Jahidur Rahman and Peter Öhman

For more information about this series, please visit www.routledge.com/Routledge-Studies-in-Accounting/book-series/SE0715

Environmental, Social and Governance Accounting and Auditing

Perspectives from China

Edited by Tarek Rana,
Md Jahidur Rahman
and Peter Öhman

Routledge
Taylor & Francis Group
LONDON AND NEW YORK

First published 2025
by Routledge
4 Park Square, Milton Park, Abingdon, Oxon OX14 4RN

and by Routledge
605 Third Avenue, New York, NY 10158

Routledge is an imprint of the Taylor & Francis Group, an informa business

British Library Cataloguing-in-Publication Data
A catalogue record for this book is available from the British Library

ISBN: 978-1-032-78673-5 (hbk)
ISBN: 978-1-032-78676-6 (pbk)
ISBN: 978-1-003-48893-4 (ebk)

DOI: 10.4324/9781003488934

Typeset in Times New Roman
by Apex CoVantage, LLC

Tarek Rana dedicates this book to his wife, Afsana Siddique, in recognition of her unconditional love, boundless inspiration, and continuous support throughout his career.

Md Jahidur Rahman dedicates this book to his beloved wife, Rakiba Sultana, with deep thanks for her endless love and support, which have been a steady source of strength and inspiration throughout his life.

Peter Öhman dedicates this book to his family and friends in gratitude for their unwavering love, steadfast encouragement, and constant support, which have been his foundation throughout his academic journey and life.

Contents

Tables

Editor Bios

Tarek Rana is an associate professor of accounting at RMIT University, Melbourne, Australia. Tarek earned a PhD at the UNSW Australia, an MBA from the University of Saskatchewan, and BCom (Hons.) and MCom from the University of Dhaka, Bangladesh. He is an FCPA (Certified Practising Accountants, Australia), ACMA (Chartered Institute of Management Accountants, UK), and CA (Chartered Accountants Australia and New Zealand). Tarek Rana teaches and researches the intersection of accounting and digitalization with a focus on risk management, performance measurement, public management, and sustainability. His research works have earned recognitions such as Dean's Award and College's Award for research excellence. He has edited many research books and guest-edited special issues in reputed journals. He has published in reputable accounting and management research journals, including *Accounting Auditing & Accountability Journal*; *British Accounting Review*; *Financial Accountability & Management*; *Public Money & Management*; *Business Strategy and the Environment*; *Intelligent Systems in Accounting, Finance and Management*; *Meditari Accountancy Research*; *Qualitative Research in Accounting & Management*; *Sustainability Accounting, Management and Policy Journal*; the *Journal of Intellectual Capital*; the *Journal of Accounting & Organizational Change*; and the *International Journal of Managerial and Financial Accounting*. Further to his academic record, Tarek Rana is a chartered accountant and chartered management accountant and has a professional record of accomplishment, including partnership in accounting firms, board membership, and governance experience as both executive and non-executive director.

Md Jahidur Rahman is an assistant professor of accounting at Wenzhou-Kean University in Wenzhou, China. He earned a PhD in accountancy from the City University of Hong Kong, an MBA in business management from Ritsumeikan Asia Pacific University in Japan, and a BBA (Hons.) and MBA in accounting from the University of Dhaka in Bangladesh. He is a Certified Practising Accountant (Australia). His exceptional contributions to education have earned him several accolades, including the Excellence in Teaching Award, the Most Dedicative Professor Award, and the Advanced Educator Award from the Wenzhou Education Bureau in China. He has edited numerous research books and has published in leading accounting and management research journals, including the *British Accounting Review*, *Accounting & Finance*, the *International Journal of Auditing*, the *Journal of Contemporary Accounting and Economics*, *Advances in Accounting*, *Meditari Accountancy Research*, the *Managerial Auditing Journal*, Oxford University Press, the *Journal of Family Business Management*, the *International Journal of Accounting & Information Management*, *Corporate Governance*, and *Business Ethics, the Environment & Responsibility*.

Peter Öhman is a professor and head of business administration at Mid Sweden University and director of the Centre for Research on Economic Relations (CER). His research focuses on behavioural issues, primarily in accounting and auditing, but also in the banking and property industries. He has published a significant number of scholarly articles in leading academic journals, for example, *Contemporary Accounting Research* and *Behavioural Research in Accounting*. He has edited and published books, book chapters, and reports and presented papers at numerous international conferences. He is a member of editorial boards and a reviewer of several well-known international journals. He has earned several scientific and educational accolades, and he supervises several doctoral student projects.

Notes on Contributors

Tongshu Cen graduated from the Department of Accounting at the College of Business and Public Management, Wenzhou-Kean University, a Sino-American university affiliated with Kean University, NJ, USA.

Hanqi He graduated from the Department of Accounting at the College of Business and Public Management, Wenzhou-Kean University, a Sino-American university affiliated with Kean University, NJ, USA.

Yu Jiayi graduated from the Department of Accounting at the College of Business and Public Management, Wenzhou-Kean University, a Sino-American university affiliated with Kean University, NJ, USA.

Sajjad Khan has been working in the Australian higher education sector for more than 20 years and has worked in five Australian universities (University of Melbourne, Charles Sturt University, La Trobe University, Federation University at MIT and ATMC, and Charles Darwin University at ATMC, Melbourne) and three universities overseas (University of Dhaka, The People's University of Bangladesh, and Bangladesh University of Engineering and Technology). He has taught a range of accounting subjects for both undergraduate and postgraduate programs, including auditing and assurance services, forensic accounting, external reporting, financial accounting, accounting systems and processes, management accounting for costs and control, strategic and sustainable accounting, and decision support tools. He has taught students from diverse academic and socio-economic backgrounds and is thoroughly familiar with a full range of educational backgrounds, needs, and aspirations. He holds an excellent rank for his teaching according to student evaluations and is popular among the student body. He also has significant experience in academic leadership roles. He is also focusing on a strong research and publication record and has published several research articles in national and international refereed and professional journals. He has a strong interest to do research on accounting and organizational change, public sector accounting, accountability and sustainable performance, management accounting, and control systems. He is enthusiastic about collaboration with a broader academic network to actively learn and grow.

Binqing Lu graduated from the Department of Accounting at the College of Business and Public Management, Wenzhou-Kean University, a Sino-American university affiliated with Kean University, NJ, USA.

Chenyu Mao graduated from the Department of Accounting at the College of Business and Public Management, Wenzhou-Kean University, a Sino-American university affiliated with Kean University, NJ, USA.

Chen Pinrun graduated from the Department of Accounting at the College of Business and Public Management, Wenzhou-Kean University, a Sino-American university affiliated with Kean University, NJ, USA.

Chong Shi graduated from the Department of Accounting at the College of Business and Public Management, Wenzhou-Kean University, a Sino-American university affiliated with Kean University, NJ, USA.

Yuxin Song graduated from the Department of Accounting at the College of Business and Public Management, Wenzhou-Kean University, a Sino-American university affiliated with Kean University, NJ, USA.

Zhang Tianyu graduated from the Department of Accounting at the College of Business and Public Management, Wenzhou-Kean University, a Sino-American university affiliated with Kean University, NJ, USA.

Tong Wu graduated from the Department of Accounting at the College of Business and Public Management, Wenzhou-Kean University, a Sino-American university affiliated with Kean University, NJ, USA.

Wang Xinyi graduated from the Department of Accounting at the College of Business and Public Management, Wenzhou-Kean University, a Sino-American university affiliated with Kean University, NJ, USA.

Xuxiaohui graduated from the Department of Accounting at the College of Business and Public Management, Wenzhou-Kean University, a Sino-American university affiliated with Kean University, NJ, USA.

Wang Yujing graduated from the Department of Accounting at the College of Business and Public Management, Wenzhou-Kean University, a Sino-American university affiliated with Kean University, NJ, USA.

Hongtao Zhu is a PhD student in the Department of Accountancy at the City University of Hong Kong. His research has been published in journals including British Accounting Review, Managerial Auditing Journal, Accounting & Finance, Journal of Contemporary Accounting & Economics, Advances in Accounting, and Meditari Accountancy Research. He is also a reviewer for academic journals in his field.

Lingna Zhuge graduated from the Department of Accounting at the College of Business and Public Management, Wenzhou-Kean University, a Sino-American university affiliated with Kean University, NJ, USA.

Chen Zhuo graduated from the Department of Accounting at the College of Business and Public Management, Wenzhou-Kean University, a Sino-American university affiliated with Kean University, NJ, USA.

Preface

In the rapidly evolving global landscape, environmental, social, and governance (ESG) considerations have emerged as critical determinants of corporate success and sustainability. The intersection of ESG factors with financial performance, corporate governance, and auditing practices has garnered significant attention from academicians, policymakers, and industry professionals alike. This book, *Environmental Social and Governance Accounting and Auditing: Perspectives from China*, edited by Tarek Rana, Md Jahidur Rahman, and Peter Öhman, provides a comprehensive exploration of these themes within the unique context of Chinese enterprises.

China's economic transformation over the past few decades has positioned it as a pivotal player in the global market. As Chinese companies increasingly engage with international stakeholders, the integration of ESG principles into their business practices becomes paramount. This volume offers empirical insights drawn from extensive research on Chinese listed companies, shedding light on the nuanced interplay between ESG performance and various aspects of corporate governance and financial outcomes.

The chapters in this book are meticulously curated to provide a robust framework for understanding how ESG factors influence corporate behaviour and performance. The research presented delves into the impacts of board governance models, ownership structures, and audit quality on ESG ratings and financial performance. Additionally, it addresses critical issues such as the role of ESG in mitigating financial distress and enhancing investment efficiency.

One of the distinguishing features of this book is its empirical approach, leveraging data from a decade-long study of Chinese A-share listed companies. The findings presented here are not only academically rigorous but also offer practical implications for a wide range of stakeholders, including investors, policymakers, managers, and auditors. By examining the relationship between ESG practices and corporate financial performance, this book provides actionable insights that can inform decision-making processes and foster sustainable business practices.

The importance of ESG considerations is further underscored by the global challenges posed by climate change, social inequalities, and governance failures. In this context, China's experiences and approaches to integrating ESG principles offer valuable lessons for the international community. This book serves as a vital resource for those seeking to understand the complexities of ESG accounting and auditing within one of the world's most dynamic economies.

We extend our gratitude to the contributors who have provided their invaluable expertise and insights to this volume. Their research not only enhances our understanding of ESG practices in China but also contributes to the broader discourse on sustainable development. We also acknowledge the support of our academic institutions and the reviewers whose feedback has enriched the quality of this work. We hope that this book will inspire further research and dialogue on ESG issues and encourage the adoption of practices that promote corporate sustainability and accountability. As we navigate the challenges and opportunities of the 21st century, the integration of ESG principles into business strategies will be crucial for building a more sustainable and equitable future.

Part 1

Corporate Governance and ESG Performance

1 ESG Accounting for Performance Measurement, Risk Management, and Accountability

Tarek Rana, Md Jahidur Rahman, and Peter Öhman

1. Introduction

In a rapidly evolving world where environmental, social, and governance (ESG) considerations are at the forefront of business and investment decisions, the intricate interplay between ESG factors and corporate performance is paramount. The concept of ESG accounting has evolved significantly over the past decade. Initially driven by regulatory requirements and investor demands, ESG accounting now encompasses a broader range of corporate activities, including environmental stewardship, social responsibility, and governance practices. The integration of ESG factors into financial reporting has been influenced by frameworks such as the Global Reporting Initiative (GRI) and the Sustainability Accounting Standards Board (SASB).

This book demystifies ESG by providing empirical evidence gathered from a decade of data analysis on Chinese listed companies, shedding light on the impact of ESG on financial performance and corporate governance. It further explores how ESG practices influence corporate financial performance (CFP) and what role audit quality plays in this equation. Drawing from a wealth of data, it provides practical insights into the effects of ESG disclosure, ownership structures, corporate governance, and more on the performance of businesses.

The aim is to provide a comprehensive exploration of the interplay among ESG factors, CFP, and auditing practices within the context of Chinese companies. The book delves into several key themes and objectives:

- Accounting and Audit Quality: It explores the role of accounting and audit quality as a moderating factor in the relationship between ESG performance and financial outcomes, shedding light on how audit practices can influence the outcomes of ESG integration.
- Empirical Insights on Performance and Corporate Governance: It is distinctive in its empirical approach, drawing on extensive data from Chinese A-share listed companies spanning several years, providing data-driven insights into the relationship between ESG factors and corporate performance.
- Practice and Policy Implications: It discusses ESG practice and policy implications, offering recommendations for stakeholders including policymakers,

DOI: 10.4324/9781003488934-2

investors, managers, and auditors. It contributes to the discourse on how ESG practices can be enhanced to drive sustainable development.

- ESG in the Chinese Context: It seeks to offer a deep understanding of how ESG considerations are integrated into the corporate landscape of China, which is of increasing global significance.

The book not only explores the evolving landscape of ESG accounting, auditing, and performance management but also offers actionable insights into how these factors impact CFP, all within the distinctive backdrop of China's corporate environment. The empirical approach, coupled with practical policy recommendations, makes it valuable for academicians, professionals, and policymakers seeking comprehensive knowledge of ESG practices in China and their implications for corporate success and sustainability.

2. Literature Review

ESG accounting has become a critical component of sustainability management and accountability within organizations. This initial literature review emphasizes recent scholarly work from accounting journals to explore the frameworks, methodologies, and impacts of ESG accounting on corporate sustainability practices. The focus is on understanding how ESG factors are integrated into accounting systems, the challenges faced, and the implications for corporate governance and performance.

Effective ESG reporting facilitates engagement with a broad range of stakeholders, including investors, customers, employees, and regulators. By addressing stakeholder concerns and demonstrating commitment to sustainability, organizations can build stronger, more resilient relationships. The GRI is among the most widely adopted ESG reporting frameworks, emphasizing transparency and accountability in sustainability reporting. The GRI framework provides guidelines for reporting on a wide range of ESG metrics, enabling organizations to communicate their sustainability performance effectively. SASB focuses on the financial materiality of ESG factors, tailored to specific industries. By aligning sustainability reporting with investor interests, these standards facilitate the integration of ESG information into financial analysis and decision-making processes. Comoli et al. (2023) explored how disruptions like the COVID-19 pandemic have affected ESG reporting. They use a systematic literature network analysis (SLNA) to examine the evolution of ESG reporting and its role in improving corporate governance and accountability. Jebe (2019) investigated the convergence of financial and ESG materiality, noting that the SASB attempts to merge sustainability and financial information to address the regulatory gap left by the Security Exchange Commission's (SEC's) inaction on sustainability reporting. As regulatory requirements for ESG disclosure continue to evolve, ESG accounting ensures compliance with local and international regulations. This compliance not only avoids legal penalties but also positions companies as leaders in corporate governance and sustainability.

ESG accounting helps organizations identify and manage ESG-related risks. By integrating ESG factors into risk assessment and management processes, companies can mitigate potential negative impacts and capitalize on sustainability opportunities. The International Integrated Reporting Council (IIRC) promotes integrated reporting, which combines financial and non-financial information into a single report. This approach aims to provide a holistic view of an organization's performance, emphasizing the interconnectedness of financial and ESG factors. Task Force on Climate-related Financial Disclosures (TCFD) recommendations guide organizations in disclosing climate-related risks and opportunities. The TCFD framework emphasizes scenario analysis and governance, helping companies manage climate risks and communicate their resilience strategies to stakeholders.

ESG accounting improves corporate transparency by providing stakeholders with comprehensive information on ESG practices. This transparency fosters trust and credibility, enhancing the company's reputation and stakeholder relationships. Szóka (2022) emphasizes the importance of sustainability accounting and green controlling in achieving medium- and long-term sustainability goals. The study highlights the compulsory nature of non-financial reporting standards within the EU and the development of the "taxonomy" for sustainable investments. Velikanov et al. (2023) discuss the necessity of developing new conceptual visions of management accounting systems to support sustainable development in the agro-industrial complex based on ESG strategies.

Kundrya-Vysotska et al. (2023) propose an extended format for accounting nomenclatures to include environmental, social, and management information, which supports integrated reporting and aligns with the triune approach of sustainability accounting. Svermova and Sander (2023) highlight methods for monetizing sustainability measures, showcasing their application in the automotive industry.

ESG accounting drives continuous improvement in sustainability performance. By tracking and reporting on ESG metrics, organizations can set targets, monitor progress, and implement corrective actions to enhance their overall sustainability performance. Buallay (2019) examines the relationship between ESG disclosures and bank performance, finding a significant positive impact on return on assets (ROA) and Tobin's Q, while corporate social responsibility (CSR) disclosure impacts vary across performance measures. Shaikh (2022) presents an international analysis showing that ESG compliance positively affects operational efficiency and market valuations, with varying impacts across the ESG dimensions. Kalbouneh et al. (2023) identify future research directions in sustainable accounting, including the integration of advanced technologies such as artificial intelligence (AI), big data, and Internet of Things (IoT), to enhance ESG reporting and accountability. The authors discuss the challenges of transforming traditional accounting practices to incorporate ESG principles in industrial organizations, proposing an algorithm for assessing sustainability.

It must also be noted that the lack of standardized ESG reporting frameworks creates inconsistencies in reporting practices, making it difficult for stakeholders to compare performance across organizations. Efforts to harmonize ESG standards, such as the merger of SASB and the IIRC, aim to address this issue.

The integration of ESG factors into accounting systems is crucial for enhancing corporate sustainability management and accountability. Integrating ESG information into traditional financial reporting systems requires significant changes in accounting practices and systems. Ensuring the alignment of ESG metrics with financial performance indicators is crucial for comprehensive reporting. Recent research highlights the development of new frameworks, methodologies, and tools to support ESG accounting. The impact of these developments on corporate governance, performance, and reporting is significant, with positive implications for transparency and stakeholder trust. Future directions suggest a growing role for advanced technologies in ESG reporting, which will further refine and improve sustainability accounting practices. Identifying material ESG factors relevant to the organization and its stakeholders is complex. Materiality assessments require robust stakeholder engagement and thorough analysis of industry-specific risks and opportunities.

3. Overview of the Chapters

Chapter 2 evaluates the impact of environmental conservation, societal obligations, and organizational guidance on a firm's financial health through an econometric model and regression analysis. This chapter employs a dual fixed-effect model to isolate the specific impacts of environmental expertise, social variability, and board governance on firm performance. To mitigate endogeneity concerns, the research adopts Heckman two-step estimation and propensity score matching (PSM) techniques. These methods address potential biases and enhance the robustness of the results. It highlights that while environmental initiatives typically lead to short-term financial costs due to significant investments in green technologies and practices, these do not immediately translate into financial gains. In contrast, the study identifies positive financial returns from investments in social responsibility and organizational governance. A strong focus on social issues enhances corporate reputation, customer trust, and employee morale, leading to increased sales, productivity, and innovation. Similarly, effective governance improves operational efficiency and financial performance. Collectively, these findings emphasize the need for a holistic corporate strategy that incorporates ESG elements to foster sustainable growth. The discussion section delves into the theoretical and practical implications of the findings. Theoretically, the study contributes to understanding how ESG factors collectively shape financial performance, supporting frameworks like the resource-based view (RBV) and agency theory. Practically, it advises organizations to integrate environmental expertise, social engagement, and strong governance into their strategic planning to enhance financial outcomes and sustainability. The chapter underscores the importance of a holistic approach to corporate strategy that incorporates ESG elements. Companies aiming for sustainable growth should leverage these interconnected factors to improve financial performance, meet stakeholder expectations, and gain competitive advantages. Future research should continue exploring the specific mechanisms and long-term impacts of these factors on corporate success.

Chapter 3 explores the relationship between board features and the ESG performance of listed firms, focusing on key aspects of board structure, behaviour, and history. Using data from ESG ratings of over 3,000 municipal firms between 2012 and 2022, the study examines five explanatory variables: the percentage of independent directors, the integration of the CEO and chairman roles, the board shareholding ratio, the number of specialized committees, and the percentage of female directors. The study reveals that the proportion of independent directors positively impacts the social responsibility score, while the combination of the CEO and chairman roles has a negative impact. Additionally, the number of specialized committees, the board shareholding ratio, and the percentage of female directors positively influence social responsibility ratings. These findings align with previous research, indicating that independent oversight, specialized governance, and diversity enhance ESG performance. To ensure robustness, the study employs the generalized method of moments (GMM) to address potential endogeneity issues. Both the Sargan test for overidentifying restrictions and the autoregressive (AR) (2) test for second-order serial correlation validate the model's reliability. The chapter highlights the practical implications of these findings, emphasizing the need for listed firms to develop comprehensive ESG management systems and integrate ESG standards into their business strategies. It also underscores the importance of board diversity and the separation of CEO and chairman roles for effective governance. Future research directions are suggested, including extending the study period, conducting comparative and sector-specific analyses, and exploring board dynamics, technology adoption, stakeholder influence, and behavioural aspects of board members. Additionally, examining ESG integration into business strategy, focusing on small and medium-sized enterprises (SMEs), and analysing policy and regulation impacts are recommended to build a more nuanced understanding of how board governance influences ESG performance. By addressing these future research avenues, scholars can further explore the complex relationship between board characteristics and ESG performance, contributing to the development of more effective governance practices and sustainable business strategies.

Chapter 4 explores the impacts of corporate governance on ESG disclosure, focusing on three specific aspects: the proportion of female management, internal executive compensation disparity, and supply chain concentration. Using a sample of Chinese listed firms from the Shanghai and Shenzhen stock markets over the period from 2018 to 2022, the study reveals that a higher proportion of female management positively affects ESG scores, while internal executive compensation disparity and supply chain concentration negatively impact ESG scores. These findings suggest that better ESG disclosure is associated with greater female representation in management, reduced disparity in executive compensation, and lower supply chain concentration. The study supports agency theory by showing that management's alignment with shareholders' goals to increase firm value is crucial for corporate ESG performance. The incentive for managers to enhance enterprise value drives the adoption of greenwashing measures and promotes the disclosure of ESG efforts in corporate reports. Female managers are found to be more proactive in integrating ESG performance into corporate policy and strategy compared to their male counterparts. Additionally, the results substantiate stakeholder theory by highlighting the increasing concerns of various stakeholders, including customers, employees, public welfare organizations, and government regulators, regarding corporate ESG practices. Effective corporate governance measures that engage these stakeholders, such as increasing the proportion of female managers, reducing internal executive compensation disparity, and diversifying supply chain networks, are essential for improving ESG performance. The chapter also aligns with legitimacy theory, suggesting that regulatory pressures and societal expectations significantly influence corporate ESG disclosure practices. Although the empirical results do not directly address legitimacy theory, the background information supports its relevance, indicating that firms must conform to societal norms and regulations to maintain legitimacy. The findings of this chapter offer valuable insights for policymakers, directors, and managers aiming to enhance corporate ESG performance. Firms should prioritize gender diversity in management and provide more opportunities for female managers, as a higher proportion of female management is associated with better ESG disclosure. Policymakers should consider adjusting executive compensation systems to better reflect ESG performance, as a lower internal executive compensation disparity correlates with improved ESG scores. This approach also contributes to establishing a fairer compensation system and minimizing bias. The study addresses a significant research gap by examining the impact of supply chain concentration on ESG disclosure. In the context of a global economy, achieving integration among all participants and links within the supply chain network is crucial for superior ESG performance. Firms should focus on balancing their reliance on different customers and suppliers to lower supply chain concentration and develop diverse supply chains, which not only enhances ESG performance but also improves operational efficiency.

Chapter 5 investigates the influence of ESG performance on financial performance, with a particular focus on Chinese enterprises during the COVID-19 pandemic. Utilizing data from companies listed on China's A-share stock market from 2011 to 2021, the study leverages ESG data from the Bloomberg database and financial data from the CSMAR database, providing a comprehensive analysis of the correlation between ESG performance and financial outcomes. The literature review reveals a strong correlation between ESG performance and financial performance. Studies indicate that board characteristics such as gender diversity, board size, and the presence of CSR committees significantly impact ESG performance. Additionally, mergers and acquisitions (M&A) can incentivize companies to adopt sustainable practices, positively influencing ESG scores. During the COVID-19 pandemic, ESG considerations have become increasingly important in investment decisions, surpassing traditional financial factors. The sample for this study comprises 11,230 valid observations from A-share listed companies in China, spanning from 2011 to 2021. The initial sample of 18,429 observations was subjected to several exclusion criteria to enhance the robustness and accuracy of the analysis. Companies in the financial and insurance sectors were excluded due to their unique characteristics, and observations with incomplete data or from poor-performing companies were also eliminated. Furthermore, all continuous variables were winsorized at the 1% and 99% levels to mitigate the influence of outliers. The findings of this study indicate a positive and substantial influence of ESG performance on financial performance within the Chinese market. Even in the aftermath of the COVID-19 pandemic, ESG performance continues to positively impact financial outcomes. These findings contribute to the existing body of international research, which has primarily relied on data from Western contexts, by providing insights into the Chinese market during a period of significant global disruption. This study enhances the understanding of the relationship between ESG performance and financial performance, offering valuable guidance for firms and policymakers. By focusing on Chinese data over a decade-long period and including the COVID-19 pandemic, the research provides a comprehensive analysis that addresses a gap in the existing literature. The results suggest that companies should prioritize ESG performance as it aligns stakeholder satisfaction with maintaining a good reputation and ensuring sustainable growth. Despite its contributions, the study has some limitations. It does not analyse the impact of ESG performance on financial performance in the post-pandemic period when conditions become relatively stable. The data used only extend to the end of 2021, a time when the pandemic significantly influenced business operations. Future research should include data from the post-pandemic period to provide a more comprehensive understanding of the relationship between ESG performance and financial performance. This chapter demonstrates the significant role of ESG performance in shaping financial outcomes in Chinese enterprises, particularly during the COVID-19 pandemic. It underscores the importance of integrating ESG considerations into business strategies to enhance financial performance and align with stakeholder expectations, providing a robust framework for future research and policy development.

Chapter 6 investigates the relationship between ESG factors and companies' financial performance, providing theoretical insights and practical implications. The study uses a quantitative approach to examine how ESG ratings influence financial metrics such as stock price, ROA, and return on equity (ROE), focusing on A-share listed companies in China from 2010 to 2021. ESG factors have become increasingly important in investment decision-making due to rising awareness of environmental and social issues. Investors use ESG metrics to evaluate corporate behaviour and potential long-term financial performance. The chapter outlines the significance of ESG in financial markets and its growing role in guiding investment strategies. The chapter integrates three dominant theoretical perspectives to explore the ESG–financial performance relationship: cash flow theory (CFT), sustainable development theory (SDT), and resource-based theory (RBT). CFT posits a strong association between ESG factors and financial performance through enhanced cash flows and reduced risks. SDT emphasizes the integration of economic, social, and environmental dimensions, aligning with ESG principles. RBT highlights that companies with superior ESG performance possess resources and capabilities that provide competitive advantages, leading to sustainable growth and profitability. The analysis confirms a positive relationship between ESG ratings and financial performance indicators. Alareeni and Hamdan (2020) found that while the environmental component positively affects Tobin's Q, it negatively impacts ROA and

ROE. The study corroborates these findings, showing that higher ESG ratings are associated with increased ROA and ROE, indicating better profitability and capital efficiency. Additionally, companies with strong ESG profiles tend to have higher stock prices, reflecting market confidence in their long-term viability. The chapter highlights several limitations in current ESG research. The varying impact of ESG across industries is a significant challenge, as different sectors benefit differently from ESG practices. Moreover, understanding how ESG factors affect different types of investors remains complex. The absence of standardized ESG metrics and reporting requirements also complicates the evaluation of ESG performance. These limitations underscore the need for industry-specific studies, global comparative research, and standardized ESG data. The chapter concludes that ESG factors positively influence companies' financial performance, particularly ROA, ROE, and stock price. These findings align with CFT and RBT, demonstrating that higher ESG ratings enhance profitability, capital efficiency, and market value. However, the study also highlights the complexities and challenges in ESG research, emphasizing the need for more detailed, industry-specific, and globally comprehensive analyses. Addressing these gaps will provide deeper insights into the ESG–financial performance relationship and guide investors and companies in implementing effective ESG strategies.

Chapter 7 explores the theoretical implications of ESG performance on corporate bankruptcy risk within the Chinese market, drawing comparisons with prior research primarily conducted in the United States. Given the distinct national contexts of China and the United States, this study examines whether the influence of ESG performance on bankruptcy risk yields similar conclusions in China. The Chinese market, characterized by rapid economic growth and a growing focus on sustainable development and corporate responsibility, provides a compelling backdrop for investigating the relationship between ESG performance and corporate bankruptcy risk (Petushkova, 2022). The chapter confirms Hypothesis 1, which posits a negative association between ESG performance and corporate bankruptcy risk. Empirical results indicate that companies with robust ESG performance are more likely to demonstrate superior financial performance, effective risk management, and long-term sustainability, thus reducing the likelihood of bankruptcy. This finding aligns with previous global research, supporting the notion that higher ESG performance contributes to lower bankruptcy risk. The chapter emphasizes the importance of ESG factors in influencing bankruptcy risk, particularly in the Chinese context. Empirical research indicates that enterprises with stronger ESG performance are less prone to bankruptcy. These companies prioritize environmental sustainability by reducing pollution, managing resources efficiently, and complying with environmental regulations. Their commitment to social responsibility is demonstrated through employee well-being, community engagement, and stakeholder relations. Furthermore, sound governance practices, such as transparent decision-making, an independent board of directors, and effective risk management, enhance their overall resilience. Several factors contribute to the positive association between ESG performance and reduced bankruptcy risk. Firstly, companies with strong ESG practices can better adapt to changing regulatory frameworks and mitigate risks associated with non-compliance and penalties. This is particularly relevant in China, where there is a growing emphasis on environmental protection and social responsibility (Wang et al., 2023). By adopting sustainable practices, companies can secure a strong market position and reduce regulatory risk. Secondly, ESG performance reflects a company's ability to manage operational risk effectively. Companies with sound governance structures and ethical business practices are better equipped to identify and address potential financial and operational risks, thereby minimizing the possibility of bankruptcy. This ability to manage risk enhances their resilience against economic and market fluctuations. The chapter also highlights the role of stakeholder pressure in driving ESG performance and reducing bankruptcy risk. In the Chinese context, companies face significant pressure from stakeholders, including investors, consumers, employees, and government regulators, to prioritize and improve their ESG performance. This pressure can manifest in demands for transparency, responsible business conduct, and compliance with regulatory requirements (Do & Vo, 2023). Stricter regulations are expected to strengthen the association between ESG performance and bankruptcy risk as companies face higher compliance requirements and increased reputational risks. This chapter contributes to the understanding of how ESG performance impacts corporate bankruptcy risk in the Chinese context. It affirms that higher ESG performance is associated with a lower likelihood of bankruptcy, providing valuable insights for stakeholders and policymakers aiming to promote sustainable business practices and enhance corporate sector stability.

Chapter 8 investigates the influence of ownership structure, specifically equity concentration and state ownership, on the ESG ratings of Chinese listed companies. The study is grounded in legitimacy theory and stakeholder theory, providing a comprehensive analysis of how different ownership structures impact corporate ESG performance. The chapter begins by outlining the theoretical framework. Legitimacy theory suggests that companies strive to conform to societal norms and values to maintain legitimacy. High-visibility firms require substantial CSR disclosure to gain legitimacy, while the ownership structure influences the type and scope of reporting. Stakeholder theory posits that a company's performance depends on the value placed on each stakeholder group. The equity concentration and the nature of the largest shareholder significantly determine how well a company fulfils its social responsibilities. The chapter conducts an empirical analysis using data from 1,134 non-financial Chinese listed companies between 2012 and 2021. A fixed-effects regression model is employed to examine the relationship between ownership structure and ESG ratings, with robustness tests and heterogeneity analyses performed to validate the results. The analysis reveals that high equity concentration is positively correlated with higher ESG ratings. Companies with concentrated equity are more likely to engage in non-profit activities and focus on long-term sustainability, aligning with the findings of Sun et al. (2024) and Kong et al. (2014). Additionally, state-owned enterprises (SOEs) demonstrate higher ESG performance compared to non-SOEs, indicating a greater commitment to social responsibility and environmental protection. This chapter makes significant theoretical contributions by confirming the positive correlation between high equity concentration and ESG performance. It extends legitimacy theory by showing that firms with high equity concentration engage in activities that enhance their legitimacy. The study also supports stakeholder theory, demonstrating that SOEs, accountable to a diverse group of stakeholders, engage in more socially responsible activities to maintain their legitimacy. The findings have several practical implications. For investors, the positive correlation between high equity concentration and high ESG ratings suggests that such companies are more stable and present lower stock risk, providing a smooth investment opportunity. Entrepreneurs are advised to concentrate equity to enhance ESG performance and reduce corporate risk. Policymakers can encourage practices that lead to higher equity concentration and support the unique structure of SOEs to promote stability and high ESG performance within the corporate sector. This chapter provides valuable insights into the relationship between ownership structure and ESG performance in Chinese listed companies. By integrating legitimacy and stakeholder theories, the study offers a comprehensive framework for understanding the motivations behind corporate engagement in ESG activities. The findings highlight the importance of equity concentration and state ownership in enhancing ESG performance, offering practical guidance for investors, entrepreneurs, and policymakers.

Chapter 9 explores the intricate relationships among ESG disclosure, financial reporting quality (FRQ), and investment efficiency within the context of Chinese A-share listed companies from 2018 to 2022. The study is grounded in the stakeholder theory and legitimacy theory, highlighting the importance of transparency and sustainability in corporate practices. Prior studies present mixed findings on the relationship between profitability and information disclosure. For instance, Mallin et al. (2013) and Taliento et al. (2019) highlight varied results, while Sharma et al. (2020) underscore a strong correlation between profitability and information disclosure. These studies emphasize that stakeholder trust, bolstered by ESG disclosure, is crucial for obtaining capital and attracting investors, ultimately enhancing investment efficiency (Liu & Tian, 2021). The chapter elucidates three mechanisms through which ESG disclosure enhances investment efficiency. Firstly, public financial disclosures mitigate agency problems by reducing information asymmetry between managers and investors, thereby enhancing economic performance and capital gains (Ellili, 2022; Bushman & Smith, 2001). Secondly, voluntary non-financial disclosures provide additional information, allowing investors to make better decisions and reduce risks (Sharma et al., 2020; Cheynel, 2013). Thirdly, high-quality non-financial information diminishes the impact of information bias on investment efficiency, enabling informed managerial decisions (Herath & Albarqi, 2017; Matten & Moon, 2008). FRQ provides fair and unbiased financial information, reducing conflicts and information asymmetry between managers and investors. This transparency fosters better corporate management and decision-making (Hope & Thomas, 2008; Bushman & Smith, 2001). High-quality FRQ influences debt contract terms and reduces investment inefficiencies by minimizing moral hazards and regulating managerial actions through executive compensation linked to profitability (Verdi, 2006; Li & Wang, 2014; Martínez-Ferrero et al., 2015). The empirical analysis, using data from Chinese

A-share listed companies, confirms a positive correlation between high-quality ESG disclosure and investment efficiency. It also reveals that detailed governance disclosures significantly enhance investment efficiency. Control variables, such as corporate performance, asset tangibility, and financial resources, further impact investment efficiency. The findings support stakeholder theory by demonstrating that ESG and FRQ disclosures provide reliable information, satisfying stakeholder needs beyond mere profit maximization (Wijnberg, 2000). Additionally, the results affirm legitimacy theory, showing that voluntary disclosures align corporate operations with social values, enhancing corporate legitimacy and stakeholder support (Gray et al., 1988; Pereira Eugénio et al., 2013). For stakeholders and investors, the study emphasizes the importance of detailed ESG disclosures and high-quality financial reporting in improving investment efficiency. Companies should enhance their environmental, social, and governance practices and align their development with sustainability goals (Liu & Tian, 2021). Governments should establish unified ESG disclosure systems to standardize reporting practices, thereby improving data quality and comparability (Cui, 2022). The chapter concludes by affirming the positive correlation between ESG and FRQ disclosures and investment efficiency. However, it acknowledges limitations, such as the study's focus on Chinese A-share listed companies and the developing stage of China's ESG disclosure system. Future research should expand to include more countries and address additional factors influencing investment efficiency as China's ESG reporting evolves. This chapter contributes to the literature by providing a nuanced analysis of ESG and FRQ disclosures' impact on investment efficiency, advocating for comprehensive and standardized reporting practices to foster sustainable corporate development.

Chapter 10 investigates the relationship between ESG performance and financial constraints in Chinese family enterprises, highlighting the influence of ESG factors on the overall effectiveness of these businesses. The research sample includes firms listed on the Shanghai and Shenzhen stock exchanges from 2012 to 2021. The findings reveal a positive correlation between ESG performance and corporate success, particularly for family firms where economic interests are prioritized. This trend has become more pronounced in recent years. The study contributes to several areas of ESG and family business research by employing the mediation effect to examine various types of family businesses, aligning with signalling theory and information asymmetry theory. Additionally, the impact of second-generation family business owners on ESG factors is explored, providing insights into how their involvement affects firm performance. The analysis also considers the influence of different years, shedding light on significant shifts in ESG performance among Chinese family firms over time. Despite its contributions, the study has limitations. It does not extrapolate the effects of individual organizations' ESG practices on broader business outcomes and identifies research gaps related to evaluating ESG impacts on business value and performance through financing constraints. The classification of family companies could also be improved. Future research could address these gaps by expanding the sample to include data from other countries and economies. This would provide a more comprehensive understanding of how ESG performance influences family businesses in different cultural and economic contexts. The chapter underscores the importance of ESG factors in mitigating financial constraints and enhancing the success of family businesses in China. Good ESG performance is associated with lower financing limitations and higher profitability, offering valuable insights for practitioners and policymakers in shaping ESG policies. By focusing on Chinese family enterprises, the research fills a gap in the literature and highlights the distinct challenges and opportunities these businesses face regarding ESG practices. The findings demonstrate that ESG performance can alleviate financial burdens, leading to improved business performance and increased competitiveness. This chapter provides a comprehensive analysis of the role of ESG performance in mitigating financial constraints and enhancing the success of Chinese family businesses. The findings underscore the need for further research to explore these dynamics in different contexts and over extended periods. Insights from this study can inform policymakers, practitioners, and academics as they seek to understand and leverage ESG practices to promote sustainable growth in family businesses, ultimately contributing to the broader understanding of ESG's impact on the global business landscape.

Chapter 11 provides an in-depth examination of the relationship between ESG practices and dividend payment policies, offering substantial contributions to the advancement of agency theory, stakeholder theory, life cycle theory, and signalling theory. The theoretical framework integrates four interconnected theories to elucidate the relationship between ESG practices and dividend payments. Agency theory suggests that reducing information asymmetry between management and shareholders can mitigate agency problems, with enhanced ESG disclosures fostering investor confidence and reducing financing costs. Stakeholder theory posits that companies with high ESG scores, reflecting strong social responsibility, can enhance financial performance and satisfy shareholder expectations. Life cycle theory argues that firms with growth potential should retain earnings for reinvestment, although our findings indicate that mature firms can engage in ESG practices without sacrificing dividend distributions. Signalling theory highlights that ESG disclosures signal a firm's commitment to sustainability and robust financial health, attracting investor support and facilitating higher dividend payments. A fixed effect model is used in the study to account for unobserved heterogeneity across industries, individual firms, and time periods, ensuring robust analysis of the relationship between ESG practices and dividend payouts. The results show a significant positive correlation between ESG scores and dividend payout ratios, supporting the hypotheses derived from the theoretical framework. Specifically, the coefficient for ESG score is 0.0461, with a 1% significance level indicating that higher ESG scores promote increased dividend payouts. To isolate the effects of ESG and audit quality on dividend policy, the study includes various control variables reflecting corporate governance factors. These include board size, CEO duality, board independence, firm size, financial leverage, free cash flow, ROA, sales growth, retained earnings, and effective tax rate. The findings reveal that financial leverage negatively impacts dividend payments, and larger firms tend to retain earnings rather than distribute dividends. Higher investments in ESG initiatives are associated with lower dividend payouts, likely due to the substantial costs involved in these practices. Among governance factors, only board independence significantly affects dividend payout ratios, with more independent boards constraining dividend distributions to prioritize long-term strategic investments. Audit quality plays a critical role in influencing ESG dividend decisions. Improved audit quality enhances the accuracy of financial statements, reduces information asymmetry, and fosters investor confidence. The study finds that while higher audit quality may temporarily negatively impact dividend payments, it remains crucial for long-term benefits. High-quality audits, particularly by Big Four auditors, provide additional credit assurance, facilitate lower-cost financing, and support ESG disclosures. These findings reinforce the importance of audit quality in promoting transparency and investor trust. The study makes significant theoretical contributions by demonstrating how ESG practices influence dividend payment policies through the lenses of agency theory, stakeholder theory, life cycle theory, and signalling theory. It extends agency theory by highlighting the role of ESG disclosures in reducing information asymmetry. It integrates stakeholder interests with financial outcomes, reinforcing stakeholder theory. The study modifies life cycle theory by showing that ESG initiatives do not preclude dividend payments in mature firms. Additionally, it supports signalling theory by demonstrating how ESG disclosures act as credible signals of corporate performance and governance quality. The research also underscores the importance of maintaining high audit quality to enhance overall corporate governance and support these theoretical frameworks.

Chapter 12 examines the relationship between ESG performance and financial distress among Chinese companies, using a dataset of 31,373 listed firms from 2009 to 2022. By leveraging Z-scores as a proxy for financial distress risk (FDR), the analysis reveals a negative correlation between ESG scores and financial distress. The results indicate that higher ESG scores are associated with lower financial distress, confirming the hypothesis that ESG performance can mitigate corporate financial risks. The research also investigates the moderating effect of firm characteristics, particularly focusing on SOEs versus non-SOEs. The findings demonstrate that the negative relationship between ESG performance and financial distress is more pronounced in non-SOEs. This distinction underscores the unique dynamics within Chinese markets, where SOEs benefit from closer ties to the government, providing them with substantial financing advantages that can buffer against financial distress. The chapter contributes significantly to the existing literature by utilizing recent data from Chinese listed companies, marking the first exploration of the ESG–financial distress relationship within this context. The robust methodology includes the use of two-stage least squares (2SLS) and GMM approaches to address potential endogeneity issues, ensuring the reliability of the results. This research enriches the theoretical framework by highlighting the differential impact of ESG on financial distress across various types of firms in China. Practically, the findings have important implications for policymakers and business managers. For policymakers, the study suggests that promoting ESG practices can enhance corporate financial stability and reduce the likelihood of bankruptcy, thus creating a more resilient economic environment. Encouraging companies to adopt better ESG practices can lead to a more stable and sustainable market. For business managers, the research highlights the economic benefits of high ESG performance, providing a compelling case for integrating ESG considerations into corporate strategy. Managers are advised to focus not only on social benefits but also on the potential financial advantages of strong ESG performance. The discussion underscores the alignment of the study's results with prior literature, reaffirming the inverse relationship between ESG and financial distress found in other contexts, such as Western and other Asian markets. However, the distinct focus on Chinese companies provides new insights into the unique market conditions and regulatory environment in China.

Chapter 13 explores the relationship between ESG factors and CFP, particularly focusing on the moderating role of audit quality within the Chinese context. The study's findings align with previous research that highlights the positive impact of ESG on CFP. However, it also introduces the unique perspective of Chinese data and incorporates audit quality as a significant moderating factor, addressing gaps in the existing literature. The chapter's findings have significant practical implications for managers, policymakers, and practitioners within Chinese enterprises. For managers, the positive impact of ESG on financial performance emphasizes the need to integrate ESG considerations into corporate strategies. This integration helps address ESG-related risks and opportunities more effectively, leading to sustainable business practices and improved financial outcomes. For policymakers, the research highlights the importance of promoting higher ESG ratings among companies. Encouraging robust ESG practices can drive sustainable development and improve overall corporate governance standards. Policymakers can use these findings to formulate regulations and incentives that support ESG initiatives, fostering a more sustainable corporate environment. For practitioners, particularly those in accounting and auditing firms, the study underscores the critical role of audit quality in ESG reporting. High-quality audits ensure the accuracy and reliability of ESG disclosures, helping companies maintain transparency and accountability. Accounting firms can leverage these insights to enhance their ESG reporting and auditing services, providing better support to companies aiming to meet ESG standards. This chapter emphasizes the positive relationship between ESG and CFP, while also highlighting the moderating role of audit quality. The findings contribute to the existing literature by incorporating a Chinese perspective and offering practical implications for various stakeholders. This comprehensive analysis provides a valuable framework for understanding the interplay among ESG factors, audit quality, and financial performance in the context of sustainable development.

Chapter 14 investigates the impact of ESG factors on the financial performance of enterprises of varying sizes, grounded in stakeholder theory. The research encompasses an analysis of ESG and corporate performance from 2011 to 2022, reviewing pertinent literature on stakeholder theory. The empirical analysis leverages data from the CSMAR database, including all Chinese A-share listed enterprises from 2011 to 2021, supplemented by ESG assessments from organizations such as China Securities, Hexun, and Bloomberg. The relationship between ESG factors and firm value is explored, highlighting the contentious debate surrounding the influence of ESG on economic success. Notable critics, such as Friedman (1970), argue against the efficacy of CSR initiatives, suggesting that they limit shareholder economic freedom and represent a distorted view of capitalism. In contrast, stakeholder theory posits that ESG initiatives can enhance financial performance by fostering positive stakeholder relationships. Empirical studies indicate that while larger companies can better withstand stakeholder pressure, smaller firms are more sensitive to stakeholder influences, particularly in the context of Chinese enterprises where government-directed CSR initiatives significantly impact performance. The chapter's findings suggest that significant stakeholders, especially those supported by government policies, positively influence company performance, corroborating stakeholder theory. This influence is particularly pronounced in smaller enterprises, which are more agile and capable of adapting their ESG practices to improve performance and societal impact. Conversely, larger firms benefit from more complex internal governance structures but must still consider the influence of key stakeholders. The study contributes valuable insights into the role of ESG factors in corporate performance, particularly within the Chinese context. It underscores the importance of ESG initiatives for firms of different sizes and offers practical implications for policymakers, investors, and corporate managers engaged in ESG strategies. Future research should aim to address the identified limitations to enhance the robustness and applicability of the results, ultimately fostering a deeper understanding of the impact of ESG on corporate performance globally.

Chapter 15 investigates the role of ESG disclosure as a strategic tool in corporate bond issuance in China. The chapter analyses data from 3,567 companies listed on China's A-shares from 2011 to 2021, employing a regression model to explore the relationship between ESG disclosure and bond issuance outcomes. The key dependent variables are the likelihood of bond issuance and the scale of corporate bond issuance. The principles of ESG disclosure, initially developed in Europe and the United States, have gained traction in China due to growing governmental and societal attention. ESG disclosure aligns with China's strategic shift towards green and sustainable production models. With the increase in investor awareness of CSR, the importance of ESG information in investment decisions has become more pronounced. Despite challenges such as inconsistent disclosure practices, the Chinese government's initiatives aim to standardize and enhance ESG reporting. The study draws on signalling and information asymmetry theories to explain how ESG disclosure influences investor behaviour and corporate financing. According to signalling theory, ESG disclosure serves as a signal to investors about a company's commitment to sustainability and social responsibility. Information asymmetry theory posits that better communication of internal information enhances trust and reduces financing costs. High-quality ESG disclosures can lower bond premiums and attract long-term investors by providing assurance about a company's stability and ethical practices. The empirical analysis utilizes regression models to test the impact of ESG disclosure on bond issuance. The study's dataset comprises 30,994 unbalanced panel data entries, providing a robust foundation for the analysis. The results confirm that ESG disclosure positively affects both the likelihood and scale of bond issuance. Specifically, companies with higher ESG scores are more successful in attracting investors and securing larger financing amounts. The findings support the hypotheses, demonstrating that ESG disclosure serves as an effective tool for enhancing corporate financing outcomes. Companies that prioritize ESG disclosure tend to have better financing results, attracting more investors and reducing financing costs. Among the three dimensions of ESG, social responsibility and corporate governance have the most significant positive impacts on bond issuance. This underscores the importance of focusing on these areas to improve financing prospects. This chapter highlights the strategic importance of ESG disclosure in the corporate bond market. By demonstrating that ESG practices can attract investors and facilitate financing, the study encourages stakeholders to adopt and enhance ESG disclosure practices. The findings have significant implications for government policies, corporate strategies, and investor decisions, promoting sustainable development and responsible business practices in China. The government is encouraged to strengthen ESG disclosure regulations, enterprises should integrate ESG into their governance frameworks, and investors are advised to consider ESG factors in their investment decisions.

Chapter 16 looks into the impact of a company's bank credit exposure (BCE) on its ESG performance, challenging traditional assumptions and offering new perspectives. The study reveals that companies with higher BCE tend to exhibit higher levels of ESG performance, countering the conventional belief that external financing negatively impacts sustainability efforts. The investigation builds upon two primary streams of literature: one focusing on public firms' BCE and its effect on financial performance, and the other examining the factors influencing ESG performance. Previous studies have suggested that companies dependent on external financing might prioritize short-term financial goals over long-term sustainability objectives. This research challenges this view by proposing that firms can leverage their relationships with banks to enhance their commitment to sustainable practices. Empirical findings support the hypothesis that higher BCE positively correlates with ESG performance. Companies with greater financial leverage can secure the resources needed to invest in ESG projects, thus improving their overall sustainability. Banks, as significant stakeholders, and creditors exert pressure on firms to maintain high ESG standards, thereby aligning financial strategies with sustainability goals. The chapter challenges the traditional notion that BCE adversely affects ESG performance, showing instead that firms under pressure from lenders and regulatory institutions are motivated to prioritize sustainability. This finding contributes to agency and stakeholder theories by highlighting how companies align their actions with stakeholder expectations to minimize financial risks and attract investment. It also advances institutional theory by demonstrating how external institutional pressures influence corporate sustainability practices. Practically, the findings offer valuable guidance for various stakeholders. Companies should recognize the benefits of BCE in ESG performance by integrating ESG considerations into their decision-making processes, developing robust ESG reporting systems, and aligning sustainability goals with stakeholder expectations. Banks can enhance their lending criteria by incorporating ESG factors, investigating ESG indicators, and creating sustainable finance products to encourage better ESG performance among borrowers. Investors should factor in ESG performance when making investment decisions, engage with companies to foster ESG advancements, and demand transparency in ESG disclosures. Regulators should promote standardized ESG reporting frameworks, consider the positive relationship between BCE and ESG performance in their regulations, and collaborate with financial institutions to incorporate ESG considerations into lending practices. The study's context in China is particularly noteworthy, given the stringent regulatory environment and the increasing focus on sustainability. The findings suggest that firms with higher BCE in China tend to have better ESG performance, a result that could extend to other developing countries with similar political, economic, and legal contexts. This chapter provides a comprehensive analysis of the interplay between BCE and ESG performance, challenging conventional wisdom and offering a nuanced understanding of how financial leverage can drive sustainable business practices. By integrating theoretical frameworks and empirical evidence, the study highlights the significant role of stakeholders, particularly banks, in promoting sustainability. These insights are crucial for companies, lenders, investors, and regulators aiming to foster sustainable economic development and create positive ESG outcomes.

Chapter 17 proposes directions for future research at the intersection of ESG accounting, performance measurement, and risk management, specifically within the context of Chinese listed companies. One important consideration is that ESG accounting is not only a technical exercise but also a social practice that reflects and reinforces societal values and norms. ESG accounting systems can enable and constrain efforts to address emerging challenges such as climate change, social inequality, corporate governance, and sustainability reporting. For instance, traditional accounting frameworks may not adequately capture the multifaceted impacts of ESG initiatives, leading to under-investment in projects that promote long-term sustainability. Similarly, accountability systems that prioritize short-term financial performance over comprehensive ESG outcomes may incentivize short-term decision-making and hinder strategic, long-term planning. ESG accounting is a dynamic and evolving field that plays a crucial role in sustainability management and corporate accountability. The integration of ESG factors into traditional financial reporting systems requires significant changes in accounting practices and systems, necessitating ongoing efforts to develop standardized frameworks and methodologies. Despite challenges related to standardization, data quality, and integration, the future of ESG accounting is promising. Regulatory developments, technological advancements, and increasing investor demand will continue to drive the evolution of ESG accounting, ensuring its central role in fostering sustainable business practices. Therefore, this chapter argues that policymakers, corporate managers, and stakeholders should engage in critical reflection and dialogue on the role of ESG accounting and accountability systems in addressing these emerging challenges. This should involve considering a range of perspectives and incorporating diverse stakeholder input into the design and implementation of these systems. Among suggested directions, the chapter contends that the corporate sector, particularly in China, faces inherent uncertainties and that future research should focus on how companies can effectively manage ESG-related risks and uncertainties. Additionally, the concluding chapter argues that innovation is crucial in enhancing ESG performance and that future research should explore how companies can effectively adopt and use advanced technologies, such as big data analytics and blockchain, to innovate and improve their ESG reporting and overall sustainability practices. By addressing these critical aspects, future research can contribute to increased knowledge of how ESG accounting can drive sustainable corporate success in an increasingly complex and dynamic global environment.

4. Conclusion

The exploration of ESG accounting within the context of China offers critical insights into the complex interplay between sustainable practices and corporate performance. This introductory chapter has illustrated that integrating ESG factors into accounting and auditing practices not only enhances transparency and accountability but also contributes to corporate financial success. Empirical data from a decade of Chinese corporate activities have highlighted the pivotal role of high-quality ESG disclosures in fostering stakeholder trust and driving sustainable business outcomes.

The findings underscore the importance of robust audit practices in ensuring the reliability and comparability of ESG information. The moderating effect of audit quality on the relationship between ESG performance and financial outcomes reveals that high-quality audits enhance the credibility of ESG disclosures, thereby facilitating better decision-making for investors and other stakeholders. This underscores the necessity for firms to invest in superior audit practices as part of their broader ESG strategies.

The distinctive characteristics of the Chinese market, as elucidated through this research, provide valuable lessons for global discourse on ESG integration. China's unique regulatory environment, ownership structures, and governance practices present both challenges and opportunities for advancing ESG objectives. This chapter contributes to a nuanced understanding of how these factors interplay within the Chinese context, offering insights that are applicable to other emerging markets with similar economic and regulatory landscapes.

The key themes explored include the role of ESG accounting in performance measurement, risk management, and corporate governance. The empirical evidence presented supports the argument that effective ESG practices are integral to long-term corporate sustainability and resilience. Moreover, the practical recommendations offered aim to guide policymakers, investors, managers, and auditors in enhancing ESG practices to support sustainable development goals.

A main message is to advocate for a comprehensive approach to ESG integration, emphasizing the importance of high-quality audit practices, stakeholder engagement, and regulatory support. By addressing these aspects, organizations are helped to achieve their sustainability goals, enhance their financial performance, and build resilient, sustainable businesses. As the discourse on ESG continues to evolve, further research could explore the long-term impacts of ESG practices on corporate success and to refine the tools and frameworks that support effective ESG accounting.

References

Buallay, A. (2019). Is sustainability reporting (ESG) associated with performance? Evidence from the European banking sector. *Management of Environmental Quality: An International Journal, 30*(1), 98–115.
Bushman, R. M., & Smith, A. J. (2001). Financial accounting information and corporate governance. *Journal of Accounting and Economics, 32*(1–3), 237–333.
Cheynel, E. (2013). A theory of voluntary disclosure and cost of capital. *Review of Accounting Studies, 18*, 987–1020.
Comoli, M., Tettamanzi, P., & Murgolo, M. (2023). Accounting for 'ESG' under disruptions: A systematic literature network analysis. *Sustainability, 15*(8), 6633.
Cui, J. (2022). Research on the impact of digital finance development on ESG performance of enterprises. *Academic Journal of Business & Management, 4*, 136–142.
Do, T. K., & Vo, X. V. (2023). Is mandatory sustainability disclosure associated with default risk? Evidence from emerging markets. *Finance Research Letters, 55*, 103818.
Ellili, N. O. D. (2022). Impact of ESG disclosure and financial reporting quality on investment efficiency. *Corporate Governance: The International Journal of Business in Society, 22*(5), 1094–1111.
Friedman, M. (1970). A theoretical framework for monetary analysis. *Journal of Political Economy, 78*(2), 193–238.
Gray, R., Owen, D., & Maunders, K. (1988). Corporate social reporting: Emerging trends in accountability and the social contract. *Accounting, Auditing & Accountability Journal, 1*(1), 6–20.
Herath, S. K., & Albarqi, N. (2017). Financial reporting quality: A literature review. *International Journal of Business Management and Commerce, 2*(2), 1–14.
Hope, O. K., & Thomas, W. B. (2008). Managerial empire building and firm disclosure. *Journal of Accounting Research, 46*(3), 591–626.
Jebe, R. (2019). The convergence of financial and ESG materiality: Taking sustainability mainstream. *American Business Law Journal, 56*(3)00000000000000000, 645–702.
Kalbouneh, A., Aburisheh, K., Shaheen, L., & Aldabbas, Q. (2023). The intellectual structure of sustainability accounting in the corporate environment: A literature review. *Cogent Business & Management, 10*(2), 2211370.
Kong, D., Liu, S., & Dai, Y. (2014). Environmental policy, company environment protection, and stock market performance: Evidence from China. *Corporate Social Responsibility and Environmental Management, 21*(2), 100–112.
Kundrya-Vysotska, O., Vagner, I., & Demko, I. (2023). Extrapolation of professional judgment in the accounting system: Significance and impact on development. *Herald of Economics, 2*, 89–102.
Li, H., & Wang, W. (2014). Impact of intangible assets on profitability of Hong Kong listed information technology companies. *Business and Economic Research, 4*(2), 98.
Liu, L., & Tian, G. G. (2021). Mandatory CSR disclosure, monitoring and investment efficiency: Evidence from China. *Accounting & Finance, 61*(1), 595–644.
Mallin, C., Michelon, G., & Raggi, D. (2013). Monitoring intensity and stakeholders' orientation: How does governance affect social and environmental disclosure? *Journal of Business Ethics, 114*, 29–43.
Martínez-Ferrero, J., Garcia-Sanchez, I. M., & Cuadrado-Ballesteros, B. (2015). Effect of financial reporting quality on sustainability information disclosure. *Corporate Social Responsibility and Environmental Management, 22*(1), 45–64.
Matten, D., & Moon, J. (2008). "Implicit" and "explicit" CSR: A conceptual framework for a comparative understanding of corporate social responsibility. *Academy of Management Review, 33*(2), 404–424.
Pereira Eugénio, T., Costa Lourenço, I., & Morais, A. I. (2013). Sustainability strategies of the company TimorL: Extending the applicability of legitimacy theory. *Management of Environmental Quality: An International Journal, 24*(5), 570–582.

Petushkova, V. V. (2022). China's experience and prospects for sustainable development. *Herald of the Russian Academy of Sciences*, *92*(2), 207–215.
Shaikh, I. (2022). Environmental, social, and governance (ESG) practice and firm performance: An international evidence. *Journal of Business Economics and Management*, *23*(1), 218–237.
Sharma, M., Kumar, R., & Kaur, R. (2020). Corporate sustainability and fair market value: A study of Indian family versus non-family firms. *Asia-Pacific Management Accounting Journal*, *15*(2), 93–121.
Sun, Q., Li, Y., & Hong, A. (2024). Integrating ESG into corporate strategy: Unveiling the moderating effect of digital transformation on green innovation through employee insights. *Systems*, *12*(5), 148.
Švermová, P., & Sander, M. (2023). ROSI and tools for monetizing sustainability (ESG) measures. In *Liberec economic forum* (p. 23).
Szóka, K. (2022). Sustainability accounting and reporting in the post-COVID times. In *6th FEB international scientific conference* (pp. 145–154).
Taliento, M., Favino, C., & Netti, A. (2019). Impact of environmental, social, and governance information on economic performance: Evidence of a corporate 'sustainability advantage' from Europe. *Sustainability*, *11*(6), 1738.
Velikanov, A., Egorova, E., Balashova, N., Melikhov, V., & Chekrygina, T. (2023). Conceptual approach to the development of accounting and information support for managing the sustainable development of economic entities in the agro-industrial complex based on the ESG strategy. In *E3S web of conferences* (Vol. 463, p. 01044). EDP Sciences.
Verdi, R. S. (2006). Information Environment and the Cost of Equity Capital. Available at SSRN: https://ssrn.com/abstract=757966 or http://dx.doi.org/10.2139/ssrn.757966
Wang, L., Le, Q., Peng, M., Zeng, H., & Kong, L. (2023). Does central environmental protection inspection improve corporate environmental, social, and governance performance? Evidence from China. *Business Strategy and the Environment*, *32*(6), 2962–2984.
Wijnberg, N. M. (2000). Normative stakeholder theory and Aristotle: The link between ethics and politics. *Journal of Business Ethics*, *25*(4), 329–342.

2 Environmental Expertise, Social Variability, and Board Governance Models' Impact on Corporate Financial Performance

Md Jahidur Rahman, Tarek Rana, Hongtao Zhu, Chen Zhuo, and Sajjad Khan

1. Introduction

This study explores the complex interaction among environmental knowledge, societal diversity, and boardroom governance, and how these factors collectively impact a company's financial performance – an area that remains underexplored in business research. While many studies have individually examined these elements, the joint effects and interplay between them warrant further investigation.

Our research is motivated by several factors. Firstly, the growing importance of environmental expertise in business strategies is well-documented. Plumlee et al. (2015) highlight the increasing relevance of environmental challenges in shaping corporate strategies, emphasizing how companies navigate these issues in their operational and strategic decisions. Furthermore, Bansal (2005) argues that companies with advanced environmental awareness are better positioned to enhance sustainability and gain a competitive advantage, potentially benefiting from cost savings, improved brand image, and customer loyalty. However, the specific mechanisms linking environmental knowledge to financial performance are not fully understood and require more detailed exploration.

Secondly, the impact of social diversity on financial outcomes has also been extensively studied. The value of a diverse workforce, encompassing differences in ethnicity, gender, education, and experience, is widely recognized as a driver of innovation and improved decision-making, leading to better financial performance. Cox (1993) was among the first to highlight the importance of diversity in fostering organizational innovation. However, the exact relationship between diversity and financial performance is complex and disputed. For example, Rose (2016) questions the straightforward impact of women in the boardroom on company performance, suggesting that the relationship is influenced by industry-specific factors and the cultural context of the business, indicating the need for further detailed studies.

Lastly, while board governance is acknowledged as vital for financial health, its interaction with environmental and social factors is largely unexplored, highlighting a key opportunity for future research.

DOI: 10.4324/9781003488934-3

This study addresses gaps by examining the combined effects of environmental expertise, societal diversity, and governance on corporate financial performance, offering new insights into their dynamic interplay.

While extensive research exists on these factors individually, their collective impact on corporate financial outcomes warrants further exploration. This study analyses data from China A shares (2011–2021) using a dual fixed effect model to assess these factors' specific impacts. To address potential endogeneity, Heckman and propensity score matching (PSM) methods are employed, along with sensitivity analyses, to ensure result robustness.

Key findings indicate that while environmental management may temporarily reduce financial performance due to increased costs, social responsibility and effective governance positively contribute. The negative effects of environmental governance are primarily observed in state-owned enterprises (SOEs), whereas strong governance significantly enhances performance in non-state-owned firms, likely due to more pronounced governance issues in state-owned entities.

The study highlights the importance of societal diversity, showing that a diverse workforce fosters innovation and broadens decision-making, leading to better financial outcomes. Additionally, effective board governance, emphasizing transparency and accountability, is confirmed as critical for financial success, enhancing the impacts of environmental knowledge and societal diversity.

These results advocate for integrating environmental expertise, societal diversity, and robust board oversight into corporate strategies, although further exploration is needed. This study contributes to the literature by exploring the interplay of these elements and emphasizing the importance of sustainable and inclusive practices for improving financial outcomes.

The growing focus on sustainability reflects a recognition that such practices not only enhance financial performance but are also essential for long-term shareholder value. Companies that effectively integrate sustainability can achieve competitive advantages and unlock new opportunities. Boards must prioritize sustainability and adapt to oversee these issues effectively, often lacking necessary ESG expertise. Recruiting individuals with strong ESG credentials is crucial for effective oversight.

Moreover, green finance plays a pivotal role in directing resources towards sustainable industries, influencing corporate behaviour through ESG considerations. This study underscores the significance of environmental expertise, board social engagement, and governance quality in enhancing corporate performance. It advises organizations to strengthen governance practices and social engagement to improve financial outcomes and fulfil corporate social responsibilities.

The paper is structured as follows: Section 2 explores the theoretical frameworks. Section 3 reviews relevant literature and formulates hypotheses. Section 4 outlines the research methodology and sample selection. Section 5 presents empirical findings. Sections 6 and 7 address endogeneity and perform robustness tests. Section 8 discusses implications, and Section 9 concludes the study.

2. Theoretical Framework

This study's conceptual framework explores the connections among environmental expertise, societal diversity, and board governance, and their combined impact on corporate financial performance. This theoretical structure is grounded in the existing literature, with each element seen as vital to the corporate ecosystem.

Firstly, environmental expertise is framed within the resource-based view (RBV), which posits that those unique resources – valuable, rare, inimitable, and non-substitutable (VRIN) – can provide a competitive advantage (Barney, 1991). Here, environmental knowledge is viewed as such a resource, enabling firms to navigate environmental challenges effectively. This capability enhances resilience and transforms challenges into opportunities, as supported by Clarkson et al. (2011), who link strong environmental acumen to sustainable practices and better financial outcomes.

Secondly, societal diversity is examined through the diversity–creativity link theory, which suggests that diverse teams foster creativity and innovation (Page, 2007). A diverse workforce can enhance business outcomes, including financial performance. Research, such as Joecks et al. (2013), supports the positive relationship between diversity and financial success, emphasizing that effective and inclusive management is crucial for maximizing these benefits.

Thirdly, the impact of board governance on financial performance is analysed through agency theory, which highlights the role of a well-functioning board in reducing agency conflicts between management and shareholders (Jensen & Meckling, 1976). Effective board oversight aligns interests and enhances financial performance, as shown by Ghosh (2006) and in more recent studies by Lu et al. (2020).

This framework integrates RBV, the diversity–creativity link theory, and agency theory, providing a solid foundation for examining how environmental expertise, societal diversity, and board governance collectively influence corporate financial performance. This comprehensive approach offers valuable insights into the interactions among these elements, contributing significantly to the existing literature.

3. Literature Review and Hypothesis Development

3.1 Literature Review

The literature on the relationship between environmental expertise, social diversity, and board governance as determinants of corporate financial performance is extensive but lacks a comprehensive synthesis of their combined effects.

Recent studies highlight the growing importance of environmental expertise in corporate decision-making. Plumlee et al. (2015) note that environmental concerns are increasingly shaping corporate strategies. Bansal (2005) argues that firms with strong environmental knowledge can sustain growth and gain a competitive edge, positively impacting financial performance. However, the mechanisms linking environmental expertise to financial outcomes remain unclear, indicating a need for further research.

Social diversity is also recognized as a valuable asset. A diverse workforce – encompassing various backgrounds, genders, and ethnicities – can drive innovation and improve decision-making, leading to better financial performance (Cox, 1993). Yet, the exact relationship between social diversity and financial outcomes is still debated. For instance, Rose (2016) questions the impact of female board representation on company performance, suggesting it varies by industry and cultural contexts.

Lastly, board governance plays a critical role in influencing corporate financial performance. Adams et al. (2010) provide insights into how boards affect governance, but the relationship between board structures and financial outcomes is not fully understood, highlighting the need for more empirical studies in this area. Several studies in China also investigate the relationship between environmental accounting and firm performance (Rahman & Wu, 2023; Rahman, Wu, et al., 2024; Rahman, Zhu, & Chen, 2023; Zhu & Rahman, 2024).

> *Hypothesis 1 (H1): There is a negative relationship between environmental proficiency and an organization's financial performance, suggesting that while environmental strategies may initially incur costs, they could lead to long-term financial benefits. This hypothesis calls for testing the immediate versus long-term impacts of environmental initiatives on financial results.*

Several studies have explored the interactions among environmental regulations, innovation, and firm performance, informing our hypothesis. Research shows that strict environmental regulations can force firms into a compliance-focused stance, potentially harming financial performance. This rigidity may hinder adaptability and limit innovative solutions that enhance fiscal outcomes (Kwon et al., 2021).

In contrast, firms that dynamically respond to environmental regulations often achieve better financial results. By proactively managing their environmental impact and embracing innovation, these firms can enhance sustainability, improve resource efficiency, reduce costs, and strengthen their competitive position, leading to improved financial performance (Kwon et al., 2021).

While the Porter hypothesis suggests that well-designed regulations can drive innovation to offset compliance costs, opinions vary on how regulation-induced technologies impact firm performance. The effects depend on the specific technologies and innovations adopted, resulting in mixed findings. Nonetheless, studies indicate that proactive environmental management and innovation can positively influence financial performance (Lundgren & Zhou, 2017).

In summary, although some research highlight the negative impacts of strict regulations, evidence supports that proactive environmental management and innovation can lead to favourable financial outcomes. Firms that strategically address environmental challenges and leverage innovation are more likely to experience a positive correlation between environmental proficiency and financial performance.

> *Hypothesis 2 (H2): There is a positive correlation between societal diversity and an organization's financial performance, suggesting that diverse*

organizational teams can drive better fiscal outcomes through enhanced creativity and decision-making capabilities.

This hypothesis suggests that societal diversity can positively influence an organization's financial performance. Numerous studies highlight the advantages of board diversity, resource diversity, and effective management practices.

Board diversity – encompassing varied gender, age, experience, and qualifications – has been linked to improved board functionality and enhanced firm performance. A diverse board helps firms better understand market dynamics and customer needs, providing a competitive advantage (Akram et al., 2020). Additionally, societal diversity fosters collaboration and learning across cultures, allowing organizations to tap into diverse talent pools and resources, leading to increased innovation and adaptability, which ultimately boost financial results. Organizations that embrace diversity and inclusive practices are better positioned to attract top talent and expand their customer base (Pless & Maak, 2004).

However, managing diversity effectively requires strong coordination and communication to address potential challenges. Diverse opinions can complicate decision-making and diminish social capital, necessitating frameworks to navigate these issues while leveraging diversity's benefits (Pless & Maak, 2004).

Empirical evidence supports the idea that societal diversity is positively correlated with financial performance. Research on board diversity, resource diversity, and robust management practices underscores the positive impacts of diversity on decision-making, innovation, and adaptability, all critical for enhancing financial outcomes. By valuing and harnessing diverse human capital, organizations can strengthen their competitive edge and achieve superior financial results.

Hypothesis 3 (H3): There is a positive relationship between exemplary board governance and an organization's financial performance, suggesting that effective governance structures enhance financial outcomes by aligning managerial actions with shareholder interests.

Research shows a positive correlation between strong board governance and organizational financial performance. Companies with effective governance structures often report better financial outcomes. Key factors, such as board independence, diversity, and expertise, significantly enhance governance and positively impact financial results (Paniagua et al., 2018).

Independent boards, free from conflicts of interest, are linked to higher profitability and increased shareholder value. Additionally, boards with diverse directors improve decision-making and financial performance (The Harvard Law School Forum on Corporate Governance, 2018). The effectiveness of board committees, like the audit and compensation committees, is also crucial for ensuring transparency, accountability, and sound financial management, which enhances performance and reduces risks (Bhatia & Gulati, 2021).

Overall, evidence supports the idea that strong board governance leads to improved financial performance. By implementing robust governance practices, organizations can enhance financial outcomes, boost investor confidence, and mitigate risks, promoting long-term sustainability and success. These findings contribute to the exploration of the intersection between environmental expertise, societal diversity, and board governance in relation to corporate financial health.

4. Research Design

4.1 Sample Selection and Data Description

Drawing on the research methodologies of Pham et al. (2022) and Cheng et al. (2023), this study examines the effects of corporate environmental responsibility, social responsibility, and governance on corporate performance. Given that comprehensive environmental, social, and governance (ESG) data started to be consistently published in 2011, for this study data from China's A-share listed companies spanning the years 2011 to 2021 were selected for empirical analysis.

The data selection process adhered to the following criteria to ensure the quality and relevance of the information:

1. Exclusion of special treatment (ST) enterprises that are under financial distress or face delisting risks;
2. Exclusion of listed financial companies due to their unique regulatory and financial reporting standards;
3. Exclusion of companies with an asset–liability ratio greater than 1, as this may indicate financial instability;
4. Removal of samples with missing key variables to maintain the integrity and completeness of the dataset;
5. A bilateral 1% trimming of continuous financial variables to mitigate the impact of extreme outliers.

After applying these filters, the study compiled a dataset of 4,418 companies, representing 32,222 observations of unbalanced panel data. The financial data for these enterprises were sourced from the CSMAR database, while the ESG ratings were obtained from assessments made by institutions such as CSI, Hexun, and Bloomberg. The process for selecting and screening variables is presented in Table 2.1, which outlines the criteria and sources for the dataset used in the empirical analysis.

Table 2.1 Variable Screening Process

Screening Criterion	*Number of Enterprises*	*Excluding Samples*
Excluding ST enterprises	529	1,192
Excluding financial banks	130	818
Samples with missing key variables were removed	499	2,620

4.2 *Variable Definitions*

4.2.1 *Explained Variables*

This study focuses on corporate performance, encompassing both financial and non-financial aspects. However, given that ESG factors predominantly influence the financial operations of enterprises, this research primarily assesses financial performance following the research approach of Wang et al. (2016). Specifically, return on assets (ROA) is chosen as the metric to gauge financial performance. In order to minimize potential estimation biases arising from the subjective selection of indicators, this study will also incorporate a robustness analysis. This analysis will follow methodologies similar to those used by Yu and Xiao (2022), updating and refining the measures of corporate performance variables. This approach ensures the accuracy and reliability of the findings by testing them under different conditions and with alternative metrics.

4.2.2 *Interpretive Variables*

ESG metrics are commonly employed to assess corporate performance in ESG domains, focusing on aspects such as resource utilization, energy consumption, waste management, carbon emissions, water resource management, and environmental protection. These environmental metrics are crucial for gauging a company's sustainable development and its environmental responsibility. Social responsibility within ESG considers a company's engagement and responsiveness to its employees, customers, suppliers, communities, and the broader public interest. This social dimension emphasizes labour rights, human rights, cultural diversity, community support, and contributions to public welfare and charitable activities. Corporate governance, another pillar of ESG, encompasses legal compliance, board governance, independence, effectiveness, and risk management. Strong corporate governance enhances transparency and accountability, which are essential for sustainable business operations. Given the varied implications of each ESG dimension on corporate operations, this study, drawing upon the framework of Cucari et al. (2018), will analyse ESG through the lens of environmental impact, social responsibility, and corporate governance. Specifically, this research will utilize the Chinese index to measure ratings in corporate environment, social responsibility, and governance. Additionally, the robustness analysis will involve adjustments to the ESG measurement criteria to ensure the reliability and applicability of the results across different contexts.

4.2.3 *Control Variables*

Wu et al. (2022) acknowledge that while this study focuses on the impacts of various ESG dimensions on enterprise performance, there are numerous other factors that can influence outcomes. Building on the approach of Gangi et al. (2018), this research aims to control for additional variables that might affect enterprise performance to enhance causal identification from the data and more accurately determine the impact of ESG factors. Specific enterprise-level control variables included in this study are as follows:

- Business Size (Size): Measured by the natural logarithm of the company's total assets (Rahman, Zhu, & Yue, 2024);
- Leverage Ratio (Lev): Calculated as the ratio of total liabilities to total assets (Rahman, Zhu, & Jiang, 2024);
- Asset Turnover Ratio (Ato): Defined as the ratio of operating income to total assets (Lam et al., 2024);
- Proportion of Fixed Assets (Inv): Calculated as the ratio of net fixed assets to total assets (Rahman, Zhu, & Zhang, 2024);
- Equity Concentration (Top1): Determined by the shareholding ratio of the top ten shareholders (Rahman et al., 2023);
- Growth Capacity: Measured by the growth rate of the company's operating income (Rahman, Zhu, & Hossain, 2023);
- Company Age (Age): Calculated using the natural logarithm of the number of years since the company was established plus one (Cahan et al., 2021);
- SOE: This variable is assigned a value of 1 if the company is state-owned, and 0 otherwise (Zhu & Rahman, 2024; Rahman & Zhu, 2024);
- Dual Leadership (Dual): Assigned a value of 1 if the roles of general manager and chairman are held by the same individual, otherwise 0 (Rahman, Zhu, & Chen, 2023).

These control variables are critical in isolating the specific effects of ESG dimensions on enterprise performance, ensuring that the analysis accounts for a broad spectrum of potentially confounding factors.

4.3 Model Construction

In order to test the impact of environmental, social responsibility, and corporate governance on corporate performance, this study draws on Bătae et al. (2021), who set the following measurement model:

$$\begin{aligned} ROA_{i,t} &= \alpha_0 + \alpha_1 E_{i,t} + \alpha_2 S_{i,t} + \alpha_3 G_{i,t} \\ &\quad + \sum Control + \sum IND + \sum YEAR + \varepsilon_{i,t} \end{aligned} \tag{1}$$

In $ROA_{i,t}$, i and t indicate the enterprise and year, respectively, indicating the performance level of the enterprise i in the first year t, and E, S, and G indicate the performance of the enterprise's environment, social responsibility, and corporate governance, respectively. $\sum IND$ and $\sum YEAR$ are the industry- and time-fixed effects, respectively. $\varepsilon_{i,c,t}$ represents random disturbance, indicating other factors that may affect enterprise performance, but have not been controlled in this study. In regression Equation (1), this study focuses on regression coefficients α_1, α_2, and α_3.

5. Empirical Results

5.1 Descriptive Statistics and Correlation Analysis

We first examine the descriptive statistical results for each variable, with the distribution outlined in Table 2.2. The maximum and minimum values for enterprise performance are 0.221 and 0.243, respectively, indicating a broad distribution for the profit margin of enterprise assets, with a mean of 0.0416 suggesting that most enterprises achieve a positive rate of return. The dimensions of E, S, and G exhibit substantial differences and high variance, indicating significant variability in performance across these areas.

From the data, it appears that the average environmental score for most companies is relatively low, which aligns with the practical context that industrial activities inherently generate pollution. This results in lower environmental scores for most companies, despite a generally high level of green technology adoption. In contrast, scores for social responsibility and corporate governance are comparatively higher, with governance scores being the highest on average. This could be attributed to the enduring impact of corporate governance on enterprise development and the increasing focus on social responsibility by companies in recent years.

Regarding the control variables, the standard deviation is large for enterprise size but small for other variables, suggesting that the distribution of each variable in this empirical analysis is relatively balanced and reasonable.

The results of the correlation analysis among various variables in the empirical study are presented in Table 2.3. Notably, the correlation coefficient between enterprise performance and environmental performance is 0.028, which is statistically significant at the 1% level. Similarly, the correlation coefficient between corporate governance and performance is 0.309, also significant at the 1% level, indicating a strong relationship. The correlation between social responsibility and performance is 0.102, suggesting a positive link.

Table 2.2 Descriptive Statistics

Variable	*Mean*	*p50*	*SD*	*Min*	*Max*	*N*
ROA	0.0416	0.0401	0.0657	–0.243	0.221	32222
E	1.908	1.500	1.120	1	8.500	32222
S	4.353	4.250	1.815	1	9	32222
G	5.381	5.750	1.330	1	9	32222
Size	22.17	21.98	1.295	19.82	26.18	32222
Lev	0.419	0.409	0.207	0.0511	0.898	32222
Ato	0.642	0.546	0.436	0.0678	2.592	32222
Inv	0.206	0.172	0.158	0.00190	0.689	32222
Top10	0.589	0.600	0.153	0.231	0.904	32222
Growth	0.173	0.111	0.401	–0.568	2.486	32222
Age	2.892	2.944	0.336	1.792	3.526	32222
SOE	0.328	0	0.469	0	1	32222
Dual	0.293	0	0.455	0	1	32222

Table 2.3 Analysis of the Variable Correlation Coefficient

Variable	*ROA*	*E*	*S*	*G*	*Size*	*Lev*	*Ato*	*Inv*	*Top10*	*Growth*	*Age*	*SOE*	*Dual*
ROA	1.000												
E	0.028***	1.000											
S	0.102***	0.296***	1.000										
G	0.309***	0.076***	0.015***	1.000									
Size	–0.022***	0.187***	0.205***	–0.000	1.000								
Lev	–0.390***	0.073***	0.087***	–0.284***	0.512***	1.000							
Ato	0.182***	0.051***	0.126***	0.004	0.047***	0.126***	1.000						
Inv	–0.087***	0.031***	–0.147***	0.032***	0.106***	0.087***	0.005	1.000					
Top10	0.268***	0.024***	0.051***	0.217***	0.111***	–0.121***	0.071***	0.004	1.000				
Growth	0.251***	–0.034***	0.022***	0.012**	0.041***	0.016***	0.133***	–0.068***	0.092***	1.000			
Age	–0.118***	0.040***	0.068***	–0.180***	0.187***	0.190***	–0.024***	0.012**	–0.208***	–0.049***	1.000		
SOE	–0.106***	0.019***	–0.034***	0.133***	0.367***	0.290***	0.033***	0.202***	–0.027***	–0.072***	0.177***	1.000	
Dual	0.058***	–0.032***	0.010*	–0.001	–0.183***	–0.145***	–0.025***	–0.102***	0.048***	0.031***	–0.109***	–0.299***	1.000

***$p < 0.01$, **$p < 0.05$, *$p < 0.1$

Table 2.4 Multicollinearity Tests

Variable	*VIF*	*1/VIF*
Size	1.67	0.5989
Lev	1.64	0.6113
SOE	1.38	0.7222
G	1.24	0.8035
S	1.19	0.8398
Top10	1.15	0.8704
Age	1.15	0.8731
E	1.13	0.8826
Dual	1.11	0.8977
Inv	1.08	0.9253
Ato	1.06	0.9423
Growth	1.04	0.9596
MeanVIF	1.24	

These findings imply that improvements in corporate governance, social responsibility, and environmental performance can all positively impact business performance, even without considering other variables, with corporate governance showing the strongest correlation.

Among the control variables, asset turnover, equity concentration, growth capability, and the dual role of leadership (two jobs held by one individual) exhibit positive correlations with enterprise performance. Conversely, variables such as enterprise size, asset–liability ratio, proportion of fixed assets, age of the enterprise, and the nature of property ownership show negative correlations with enterprise performance. These results highlight the complex interplay of factors that can influence the financial outcomes of a business.

The validity of the findings in this study might be questioned due to potential multicollinearity, given the strong correlations that can exist among corporate financial characteristics and the extensive number of financial variables used. To address this concern, a variance inflation factor (VIF) test was conducted for each financial variable. The results, displayed in Table 2.4, indicate that multicollinearity is not a significant issue in this analysis. This is evidenced by the VIF values for each variable, all of which are below 10, with an average VIF of only 1.24, close to 1. These results enhance the reliability of the estimated outcomes presented in this chapter.

5.2 Benchmark Regression

This section empirically examines the impact of environmental performance, social responsibility, and corporate governance on firm performance, utilizing data alongside the established econometric model (1). Table 2.5 presents the matching regression estimation results. Initially, the first column shows that environmental performance has a significant negative coefficient, while social responsibility and corporate governance have a significant positive coefficient. In the second column,

Table 2.5 Benchmark Regression Results

	(1) ROA	(2) ROA	(3) ROA	(4) ROA
E	−0.0015***	−0.0004	−0.0010**	−0.0009**
	(−2.8300)	(−0.9029)	(−2.1900)	(−2.0279)
S	0.0038***	0.0022***	0.0027***	0.0032***
	(12.2888)	(7.8093)	(9.1422)	(10.2910)
G	0.0153***	0.0081***	0.0079***	0.0074***
	(34.5361)	(20.0521)	(19.9170)	(18.0359)
Size		0.0091***	0.0090***	0.0095***
		(16.9100)	(16.6968)	(17.2634)
Lev		−0.1380***	−0.1390***	−0.1413***
		(−40.1914)	(−39.6230)	(−39.8538)
Ato		0.0281***	0.0360***	0.0356***
		(18.5801)	(21.3690)	(21.1544)
Inv		−0.0176***	−0.0289***	−0.0302***
		(−5.4328)	(−6.9799)	(−7.2536)
Top10		0.0539***	0.0498***	0.0521***
		(15.1364)	(14.4484)	(15.0365)
Growth		0.0336***	0.0320***	0.0318***
		(30.2992)	(29.3601)	(28.6525)
Age		0.0012	−0.0011	0.0041**
		(0.7500)	(−0.6876)	(2.2903)
SOE		−0.0063***	−0.0057***	−0.0066***
		(−5.0386)	(−4.4089)	(−5.1397)
Dual		0.0004	0.0010	0.0014
		(0.3353)	(0.9359)	(1.3904)
Ind	No	No	Yes	Yes
Year	No	No	No	Yes
_cons	−0.0543***	−0.2075***	−0.2085***	−0.2217***
	(−18.6360)	(−18.0070)	(−13.2616)	(−13.7898)
N	32,222	32,222	32,222	32,222
Adj. R^2	0.106	0.349	0.376	0.380

Note: The value in parentheses is the *t*-statistic, cluster value at the enterprise level; *, **, and *** are significant at 10%, 5%, and 1%, respectively, the same as the latter table.

including enterprise-level control variables leads to the loss of significance for environmental performance, but the other variables remain largely unchanged. The third column adjusts for industry-specific fixed effects, and the fourth includes both industry- and time-fixed effects, providing benchmark regression estimates due to improved model fit.

The regression outcomes indicate that a one-percentage-point increase in environmental performance corresponds to a 0.0009 percentage-point decline in financial performance, significant at the 5% level. This negative impact may arise from initial costs related to adopting environmentally friendly practices, such as clean technologies and waste reduction, which often require substantial investments and can lead to higher operational costs. Additionally, the financial benefits of these investments may take years to materialize, further affecting profit margins in the short term. This aligns with findings from Ren et al. (2020) and similar studies indicating that environmental governance can adversely affect short-term financial performance.

Conversely, the results show that a one-percentage-point increase in corporate social responsibility leads to a 0.0032 percentage-point increase in corporate performance. Positive social responsibility enhances a company's reputation, boosts consumer confidence, and ultimately improves sales and market share. It also enhances employee morale and productivity, as alignment with corporate values can increase job satisfaction and loyalty. Le et al. (2022) support this positive impact using cross-national data.

The regression coefficient for corporate governance is 0.0074, significant at the 1% level, indicating that each percentage-point increase in corporate governance results in a 0.0074 percentage-point increase in corporate performance. Effective corporate governance reduces agency problems and improves operational efficiency, positively influencing performance. Nasrallah and Khoury (2022) observed similar results in smaller enterprises in France, reinforcing the value of robust corporate governance in enhancing enterprise performance.

5.3 Heterogeneity Analysis of Property Properties

The analysis above reflects average effects across enterprises, but the nature of property rights can influence how environmental efforts, social responsibility, and corporate governance affect performance. In China, SOEs usually have better access to credit and management support due to political backing, while non-SOEs rely more on business merits to attract investors. This distinction may lead to different impacts of ESG factors on SOE and non-SOE performance.

To investigate these differences, the sample is divided into SOEs and non-SOEs, with regression results shown in Table 2.6. The analysis reveals that while social responsibility and corporate governance have significant positive coefficients in non-SOEs, the coefficient for environmental performance is negative but not significant. In contrast, SOEs exhibit a significant negative coefficient for environmental performance, while social responsibility and corporate governance remain positively impactful.

Social responsibility's influence is similar in both types of enterprises, but corporate governance has a much stronger positive effect on non-SOEs. This suggests that non-SOEs may achieve higher returns through targeted ESG strategies compared to SOEs. The results highlight the importance of considering ownership type when evaluating the impact of ESG factors on business performance.

Table 2.6 Results of Different Property Properties

	(1) Non-SOEs	(2) SOEs
E	−0.0001	−0.0020***
	(−0.2471)	(−2.9423)
S	0.0030***	0.0031***
	(7.8018)	(6.8359)
G	0.0090***	0.0023***
	(18.4275)	(3.2945)
Size	0.0116***	0.0095***
	(16.6939)	(10.6882)
Lev	−0.1451***	−0.1413***
	(−33.2344)	(−24.4641)
Ato	0.0435***	0.0223***
	(18.5821)	(10.1144)
Inv	−0.0293***	−0.0336***
	(−5.6819)	(−5.1093)
Top10	0.0624***	0.0239***
	(14.6056)	(4.1115)
Growth	0.0338***	0.0237***
	(23.7859)	(15.9860)
Age	0.0037*	0.0043
	(1.8390)	(1.2935)
SOE	0.0000	0.0000
	(.)	(.)
Dual	0.0009	0.0021
	(0.7723)	(0.9619)
Ind	Yes	Yes
Year	Yes	Yes
_cons	−0.2774***	−0.1729***
	(−12.3900)	(−8.0118)
N	21,663	10,559
Adj. R^2	0.397	0.369

6. Endogenous Discussion

6.1 Heckman Method

The estimation results of this study might be affected by endogeneity issues, such as the possibility that enterprises with better performance are more inclined to make substantial investments in ESG initiatives. To mitigate the impact of endogeneity on the findings of this study, we adopt the methodology proposed by Bose et al. (2022), using a Heckman two-step estimation process.

To implement this, we construct a treatment variable based on whether an enterprise has received a Bloomberg ESG rating. Bloomberg is recognized as a global ESG rating agency with a comprehensive understanding and well-developed evaluation system for ESG performance. Therefore, if an enterprise has been rated by

Table 2.7 Heckman Phase 1

Variable	*(1)* *Treat*
Size	0.9422*** (31.5749)
Lev	−1.1301*** (−8.0901)
Ato	0.1050* (1.6755)
Inv	0.2083 (1.1680)
Top10	−0.0435 (−0.2829)
Growth	−0.0717*** (−2.9679)
Age	−0.0555 (−0.6613)
SOE	0.0882 (1.4347)
Dual	−0.0513 (−1.2077)
Ind	Yes
Year	Yes
Constant	−19.4441*** (−25.8623)
Observations	32,130

Bloomberg, the treatment variable is assigned a value of 1; if not, it is set to 0. This treatment variable is then used as the explanatory variable in the first stage of the Heckman model, resulting in the calculation of the inverse Mills ratio (IMR).

The IMR is subsequently used in the second stage of the regression to adjust for any selection bias, ensuring that the estimation of the impact of ESG on corporate performance is more robust and reliable. This approach helps clarify whether the observed correlations are genuinely due to ESG actions or are merely a reflection of underlying differences in enterprise performance.

The IMR derived from the Heckman model is incorporated into the benchmark regression model to address potential endogeneity issues. The estimated results are displayed in Table 2.8. The first column presents the estimates without any control variables, while the second column includes these variables. The findings indicate that the regression coefficients for both social responsibility and corporate governance are significantly positive, both with and without the control variables. However, the coefficients turn negative, although not significantly so, after the control variables are added.

These results underscore the positive influence of social responsibility and corporate governance on corporate performance. Nonetheless, when considering the Heckman correction, the negative impact of environmental performance

Table 2.8 Heckman Model: Estimated Results

	(1) *ROA*	*(2)* *ROA*
E	−0.0035***	−0.0007
	(−6.4381)	(−1.6071)
S	0.0047***	0.0031***
	(13.4578)	(9.9079)
G	0.0151***	0.0076***
	(34.3007)	(18.5322)
IMR	−0.0077***	−0.0184***
	(−7.8027)	(−5.9299)
Size		−0.0006
		(−0.3257)
Lev		−0.1272***
		(−29.6781)
Ato		0.0344***
		(20.3221)
Inv		−0.0323***
		(−7.8418)
Top10		0.0555***
		(15.8156)
Growth		0.0323***
		(29.1789)
Age		0.0045**
		(2.5356)
SOE		−0.0077***
		(−5.8172)
Dual		0.0024**
		(2.3611)
Ind	Yes	Yes
Year	Yes	Yes
_cons	−0.0652***	−0.0011
	(−5.7758)	(−0.0268)
N	32,130	32,130
Adj. R^2	0.155	0.382

on enterprise performance becomes less pronounced, suggesting that the initial adverse effects may be mitigated when adjusting for potential biases in the model. This adjustment provides a clearer picture of the complex relationships between ESG factors and corporate performance.

6.2 PSM

Referencing the research methodologies of Gao and Liu (2023), Tang et al. (2023), and others, this chapter acknowledges potential endogeneity issues arising from sample selection, as well as systematic differences between enterprises that might impact the estimation results. To address these concerns, PSM is employed to mitigate the possible endogeneity in model estimation.

Specifically, the previously constructed treatment variables are used to estimate a logit model, employing the nearest neighbour 1:1 matching criterion to select closely matched samples for analysis. After re-matching the sample and conducting benchmark regression estimations, the results are displayed in Table 2.9. The findings indicate that even after applying PSM, the impact of environmental performance on enterprise performance remains significantly negative, while the effects of social responsibility and corporate governance on enterprise performance are significantly positive.

Therefore, even when considering endogeneity, the conclusion that social responsibility and corporate governance positively influence enterprise performance, while environmental performance has a negative effect, remains unchanged. This reinforces the robustness of our findings against potential biases in sample selection and model estimation.

6.3 Change in the Fixed Effect

In earlier analyses, a dual fixed effect model for industry and time was used, but endogeneity issues may arise from omitted enterprise-level variables that could affect performance. To address this, the study now employs an individual and time double-fixed-effect model, and the results are shown in Table 2.10.

After applying this model, the regression coefficient for environmental performance is positive but not statistically significant. In contrast, the impacts of social responsibility and corporate governance on enterprise performance remain significantly positive. These findings indicate that the previously observed effect of environmental performance may be influenced by omitted enterprise-level variables, while the positive effects of social responsibility and corporate governance appear more consistent and robust against such biases.

7. Robustness Test

To enhance result accuracy, a robustness test is conducted by altering variable measurement methods. Initially, the dependent variable is measured using return on equity (ROE) to assess enterprise performance, and the results are shown in the first column of Table 2.11. Here, environmental performance has a noticeable negative regression coefficient, while social responsibility and corporate governance show positive significance, reinforcing the findings.

The robustness test also includes Tobin's Q, with results presented in Table 2.11 confirming previous findings: social responsibility and corporate governance remain positively significant, while environmental performance is negatively significant. Next, ESG ratings from Bloomberg and Hexun replace the initial explanatory variables. The results presented in Table 2.11 indicate that the significance and direction of the coefficients for the main variables remain largely unchanged, further validating the study.

Finally, additional control variables – board size (Board), board independence (Indip), and management expenses (Mfee) – are introduced. Regression estimates in the fifth column of Table 2.11 demonstrate that the study's conclusions remain robust with the inclusion of these controls.

Table 2.9 Results of the PSM Regression

	(1) ROA	(2) ROA
E	−0.0037***	−0.0012**
	(−5.6060)	(−2.3515)
S	0.0047***	0.0029***
	(10.4376)	(7.6785)
G	0.0132***	0.0065***
	(23.0789)	(12.9806)
Size		0.0104***
		(14.0915)
Lev		−0.1510***
		(−33.7968)
Ato		0.0340***
		(17.9101)
Inv		−0.0262***
		(−5.2340)
Top10		0.0484***
		(11.4407)
Growth		0.0296***
		(21.1528)
Age		0.0064***
		(2.7102)
SOE		−0.0091***
		(−6.0472)
Dual		0.0021
		(1.4743)
Ind	Yes	Yes
Year	Yes	Yes
_cons	−0.0362***	−0.2149***
	(−2.9867)	(−10.7944)
N	18,501	18,501
Adj. R^2	0.143	0.393

8 Discussion

8.1 Relationship with Prior Literature

Understanding prior literature is essential for advancing knowledge on environmental expertise, social variability, and board governance regarding corporate financial performance. Several sources highlight important aspects of this relationship:

> For instance, the study "Boards Are Obstructing ESG – at Their Own Peril" highlights corporate boards' failure to recognize the financial implications of ESG issues, noting a lack of ESG expertise among members. It suggests appointing directors with ESG experience and requiring reports on

Table 2.10 Change in the Fixed-Effect Estimation Results

	(1) *ROA*	*(2)* *ROA*
E	0.0001	0.0001
	(0.1829)	(0.1829)
S	0.0014***	0.0014***
	(4.0927)	(4.0927)
G	0.0025***	0.0025***
	(5.8601)	(5.8601)
Size	0.0164***	0.0164***
	(12.3203)	(12.3203)
Lev	−0.1757***	−0.1757***
	(−34.2289)	(−34.2289)
Ato	0.0564***	0.0564***
	(18.3354)	(18.3354)
Inv	−0.0577***	−0.0577***
	(−8.5830)	(−8.5830)
Top10	0.0423***	0.0423***
	(6.9517)	(6.9517)
Growth	0.0256***	0.0256***
	(25.9526)	(25.9526)
Age	0.0079	0.0079
	(1.0019)	(1.0019)
SOE	−0.0089***	−0.0089***
	(−2.9569)	(−2.9569)
Dual	0.0011	0.0011
	(0.9064)	(0.9064)
Firm	Yes	Yes
Year	Yes	Yes
_cons	−0.3209***	−0.3209***
	(−9.5885)	(−9.5885)
N	32,222	32,222
Adj. R^2	0.306	0.306

the financial impacts of ESG investments, revealing challenges in adopting sustainability.

Kim et al. (2024) present a model showing how board governance, environmental competence, and social involvement affect a company's environmental performance. Enhancing board social engagement (BSE) and board environmental expertise (BEE) leads to better environmental outcomes, emphasizing the need to integrate these factors with traditional governance metrics. Moreover, S. H. Kim and Li (2021) discuss the critical role of boards in promoting sustainability and the need to shift from short-term profit maximization to long-term value creation, advocating for a corporate purpose aligned with ESG priorities.

The literature reveals a gap between the recognition of ESG importance by investors and corporate boards. Many boards lack ESG expertise and struggle with

Table 2.11 Test of Robustness

	(1) *ROE*	*(2)* *Tobin's Q*	*(3)* *ROA*	*(4)* *ROA*	*(5)* *ROA*
E	−0.0018**	−0.0295**			−0.0010**
	(−2.0074)	(−2.2243)			(−2.1865)
S	0.0061***	0.0593***			0.0031***
	(10.0651)	(5.8206)			(10.1843)
G	0.0128***	0.0482***			0.0077***
	(15.8788)	(3.9477)			(18.7640)
E_BP			−0.0001*		
			(−1.7106)		
S_BP			0.0003***		
			(2.7271)		
G_BP			0.0002***		
			(3.0081)		
E_HX				−0.0009***	
				(−14.6061)	
S_HX				0.0002***	
				(3.3726)	
G_HX				0.0077***	
				(101.3751)	
Size	0.0234***	−0.5926***	0.0094***	−0.0026***	0.0094***
	(20.0720)	(−22.9046)	(9.2049)	(−6.7969)	(16.9337)
Lev	−0.2105***	−1.4026***	−0.1765***	−0.0352***	−0.1403***
	(−25.3191)	(−10.1407)	(−29.0308)	(−14.8802)	(−39.7853)
Ato	0.0732***	0.1321***	0.0354***	0.0137***	0.0354***
	(21.0081)	(2.6568)	(13.3295)	(13.7374)	(21.0829)
Inv	−0.0468***	−0.7191***	−0.0339***	−0.0044*	−0.0303***
	(−5.5349)	(−5.7772)	(−4.8663)	(−1.7597)	(−7.2868)
Top10	0.0877***	1.2210***	0.0432***	−0.0058**	0.0522***
	(13.1592)	(10.3450)	(7.2779)	(−2.5730)	(15.1590)
Growth	0.0653***	0.3003***	0.0309***	0.0156***	0.0317***
	(27.6990)	(9.1078)	(16.2999)	(22.6088)	(28.4903)
Age	0.0108***	0.1670***	0.0073**	0.0038***	0.0040**
	(3.2945)	(2.7595)	(2.3228)	(3.5133)	(2.2535)
SOE	−0.0087***	−0.2880***	−0.0121***	0.0008	−0.0070***
	(−3.3919)	(−6.6777)	(−5.9504)	(0.9716)	(−5.4027)
Dual	0.0027	0.0595	0.0037*	0.0008	0.0019*
	(1.3554)	(1.5363)	(1.7856)	(1.2552)	(1.8618)
Board					0.0024
					(0.7871)
Indep					−0.0368***
					(−3.7513)
Mfee					−0.0008***
					(−4.3134)
Ind	Yes	Yes	Yes	Yes	Yes
Year	Yes	Yes	Yes	Yes	Yes
_cons	−0.5740***	14.0070***	−0.1418***	0.0006	−0.2116***
	(−18.4735)	(24.0985)	(−5.3409)	(0.0658)	(−12.0620)
N	32189	25612	11263	28355	32219
Adj. R^2	0.284	0.443	0.424	0.734	0.381

sustainable practices. However, there is growing acknowledgement of the need to enhance governance through environmental expertise and social engagement, which positively impacts firm environmental performance. A well-defined corporate purpose is crucial for integrating ESG concerns into decision-making and strategic planning. Future research should explore how environmental expertise, social engagement, and improved governance affect corporate financial performance, as well as the links between ESG performance and broader financial outcomes.

8.2 Theoretical Contribution

The connection between environmental expertise, social diversity, board governance, and corporate financial performance has received significant attention in recent academic discussions. Numerous studies highlight the substantial impact of environmental and social factors on firm performance. To address potential endogeneity issues that could skew results, this research employs Heckman and PSM methods. These approaches enhance the robustness of the findings by mitigating biases and ensuring result credibility. Additionally, a robustness test is conducted by varying measurement methods, providing insights into the stability and generalizability of the observed relationships. Overall, this study contributes significantly to our understanding of how corporate governance, social responsibility, and environmental factors influence business success. The empirical evidence generated can inform academics, investors, and policymakers, enabling them to make informed decisions and implement effective strategies.

8.3 Practical Implications

The impact of environmental expertise, social variability, and board governance on corporate financial performance has become a key focus of interest and research. Several studies highlight how these factors collectively influence financial outcomes. Firstly, while environmental expertise is essential, research shows it does not directly lead to improved short-term financial performance. Horváthová (2012) suggests that having environmental knowledge alone is not enough; companies must integrate this expertise with strategic practices to realize long-term financial benefits. Secondly, social variability, or board social engagement, plays a significant role in influencing financial performance. Boards that actively address societal issues and promote social initiatives tend to perform better. This engagement includes human rights, employee welfare, and diversity, with Kim et al. (2023) noting that incorporating these social factors into governance fosters a positive corporate image and drives financial success. Moreover, the governance structure is crucial for determining financial outcomes. Effective practices characterized by board independence, diversity, and transparency are linked to better financial performance (Whelan, 2021). Boards that prioritize environmental and social considerations in their decision-making are better positioned to achieve favourable results. Corporate boards must recognize the importance of integrating environmental expertise, embracing social variability, and maintaining strong governance practices to enhance financial performance. By doing so, organizations can achieve sustainable growth, meet stakeholder expectations, and strengthen their competitive advantage.

9. Conclusion

This study examines the impact of environmental conservation, societal obligations, and organizational governance on a firm's financial health, utilizing the econometric framework in model (1) and regression results in Table 2.5. The analysis reveals a negative coefficient for environmental performance, indicating that each percentage-point improvement in ecological health corresponds to a 0.0009 percentage-point decrease in financial performance. This paradox suggests that environmental initiatives often require significant investments – such as adopting cleaner technologies and improving energy efficiency – that can lead to short-term financial burdens.

Investments in green technologies may increase capital expenditures, R&D costs, or operational expenses, affecting profitability. Additionally, these investments can take time to yield financial returns, with costs related to R&D and training potentially impacting performance in the interim. Conversely, the study finds a positive coefficient for social responsibility, where each percentage-point increase leads to a 0.0032 percentage-point improvement in corporate performance. This aligns with research indicating that engagement in societal issues enhances brand image, builds consumer trust, and increases sales. A strong commitment to social responsibility can also boost employee morale and productivity, further enhancing competitiveness. Moreover, organizational governance positively affects financial performance, with each percentage-point improvement linked to a 0.0074 percentage-point increase in corporate results. This supports the view that effective governance mitigates internal conflicts and enhances operational efficiency.

Overall, the study emphasizes the need for a comprehensive corporate strategy that integrates ESG elements, as these dimensions collectively influence financial health. However, it does not explore the detailed mechanisms by which ESG factors impact performance, suggesting opportunities for future research. Further studies could investigate how ESG components contribute to financial health and aid companies in developing balanced strategies that incorporate environmental and social responsibilities alongside governance.

References

Adams, R. B., Hermalin, B. E., & Weisbach, M. S. (2010). The role of boards of directors in corporate governance: A conceptual framework and survey. *Journal of Economic Literature*, *48*(1), 58–107.

Akram, F., Haq, M. a. U., Natarajan, V. K., & Chellakan, R. S. (2020). Board heterogeneity and corporate performance: An insight beyond agency issues. *Cogent Business & Management*, *7*(1), 1809299.

Bansal, P. (2005). Evolving sustainably: A longitudinal study of corporate sustainable development. *Strategic Management Journal*, *26*(3), 197–218.

Barney, J. (1991). Firm resources and sustained competitive advantage. *Journal of Management*, *17*(1), 99–120.

Bătae, O. M., Dragomir, V. D., & Feleagă, L. (2021). The relationship between environmental, social, and financial performance in the banking sector: A European study. *Journal of Cleaner Production*, *290*, 125791.
Bhatia, M., & Gulati, R. (2021). Board governance and bank performance: A meta-analysis. *Research in International Business and Finance*, *58*, 101425.
Bose, S., Ali, M. J., Hossain, S., & Shamsuddin, A. (2022). Does CEO – audit committee/board interlocking matter for corporate social responsibility? *Journal of Business Ethics*, *179*(3), 819–847.
Cahan, S., Lam, B. M., Li, L. Z., & Rahman, M. J. (2021). Information environment and stock price synchronicity: Evidence from auditor characteristics. *International Journal of Auditing*, *25*(2), 332–350.
Cheng, R., Kim, H., & Ryu, D. (2023). ESG performance and firm value in the Chinese market. *Investment Analysts Journal*, 1–15.
Clarkson, P. M., Li, Y., Richardson, G. D., & Vasvari, F. P. (2011). Does it really pay to be green? Determinants and consequences of proactive environmental strategies. *Journal of Accounting and Public Policy*, *30*(2), 122–144.
Cox, D. D. (1993). An analysis of Bayesian inference for nonparametric regression. *The Annals of Statistics*, *21*(2), 903–923.
Cucari, N., Esposito De Falco, S., & Orlando, B. (2018). Diversity of board of directors and environmental social governance: Evidence from Italian listed companies. *Corporate Social Responsibility and Environmental Management*, *25*(3), 250–266.
Gangi, F., Mustilli, M., & Varrone, N. (2018). The impact of corporate social responsibility (CSR) knowledge on corporate financial performance: Evidence from the European banking industry. *Journal of Knowledge Management*, *23*(1), 110–134.
Gao, W., & Liu, Z. (2023). Green credit and corporate ESG performance: Evidence from China. *Finance Research Letters*, *55*, 103940.
Ghosh, S. (2006). Do board characteristics affect corporate performance? Firm-level evidence for India. *Applied Economics Letters*, *13*(7), 435–443.
Horváthová, E. (2012). The impact of environmental performance on firm performance: Short-term costs and long-term benefits? *Ecological Economics*, *84*, 91–97.
Jensen, M. C., & Meckling, W. H. (1976). Theory of the firm: Executive behavior, agency expenses and ownership structure. *Journal of Financial Economics*, *3*(4), 305–360.
Joecks, J., Pull, K., & Vetter, K. (2013). Gender diversity in the boardroom and firm performance: What exactly constitutes a "Critical Mass?". *Journal of Business Ethics*, *118*(1), 61–72.
Kim, M. J., Hall, C. M., Chung, N., Kim, M., & Sohn, K. (2024). What makes tourists use public transport? Value-belief-norm theory, environmental, social, and governance factors, and the sustainable development goals. *Journal of Travel Research*, *63*(6), 1426–1441.
Kim, S., & Li, Z. (2021). Understanding the impact of ESG practices in corporate finance. *Sustainability*, *13*(7), 3746.
Kim, D., Marin, M. J., Richardson, G. D., Salterio, S. E., & Tsang, A. (2023). Modeling board governance, environmental expertise, and social engagement effects on firm environmental performance: Panel data evidence. *Journal of Contemporary Accounting & Economics*, *19*(2), 100364.
Kwon, H., Lee, J., & Choi, L. (2021). Dynamic interplay of environmental sustainability and corporate reputation: A combined parametric and nonparametric approach. *Annals of Operations Research*, *324*(1–2), 687–719.
Lam, B. M., Mo, P. L. L., & Rahman, M. J. (2024). Secrecy culture, client importance, and auditor reporting behavior: An international study. *Managerial Auditing Journal*, *39*(2), 113–137.
Le, M. H., Lu, W. M., & Kweh, Q. L. (2022). The moderating effects of power distance on corporate social responsibility and multinational enterprises performance. *Review of Managerial Science*, 1–31.
Lu, Y., Wang, W., & Zhang, T. (2020). The interplay of board autonomy, corporate social responsibility, and company performance. *Sustainability*, *12*(3), 836.

Lundgren, T., & Zhou, W. (2017). Firm performance and the role of environmental management. *Journal of Environmental Management, 203*, 330–341.
Nasrallah, N., & El Khoury, R. (2022). Is corporate governance a good predictor of SMEs financial performance? Evidence from developing countries (the case of Lebanon). *Journal of Sustainable Finance & Investment, 12*(1), 13–43.
Page, S. E. (2007). *The difference: How the power of diversity creates better groups, firms, schools, and societies*. Princeton University Press.
Paniagua, J., Rivelles, R. P., & Sapena, J. (2018). Corporate governance and financial performance: The role of ownership and board structure. *Journal of Business Research, 89*, 229–234.
Pham, T. N., Tran, P. P., Le, M. H., Vo, H. N., Pham, C. D., & Nguyen, H. D. (2022). The effects of ESG combined score on business performance of enterprises in the transportation industry. *Sustainability, 14*(14), 8354.
Pless, N., & Maak, T. (2004). Building an inclusive diversity culture: Principles, processes and practice. *Journal of Business Ethics, 54*, 129–147.
Plumlee, M., Brown, D., Hayes, R. M., & Marshall, R. S. (2015). Voluntary environmental disclosure quality and firm value: Further evidence. *Journal of Accounting and Public Policy, 34*(4), 336–361.
Rahman, J., & Wu, J. (2023). M&A activity and ESG performance: Evidence from China. *Managerial Finance, 50*(1), 179–197.
Rahman, M. J., Wu, Q., & Zhu, H. (2024). Corporate social responsibility in times of social distancing: Evidence from China. *Business Ethics, the Environment & Responsibility*.
Rahman, M. J., & Zhu, H. (2024). Detecting accounting fraud in family firms: Evidence from machine learning approaches. *Advances in Accounting, 64*, 100722.
Rahman, M. J., Zhu, H., & Chen, S. (2023). Does CSR reduce financial distress? Moderating effect of firm characteristics, auditor characteristics, and covid-19. *International Journal of Accounting & Information Management, 31*(5), 756–784.
Rahman, M. J., Zhu, H., & Hossain, M. M. (2023). Auditor choice and audit fees through the lens of agency theory: Evidence from Chinese family firms. *Journal of Family Business Management, 13*(4), 1248–1276.
Rahman, M. J., Zhu, H., & Jiang, X. (2024). Family firms, client importance, and auditor reporting behavior: Evidence from China. *Meditari Accountancy Research, 32*(2), 543–578.
Rahman, M. J., Zhu, H., & Yue, L. (2024). Does the adoption of artificial intelligence by audit firms and their clients affect audit quality and efficiency? Evidence from China. *Managerial Auditing Journal, 39*(6), 668–699.
Rahman, M. J., Zhu, H., Zhang, Y., & Hossain, M. M. (2024). Effect of female representation in audit committees on non-audit fees: Evidence from China. *Meditari Accountancy Research*.
Ren, S., Wei, W., Sun, H., Xu, Q., Hu, Y., & Chen, X. (2020). Can mandatory environmental information disclosure achieve a win-win for a firm's environmental and economic performance? *Journal of Cleaner Production, 250*, 119530.
Rose, J. (2016). Who do you think you are? Jacqueline Rose on trans. *London Review of Books, 38*(9), 3–13.
The Harvard Law School Forum on Corporate Governance. (2018, May 18). *Board performance evaluations that add value*. https://corpgov.law.harvard.edu/2018/05/18/board-performance-evaluations-that-add-value/
Tang, S., He, L., Su, F., & Zhou, X. (2023). Does directors' and officers' liability insurance improve corporate ESG performance? Evidence from China. *International Journal of Finance & Economics, 29*(3), 3713–3737.
Wang, Q., Dou, J., & Jia, S. (2016). A meta-analytic review of corporate social responsibility and corporate financial performance: The moderating effect of contextual factors. *Business & Society, 55*(8), 1083–1121.

Whelan, T. (2021, January 22). Boards are obstructing ESG – at their own peril. *Harvard Business Review*.
Wu, S. H., Lin, F. J., & Perng, C. (2022). The affecting factors of small and medium enterprise performance. *Journal of Business Research, 143*, 94–104.
Yu, X., & Xiao, K. (2022). Does ESG performance affect firm value? Evidence from a new ESG-scoring approach for Chinese enterprises. *Sustainability, 14*(24), 16940.
Zhu, H., & Rahman, M. J. (2024). Ex-ante expected changes in ESG and future stock returns based on machine learning. *The British Accounting Review*, 101457.

3 Board Structure and Board Composition in China and ESG Performance

Md Jahidur Rahman, Tarek Rana, Hongtao Zhu, and Tong Wu

1. Introduction

This chapter examines the board of directors of listed companies, detailing how various board characteristics influence corporate ESG performance. It also discusses the upgrade path of board characteristics for GEM listed companies and analyses relevant policies and measures to enhance the ESG performance of these companies, starting with the current situation and future trends of ESG development among A-share listed companies.

The board of directors, responsible for authorizing and supervising the implementation of strategic goals, management systems, and corporate culture (BCBS, 2015), plays a crucial role in a company's success (García-Sánchez et al., 2018). Effective governance also emphasizes corporate responsibility and business ethics (HLEG, 2017). An increasing body of research shows a significant positive relationship between a company's profitability and its sustainability performance: firms with high sustainability ratings significantly outperform their peers in market value and accounting performance (Eccles et al., 2014). In other words, adopting best practices in environmental, social, and corporate governance (ESG) leads to long-term competitive advantages. Companies recognize that achieving one or more sustainable development goals (SDGs), especially those related to climate change, is essential for their survival.

In this chapter, we investigate the link between the ESG performance of class A stocks and board quality. We focus on three key aspects of boards: structure, behaviour, and history. By analysing a large dataset of ESG ratings for public A-share companies from 2012 to 2022, we aim to clarify the relationship between these board features and ESG performance. We consider the number of special committees, the percentage of independent directors, the dual role combination, directors' ownership ratio, and the proportion of female directors. Our analysis uses a multiple regression model to determine the precise effect of each board attribute on ESG performance. We rigorously examined our model's endogeneity to validate our findings.

A growing body of research explores the connection between board functions and ESG performance, providing insights into how boards can support sustainable business practices and good corporate governance. For instance, Smith and Wang's

DOI: 10.4324/9781003488934-4

(2017) study on board composition and ESG performance found that independent directors positively influenced a company's ESG ratings. This finding aligns with agency theory, which posits that independent directors can effectively monitor management and ensure accountability for SDGs.

Studies by Johnson et al. (2018) and Garcia-Meca et al. (2020) also highlighted the importance of board diversity, particularly the proportion of female board members, in achieving ESG success. They suggested that diverse boards offer varied perspectives, leading to better decision-making and a stronger focus on long-term sustainability goals. While these studies have illuminated specific board duties and their impact on ESG performance, further research is needed to fully understand the topic. This study aims to fill this gap by analysing the combined effect of board structure, behaviour, and history on the ESG performance of A-rated securities. It offers empirical insights for policymakers, corporate governance experts, and investors, advancing sustainable investing discussions and guiding stakeholders. Several studies in China also investigate the relationship of environmental accounting and firm performance (Rahman & Wu, 2023; Rahman, Wu, et al., 2024; Rahman et al., 2023; Zhu & Rahman, 2024).

The rest of the chapter is organized as follows: literature review: previous studies on board structure and ESG performance; and methodology: endogeneity testing, robustness test, descriptive statistics, and collinearity analysis. Findings of the analysis show that the proportion of independent directors positively affects the corporate responsibility score, while the dual role combination negatively affects the corporate responsibility score. The shareholding ratio of the board, the number of committees, and the proportion of female directors all significantly impact the corporate responsibility score. Relationship with previous literature, theoretical implications, and practical implications are dealt with in Discussion. A summary of key findings and contributions to the field is provided in Conclusion.

2. Literature Review and Hypotheses Development

2.1 Structural Characteristics of the Board of Directors and ESG Performance of Enterprises

This research explores three main perspectives from mainstream Western economic theory: the impact of the percentage of independent directors on corporate social responsibility (CSR), the effect of combining the chairman and CEO positions on CSR, and the influence of the number of professional directors on CSR. These stages are thoroughly explained from both local and international viewpoints.

Independent directors are external members who can make independent and objective judgements, unaffected by the interests of other shareholders, and hold no other positions within the firm. They represent the interests of all shareholders and maintain independence in decision-making, property, and tenure. A review of foreign studies on the proportion of independent directors and their correlation with company ESG performance focuses on several key aspects. Birindelli, Dell'Atti, Iannuzzi & Savioli (2018) highlighted that increasing the proportion of independent directors can enhance corporate governance by rationalizing executive policies. Independent directors provide informed, scientific, robust, and objective assessments, which promote commercial interests. Birindelli et al. (2018) asserted that independent directors improve the rationality of management decisions and propose business strategies that serve the company's interests impartially.

The scenario where the chairman and CEO are the same person is known as "two in one." Jensen (1993) argued that when the number of board members exceeds a certain limit, they may be subject to managerial constraints, which could harm stakeholders' rights and the fulfilment of supervisory duties. Major shareholders serving as both chairman and CEO can lead to insufficient regulation of business activities, increasing the company's tendency to neglect environmental protection obligations. Jensen (1993) also noted that appointing directors as CEOs can weaken the company's internal control system. Effective supervision is only achieved when these roles are held by different individuals. Zhang and Duan (2008) empirically tested 559 Chinese companies listed on the Shanghai Stock Exchange and found that voluntary information disclosure significantly decreased when the chairman also served as CEO. Other experts have shown that there may be no direct link between certain personal characteristics of the general manager and specific business actions.

The Professional Committee of the Board of Directors was established to provide fair, professional, and independent advice. In 2018, the China Securities Regulatory Commission updated the "Governance Standards for Listed Companies" and introduced a separate audit committee, along with strategy, nominating, and remuneration committees. Beckman and Haunschild (2002) suggested that a diverse board can offer better technical support and foster relationships with stakeholders, enhancing CSR management. The enterprise development strategy committee conducts strategic research and planning on long-term company development, including key strategic decisions. Although there is limited literature on the number of specialized committees and their direct impact on ESG performance, it is evident that strategic committees must prioritize ESG as a crucial sustainable development plan. Therefore, the number of specialized committees can reflect the level of governance of the board of directors. More specialized committees often correlate with better ESG performance. Therefore, the structural characteristics of the board of directors, including the proportion of independent directors, the combination of chairman and CEO roles, and the presence of professional committees, significantly impact a company's ESG performance.

2.2 Board Incentive Characteristics and ESG Performance of Enterprises

The existing literature primarily focuses on two aspects: the impact of board compensation ratio on CSR and the impact of board shareholding ratio on corporate ESG performance. Board shares act as a long-term incentive mechanism for board compensation. The board of directors is traditionally responsible for monitoring and regulating the interaction between management and shareholders. As rational managers, directors often prioritize their own interests, which can sometimes conflict with the interests of the business and shareholders. The company's annual report and social responsibility reports can indicate that directors are optimistic about the company's future, improve its social reputation, and create a positive corporate image among external shareholders. By fulfilling their control and management responsibilities, directors can safeguard the interests of the owners. Research by Chen et al. (2018) suggests a positive correlation among shareholder size, board ownership rate, and CSR. In practice, CSR can help establish a positive reputation, thereby boosting the company's stock price. This chapter posits that a higher equity ratio enables board members to align their personal careers with corporate profit goals, encouraging them to pay more attention to CSR disclosure, adhere to CSR standards, focus on environmental protection, and enhance social reputation. This attention to corporate governance can further improve the ESG performance of companies.

2.3 Proportion of Female Board Members and Enterprise ESG Performance

The personal history of board members, including age, gender, educational background, and professional experience, significantly influences corporate governance. Despite the challenges in measuring personal background information, the existing literature has primarily focused on the effects of board members' international experiences and the number of female board members on corporate ESG performance and social responsibility. A considerable amount of international research has examined the relationship between female board members, CSR, and corporate finance. Ibrahim and Angelidis (1995) found that male boards tend to prioritize a company's financial management performance more than female boards. Studies by Pereira and Shrestha (2015), Ahern and Dittmar (2012), and Rahman, Zhu, Zhang, et al. (2024) indicate that companies with a higher percentage of female directors tend to perform better in areas such as charitable contributions, employee benefits, and environmental protection. Domestic researchers have also explored this topic. Rahman, Zhu, Zhang, et al. (2024) used agency theory to find similar results, showing that a higher proportion of female shareholders correlates with commercial banks offering higher cash dividends to shareholders. Thus, the presence of female board members positively impacts corporate ESG performance. This includes better engagement in CSR activities, enhanced employee welfare, and improved environmental stewardship. Female directors contribute to a diverse and balanced board, leading to more comprehensive and socially responsible corporate governance.

3. Research Design

3.1 Dependent Variable

The data on Huazheng's social responsibility ratings, released by A-rated companies from 2012 to 2022, constitute the majority of the dependent variables in this chapter. This study illustrates this idea using ESG variable symbols. China's ESG rating system is still in an exploratory phase and has not yet established a common standard. To evaluate the data provided by companies, we use the Huazheng ESG database, which currently contains information up to 2022. Note that changes to other databases may cause delays. ESG analysis is mainly applied to A-level companies in China. The key elements of the assessment include the collection of public data; the creation of tools to evaluate the operating environment, company development, and governance; and the assignment of appropriate text levels. When crafting an ESG assessment methodology with Chinese characteristics, the specifics of the country, including policies, guidelines, corporate governance practices, industry development status, and data availability, must be considered. Understanding Chinese culture and mentality is also crucial in deciding which control points in the scoring system to investigate and improve. The ESG rating system itself needs to be dynamic and updated to keep pace with the continuous evolution of the market. By adapting our stance, we can make the ESG rating system more relevant to organizations and individual ratings, making the results more useful and widely accepted. Examples of specific ESG variables include energy conservation, pollution reduction, social supply chain management, shareholder diversity, and general ESG practices in corporate governance. For company valuation, variables such as market prices, book value versus book value, return on investments, costs, and revenues can be used. The ESG framework sets general standards like localization and dynamic updates of rating systems. However, when applying these to different regions and departments, the unique circumstances of each must be considered. This comprehensive approach ensures that the ESG rating system remains relevant and accurately reflects the performance and sustainability practices of companies within the Chinese context.

3.2 Independent Variable

The explanatory variable in this study is the board structure variable, as it examines how board structure affects CSR performance. Specifically, five indicators are used as explanatory variables: the percentage of independent directors, the integration of the chairman and CEO roles, the directors' shareholding ratio, the number of technical committees established by directors, and the percentage of female directors. The descriptions of each explanatory variable are as follows:

1. *Independent Directors Ratio:* This is the proportion of independent directors to total directors as at the end of the previous fiscal year.
2. *Integration of Chairman and CEO Roles:* This variable takes the value of 0 if the roles of chairman and CEO are combined, and 1 if they are separate.
3. *Directors' Shareholding Ratio*: This is the ratio of the total number of shares held by the board to the total number of shares outstanding.
4. *Number of Technical Committees for Directors:* This is the natural logarithm of the number of technical committees established by directors.
5. *Female Director Representation:* This is the proportion of female directors to the total number of directors at the end of the fiscal year.

3.3 Control Variable

This study also considers the possibility that other factors could interact with management traits to affect a company's ESG performance. Based on findings from recent national and international research, five crucial control variables were incorporated into the model: company size, foundation period (Age), real estate debt ratio (Lev), company type (state), and product market competitiveness [Herfindahl–Hirschman Index (HHI)]. The accounting year and firm size are logarithmically transformed in this analysis.

1. *Company Size*: This variable is typically expressed as the logarithm of the company's total assets at the end of the year and is often used as a control in similar studies. Previous research suggests that larger organizations find it easier to invest in CSR.
2. *Foundation Period (Age)*: This is the incorporation date of the company. Investor awareness of CSR investments varies with the age of the company. Older companies tend to focus more on ESG, making it easier to improve ESG disclosure.
3. *Asset–Liability Ratio (Lev)*: The ratio of total liabilities to total assets. Different companies' asset–liability ratios can affect their ESG performance in various ways.
4. *Company Type*: Different types of businesses have distinct ESG investment strategies. Companies across industries face unique ESG opportunities and challenges based on their business strategies and values, which in turn affect their environmental and social impacts.
5. *HHI*: This index measures market concentration by summing the squares of the market shares of the top *n* companies in a particular industry. It helps determine how concentrated a company's product market is.

Including these control variables helps diminish the impact of other factors on management traits and the company's ESG performance, thereby making the analysis more accurate. Detailed definitions of each variable are provided in Table 3.1.

3.4 Data Sources and Preprocessing

The companies included for this empirical study's sample were all companies with an A rating for the years 2012–2022. The main data source is the Wind database. To reduce the impact of outliers on the findings of the empirical test, missing values have been eliminated and the data have been trimmed.

Establishment of the Model

Considering the selection of variables and relevant research hypotheses in this chapter, the ordinary least squares (OLS) model used in this empirical study is specifically as follows:

$$\begin{aligned} ESG_t = \alpha_1 + \alpha_2 * indir_t + \alpha_3 * size_t + \alpha_4 * lev_t + \alpha_5 * age_t + \alpha_6 * lev_t \\ + \alpha_7 * state_t + \alpha_8 * hhi_t + \varepsilon_t \end{aligned} \tag{1}$$

Table 3.1 Variable Definition

Variable Type	*Variable Name*	*Variable Code*	*Definition*	*Reference*
Dependent variable	ESG comprehensive rating	ESG	Bloomberg database ESG data /100	Zhu and Rahman (2024)
Independent variable	Proportion of independent directors	Indir	Number of independent directors at the end of the year/total number of board members at the end of the year	Rahman et al. (2023)
	Duality	Dual	Value for both chairman and general manager is 1; otherwise, it is 0	Rahman et al. (2023)
	Shareholding ratio of directors	Boardr	Sum of directors' shareholding at the end of the year/total number of shares of the company at the end of the year	Rahman et al. (2023)
	Number of specialized committees established by the board of directors	Sum	Ln (1 + number of special committees established by the board of directors)	Rahman et al. (2023)
	Proportion of female directors	Female	Number of female directors at the end of the year/total number of directors at the end of the year	Rahman, Zhu, Zhang, and Hossain (2024)
Control variable	Enterprise size	Size	Ln (1 + total assets of the company at the end of the year)	Rahman, Zhu, and Yue (2024)
	Listing period	Age	Calculated using the natural logarithm of the number of years since the company was established plus one	Rahman, Zhu, and Jiang (2024)
	Asset liability ratio	Lev	Lev = (total liabilities ÷ total assets) × 100%	Lam et al. (2024)
	Enterprise nature	State	State owned 1, non-state-owned 0	Rahman and Zhu (2024)
	Market competitiveness	HHI	–	Rahman and Zhu (2023)

$$ESG_t = \alpha_1 + \alpha_2 * dual_t + \alpha_3 * size_t + \alpha_4 * lev_t + \alpha_5 * age_t + \alpha_6 * lev_t + \alpha_7 * state_t + \alpha_8 * hhi_t + \varepsilon_t \tag{2}$$

$$ESG_t = \alpha_1 + \alpha_2 * boardr_t + \alpha_3 * size_t + \alpha_4 * lev_t + \alpha_5 * age_t + \alpha_6 * lev_t + \alpha_7 * state_t + \alpha_8 * hhi_t + \varepsilon_t \tag{3}$$

$$ESG_t = \alpha_1 + \alpha_2 * sum_t + \alpha_3 * size_t + \alpha_4 * lev_t + \alpha_5 * age_t + \alpha_6 * lev_t + \alpha_7 * state_t + \alpha_8 * hhi_t + \varepsilon_t \quad (4)$$

$$ESG_t = \alpha_1 + \alpha_2 * female_t + \alpha_3 * size_t + \alpha_4 * lev_t + \alpha_5 * age_t + \alpha_6 * lev_t + \alpha_7 * state_t + \alpha_8 * hhi_t + \varepsilon_t \quad (5)$$

Here, α_t represents the estimation coefficient of the explanatory variable and the control variable, and ε_t represents the random disturbance term subject to normal distribution. The five models correspond to the five assumptions mentioned in the previous section.

4. Empirical Results

4.1 Descriptive Statistics

Table 3.2 presents the descriptive statistics, including sample size, mean, standard deviation, and maximum and lowest values for the key variables in this empirical model. Using descriptive statistics, no moderately poor data points were discovered, and each data point's sample size is 38,131 with no missing values. Below that, the dependent variable ESG has an average value of 72.929, a standard deviation of 56.450, and a maximum value of 81.110.

4.2 Collinearity Analysis

The individual's correlation coefficient for the dependent variable, the explanatory variable, and the control variable is displayed in Table 3.3. Just take a look at the first data column's attributes. We may infer from the first column of data that there is a 0.053 correlation coefficient, which is significant at the 0.01 level, between the explanatory variable ESG and the percentage of independent directors Indir. ESG and double markup have a −0.006 association coefficient, which is not statistically significant. The explanatory variable ESG and the participation coefficient

Table 3.2 Descriptive Statistics of Main Variables

Variable	*Sample Size*	*Mean Value*	*Standard Deviation*	*Minimum Value*	*Maximum Value*
ESG	38,313	72.929	5.080	56.450	81.110
Indir	38,313	0.376	0.050	0.333	0.500
Dual	38,313	0.300	0.458	0.000	1.000
Boardr	38,313	0.130	0.184	0.000	0.551
Sum	38,313	1.601	0.095	1.099	1.792
Female	38,313	0.154	0.127	0.000	0.429
Size	38,313	22.193	1.296	19.621	25.014
Age	38,313	9.969	7.756	0.000	24.000
Lev	38,313	0.427	0.211	0.053	0.823
HHI	38,313	0.087	0.077	0.000	0.302

Table 3.3 Correlation Analysis

	ESG	*Indir*	*Dual*	*Boardr*	*Sum*	*Female*	*Size*	*Age*	*Lev*	*HHI*
ESG	1.000									
Indir	0.053***	1.000								
Dual	–0.006	0.114***	1.000							
Boardr	0.096***	0.074***	0.258***	1.000						
Sum	0.054***	0.005	–0.032***	–0.045***	1.000					
Female	–0.008	0.031***	0.111***	0.121***	–0.003	1.000				
Size	0.215***	–0.035***	–0.201***	–0.352***	0.131***	–0.127***	1.000			
Age	–0.134***	–0.032***	–0.249***	–0.542***	0.007	–0.086***	0.369***	1.000		
Lev	–0.108***	–0.014***	–0.152***	–0.328***	0.109***	–0.084***	0.503***	0.349***	1.000	
HHI	–0.070***	–0.010*	–0.082***	–0.143***	0.043***	–0.038***	0.133***	0.107***	0.131***	1.000

* $p < 0.1$, ** $p < 0.05$, *** $p < 0.01$

Boardr have a correlation coefficient of 0.096, which is significant at the 0.01 level. The explanatory variable ESG and the total number of committee members have a 0.054 correlation coefficient, which is significant at the 0.01 level. Women have a −0.008 correlation coefficient, which is irrelevant. Here, we can conduct preliminary testing for Hypotheses 1, 3, and 4.

In addition, the results of the collinearity test are also output here, as shown in Table 3.4. The results of the collinearity test show that none of the indicators are collinear, which means that the VIF value is less than 10, indicating that the chosen indicators are independent and non-interactive and that there is no overfitting that may be utilized to create regression models.

4.3 Benchmark Regression

After controlling the industry and year factors, OLS regression was performed on the five models, and the results are shown in Table 3.5. The adjusted *R2* value of each model is 0.215, 0.212, 0.215, 0.212, and 0.212, respectively, and the fitting effect was satisfactory.

Independent directors provide expert guidance and advice on corporate management due to their expertise in economics, law, and environmental protection. A certain percentage of independent directors significantly contributes to the protection and promotion of stakeholders' rights and interests. They also influence top-down reporting practices and information disclosure for GEM listed businesses, enhancing their ESG performance rankings. In the context of principal–agent theory, combining the roles of chairman and CEO significantly increases the CEO's decision-making independence and reduces communication and agency costs across departments. However, this merger can diminish the oversight of the CEO's decisions. As supervisory responsibilities gradually shift from directors to operators, and with the lack of corresponding independence, the chairman is more likely to control the overall operation of the enterprise. This centralization of power can lead to the chairman abusing their authority, potentially infringing on enterprise assets and harming the rights and interests of minority shareholders.

Table 3.4 Collinearity Diagnosis

Variable	*VIF*	*1/VIF*
Age	1.540	0.649
Boardr	1.530	0.655
Size	1.490	0.670
Lev	1.440	0.696
Dual	1.120	0.895
HHI	1.030	0.967
Female	1.030	0.971
Sum	1.030	0.975
Indir	1.020	0.983
Mean	VIF	1.250

Table 3.5 Baseline Regression

	ESG	*ESG*	*ESG*	*ESG*	*ESG*
Indir	5.628***				
	(11.54)				
Size	1.689***	1.677***	1.711***	1.679***	1.684***
	(68.31)	(67.53)	(68.78)	(67.82)	(67.74)
Age	−0.129***	−0.132***	−0.111***	−0.130***	−0.130***
	(−35.76)	(−35.76)	(−27.71)	(−35.66)	(−35.80)
Lev	−7.002***	−6.996***	−6.829***	7.012***	−6.997***
	(−46.68)	(−46.57)	(−45.31)	(−46.63)	(−46.58)
HHI	0.079	0.146	0.136	0.146	0.134
	(0.11)	(0.20)	(0.19)	(0.20)	(0.19)
Dual		−0.156***			
		(−2.85)			
Boardr			1.860***		
			(12.02)		
Sum				0.863***	
				(3.47)	
Female					0.128***
					(6.66)
_cons	39.704***	42.057***	40.884***	40.628***	41.851***
	(66.99)	(74.09)	(71.23)	(60.38)	(73.37)
r2_a	0.215	0.212	0.215	0.212	0.212
F	113.901	112.053	113.604	111.893	111.795
N	38313	38313	38313	38313	38313

t statistics is given in parentheses.

$^{*}p < 0.1$, $^{**}p < 0.05$, $^{***}p < 0.01$

The combination of the roles of CEO and chairman can lead to adverse selection issues, reducing the chairman's supervisory responsibilities and thus negatively impacting ESG performance. Additionally, if majority or controlling shareholders possess more information and voting rights, they can more effectively supervise the company. Bernardi et al. (2009) research indicates that companies with a higher number of female directors tend to engage in more active social responsibility behaviours and are more likely to be listed among the "world's most ethical businesses." The theory of female concern emphasizes that women who pay more attention to social environments and ethics are more responsive to environmental pollution and community damage caused by corporate actions. This differs significantly from males, as women's particular compassion and social roles promote their moral and ethical beliefs. Rahman, Zhu, Zhang, et al. (2024) also found that while male directors focused more on the firm's overall financial success, female directors prioritized CSR. These arguments align with the empirical findings of this study, which show that the percentage of women on the board of directors positively impacts the performance of ESG factors.

(1) Independent Directors' % in Relation to ESG

The fitting outcome of model 1 is displayed in the first column. The coefficient of Indir for independent directors is 5.628, which, as the result demonstrates, is significant at the significance level of 0.01, indicating that Indir for independent directors significantly improves social responsibility. That is, the higher the ESG of the social responsibility score, the higher the share of independent directors.

(2) Connection between ESG and the Integration of Two Positions

The results of model 2's fitting are shown in the second column. The coefficient of dual for dual roles is 1.677, which is significant at the 0.01 level and indicates a substantial inverse relationship between dual roles and social responsibility, as demonstrated in the data. The lower their social responsibility score (ESG), the more instances there are of two positions being combined.

(3) Proportion of Comitology Agreements to the ESG

The results of fitting model 4 are displayed in the fourth column. According to the findings, there is a statistically significant positive correlation between social responsibility and the total number of rejects, as indicated by the coefficient of the sum of comitology agreements, which is 0.863 and has a significance level of 0.01. The ESG indicator for a body's social responsibility increases with an increase in the number of bodies.

(4) Percentage of Women on the Board to the Governance-related Sustainability Standard (GSS)

The matching outcomes for model 5 are displayed in the fifth column. As the findings indicate, there are 0.128 women on the board, which is significant at 0.01 and clearly demonstrates a positive relationship between social responsibility and the percentage of women on executive boards. The evaluation of their social responsibility increases with an increase in the percentage of women on the board.

4 Endogeneity Testing

This section mainly uses the generalized method of moments (GMM) technique to test and correct the possible endogenous problems in the baseline regression. There are two GMM approaches: differential GMM and system GMM. Compared with the differential GMM, system GMM is better in testing endogeneity. Therefore, this study adopts system GMM, which needs to test the validity of explanatory variable lag value as an instrumental variable to test the validity of GMM estimation. Therefore, the following two methods are used for the test: (1) the Sargan transition identification method is used to judge whether the instrumental variables cited in this chapter are valid. If the null hypothesis is not rejected, it indicates that the instrumental variables selected in this study are appropriate; and (2) the non-autocorrelation of residual terms, that is, whether there is second-order sequence autocorrelation of residual terms, is verified. Specifically, the method adopted is AR (2). If the null hypothesis is not rejected, it indicates that there is

Table 3.6 Endogeneity Test Regression

	ESG	*ESG*	*ESG*	*ESG*	*ESG*
Indir	5.795***				
	(6.34)				
Size	1.527***	1.698***	1.730***	1.624***	1.879***
	(11.52)	(10.79)	(51.90)	(33.26)	(12.02)
Age	−0.144***	−0.126**	−0.100***	−0.117***	−0.110***
	(−10.18)	(−2.13)	(−5.98)	(−14.80)	(−7.35)
Lev	−6.812***	−7.019***	−6.779***	−7.385***	−6.924***
	(−21.32)	(−44.29)	(−32.97)	(−27.28)	(−37.26)
HHI	1.422	0.151	0.153	0.393	0.028
	(0.84)	(0.18)	(0.21)	(0.47)	(0.03)
Dual		−0.177***			
		(−8.04)			
Boardr			2.607*		
			(1.73)		
Sum				18.189*	
				(1.68)	
Female					17.180***
					(5.22)
_cons	97.688**	41.395***	40.161***	14.625	35.077***
	(2.33)	(8.91)	(39.86)	(0.91)	(6.53)
r2_a	0.225	0.209	0.212	0.113	0.221
F					
N	38313	38313	38313	38313	38313

t statistics values are given in parentheses.

$^{*}p < 0.1$, $^{**}p < 0.05$, $^{***}p < 0.01$

no second-order sequence autocorrelation of residual terms. Both AR (2) and Sargon test results from this study accept the null hypothesis, that is, the test passes. Table 3.6 shows the results.

5. Robustness Test

In order to ensure the robustness of the model, the corresponding robustness test is conducted in this study. The robustness test mainly adopts the fixed-effect model of panel regression. Since only time and industry effects are controlled in the benchmark regression and the data also have the characteristics of panel data, the fixed-effect model used for panel regression is used here. Individual effects are controlled to achieve a robust effect.

Table 3.7 displays the robustness findings after the dependent variable is changed. This leads to the conclusion that the model is resilient with no significant variations in the coefficients and significance of other control variables, and the robustness results are consistent with the baseline regression. As a result, the findings of the comparative regression analysis and the conclusions reached in this study are reliable and accurate.

Table 3.7 Robust Regression Coefficients

	ESG	*ESG*	*ESG*	*ESG*	*ESG*
Indir	5.999***				
	(12.13)				
Size	1.716***	1.701***	1.747***	1.693***	1.712***
	(74.48)	(73.31)	(75.15)	(73.12)	(73.81)
Age	−0.127***	−0.130***	−0.106***	−0.127***	−0.128***
	(−36.20)	(−36.34)	(−26.91)	(−36.01)	(−36.34)
Lev	−6.127***	−6.113***	−5.944***	−6.167***	−6.110***
	(−44.11)	(−43.93)	(−42.61)	(−44.25)	(−43.90)
HHI	−5.143***	−5.154***	−4.852***	−5.197***	−5.121***
	(−15.84)	(−15.83)	(−14.91)	(−15.97)	(−15.74)
Dual		−0.149***			
		(−2.65)			
Boardr			2.074***		
			(12.54)		
Sum				1.711***	
				(6.54)	
Female					0.396**
					(2.02)
_cons	36.872***	39.539***	37.864***	36.915***	39.152***
	(70.82)	(81.24)	(76.73)	(60.94)	(80.25)
r2_a	0.155	0.152	0.155	0.153	0.152
F	1338.215	1305.189	1340.621	1313.631	1304.771
N	38313	38313	38313	38313	38313

t statistics in parentheses.

* $p < 0.1$, ** $p < 0.05$, *** $p < 0.01$

6 Discussion and Conclusion

6.1 Relationship with Prior Studies

Scholars have long studied the characteristics of boards of directors to understand how their managerial abilities can enhance CSR and ESG performance. A review of the literature reveals that most experts identify board features through comprehensive checklists. For example, Ge et al. (2024) highlighted characteristics such as the capacity to act independently, motivation mechanisms, stable behaviour, years of experience, and the ability to acquire expertise. Ping et al. (2011) further detailed the characteristics of boards, including board size, shareholder characteristics, management characteristics, the structure of directors, the status of meeting completions, and the quality of supervisory board members.

This study shows that the combination of the CEO and chairman roles negatively affects corporate responsibility ratings, while the proportion of independent directors has a positive impact. Additionally, the number of committees, the percentage of female directors, and the board ownership ratio significantly improve corporate responsibility ratings. The study by Birindelli et al. (2018) supports this finding, showing that increasing the number of independent directors can enhance the soundness of management decisions. Independent directors can make decisions that are in the best interests of the company from an impartial standpoint and provide informed, reasonable, and objective assessments. Jensen (1993), in his study of board governance structures abroad, noted that having directors also serve as chief executives can weaken a company's internal control system. Fair and reasonable management oversight is only achieved when the roles of director and chief executive are held by different individuals. Supporting this, Chen et al. (2018) found a strong association between shareholder size, board shareholding percentage, and CSR. The findings of this study are consistent with prior research, demonstrating that independent directors, board diversity, and separation of CEO and chairman roles are crucial for enhancing corporate ESG performance.

Practical Implications

Based on the findings of the aforementioned empirical research, it can be concluded that ESG performance among ChiNext board listed companies has shown an upward trend year after year. This improvement is due to the increasing importance these companies place on actively disclosing their ESG reports as part of their board strategic decisions and ideological commitments. However, the ESG research group of listed firms in China has found that managers' performance levels are inconsistent, and Chinese listed businesses have not yet given ESG management enough attention to reach the pinnacle of applied enterprise strategy. The primary focus for most organizations remains the publication of corporate ESG statements. To truly integrate ESG principles, listed firms must develop comprehensive ESG management systems, incorporate ESG standards into their overall management, and establish management systems with strategic risk control index targets, in addition to creating ESG reports.

Low governance effectiveness and strict internal personnel control have plagued the boards of directors of ChiNext board listed companies in China. Optimizing and modernizing the boards of these companies have long been a focus of academic research and business attention. There is currently limited literature specifically concentrating on the link between ESG performance and the board features of GEM listed businesses. Most research, both domestic and international, focuses on the ESG disclosure of listed companies rather than the specific attributes of their boards.

In terms of variable selection, this article uses the characteristics of the board of directors as the explanatory variable and the enterprise's ESG performance as the dependent variable to examine the correlation between the two. The objectives are twofold: firstly, to identify the elements that genuinely support ESG performance and help enhance the governance of GEM listed companies' boards of directors through empirical findings and, secondly, based on the positive impacts of specific board characteristics, to provide constructive recommendations for improving board governance and boosting the ESG performance of organizations. This approach helps listed firms achieve long-term sustainable development and encourages boards of directors to apply ESG principles effectively.

Theoretical Contributions

This chapter focuses on the influence of board features on the ESG performance of listed firms. Five explanatory variables were selected to represent board characteristics based on ESG rating data of A-share companies from 2012 to 2022: the proportion of independent directors, the integration of the CEO and chairman positions, the board shareholding ratio, the number of specialized committees, and the number of female directors. The proportion of independent directors does not significantly correlate with the ESG performance of companies listed on the ChiNext board. This finding challenges the commonly held belief that independent directors inherently enhance ESG performance through improved oversight and governance. There is a negative correlation between integration of the CEO and chairman positions and the ESG performance of enterprises. This supports the notion that combining these roles can reduce the effectiveness of oversight and lead to potential conflicts of interest. Previous research suggests that this merger diminishes the CEO's decision-making oversight, as the chairman's increased control can lead to misuse of power, infringing on enterprise assets, and harming minority shareholders' rights. The number of specialized committees under the board of directors is positively correlated with the ESG performance of the enterprise. This indicates that specialized committees contribute to more effective governance by addressing specific areas of concern and enhancing the board's overall functionality. While the specific impacts of the board shareholding ratio and the number of female directors are not detailed in this summary, their inclusion as explanatory variables highlights the importance of diverse board characteristics in assessing ESG performance.

These findings contribute to the existing literature by providing empirical evidence on the complex relationship between board characteristics and ESG performance. They emphasize the need for a nuanced understanding of how different aspects of board composition and structure can influence corporate governance and sustainability outcomes. This research underscores the importance of specialized committees and the risks associated with the CEO–chairman role integration, offering valuable insights for both scholars and practitioners aiming to improve ESG performance through board governance.

This study examines the impact of board features on the ESG performance of A-rated stocks, focusing on three key aspects: board structure, board behaviour, and board history. The data for this analysis were sourced from the ESG ratings of over 3,000 municipal firms between 2012 and 2022. Five explanatory factors were selected to reflect board characteristics: the percentage of independent directors, the number of technical committees, the combination of general manager and chairman roles, the board shareholding ratio, and the percentage of female board members. A multiple regression model was developed for analysis and testing, with robustness and endogeneity thoroughly examined to ensure reliable conclusions.

The percentage of independent directors positively impacts the social responsibility score. This underscores the value of independent oversight in enhancing corporate governance and social responsibility. The combination of the general manager and chairman roles has a negative impact on the social responsibility score. This finding highlights the risks associated with consolidating these roles, which can reduce oversight and lead to potential conflicts of interest. The management of board ownership and the number of technical committees positively influence social responsibility ratings. These factors contribute to more effective governance and decision-making processes. The percentage of female directors significantly and positively impacts social responsibility ratings, emphasizing the importance of gender diversity in enhancing board effectiveness and ESG performance. The study provides robust empirical evidence on the relationship between board characteristics and ESG performance, offering valuable insights for both academic research and practical governance strategies. By highlighting the importance of independent directors, specialized committees, and gender diversity, this research contributes to a deeper understanding of how board composition and structure can drive better ESG outcomes.

Based on the findings and limitations of this study, several avenues for future research can be suggested to further explore the relationship between board features and ESG performance. Future research could extend the timeframe of the study beyond 2022 to include more recent data. This would allow for an analysis of long-term trends and the impact of evolving corporate governance practices on ESG performance. Conducting comparative studies across different regions or countries could provide insights into how cultural, regulatory, and economic differences influence the relationship between board characteristics and ESG performance. This could help identify best practices and contextual factors that enhance ESG outcomes. Examining the impact of board features on ESG performance within specific industries could uncover industry-specific dynamics and challenges. This would allow for more tailored governance recommendations and strategies. Future research could investigate the role of board dynamics, such as board meetings' frequency, board member interactions, and decision-making processes, on ESG performance. Understanding how these dynamics influence ESG outcomes could provide deeper insights into effective board governance. Exploring how the adoption of new technologies and innovative practices within board governance affects ESG performance could be a fruitful area of research. This includes the use of digital tools for monitoring and reporting ESG metrics and the impact of technological expertise among board members. Analysing how different stakeholders, such as institutional investors, activists, and regulators, influence board decisions related to ESG could provide a more comprehensive understanding of the external pressures shaping corporate governance practices. Investigating the behavioural aspects of board members, including their values, attitudes, and motivations towards ESG, could offer insights into the human factors driving governance practices. This could include studies on the psychological and sociological aspects of board decision-making. Future research could examine how boards integrate ESG considerations into overall business strategy and the long-term impact of such integration on company performance and sustainability. Most studies, including this one, focus on larger, publicly traded companies. Future research could explore the relationship between board features and ESG performance in small and medium-sized enterprises, which face different governance challenges and opportunities. Analysing the impact of various policy and regulatory frameworks on the effectiveness of board governance in promoting ESG performance could provide valuable insights for policymakers and regulators aiming to enhance corporate sustainability. By exploring these future research directions, scholars can build on the current study's findings and contribute to a more nuanced and comprehensive understanding of how board governance influences ESG performance across different contexts and dimensions.

References

Ahern, K. R., & Dittmar, A. K. (2012). The changing of the boards: The impact on firm valuation of mandated female board representation. *The Quarterly Journal of Economics, 127*(1), 137–197.

BCBS – Basel Committee on Banking Supervision. (2015). *Guidelines: Corporate governance principles for banks*. BCBS.

Beckman, C. M., & Haunschild, P. R. (2002). Network learning: The effects of partners' heterogeneity of experience on corporate acquisitions. *Administrative Science Quarterly, 47*, 92–124.

Bernardi, R. A., Bosco, S. M., & Columb, V. L. (2009). Does female representation on boards of directors associate with the 'most ethical companies' list? *Corporate Reputation Review, 12*, 270–280.

Birindelli, G., Dell'Atti, S., Iannuzzi, A. P., & Savioli, M. (2018). Composition and activity of the board of directors: Impact on ESG performance in the banking system. *Sustainability, 10*(12), 4699.

Chen, Y. C., Hung, M., & Wang, Y. (2018). The effect of mandatory CSR disclosure on firm profitability and social externalities: Evidence from China. *Journal of Accounting and Economics, 65*(1), 169–190.

Eccles, R. G., Ioannou, I., & Serafeim, G. (2014). The impact of corporate sustainability on organizational processes and performance. *Management Science, 60*, 2835–2857. https://doi.org/10.1287/mnsc.2013.1849

Garcia-Meca, E., Garcia-Sanchez, I. M., & Cuadrado-Ballesteros, B. (2020). Board gender diversity and corporate social performance: The role of business risk and corporate reputation as mediating mechanisms. *Corporate Social Responsibility and Environmental Management, 27*(6), 2528–2540. https://doi.org/10.1002/csr.1932

García-Sánchez, I. M., Martánez-Ferrero, J., & García-Meca, E. (2018). Board of directors and CSR in banking: The moderating role of bank regulation and investor protection strength. *Australian Accounting Review, 86*, 428–445. https://doi.org/10.1111/auar.12247

Ge, E., DongZhi, C., & Mace, R. (2024). Religiosity and gender bias structure social networks. *Evolutionary Human Sciences, 6*, e23.

HLEG – High-Level Expert Group on Sustainable Finance. (2017). *Financing a sustainable European economy, interim report 2017*. https://ec.europa.eu/info/publications/170713-sustainable-finance-report_en

Ibrahim, N. A., & Angelidis, J. P. (1995). The corporate social responsiveness orientation of board members: Are there differences between inside and outside directors? *Journal of Business Ethics, 14*, 405–410.

Jensen, M. C. (1993). The modern industrial revolution, exit and failure of internal control system. *The Journal of Finance, 1993*(3), 831–880.

Johnson, R. A., Meyer, K. E., & Sakai, M. (2018). Board diversity and corporate social responsibility: Evidence from Japan. *Journal of Business Ethics, 149*(2), 401–414. https://doi.org/10.1007/s10551-016-3060-5

Lam, B. M., Mo, P. L. L., & Rahman, M. J. (2024). Secrecy culture, client importance, and auditor reporting behavior: An international study. *Managerial Auditing Journal, 39*(2), 113–137

Pereira, V., & Shrestha, K. (2015). Women directors and corporate social responsibility. *Journal of Business Ethics*, *136*(2), 399–417.
Ping, T., Chang-qing, S., & Li, S. (2011, September). Empirical research on the interactive relationship between cash holdings and corporate performance of listed companies in China. In *2011 international conference on management science & engineering 18th annual conference proceedings* (pp. 938–949). IEEE.
Rahman, J., & Wu, J. (2023). M&A activity and ESG performance: Evidence from China. *Managerial Finance*, *50*(1), 179–197.
Rahman, M. J., Wu, Q., & Zhu, H. (2024). Corporate social responsibility in times of social distancing: Evidence from China. *Business Ethics, the Environment & Responsibility*.
Rahman, M. J., & Zhu, H. (2023). Predicting accounting fraud using imbalanced ensemble learning classifiers – evidence from China. *Accounting & Finance*, *63*(3), 3455–3486
Rahman, M. J., & Zhu, H. (2024). Detecting accounting fraud in family firms: Evidence from machine learning approaches. *Advances in Accounting*, *64*, 100722.
Rahman, M. J., Zhu, H., & Chen, S. (2023). Does CSR reduce financial distress? Moderating effect of firm characteristics, auditor characteristics, and covid-19. *International Journal of Accounting & Information Management*, *31*(5), 756–784.
Rahman, M. J., Zhu, H., & Jiang, X. (2024). Family firms, client importance, and auditor reporting behavior: Evidence from China. *Meditari Accountancy Research*, *32*(2), 543–578.
Rahman, M. J., Zhu, H., & Yue, L. (2024). Does the adoption of artificial intelligence by audit firms and their clients affect audit quality and efficiency? Evidence from China. *Managerial Auditing Journal*. *39*(6), 668–699. https://doi.org/10.1108/ MAJ-03-2023-3846
Rahman, M. J., Zhu, H., Zhang, Y., & Hossain, M. M. (2024). Effect of female representation in audit committees on non-audit fees: Evidence from China. *Meditari Accountancy Research*, *32*(4), 1258–1290. https://doi.org/10.1108/MEDAR-05-2023-1996
Smith, J., & Wang, Y. (2017). Board structure and corporate social responsibility: Evidence from the United States. *Journal of Business Ethics*, *144*(3), 623–644. https://doi.org/10.1007/s10551-015-2865-2
Zhang, C., & Duan, N. (2008). An empirical study of the relationship between board size and performance in private listed companies in China. *Audit Research*, *06*, 71–78.
Zhu, H., & Rahman, M. J. (2024). Ex-ante expected changes in ESG and future stock returns based on machine learning. *The British Accounting Review*, 101457.

4 Corporate Governance and ESG Disclosure in China

Md Jahidur Rahman, Tarek Rana, Hongtao Zhu, and Chen Pinrun

1. Introduction

This chapter explores the effects of corporate governance on environmental, social, and governance (ESG) disclosure in the Chinese stock market, drawing inspiration from Bamahros et al. (2022) and the increasing emphasis on ESG reporting in China. It focuses on three key aspects of governance: the management personnel structure, internal executive compensation disparity, and supply chain concentration. The study addresses three main questions: (1) does a higher proportion of female management improve ESG disclosure? (2) Is reducing internal executive compensation disparity significant for ESG disclosure? (3) Can lower supply chain concentration enhance ESG disclosure?

The motivations for this research are threefold. Firstly, companies have become more aware of ESG issues over the past decade, linking their ESG activities to market preferences, managerial behaviour, and brand value (Khan, 2019; Gillan et al., 2021). Firms with strong sustainability awareness often exhibit better management and financial performance (Zumente & Bistrova, 2021). Secondly, research shows that promoting gender diversity positively impacts ESG performance (e.g., Velte, 2016). However, some studies question the relationship between gender-diverse boards and corporate performance (e.g., Manita et al., 2018). This study aims to clarify the impact of female management on ESG performance. Additionally, integrating ESG metrics into executive compensation has been shown to improve corporate ESG performance (Cohen et al., 2022), yet the relationship between internal compensation disparity and ESG disclosure in China remains unexplored. Thirdly, as China aims for carbon peak by 2030 and carbon neutrality by 2060 (Sun et al., 2022), firms must disclose ESG information to comply with government mandates (Li et al., 2023). Enhancing ESG disclosure is vital for sustainable development.

In this chapter, we empirically examine the research questions using data from Chinese listed firms between 2018 and 2022. The dependent variable is the corporate ESG score, while the independent variables include the proportion of female management, internal executive compensation disparity, and supply chain concentration. The study employs the generalized method of moments (GMM) and Hausman fixed-effect model to address endogeneity, along with robustness tests using lagged variable models. Results indicate a positive relationship between corporate

DOI: 10.4324/9781003488934-5

governance and ESG disclosure. Specifically, a higher proportion of female management, lower internal executive compensation disparity, and reduced supply chain concentration contribute to improved ESG disclosure quality.

This chapter contributes to the literature by demonstrating that female managers are more motivated to enhance ESG performance, supporting previous findings (Borghesi et al., 2014). We also uniquely examine the effects of internal executive compensation disparity and supply chain concentration on ESG performance in Chinese firms. Theoretical contributions include support for agency theory, stakeholder value theory, and legitimacy theory, showing that management's pursuit of ESG goals aligns with shareholder interests. Practically, the findings offer insights for policymakers and corporate leaders on improving ESG performance through diversity and equitable compensation.

The chapter is structured as follows: Section 2 covers ESG background in China; Section 3 presents theoretical perspectives; Section 4 reviews the literature and proposes hypotheses; Section 5 outlines the research design; Section 6 details empirical results; Section 7 addresses endogeneity; Section 8 presents robustness tests; Section 9 discusses findings; and Section 10 concludes the study.

2. Background

The term ESG, introduced in 2004, has recently become a key focus in global corporate strategies (Zhang, 2022). In China, the drive to adopt ESG practices is largely motivated by the nation's goal of transitioning to a green economy. As the Chinese economy shifts from rapid growth to high-quality development, it aims for sustainable and efficient economic progress (Tang et al., 2023). With a national sustainable development strategy in place, regulators are increasingly prioritizing ESG, and China, as the largest emerging economy, is actively promoting a green innovation strategy (Tan & Zhu, 2022). The government is committed to facilitating ESG development through top-down initiatives, essential for sustainable growth in the global economy (Li et al., 2021).

China has made significant progress in ESG promotion, establishing cooperation agreements for environmental information disclosure, introducing governance codes for listed firms, setting ambitious carbon targets, and mandating legal disclosure of environmental data (Zhang, 2022). Companies are motivated by external policy pressures, internal growth needs, and the importance of maintaining positive community relations (Cong et al., 2022). Transitioning to a lower-carbon model is vital for achieving China's peak carbon goal by 2030 and carbon neutrality by 2060 (Mneimneh et al., 2023). Several studies in China also investigate the relationship between environmental accounting and firm performance (Rahman & Wu, 2023; Rahman et al., 2024, 2023; Zhu & Rahman, 2024).

Additionally, a new generation of investors is increasingly incorporating ESG strategies into their practices (Chen & Mussalli, 2020). ESG considerations are becoming essential in investment assessments by portfolio managers and analysts (Orsagh et al., 2019). However, a Chartered Financial Analyst (CFA) Institute report notes that most Chinese investors focus more on learning about ESG investing than on implementing it, with 80%–90% lacking a framework for ESG investments. Despite this, Chinese listed firms have become more proactive in ESG disclosure; by the end of 2020, over 25% of A-share companies had published their annual corporate social responsibility (CSR) and ESG reports, a significant increase (Zhang, 2022). Nonetheless, many companies and sectors still face challenges with ESG performance ratings. While some improved their Morgan Stanley Capital International (MSCI) ESG ratings from 2018 to 2020, most continue to struggle with low scores on the AAA-CCC scale (World Economic Forum, 2021).

3. Theoretical Perspectives

In response to the increasing interest in CSR, a comprehensive set of ESG metrics has been proposed to evaluate CSR performance (Cohen et al., 2022). Investors often use ESG ratings to assess companies based on stakeholder treatment, corporate governance, and potential environmental impact (Signori et al., 2021). Corporate governance is crucial to a company's ESG performance (Buchetti et al., 2022), with several theories – such as agency theory, stakeholder value theory, and legitimacy theory – offering insights into why companies disclose their ESG performance (Alsayegh et al., 2020).

Agency theory suggests that shareholders and management share a common goal of maximizing shareholder value (Jensen & Meckling, 1976). This focus on value creation is linked to the corporation's ability to generate profit, which may lead managers to engage in greenwashing or promote ESG disclosures (Friedman et al., 2021).

Research indicates that firms responsive to stakeholder demands tend to outperform their peers (Li et al., 2021). Stakeholder theory emphasizes the importance of stakeholder support for a corporation's long-term success (Gray et al., 1995). Effective stakeholder engagement enhances environmental policies and promotes sustainable development (Lokuwaduge & Heenetigala, 2016). Increasingly, diverse groups – including customers, employees, and regulators – are focusing on how companies address ESG issues (Khan, 2019).

Government regulators are implementing policies and disclosure systems to standardize business practices (Li et al., 2021). Legitimacy theory argues that ESG disclosure is a necessary requirement, heavily influenced by regulatory frameworks (Lokuwaduge & Heenetigala, 2016).

Integrating these theories shows that corporate governance significantly affects ESG performance and disclosure. Effective governance aligns management goals with shareholder interests, addresses stakeholder concerns, and meets regulatory requirements, ultimately enhancing ESG performance and transparency.

4. Literature Review and Hypothesis Development

4.1 Role of Female Management

The board of directors plays a crucial role in a corporation's success and is vital for effective governance (García-Sánchez et al., 2017; Demirbas & Yukhanaev, 2011).

One key method for boards to address governance issues and create value is through performance evaluation (Kiel & Nicholson, 2005). Therefore, both the board and management should prioritize ESG factors in their evaluations and disclosures. With a strong positive correlation between sustainability performance and profitability, companies understand that achieving sustainable development is essential for survival (Birindelli et al., 2018). Transparency in ESG practices can help reduce fraud risks, lower production costs, and improve quality and productivity (Suttipun, 2021).

Gender diversity in the board and management significantly influences ESG disclosure. Female CEOs and managers are generally more committed to CSR and more likely to invest in CSR initiatives (Borghesi et al., 2014). Female directors often excel at addressing stakeholders' interests due to their greater concern for welfare (Adams et al., 2011). Additionally, equitable power distribution within the board enhances the link between female representation and social performance (Byron & Post, 2016). Research consistently shows that female board members positively affect ESG performance (Velte, 2016), and increasing the number of female executives leads to notable improvements in corporate ESG outcomes (Meng & Zhu, 2023).

However, some studies question the strength of the relationship between corporate performance and gender-diverse boards. Manita et al. (2018) found no significant correlation, and Aabo and Giorici (2022) reported no link between CEO gender and CSR performance using Refinitiv ESG data. Furthermore, female CFOs may adopt conservative financial reporting practices, potentially leading to lower budgets for ESG initiatives, which contradicts the observed positive relationship.

Overall, in this chapter, we argue that a higher proportion of female management will result in better ESG disclosure scores. Here, "management" includes directors, superiors, and executives. Thus, the proposed hypothesis is as follows:

H1: A corporation achieves better ESG disclosure with an increasing proportion of female management.

4.2 Importance of Appropriate Executive Compensation

Corporate governance includes managing executive compensation, which varies among firms due to differing capacities to pay (Porcuna Enguix, 2021). Traditionally, compensation comprises fixed and variable elements (Murphy, 2005), with salary directly influencing executive productivity (Ahamed, 2022). Increasingly, companies are linking executive pay to ESG metrics. Executives with backgrounds in business, economics, and law tend to engage more in social responsibility and support CSR investments based on a mix of financial and non-financial metrics (Li et al., 2021). Effective governance mechanisms that tie compensation to firm performance can mitigate executive opportunism (Sheikh et al., 2017). Including ESG criteria in performance evaluations leads to meaningful changes in compensation and improvements in ESG outcomes (Ormazabal et al., 2022). Additionally, firms with higher top management compensation often achieve greater eco-innovation scores (Phung et al., 2022).

However, reliability of disclosed ESG information is crucial. Trade-offs exist between managers' ESG efforts and potential reporting biases, which can lead to inconsistent outcomes (Friedman et al., 2021). Unreliable ESG disclosures may encourage greenwashing (Yu et al., 2020). Phung et al. (2022) warn of inadequate incentives for executives to genuinely enhance societal and environmental conditions, alongside issues with non-standardized ESG frameworks.

Efforts are being made to motivate executives to meet ESG expectations of stakeholders, including shareholders (Krueger et al., 2020). Stakeholders are increasingly concerned about issues like the wage gap between executives and employees, decarbonization, diversity, and equity (Matemane et al., 2022). The Chinese public, in particular, has expressed concern about executive–worker wage disparities (Jiang et al., 2019). Thus, internal executive compensation disparity is an important factor to consider. Based on this rationale, the proposed hypothesis is

H2: Mitigating the internal executive compensation disparity positively impacts the quality of ESG disclosure.

4.3 Supply Chain Concentration

Supply chain management is a vital aspect of corporate governance, with recent research highlighting a shift towards low-carbon and green supply chain practices. ESG factors play a significant role in this area, making eco-friendly business decisions and selecting sustainable partners essential for creating a green supply chain (Zeng et al., 2022). Effective eco-friendly supply chain governance involves integrating ESG indicators at various stages, facilitating the transition to lower-carbon operations. Incorporating ESG risks into supply chain management is increasingly critical; without this integration, ESG measures lack effectiveness (Dai & Tang, 2021). As stakeholders demand greater integrity in supply chains, companies must provide accurate carbon disclosures and verification reports to support low-carbon initiatives (Mohter & Fernando, 2020).

Furthermore, modern supply chains are complex networks that connect customers and suppliers rather than functioning in a linear fashion. These networks include various partners with distinct goals (Klimkiewicz, 2017), evolving from isolated companies to integrated systems comprising clients, suppliers, manufacturers, service providers, and retailers (Chatchawanchanchanakij et al., 2019). Engaging diverse stakeholders, including internal departments and customers, enhances ESG management practices through comprehensive planning, goal setting, decision-making, and knowledge sharing (George Whitelock, 2015). This chapter thus explores the influence of supply chain concentration on ESG disclosure and proposes the following hypothesis:

H3: Lower supply chain concentration promotes ESG disclosure.

5. Research Design

5.1 Sample and Data

The original sample consists of Chinese listed firms from the Shanghai and Shenzhen stock markets, covering the period from 2018 to 2022. The dependent variable ESG scores, which serve as the metric for ESG disclosure, are obtained from the Wind database. Data for the independent and control variables are sourced from the China Stock Market & Accounting Research (CSMAR) database. As shown in Table 4.1, thc initial dataset includes 5,126 corporations and 25,632 observations. After excluding observations with missing data for the dependent, independent, and control variables, the number of observations is reduced to 12,032. Additionally, to mitigate the influence of extreme values, the winsorization method is applied to replace the top and bottom 1% of the data. Consequently, the final sample size comprises 12,032 observations.

5.2 Variable Measurement

5.2.1 Dependent Variable

Corporate ESG disclosure is the dependent variable in this study, measured by the ESG scores from the Wind database.

5.2.2 Independent Variable

Proportion of Female Management

Following Velte (2016), Meng and Zhu (2023), and Peng and Chandarasupsang (2023), the explanatory variable is the proportion of female management, measured by the number of female managers over the number of total managers. To better define managers, directors, superiors, and executives are included in the number of managers gauged here. The formula for calculating the proportion of female management is as follows:

$$\text{Proportion of Female Management} = \frac{\text{Number of Female Managers}}{\text{Number of Total Managers}}$$

Table 4.1 Results of Sample Selection

Sample Selection Criteria	*No. of Firms*	*No. of Observations*
Total number	5126	25632
Less: missing sample data	1186	13600
Winsor2 all variables, cuts (1 99) replace	3940	12032
Equal to = final sample	3940	12032

Source: Created by the author

Internal Executive Compensation Disparity

Referring to Yang and Yang (2009), the author uses the percentage of top 3 total executive compensation over total executive compensation to define the internal executive compensation disparity. The formula is proposed as follows:

$$\text{Internal Executive Compensation Disparity} = \frac{\text{Top3 Total Executive Compensation}}{\text{Total Executive Compensation}}$$

Supply Chain Concentration

The explanatory variable supply chain concentration defines the dependency of the supply chain on customers and suppliers, computed by the average of the sum of purchasing and sales ratios from the top 5 suppliers and customers. Purchasing ratio means the purchasing amount from one supplier divided by the total purchasing amount from all suppliers; similarly, sales ratio means the sales amount to one customer divided by the total sales amount to all customers. The formula for supply chain concentration is as follows:

$$\text{Supply Chain Concencntration} = \left(\frac{\sum \text{Top 5 Purchasing Ratio} + \sum \text{Top 5 Sales Ratio}}{2}\right) * 100\%$$

5.2.3 *Control Variable*

Referring to the studies by Jiraporn and Chintrakarn (2013) and Meng and Zhu (2023), several control variables are included in the analysis. These variables are the number of directors, the number of independent directors, and CEO duality (whether the chairman of the board simultaneously serves as the general manager). CEO duality is quantified with a value of 1 if the chairman serves as the general manager, and 0 otherwise. Additionally, following Wu et al. (2022) and Wang et al. (2023), the control variables also include the percentage of shares held by the chairman and whether there is a change in capital structure during the year. A capital structure change is assigned a value of 1 if it occurs; otherwise, it is assigned a value of 0.

Further control variables include the presence of valid internal control, internal control deficiencies, the type of audit opinion, and engagement with foreign auditing firms. These variables are converted into dummy variables for quantification: valid internal control takes a value of 1 if present, and otherwise 0; an internal control deficiency is assigned a value of 1 if present, and otherwise 0. Valid internal control and internal control deficiency are not mutually exclusive; deficiencies can exist even with valid internal control.

Audit opinions are categorized into five types for Chinese listed firms (Wang et al., 2023). In this study, an unqualified audit opinion is assigned a value of 0, while all other types are assigned a value of 1. Engagement with a foreign audit firm is indicated by a value of 1, and otherwise 0.

To control for year and industry effects on enterprise ESG scores and mitigate the influence of omitted variables, year-fixed effects and industry-fixed effects are included in the empirical analysis.

5.3 Model Specification

Based on the study question and hypotheses, the ordinary least squares (OLS) regression model is constructed as follows:

$$ESG = \beta_0 + \beta_1 FM + \beta_2 EC + \beta_3 SCC + \beta_4 ND + \beta_5 NID + \beta_6 CCG + \beta_7 SHC + \beta_8 CSC + \beta_9 VIC + \beta_{10} DIC + \beta_{11} AOT + \beta_{12} FAF + \textit{Year-fixed Effect} + \textit{Industry-fixed Effect} + \varepsilon, \quad (1)$$

where

ESG = Corporate ESG score
FM = Proportion of female managers, calculated by the number of female managers divided by the number of total managers
EC = Internal executive compensation disparity, calculated by the percentage of top three total executive compensation over total executive compensation
SCC = Supply chain concentration, calculated by the average of the sum of purchasing and sales ratios from the top five suppliers and customers
ND = Number of directors
NID = Number of independent directors
CCG = Concurrent relationship between the chairman of the board and the general manager (CEO duality), which is assigned a value of 1 if the chairman simultaneously serves as the general manager; otherwise 0
SHC = Proportion of shares held by the chairman of the board
CSC = Capital structure change, which is assigned a value of 1 if the enterprise capital structure is changed during the year; otherwise 0
VIC = Valid internal control, which takes a value of 1; otherwise 0
DIC = Internal control deficiency, which is assigned a value of 1 if there is internal control deficiency; otherwise 0
AOT = Type of audit opinion, therein, only the unqualified opinion is assigned a value of 0; the other types of audit opinions are assigned a value of 1
FAF = Foreign auditing firm, which is assigned a value of 1 if there is a foreign audit firm engaged in enterprise auditing; otherwise 0.

6. Empirical Results

6.1 Descriptive Statistics

6.1.1 Summary Statistics

Table 4.2 presents the summary statistics of the 12,032 samples from 2018 to 2022. On average, the corporate ESG score is 5.971, with a significant variation in ESG scores among different companies as indicated by the standard deviation. The mean proportion of female management is 0.211, suggesting that around one-fifth of managers are female. Additionally, the average percentage of the top three

Table 4.2 Summary Statistics

Variable	*N*	*Mean*	*Std. Dev.*	*Min*	*Max*
ESG	12032	5.971	0.815	4.16	8.27
FM	12032	.211	0.123	0	.545
EC	12032	.646	0.186	.297	1
SCC	12032	33.453	17.107	4.9	83.87
ND	12032	8.391	1.600	5	14
NID	12032	3.119	0.519	2	5
CCG	12032	.69	0.463	0	1
SHC	12032	8.675	14.017	0	55.73
CSC	12032	.697	0.460	0	1
VIC	12032	.985	0.121	0	1
DIC	12032	.395	0.489	0	1
AOT	12032	.035	0.185	0	1
FAF	12032	.022	0.148	0	1

Source: Created by the author

Note: Summary statistics of the sample from 2018 to 2022 are presented.

total executive compensation is 64.6%. The average supply chain concentration is 33.453%, but this measure varies substantially among firms, as evidenced by a standard deviation of 17.107.

6.1.2 Correlations

Table 4.3 presents the correlation results among all variables. The variables FM, EC, and SCC show a negative relationship with ESG scores. EC and SCC are significant at the 1% significance level, while FM is not significant even at the 10% significance level. The correlations suggest that lower internal executive compensation disparity and reduced SCC are more likely to enhance corporate ESG scores. It is important to note that correlation is a direct and elementary measurement of the relationship between two variables, unlike regression analysis, which can examine multiple variables simultaneously. Therefore, while FM may not show a significant correlation with ESG in this preliminary analysis, it could still have a significant relationship in a more comprehensive regression analysis. Further conclusions will be drawn from the regression results.

6.2 OLS Regression Results

Table 4.4 presents the results of the OLS regression. Column 1 displays the OLS regression results without control variables, while column 2 includes the OLS regression results with control variables.

In column 1, the coefficient of FM is significantly positive (coefficient = 0.158, *t*-stat = 2.711), indicating that higher ESG disclosure quality is associated with a higher proportion of FM. Column 2 confirms this conclusion, showing that even with the inclusion of control variables, FM remains positively related to ESG at the 1%

Table 4.3 Correlation between Variables

	(1) ESG	*FM*	*EC*	*SCC*	*ND*	*NID*	*CCG*	*SHC*	*CSC*	*VIC*	*DIC*	*AOT*	*FAF*
ESG	1.000												
FM	−0.011	1.000											
EC	−0.134***	0.175***	1.000										
SCC	−0.068***	0.024***	0.138***	1.000									
ND	0.056***	−0.152***	−0.234***	−0.091***	1.000								
NID	0.081***	−0.128***	−0.191***	−0.104***	0.736***	1.000							
CCG	0.007	−0.117***	−0.066***	−0.047***	0.194***	0.130***	1.000						
SHC	0.073***	0.123***	0.043***	0.055***	−0.215***	−0.178***	−0.268***	1.000					
CSC	0.115***	0.058***	−0.042***	−0.023**	-0.062***	−0.077***	−0.132***	0.208***	1.000				
VIC	0.117***	−0.016*	−0.055***	−0.025***	0.020**	0.018*	−0.003	0.025***	0.023**	1.000			
DIC	0.006	−0.061***	−0.029***	−0.031***	0.083***	0.094***	0.078***	−0.131***	−0.196***	−0.152***	1.000		
AOT	−0.152***	0.003	0.071***	0.031***	−0.032***	−0.022**	0.009	−0.037***	−0.019**	−0.631***	0.168***	1.000	
FAF	0.164***	−0.036***	−0.045***	−0.044***	0.051***	0.098***	0.025***	−0.033***	−0.026***	0.014	0.047***	−0.020**	1.000

Source: Created by the author

* $p < 0.1$, ** $p < 0.05$, *** $p < 0.01$

Table 4.4 OLS Regression Results

	(1)		(2)	
	Coefficient	*t-stat*	*Coefficient*	*t-stat*
FM	0.158***	[2.711]	0.174***	[3.022]
EC	−0.549***	[−14.154]	−0.436***	[−11.440]
SCC	−0.005***	[−11.466]	−0.004***	[−8.943]
ND			−0.011	[−1.630]
NID			0.124***	[6.116]
CCG			0.095***	[6.314]
SHC			0.002***	[5.024]
CSC			0.113***	[7.196]
VIC			0.230***	[3.219]
DIC			0.079***	[5.468]
AOT			−0.466***	[−9.838]
FAF			0.838***	[13.955]
_cons	6.465***	[218.575]	5.623***	[57.314]
Industry	Yes		Yes	
Year	Yes		Yes	
r2_within	0.032		0.091	
N	12,032.000		12,032.000	

Source: Created by the author

* $p < 0.1$, ** $p < 0.05$, *** $p < 0.01$

significance level (coefficient = 0.174, *t*-stat = 3.022). This suggests that the correlation coefficient of FM and ESG in the correlation analysis should be reconsidered.

Similarly, the regression results from both columns 1 and 2 indicate that EC and SCC are significant and negatively related to ESG at the 1% significance level. This implies that a higher proportion of FM, lesser internal executive compensation disparity, and lower SCC can lead to better ESG disclosure.

7. Endogeneity Test

7.1 Endogeneity Concerns

Endogeneity issues arise from the correlation between independent variables and the regression error term (Semadeni et al., 2013). These problems can result from omitted variables, simultaneity, measurement error, and sample selection (Kim & Washington, 2006; Chib et al., 2009; Gordon, 2013; Abdallah et al., 2015). In this analysis, we found that endogeneity in the model may arise from several factors.

Firstly, omitted variables in the regression model can lead to endogeneity (Gordon, 2013). Secondly, the absence of a random sampling method in the sample selection process may introduce bias (Chib et al., 2009). Thirdly, missing values might be due to measurement bias rather than randomness; some firms may selectively disclose their corporate ESG performance, resulting in incomplete data (Abdallah et al., 2015). To address these endogeneity issues, this study employs the GMM test, which helps mitigate these problems in the regression model.

7.2 GMM Test

Referring to Kripfganz (2016), the dynamic panel data estimation for two-step difference GMM is used to test endogeneity. One-period lagged ESG, one-period to three-period lagged FM and EC, one-period to four-period lagged SCC, and three-period to six-period lagged control variables are set as endogenous variables and predetermined variables. The industry variable is set as an exogenous variable. Moreover, the fixed year-effect is involved in the dynamic panel data estimation for two-step difference GMM.

Table 4.5 shows the results of the dynamic panel data estimation for two-step difference GMM. Consistently, FM (coefficient = 0.889, *t*-stat = 2.217) is positively

Table 4.5 GMM Test on Endogeneity

	Coefficient	*t-stat*
L.ESG	0.258***	[3.752]
FM	0.889**	[2.217]
EC	−0.783***	[−3.247]
SCC	−0.007**	[−2.510]
ND	−0.131*	[−1.848]
NID	0.368	[1.118]
CCG	0.071	[0.472]
SHC	0.001	[0.112]
CSC	0.074	[1.009]
VIC	−1.122*	[−1.692]
DIC	0.376***	[5.388]
AOT	−0.045	[−0.201]
FAF	1.906*	[1.658]
2019.year	−0.009	[−0.444]
2021.year	0.098***	[5.501]
2022.year	0.070**	[2.361]
ar1p	0.000	
ar2p	0.428	
Sarganp	0.465	
Hansenp	0.172	
N	4,212.000	

Source: Created by the author

* $p < 0.1$, ** $p < 0.05$, *** $p < 0.01$

related to ESG at the 5% significance level. While EC and SCC are negatively related to ESG, with EC (coefficient = –0.783, *t*-stat = –3.247) at the 1% significance level and SCC (coefficient = –0.007, *t*-stat = –2.510) at the 5% significance level. Moreover, the Arellano–Bond test for AR (2) in first differences is 0.428, more than 0.1; simultaneously, the values of Sargon (0.465) and Hansen (0.172) tests are more than 0.1. Therefore, the dynamic panel data estimation for two-step difference GMM and conclusions are effective.

7.3 Fixed or Random Individual-Effect Model (Based on Hausman Test)

The fixed or random individual-effect test explores the individual firm effects on the model. Table 4.6 shows the results of the coefficient and *t*-stat of the fixed individual-effect model and the random individual-effect model. Based on the Hausman test, fixed individual effects should be used.

Table 4.7 shows the regression results based on the fixed year-effect and the individual-effect. Column 2 shows the results with the constraint of control variables. At the 10% significance level, FM (coefficient = 0.170, *t*-stat = 1.898) maintains a consistent positive relationship with ESG. At the 10% significance level, EC (coefficient = −0.100, *t*-stat = −1.936) is negatively related to ESG, while at the 1% significance level, SCC (coefficient = −0.002, *t*-stat = −3.112) maintains a consistent negative relationship with ESG. Consequently, the results are robust to the model involving fixed individual effects.

8. Robustness Check

8.1 Alternative Measure

Referring to Meng and Zhu (2023), the one-period lagged variable of the proportion of female managers is an alternative variable for female managers. Likewise, one-period lagged variables of internal executive compensation and SCC are used in the alternative measure equation. The dependent variable ESG is replaced by the ESG score in the current year. Consequently, the regression results and conclusions are general if the relationship remains the same between the last-period independent variables and the current-period dependent variable. The new equation model is as follows:

$$\begin{aligned} ESG_t = {} & \beta_0 + \beta_1 L.FM + \beta_2 L.EC + \beta_3 L.SCC + \beta_4 ND + \beta_5 NID + \beta_6 CCG \\ & + \beta_7 SHC + \beta_8 CSC + \beta_9 VIC + \beta_{10} DIC + \beta_{11} AOT + \beta_{12} FAF \\ & + \text{Year-fixed Effect} + \text{Industry-fixed Effect} + \varepsilon, \end{aligned} \tag{2}$$

where ESG_t is the corporate ESG score in the current year, L.FM is the proportion of FM in the last year, L.EC is the internal executive compensation disparity in the last year, and L.SCC is the SCC in the last year. This chapter adopts the lagged variable model to test the robustness of the prior empirical results. The robustness

Table 4.6 Fixed or Random Individual-Effect Model

	Fe *ESG*	*Re* *ESG*
FM	0.170*	0.065
	(1.90)	(1.00)
EC	−0.100*	−0.302***
	(−1.94)	(−7.34)
SCC	−0.002***	−0.002***
	(−3.11)	(−3.95)
ND	−0.007	−0.010
	(−0.77)	(−1.39)
NID	0.098***	0.115***
	(3.66)	(5.43)
CCG	0.090***	0.068***
	(4.62)	(4.32)
SHC	0.003***	0.005***
	(2.64)	(6.95)
CSC	0.057***	0.090***
	(4.11)	(7.01)
VIC	−0.097*	0.003
	(−1.77)	(0.05)
DIC	−0.016	0.025
	(−0.69)	(1.50)
AOT	−0.081**	−0.185***
	(−2.26)	(−5.39)
FAF	0.163*	0.566***
	(1.90)	(9.63)
2018.year	0.000	0.000
	(.)	(.)
2019.year	0.041***	0.048***
	(2.98)	(3.53)
2020.year	0.081***	0.092***
	(6.01)	(6.88)
2021.year	0.197***	0.216***
	(14.46)	(16.31)
2022.year	0.197***	0.224***
	(12.53)	(14.68)
_cons	5.692***	5.657***
	(51.45)	(63.33)
N	12032	12032
R^2	0.0473	

Source: Created by the author

* $p < 0.1$, ** $p < 0.05$, *** $p < 0.01$

of empirical results can be confirmed if there are consistent relationships between the independent and dependent variables after replacing the independent variables with lagged variables. As such, replace FM, EC, and SCC with one-period lagged independent variables FM, EC, and SCC. Likewise, if the relationship between L.FM, L.EC, L.SCC, and ESG remains consistent, it is reasonable to believe that the empirical results are robust and precise.

Table 4.7 Fixed Individual-Effect

	(1)		*(2)*	
	Coefficient	*t-stat*	*Coefficient*	*t-stat*
FM	0.164*	[1.825]	0.170*	[1.898]
EC	−0.115**	[−2.240]	−0.100*	[−1.936]
SCC	−0.002***	[−3.329]	−0.002***	[−3.112]
ND			−0.007	[−0.772]
NID			0.098***	[3.657]
CCG			0.090***	[4.618]
SHC			0.003***	[2.640]
CSC			0.057***	[4.112]
VIC			−0.097*	[−1.769]
DIC			−0.016	[−0.693]
AOT			−0.081**	[−2.255]
FAF			0.163*	[1.900]
_cons	5.990***	[135.349]	5.692***	[51.454]
Individual	Yes		Yes	
Year	Yes		Yes	
r2_within				
N	12,032.000		12,032.000	

Source: Created by the author

* $p < 0.1$, ** $p < 0.05$, *** $p < 0.01$

Table 4.8 shows the results of the lagged variable model. Column 1 shows the test results without control variables; column 2 shows the test results with the constraint of control variables. At the 1% significance level, L.EC (coefficient = –0.391, *t*-stat = –7.721) and L.SCC (coefficient = –0.004, *t*-stat = –6.391) still maintain consistent negative relationships with ESG under the constraint of control variables. The difference from the regression results is that the significance of L.FM decreases. At the 10% significance level, L.FM (coefficient = 0.134, *t*-stat = 1.696) is positively related to ESG under the control variables. Despite the significance decrease in FM in the robustness test, it is acceptable that L.FM is still significant at the 10% significance level. Therefore, based on the analysis, the coefficient and significance are close to the regression results, which indicates that the prior empirical results are robust, and the conclusions are valuable as a reference.

8.2 Multicollinearity Test

Referring to Saidu (2019), this analysis uses variance inflation factors (VIFs) to confirm multicollinearity. Table 4.9 shows the VIFs of each variable. The VIF

Table 4.8 Lagged Variable Model on Robustness

	(1)		*(2)*	
	Coefficient	*t-stat*	*Coefficient*	*t-stat*
L.FM	0.113	[1.416]	0.134*	[1.696]
L.EC	−0.516***	[−9.882]	−0.391***	[−7.721]
L.SCC	−0.005***	[−8.278]	−0.004***	[−6.391]
ND			0.006	[0.712]
NID			0.094***	[3.469]
CCG			0.078***	[3.747]
SHC			0.003***	[5.075]
CSC			0.133***	[6.517]
VIC			0.233**	[2.265]
DIC			0.093***	[4.880]
AOT			−0.501***	[−7.508]
FAF			0.885***	[11.429]
_cons	6.482***	[163.543]	5.563***	[41.080]
Industry	Yes		Yes	
Year	Yes		Yes	
r2_within	0.028		0.093	
N	6,994.000		6,994.000	

Source: Created by the author

* $p < 0.1$, ** $p < 0.05$, *** $p < 0.01$

value of all variables is less than 5, and the mean value of the VIF is 1.38, also less than 5. Therefore, there is no multicollinearity. The regression conclusion is comparatively precise because there are no highly close correlations between independent variables.

9. Discussion

9.1 Relationship with Prior Literature

No prior research has specifically examined the impact of internal executive compensation disparity and SCC on corporate ESG performance in the Chinese context. This chapter demonstrates that reducing internal executive compensation disparity and lowering SCC positively influence ESG disclosure. While studies on compensation disparity are limited, related research shows that many corporations aim to establish fairer executive compensation systems. Eklund and Stern (2021) highlight the importance of creating equitable compensation schemes linked to ESG performance. Firms that implement ESG-based remuneration find

Table 4.9 Multicollinearity Test

	VIF	*1/VIF*
ND	2.304	0.434
NID	2.219	0.451
AOT	1.686	0.593
VIC	1.67	0.599
SHC	1.161	0.861
CCG	1.116	0.896
EC	1.108	0.903
DIC	1.094	0.914
CSC	1.093	0.915
FM	1.064	0.94
SCC	1.031	0.97
FAF	1.016	0.985
Mean VIF	1.38	–

Source: Created by the author

that integrating executive pay with non-financial performance improves overall effectiveness (Haque & Ntim, 2020). Thus, efforts to reduce internal compensation disparities contribute to a more just and resilient system.

Diverse supply chain governance also enhances ESG performance. Engaging various stakeholders – such as internal departments, suppliers, and customers – is crucial for effective ESG management practices, including joint planning, goal-setting, and knowledge sharing (Whitelock, 2015). Sardanelli et al. (2022) suggest that value-chain data can help firms operate within effective frameworks to meet ESG indicators. Additionally, customers' ESG practices can influence their suppliers, as major customers often ensure that vendors comply with similar standards (Tang et al., 2023).

Moreover, the positive relationship between the proportion of FM and ESG disclosure aligns with findings from Borghesi et al. (2014), Velte (2016), and Meng and Zhu (2023), although it contrasts with Manita et al. (2018). Overall, enterprise ESG performance tends to improve with greater female involvement in decision-making.

9.2 Theoretical Implications

The findings of this study strongly support agency theory, which suggests that management and shareholders share the common goal of enhancing corporate ESG performance to boost firm value. The drive for managers to increase enterprise value can lead to greenwashing practices and promote ESG performance disclosure in corporate reports (Friedman et al., 2021). This study shows that female managers are more proactive than their male counterparts in integrating ESG performance and disclosure into corporate policies.

The results also validate stakeholder theory, highlighting the growing concerns of various stakeholders – such as customers, employees, public welfare organizations, and government regulators – regarding corporate ESG practices (Khan, 2019). Key stakeholders, including female managers and supply chain partners, play critical roles. Effective strategies to engage these stakeholders in ESG issues include increasing FM representation, reducing internal executive compensation disparity, and diversifying supply chain networks.

Additionally, the findings are consistent with legitimacy theory, which posits that companies must adhere to societal norms and regulations to maintain legitimacy. While the empirical results are not directly linked to legitimacy theory, the supporting background indicates that regulatory pressures and societal expectations significantly impact corporate ESG disclosure practices.

9.3 Practical Implications

This study provides valuable insights for policymakers, directors, and managers looking to enhance corporate ESG performance. The findings show that a higher proportion of FM, reduced internal executive compensation disparity, and a diverse supply chain are linked to better ESG disclosure and higher performance scores. Therefore, firms should prioritize gender diversity in management and create more opportunities for female leaders.

Additionally, this chapter addresses a significant research gap by exploring the impact of SCC on ESG disclosure. In a global economy, supply chain networks involve various clients and suppliers, making integration among all participants essential for achieving strong ESG performance. Different customers and suppliers can influence the transition to a low-carbon supply chain in distinct ways. The findings suggest that firms should aim to balance their reliance on various partners, as lower SCC and diverse supply chains can enhance ESG performance and improve overall operational efficiency.

10. Conclusion

This chapter examines the impact of corporate governance on ESG disclosure, focusing on the proportion of FM, internal executive compensation disparity, and supply chain concentration. Using data from Chinese listed firms on the Shanghai and Shenzhen stock markets between 2018 and 2022, the findings show that a higher proportion of FM positively influences ESG scores, while internal executive compensation disparity and SCC negatively affect them. In summary, better ESG disclosure is linked to more FM, reduced compensation disparity, and lower SCC.

The chapter significantly contributes to the literature on corporate governance and ESG disclosure. It offers insights from agency theory, stakeholder value theory, and legitimacy theory, enriching existing knowledge. It also pioneers the investigation of internal executive compensation disparity and SCC in the Chinese context. Addressing compensation disparity can enhance corporate governance and promote fairness, while analysing SCC aids in developing efficient, low-carbon management practices. However, the study has limitations. The model lacks robust theoretical foundations, relies on a single ESG evaluation system, and does not identify optimal levels for FM, compensation disparity, and SCC to maximize ESG disclosure, which could be explored in future research.

Future studies should incorporate a wider range of theoretical frameworks, such as institutional theory and resource dependency theory, to strengthen model construction. Using multiple ESG rating systems can validate findings and avoid biases associated with a single system. Research should also aim to determine optimal levels for governance factors influencing ESG performance. Longitudinal studies could provide insights into how changes in governance practices impact ESG disclosure over time, while comparative studies across different countries could reveal variations influenced by regulatory environments and cultural factors. Investigating corporate governance within specific industries could uncover unique dynamics and best practices. Qualitative methods, like interviews and case studies, could enhance the understanding of firms' motivations and challenges in improving ESG performance. Future research should also explore how technological innovations, such as blockchain and big data analytics, affect corporate governance and ESG disclosure. Examining stakeholder perspectives – including investors and regulators – could offer a holistic view of the importance of ESG disclosure. Investigating how specific policies impact ESG practices could inform more effective regulatory interventions.

In conclusion, this chapter provides valuable insights into how corporate governance influences ESG disclosure, offering practical implications for policymakers and managers to enhance ESG performance through strategic adjustments in management diversity, executive compensation, and supply chain practices.

References

Aabo, T., & Giorici, I. C. (2022). Do female CEOs matter for ESG scores? *Global Finance Journal*, *56*, 100722.

Abdallah, W., Goergen, M., & O'Sullivan, N. (2015, July 16). Endogeneity: How failure to correct for it can cause wrong inferences and some remedies. *British Journal of Management*, *26*(4), 791–804.

Adams, R. B., Licht, A. N., & Sagiv, L. (2011, June 1). Shareholders and stakeholders: How do directors decide? *Strategic Management Journal*, *32*(12), 1331–1355.

Ahamed, F. (2022, January 22). CEO compensation and performance of banks. *European Journal of Business and Management Research*, *7*(1), 100–103.

Alsayegh, M. F., Abdul Rahman, R., & Homayoun, S. (2020, May 11). Corporate economic, environmental, and social sustainability performance transformation through ESG disclosure. *Sustainability*, *12*(9), 3910.

Bamahros, H. M., Alquhaif, A., Qasem, A., Wan-Hussin, W. N., Thomran, M., Al-Duais, S. D., Shukeri, S. N., & Khojally, H. M. A. (2022, May 19). Corporate Governance mechanisms and ESG reporting: Evidence from the Saudi stock market. *Sustainability*, *14*(10), 6202.

Birindelli, G., Dell'Atti, S., Iannuzzi, A., & Savioli, M. (2018, December 10). Composition and activity of the board of directors: Impact on ESG performance in the banking system. *Sustainability*, *10*(12), 4699.

Borghesi, R., Houston, J. F., & Naranjo, A. (2014, June). Corporate socially responsible investments: CEO altruism, reputation, and shareholder interests. *Journal of Corporate Finance*, *26*, 164–181.

Buchetti, B., Arduino, F. R., & De Vito, A. (2022). A systematic literature review on corporate governance and ESG research: Trends and future directions. *SSRN Electronic Journal*.

Byron, K., & Post, C. (2016, June 12). Women on boards of directors and corporate social performance: A meta-analysis. *Corporate Governance: An International Review*, *24*(4), 428–442.

CFA Institute. (2019). *ESG Integration in China: Guidance and case studies*. CFA Institute.

Chatchawanchanchanakij, P., Arpornpisal, C., & Jermsittiparsert, K. (2019). The role of corporate governance in creating a capable supply chain: A case of Indonesian Tin industry. *International Journal of Supply Chain Management*, *8*(3), 854–864.

Chen, M., & Mussalli, G. (2020, January 18). An integrated approach to quantitative ESG investing. *The Journal of Portfolio Management*, *46*(3), 65–74.

Chib, S., Greenberg, E., & Jeliazkov, I. (2009, January). Estimation of semiparametric models in the presence of endogeneity and sample selection. *Journal of Computational and Graphical Statistics*, *18*(2), 321–348.

Cong, Y., Zhu, C., Hou, Y., Tian, S., & Cai, X. (2022, October 12). Does ESG investment reduce carbon emissions in China? *Frontiers in Environmental Science*, *10*.

Dai, T., & Tang, C. S. (2021). Integrating ESG measures and supply chain management: Research opportunities in the post-pandemic era. *SSRN Electronic Journal*.

Demirbas, D., & Yukhanaev, A. (2011, June 28). Independence of board of directors, employee relation and harmonisation of corporate governance. *Employee Relations*, *33*(4), 444–471.

Eklund, M. A., & Stern, H. J. (2021). How COVID-19 reshapes businesses and executive pay for sustainability. *Corporate Governance and Sustainability Review*, *5*(1, Special Issue), 107–119.

Friedman, H. L., Heinle, M. S., & Luneva, I. (2021, October 11). *A theoretical framework for ESG reporting to investors*. A Theoretical Framework for ESG Reporting to Investors by Henry L. Friedman, Mirko Stanislav Heinle, Irina Luneva.

García-Sánchez, I. M., Martínez-Ferrero, J., & García-Meca, E. (2017, November 9). Board of directors and CSR in banking: The moderating role of bank regulation and investor protection strength. *Australian Accounting Review*, *28*(3), 428–445.

Gillan, S. L., Koch, A., & Starks, L. T. (2021, February). Firms and social responsibility: A review of ESG and CSR research in corporate finance. *Journal of Corporate Finance*, *66*, 101889.

Gordon, D. V. (2013, November 16). The endogeneity problem in applied fisheries econometrics: A critical review. *Environmental and Resource Economics*, *61*(1), 115–125.

Gray, R., Kouhy, R., & Lavers, S. (1995, May 1). Corporate social and environmental reporting. *Accounting, Auditing & Accountability Journal*, *8*(2), 47–77.

Haque, F., & Ntim, C. G. (2020). Executive compensation, sustainable compensation policy, carbon performance and market value. *British Journal of Management*, *31*(3), 525–546.

Jensen, M. C., & Meckling, W. H. (1976, October). Theory of the firm: Managerial behavior, agency costs and ownership structure. *Journal of Financial Economics*, *3*(4), 305–360.

Jiang, W., Lin, B., Liu, Y., & Xu, Y. (2019, March 25). Chairperson collectivism and the compensation gap between managers and employees: Evidence from China. *Corporate Governance: An International Review*, *27*(4), 261–282.

Jiraporn, P., & Chintrakarn, P. (2013). How do powerful CEOs view corporate social responsibility (CSR)? An empirical note. *Economics Letters*, *119*(3), 344–347.

Khan, M. (2019, October 1). Corporate governance, ESG, and stock returns around the world. *Financial Analysts Journal*, *75*(4), 103–123.

Kiel, G. C., & Nicholson, G. J. (2005, September). Evaluating boards and directors. *Corporate Governance: An International Review*, *13*(5), 613–631.

Kim, D. G., & Washington, S. (2006, November). The significance of endogeneity problems in crash models: An examination of left-turn lanes in intersection crash models. *Accident Analysis & Prevention*, *38*(6), 1094–1100.

Klimkiewicz, K. (2017). The role of ESG – based compensation in sustaining the supply chain. *Journal of Reverse Logistics*, *3*, 12–17.

Kripfganz, S. (2016, December). Quasi – maximum likelihood estimation of linear dynamic short-T panel-data models. *The Stata Journal: Promoting Communications on Statistics and Stata*, *16*(4), 1013–1038.

Krueger, P., Sautner, Z., & Starks, L. T. (2020, February 14). The importance of climate risks for institutional investors. *The Review of Financial Studies*, *33*(3), 1067–1111.

Li, R. Y. M., Wang, Q., Zeng, L., & Chen, H. (2023, January 3). A study on public perceptions of carbon neutrality in China: Has the idea of ESG been encompassed? *Frontiers in Environmental Science*, *10*.

Li, T. T., Wang, K., Sueyoshi, T., & Wang, D. D. (2021, October 21). ESG: Research progress and future prospects. *Sustainability*, *13*(21), 11663.

Lokuwaduge, C. S. D. S., & Heenetigala, K. (2016, December 9). Integrating environmental, social and governance (ESG) disclosure for a sustainable development: An Australian study. *Business Strategy and the Environment*, *26*(4), 438–450.

Manita, R., Bruna, M. G., Dang, R., & Houanti, L. (2018, May 14). Board gender diversity and ESG disclosure: evidence from the USA. *Journal of Applied Accounting Research*, *19*(2), 206–224.

Matemane, R., Moloi, T., & Adelowotan, M. (2022, October 17). Appraising executive compensation ESG-based indicators using analytical hierarchical process and Delphi techniques. *Journal of Risk and Financial Management*, *15*(10), 469.

Meng, X., & Zhu, P. (2023, February 20). Females' social responsibility: The impact of female executives on ESG performance. *Applied Economics Letters*, 1–6.

Mneimneh, F., Al Kodsi, M., Chamoun, M., Basharoush, M., & Ramakrishna, S. (2023). How can green energy technology innovations improve the carbon-related environmental dimension of ESG rating? *Circular Economy and Sustainability*, *3*(4), 2183–2199.

Mohter, N., & Fernando, Y. (2020, October 6). Corporate governance and low carbon supply chains: Why integrity matters? *Journal of Governance and Integrity*, *3*(2).

Murphy, K. J. (2005, April 6). *Executive compensation*. Executive Compensation – ScienceDirect.

Ormazabal, G., Cohen, S., Kadach, I., Ormazabal, G., & Reichelstein, S. (2022). Executive compensation tied to ESG performance: International evidence (No. 17267). CEPR Discussion Papers.

Orsagh, M., Allen, J., Sloggett, J., Bartholdy, S., Georgieva, A., Dehman, N. A., & Sofronova, Y. (2019). *ESG integration in Europe, the Middle East, and Africa: Markets, practices, and data*. CFA Institute, Principles for Responsible Investment (PRI). Retrieved January 28, 2023, from https://www.unpri.org/download?ac=6036

Peng, H., & Chandarasupsang, T. (2023, April 27). The effect of female directors on ESG practice: Evidence from China. *International Journal of Financial Studies*, *11*(2), 66.

Phung, G., Trinh, H. H., Nguyen, T. H., & Trinh, V. Q. (2022, July 12). Top-management compensation and environmental innovation strategy. *Business Strategy and the Environment*, *32*(4), 1634–1649.

Porcuna Enguix, L. (2021, May 13). The new EU remuneration policy as good but not desired corporate governance mechanism and the role of CSR disclosing. *Sustainability*, *13*(10), 5476.

Rahman, J., & Wu, J. (2023). M&A activity and ESG performance: Evidence from China. *Managerial Finance*, *50*(1), 179–197.

Rahman, M. J., Wu, Q., & Zhu, H. (2024). Corporate social responsibility in times of social distancing: Evidence from China. *Business Ethics, the Environment & Responsibility*.

Rahman, M. J., Zhu, H., & Chen, S. (2023). Does CSR reduce financial distress? Moderating effect of firm characteristics, auditor characteristics, and covid-19. *International Journal of Accounting & Information Management*, *31*(5), 756–784.

Saidu, S. (2019, March 4). CEO characteristics and firm performance: Focus on origin, education and ownership. *Journal of Global Entrepreneurship Research*, *9*(1).

Sardanelli, D., Bittucci, L., Mirone, F., & Marzioni, S. (2022, May 7). An integrative framework for supply chain rating: From financial-based to ESG-based rating models. *Total Quality Management & Business Excellence*, 1–20.

Semadeni, M., Withers, M. C., & Trevis Certo, S. (2013, June 25). The perils of endogeneity and instrumental variables in strategy research: Understanding through simulations. *Strategic Management Journal*, *35*(7).

Sheikh, M. F., Shah, S. Z. A., & Akbar, S. (2017, October 9). Firm performance, corporate governance and executive compensation in Pakistan. *Applied Economics*, *50*(18), 2012–2027.

Signori, S., San-Jose, L., Retolaza, J. L., & Rusconi, G. (2021, January 29). Stakeholder value creation: Comparing ESG and value added in European companies. *Sustainability*, *13*(3), 1392.

Sun, L. L., Cui, H. J., & Ge, Q. S. (2022, April). Will China achieve its 2060 carbon neutral commitment from the provincial perspective? *Advances in Climate Change Research*, *13*(2), 169–178.

Suttipun, M. (2021, March 24). The influence of board composition on environmental, social and governance (ESG) disclosure of Thai listed companies. *International Journal of Disclosure and Governance*, *18*(4), 391–402.

Tan, Y., & Zhu, Z. (2022, February). The effect of ESG rating events on corporate green innovation in China: The mediating role of financial constraints and managers' environmental awareness. *Technology in Society*, *68*, 101906.

Tang, J., Wang, X., & Liu, Q. (2023, April). The spillover effect of customers' ESG to suppliers. *Pacific-Basin Finance Journal*, *78*, 101947.

Velte, P. (2016, May 9). Women on management board and ESG performance. *Journal of Global Responsibility*, *7*(1), 98–109.

Wang, X., Song, X., & Sun, M. (2023, February 22). How does a company's ESG performance affect the issuance of an audit opinion? The moderating role of auditor experience. *International Journal of Environmental Research and Public Health*, *20*(5), 3878.

Whitelock, V. G. (2015, January 1). *Relationship between environmental social governance (ESG) management and performance–the role of collaboration in the supply chain* [Doctoral dissertation, University of Toledo].

World Economic Forum. (2021, March 25). *Are Chinese firms at a 'leapfrog moment' in ESG reporting?* World Economic Forum.

Wu, S., Li, X., Du, X., & Li, Z. (2022, November 4). The impact of ESG performance on firm value: The moderating role of ownership structure. *Sustainability*, *14*(21), 14507.

Yang, R., & Yang, J. (2009, December). Why has top executive compensation increased so much in China: An explanation of peer-effects. *Pacific Economic Review*, *14*(5), 705–716.

Yu, E. P. Y., Luu, B. V., & Chen, C. H. (2020, April). Greenwashing in environmental, social and governance disclosures. *Research in International Business and Finance*, *52*, 101192.

Zeng, H., Li, R. Y. M., & Zeng, L. (2022, September 29). Evaluating green supply chain performance based on ESG and financial indicators. *Frontiers in Environmental Science*, *10*.

Zhang, Z. (2022, January 13). ESG reporting in China: Trends, challenges, and outlook. *China Briefing News*.

Zhu, H., & Rahman, M. J. (2024). Ex-ante expected changes in ESG and future stock returns based on machine learning. *The British Accounting Review*, 101457.

Zumente, I., & Bistrova, J. (2021, June). ESG importance for long-term shareholder value creation: Literature vs. practice. *Journal of Open Innovation: Technology, Market, and Complexity*, *7*(2), 127.

Part 2

ESG Impact on Financial Performance

5 The Impact of Corporate ESG Performance on Financial Performance

Md Jahidur Rahman, Tarek Rana, Hongtao Zhu, and Hanqi He

1. Introduction

This research examines the impact of environmental, social, and governance (ESG) activities on financial reporting in Chinese enterprises. ESG includes environmental factors like climate change and biodiversity; social factors such as employee welfare and community contributions; and governance factors like board transitions and executive compensation. The ESG data were sourced from the Bloomberg database (2011–2021) and financial data from the China Stock Market & Accounting Research (CSMAR) database.

The COVID-19 pandemic has significantly affected global dynamics, with China's strict measures highlighting the need to explore ESG performance's influence on financial outcomes during this period. There is a growing emphasis on ESG research. In November 2019, Hu Jiafu, vice president of Asset Management Association of China (AMAC), stressed the need for ESG development suited to Chinese market characteristics. The 2020 China Responsible Investment Forum also called for standardizing ESG investment.

Additionally, the Chinese government has introduced regulations aligning with the UN sustainable development goals (SDG) 2030 and the Paris Agreement 2°C target, promoting resource conservation and green finance. The "China's Green Development in the New Era" white paper (January 2023) emphasized the importance of energy conservation and environmental protection in corporate practices.

This chapter outlines a structured research process. It begins with a comprehensive literature review to synthesize contributions to ESG and financial performance, identifying gaps for further exploration and formulating hypotheses. Data will be collected from the Bloomberg and CSMAR databases, ensuring objectivity by excluding incomplete records, financial and insurance data, and outliers beyond the 1% and 99% thresholds. Independent and dependent variables will then be defined, along with specific calculation and measurement methods. Finally, endogeneity and robustness tests will validate the relationships between the variables.

The analysis indicates that ESG performance positively influences financial performance among Chinese companies, particularly during the COVID-19 pandemic. Supporting literature shows a complementary relationship between ESG disclosure and investor interest. For example, Chen et al. (2022) found that ESG disclosure

DOI: 10.4324/9781003488934-7

attracts investors and enhances their willingness to invest, moderating the link between ESG ratings and financial performance. Velte (2017) also reported a positive correlation between ESG and account-based financial performance. However, Mardini (2022) noted that social factors within ESG can negatively impact cash flow performance, although the effect on accounting indicators is minimal, attributed to resource drain and reputational risks.

This chapter aims to address the following research questions: *Given the distinctive national contexts of China and Germany, can ESG performance positively influence financial performance in Chinese enterprises? Amid the COVID-19 pandemic and regional economic challenges in 2020, does ESG performance continue to exert a positive influence on financial performance?*

By investigating these questions, this study contributes to the existing literature by examining whether social factors within ESG adversely affect the financial performance of Chinese companies. Utilizing Bloomberg and CSMAR data, the study concludes that ESG performance positively influences financial performance in Chinese enterprises under current political and pandemic conditions. Based on these findings, the study offers relevant recommendations for government policymakers and corporate managers.

2. Theoretical Framework

This section explores the foundational theories connecting ESG performance to financial outcomes, focusing on stakeholder theory and sustainability management. Freeman's (1984) stakeholder theory is central to this framework, highlighting the interconnectedness between enterprises and various stakeholders. It posits that a company's success depends on its ability to meet the needs of employees, customers, suppliers, investors, and the community. According to Freeman, businesses thrive through collaborative relationships with stakeholders, which significantly influence their strategic decisions and performance.

In contrast, traditional principal–agent theory, as described by Ross (1973) and developed by Meckling and Jensen (1976), views the relationship between managers (agents) and shareholders (principals) primarily through the lens of agency costs and contractual obligations. An alternative perspective considers enterprises as integral parts of society, where value creation is assessed based on societal expectations. This aligns with sustainability management theories that stress the importance of sustainability activities for effective stakeholder communication. Roberts (1992) suggests that sustainability performance is shaped by stakeholder power, indicating that meeting stakeholder expectations enhances corporate reputation.

Empirical studies reinforce the theoretical link between ESG performance and corporate outcomes. Clarkson et al. (2008) found that comprehensive ESG reporting positively affects corporate social responsibility (CSR) indicators, such as social responsibility ratings and reputation. This relationship arises from stakeholders' interest in a firm's sustainability strategy and its perceived commitment to responsible practices. Companies with strong ESG practices are viewed more favourably, enhancing market position and financial performance.

Based on these theories, a strong correlation between ESG performance and financial outcomes can be hypothesized. Stakeholders are concerned not only with a company's operations but also with its financial results. Thus, improving ESG indicators is strategically important for long-term success. It is reasonable to posit a positive correlation between ESG performance and financial performance, as enhanced ESG practices can improve stakeholder relations, corporate reputation, and ultimately financial outcomes.

This study integrates stakeholder theory and sustainability management to elucidate the relationship between ESG performance and financial performance. By meeting stakeholder expectations through robust ESG practices, companies can achieve better financial results, affirming the strategic importance of sustainability in modern business management.

3. Literature Review and Hypothesis Development

Research on ESG performance has a long history, with early references dating back to 1962 in the book *Principles and Practice*, which discusses ESG concepts and risks related to sustainable development. While international research on ESG has been well-established for decades, domestic research in China has gained momentum only recently. Despite the relatively nascent stage of global ESG research, significant progress has been made in both domestic and international academic circles.

A review of relevant studies highlights several key insights into ESG performance. Many studies indicate that female board members positively influence ESG outcomes. Additionally, the presence of CSR committees is significantly associated with improved ESG performance, although CSR expertise alone does not show a significant impact (Velte, 2016). Firms in sensitive industries often exhibit stronger ESG performance compared to those in less sensitive sectors, as they proactively disclose ESG activities to protect their reputations, attracting greater investments (Garcia et al., 2017). Other board characteristics, such as gender diversity, board size, and CSR committees, are crucial for enhancing the ESG performance of banks, while board independence has been found to negatively correlate with ESG performance (Birindelli et al., 2018).

Mergers and acquisitions (M&A) also significantly affect ESG performance. These transactions can incentivize companies to adopt sustainable practices, enhancing the disclosure of relevant information, with positive impacts on ESG scores typically evident after one year (Song et al., 2021; Barros et al., 2022). As stakeholder demand for ESG-related information grows, companies increasingly disclose this information, creating a positive feedback loop (Madison et al., 2021).

ESG factors are now critical in business operations, influenced by external factors and societal emphasis on environmental protection and social responsibility. During the COVID-19 pandemic, ESG considerations gained prominence in investment decisions, surpassing traditional Fama–French factors. Investors are now considering overall ESG evaluations and assessments of individual factors in their analyses (Díaz et al., 2021). CSR activities positively impact market value, with

CSR investments enhancing market value directly or indirectly. For instance, due to Chaebol governance reforms, ESG performance shows varied valuation effects on industries sensitive to the Korean market (Yoon et al., 2018). Comprehensive ESG performance positively impacts account-based financial performance, notably return on assets (ROA) (Velte, 2017).

Despite extensive research, there remains a compelling interest in exploring the impact of ESG performance, particularly in diverse national contexts and under unique conditions, such as the COVID-19 pandemic. Previous studies have primarily focused on data from Germany, yet different countries exhibit distinct conditions that can influence ESG outcomes (Velte, 2017). The pandemic has significantly impacted businesses, altered investor priorities, and shifted focus from short-term gains to sustainable development, with a greater emphasis on ESG ratings. Several studies in China also investigate the relationship of environmental accounting and firm performance (Rahman & Wu, 2023; Rahman, Wu, et al., 2024; Rahman et al., 2023; Zhu & Rahman, 2024). Therefore, there is a positive relationship between environmental cost and firm performance.

Based on these considerations, this study aims to fill the research gap by examining the ESG performance of Chinese enterprises, particularly in the context of the COVID-19 pandemic. This leads to the formulation of the following hypotheses:

Hypothesis 1: ESG performance of enterprises plays a significant role in shaping financial performance in the Chinese market.
Hypothesis 2: Despite the challenges posed by the epidemic, the influence of ESG performance on financial performance remains crucial for Chinese companies.

These hypotheses will be tested using data from the Bloomberg and CSMAR databases, focusing on the unique political and economic conditions in China during the COVID-19 pandemic. This approach aims to provide a deeper understanding of the relationship between ESG performance and financial outcomes in Chinese enterprises, offering valuable insights for policymakers and corporate managers.

4. Research Design/Methodology

4.1 Sample and Data

The sample size of this study consists of A-share listed companies spanning from 2011 to 2021, totalling 11,230 valid samples. The ESG data used in the analysis were obtained from the Bloomberg database, a renowned global provider of business and financial information. Additionally, financial data from the CSMAR database, a comprehensive research database focusing on China's financial economy, were utilized. The combination of these databases allowed for a comprehensive examination of the correlation between ESG performance and financial results. The data obtained from these two databases are valid and reliable.

In this chapter, the data on the companies listed on Stock Exchange A is sampled from 2011 to 2021, with the initial sample totalling 18,429 dates. Due to the need for data in the model, the first sample is eliminated as follows. (1) Excluding companies in the financial and insurance industry, there are 1,035 articles in total. Since the accruals of companies in the financial and insurance industry have their own characteristics compared with other industries, for example, the profit model, capital structure and risk management strategy of the financial and insurance industry are different from those of other industries. The ESG performance of companies in the finance and insurance industry can be influenced by regulatory requirements, industry standards, and financial risk management, which masks the potential relationship between ESG and financial performance across industries. In order to avoid the interference of industry differences in the analysis results, these were eliminated in this study. (2) Excluding all samples with incomplete data, a total of 3647 data were obtained. This was done to avoid bias due to missing data and to improve the reliability and reproducibility of the study. (3) Excluding special treatment (ST) and PT companies, companies whose listing is suspended, with poor performance, a total of 2,479 data were obtained. Such companies usually have large losses. ST firms are those that have suffered two consecutive years of losses and may be suspended from listing. A firm that is considered "ST" is considered to be equivalent to a firm under the financial distress measure (Qin et al., 2020), and once a company loses money for two consecutive years, the exchange may impose special supervision and penalties, including the possible suspension of its stock listing. A PT firm means that trading in the shares of these companies has been suspended. A PT company may be suspended from listing due to violation of the rules of the exchange, suspected violations of laws and regulations, or other serious issues. During the suspension, the companies' shares cannot be traded on exchanges, and investors cannot buy or sell the stock. Due to their extreme performance differences, they may have a significant impact on the statistical results of the overall sample, but these companies only account for a small proportion of the total sample. At the same time, due to the special circumstances of these companies, their financial data may not accurately reflect ESG and financial performance under normal operating conditions. Eliminating these data can improve the representativeness and consistency of the sample. (4) In order to exclude the influence of extreme values, all continuous variables are winsorized by 1% and 99%, and 38 pieces of data are eliminated in this process.

After the above screening, the sample data of 11,230 qualified listed companies are finally obtained. Six variables will be analysed in this study, namely, return on equity (ROE), esg, Size (company size), Lev (asset–liability ratio), Growth (growth rate of operating income), FirmAge (years of company establishment), and Cashflow. Due to the existence of data that are difficult to measure numerically, for the convenience of analysis. In this study, company size is defined as the natural logarithm of annual total assets, while the age of the company is calculated as the current year minus the year of establishment, minus one. We will adopt the following formula to express the relationship between the various variables.

$$\mathrm{ROEi,t} = \alpha 0 + \alpha 1\mathrm{ESGi,t} + \sum \mathrm{Controlsi,t} + \sum \mathrm{Industryi} + \sum \mathrm{Yeart} + \epsilon \mathrm{i,t}$$

This is followed by the measurement of the variables. In the above formula, controls is the control variable, industry is the industry fixed effect, year is the year

Table 5.1 Sample Selection

Total number	18,429
Less financial and insurance industry samples	1,035
Less samples with incomplete data	3,647
Less ST and PT companies	2,479
Less winsorized by 1% and 99%	38
Sample data	**11,230**

fixed effect, i is different enterprises, t is different years, ε is the random disturbance term, and $a0$ is the intercept term. Table 5.1 shows the sample selection process.

4.2 *Variable Measurements*

4.2.1 *Dependent Variable*

The primary emphasis of this research revolves around the financial performance of the company, with the ROE serving as the dependent variable for measurement. Descriptive statistics were conducted to analyse this variable, yielding the following results. The average ROE is 0.0881, with a standard deviation of 0.1226. The minimum ROE value observed is −0.5268, while the maximum value is 0.4050. These statistics indicate that the ROE of the sampled companies exhibits some variability and, on average, is relatively low. Table 5.2 describes the variable definition.

4.2.2 *Independent Variables*

Our study includes the following independent variables:

The first is companies' performance in ESG aspects, which is the main research topic of this work. The ESG is broken down into three sections: environmental, social and governance. Because the impact of ESG on financial performance is assessed, these three components are not calculated separately. In this study, ESG factors collectively serve as independent variables. The second is company size (size). Company size usually depends on number of employees, asset size, market share, and other factors. Due to the complexity of directly measuring company size using various methods, this study adopts the natural logarithm of annual total assets as a proxy for company size. The thiird is the asset–liability ratio (Lev). This ratio is derived by dividing the company's total liabilities by its total assets. The fourth is growth in operating income (growth). You can use this formula to calculate the growth rate of farm income. Operating income growth rate = (Current period operating income – Previous period operating income)/Previous period operating income × 100%. The fifth is the company's age. This can be calculated as (year of establishment of company in current year – 1). The sixth is the cash flow ratio. This is used as a metric to assess the liquidity of a company's cash flow and can be calculated using the following formula: Cash flow ratio = Net cash flow from operating activities/Average total assets.

Table 5.2 Variable Definition

Variable Abbreviation	*Variable Full Name*	*Variable Definition*	*Reference*
ROE	Return on equity	Net profit/average balance of shareholders' equity	Rahman and Zhu (2024)
esg	ESG performance	Bloomberg database ESG data/100	Zhu and Rahman (2024)
Size	Scale of the company	Natural logarithm of annual total assets	Rahman, Zhu, and Yue (2024)
Lev	Asset–liability ratio	Total liabilities at year-end divided by total assets at year-end	Rahman, Zhu, and Jiang (2024)
Growth	Operating income growth rate	Current year's operating income/ previous year's operating income − 1	Lam et al. (2024)
Firm age	Years of establishment of the company	In(Year of the current year – year of establishment of the company − 1	Rahman, Wu, et al. (2024)
Cashflow	Cash flow ratio	Net cash flow from operating activities divided by total assets	Cahan et al. (2021)

4.2.3 Control Variables

The control variables of this study are as follows:

> Like previous similar studies, this study takes firm risk as a control variable (Velte, 2017). The literature suggests that corporate risk is related to stakeholder relations and financial performance (Waddock & Graves, 1997). Companies that exhibit strong ESG performance are viewed as having reduced risk, leading to lower costs of debt capital due to the "insurance effect" (Orlitzky & Benjamin, 2001; Godfrey et al., 2009). Corporate risk includes market risk, operational risk, and financial risk. In order to simplify the research and provide a clearer understanding of the relationship between ESG performance and financial performance, this study will include firm risk as a control variable. By doing so, the complexity of the analysis is reduced, allowing for a more focused examination of the influence of ESG performance on financial performance.

R&D intensity is a commonly used control variable in this field (Fischer & Sawczyn, 2013; Choi & Wang, 2009), so it appears as a control variable in this study. R&D intensity represents a company's investment in new R&D projects and generally symbolizes the importance a company places on technology and intellectual property. This variable can be expressed in the financial statements as research and development expenses. Consistent with previous research, we expect the results to be positive (Kogut & Zander, 1992), meaning that R&D intensity is positively correlated with financial performance.

5. Empirical Results/Findings

5.1. Descriptive Statistics

This study examines the correlation between the ESG performance of firms and their financial performance. To gain a better understanding of the variables, descriptive statistical analysis was performed. The results are as follows: the average ROE is 0.0881, with a standard deviation of 0.1226. The lowest and highest values of ROE are −0.5268 and 0.4050, respectively, indicating some fluctuation in ROE with a relatively low average level. The average ESG performance is 0.2825, with a standard deviation of 0.0894. The minimum and maximum values of ESG performance are 0.1172 and 0.5591, respectively, suggesting slight variation in the ESG performance of the sampled firms with a higher average level. The average firm size (size) is 23.2248, with a standard deviation of 1.3573. The minimum and maximum values of company size are 20.4915 and 27.3074, respectively, indicating significant variation in firm size with a larger average size. The average asset–liability ratio (Lev) is 0.4778, with a standard deviation of 0.2016. The minimum and maximum values of the asset–liability ratio are 0.0673 and 0.8937, respectively, suggesting some differences in the asset–liability ratios of the sampled firms, with a higher average level. The average operating income growth (Growth) is 0.1748, with a standard deviation of 0.3702. The minimum and maximum values of operating income growth rate are –0.4885 and 2.2531, respectively, indicating significant fluctuation in the growth rate of operating income among the sampled firms with a relatively low average level. The average firm age is 2.9200 years, with a standard deviation of 0.3404. The lowest and highest values of firm age are 1.7918 and 3.5264 years, respectively, indicating a wide variation in the establishment years of the sampled firms, with a longer average duration. The average cash flow ratio is 0.0596, with a standard deviation of 0.0687. The minimum and maximum values of the cash flow ratio are –0.1288 and 0.2552, respectively, indicating some variation in the cash flow ratio among the sampled firms with a relatively low average level.

5.2 Economic and Political Implications

The study reveals a significant positive correlation between the ESG performance of companies and their financial performance in the Chinese market. This finding underscores the importance of ESG activities, aligning with the characteristics of the Chinese market. By prioritizing ESG performance, companies can enhance their financial outcomes, reduce environmental pollution, and promote sustainable economic growth while improving social welfare. From a governmental perspective, policy guidance and regulation can encourage enterprises to enhance their ESG practices. The Chinese government can foster improvements in ESG performance, thereby boosting financial results and refining market mechanisms. This includes promoting green finance to achieve sustainable development and a win–win relationship between economic growth and environmental stewardship.

Additionally, the data indicate that even during the pandemic, ESG performance continues to positively affect financial outcomes. Despite the challenges posed by COVID-19, such as significant losses and layoffs, companies are actively implementing strategies to manage these risks. As employee health declines and job security wavers, firms focusing on ESG are likely to take measures to support their workforce and alleviate negative sentiments. The pandemic has heightened public awareness of health issues, influenced investor perspectives, and increased the importance of corporate reputation and brand value. Strong ESG performance helps companies build a positive corporate image and enhance brand value, which can boost market competitiveness and attract customers and partners, ultimately expanding market share.

This study confirms that ESG performance is positively related to financial performance and illustrates that focusing on ESG is a sustainable business strategy. It can lead to a more resilient supply chain, improved employee relations, and better crisis management, helping mitigate the pandemic's adverse effects. In terms of policy, the government can incentivize companies to prioritize ESG through rewards and penalties, similar to initiatives outlined in the white paper on "China's Green Development in the New Era" (Chen et al., 2022).

5.3 Baseline Regression Results

Through our benchmark regression analysis, we obtained the following results (Table 5.3): the regression model reveals a significant positive impact of ESG activities on ROE ($t = 2.5186$, $p < 0.05$), indicating a positive relationship between increased ESG performance and the financial performance of companies. Additionally, company size (Size) demonstrates a significant positive influence on ROE ($t = 19.5897$, $p < 0.001$), while the asset–liability ratio (Lev) exhibits a significant negative impact on ROE ($t = -28.8900$, $p < 0.001$).

Additionally, the growth rate of operating profit (Growth) has a considerably positive impact on ROE ($t = 30.5596$, $p < 0.001$), and cash flow also displays a significant positive effect on ROE ($t = 40.6987$, $p < 0.001$). However, the company's nature does not have a significant influence on ROE ($t = -0.0062$, $p < 0.1$). With an F-statistic value of 60.8431 ($p < 0.001$) and an $R2$ value of 0.3296, the benchmark regression model demonstrates a strong fit and explanatory power for the sample data, surpassing other variables.

In conclusion, according to the results of the benchmark regression analysis, we can affirm that ESG performance, company size, asset–liability ratio, growth rate of operating income, and cash flow ratio significantly influence a company's ROE. These results provide an important reference for enterprises and policymakers to better understand the association between ESG performance and financial

Table 5.3 Baseline Regression Results

	ROE
Esg	0.0415** (2.5186)
Size	0.0206*** (19.5897)
Lev	−0.1873*** (−28.8900)
Growth	0.0809*** (30.5596)
FirmAge	−0.0000 (−0.0062)
Cashflow	0.6221*** (40.6987)
_cons	−0.3226*** (−12.2747)
Industry	Yes
Year	Yes
N	11,230
F	60.8431
R^2	0.3296

Note: *, **, and *** represent significance at the 10%, 5%, and 1% levels, respectively, with *t*-values in parentheses.

performance. Based on the obtained results, firm *h* and the decision-maker can make effective countermeasures and formulate reasonable plans.

6. Endogeneity Tests

To address the potential endogeneity issue between ESG and financial performance, this study employs the instrumental variable approach. Specifically, the average ESG value within the same industry and the current year is utilized as the instrumental variable. The model is then re-estimated using a two-step regression method. After examining the instrumental variables, we conducted tests to assess their validity and appropriateness for addressing endogeneity concerns. Table 5.4 shows the results.

To assess the unidentifiability of the instrumental variables, we used the Kleibergen–Paap (K-P) LM statistics as the first step. K-P LM statistics is a statistical test method used to test the endogeneity of instrumental variables in linear regression models. If the K-P LM statistical value is large and significant, it means that the instrumental variable can effectively correct endogeneity and provide reliable estimation results. Conversely, if the K-P LM statistic value is small, it indicates that the instrumental variables may not be able to effectively solve the endogeneity problem, and further testing or other methods should be used to deal with endogeneity. The results obtained show a statistical K-P LM value of 353.176, with a *p* value of less than 0.01.

Table 5.4 Endogeneity Tests

	(1) *Esg*	*(2)* *ROE*
Iv	0.9332***	
	(21.6931)	
Esg		0.4966***
		(5.9174)
Size	0.0258***	0.0087***
	(47.7313)	(3.4120)
Lev	−0.0290***	−0.1728***
	(−7.9632)	(−16.6340)
Growth	−0.0011	0.0810***
	(−0.7493)	(21.1963)
FirmAge	0.0048**	−0.0025
	(2.5138)	(−0.7125)
Cashflow	0.0382***	0.6017***
	(4.4377)	(30.2031)
_cons	−0.5576***	−0.1349***
	(−35.3028)	(−2.9533)
Industry	Yes	Yes
Year	Yes	Yes
N	11,230	11,230
F	185.1824	186.8986
K-P LM	353.176	353.176
	[0.000]	[0.000]
K-P Wald *F*	477.770	477.770
	{16.38}	{16.38}
R^2	0.5994	0.2836

Note: Significance levels are denoted as *, **, and *** for 10%, 5%, and 1%, respectively. The critical value at the 10% level of the Stock–Yogo test is indicated in {}.

The findings suggest that the instrumental variable successfully passed the unidentifiability test. Consequently, we can assume the instrumental variables are both valid and reliable for our analysis. Secondly, we conducted a weak instrumental variable test to ensure the validity of the instrumental variables. Weak instrumental variable test is a statistical test method used to evaluate the validity and reliability of instrumental variables in solving endogeneity problems. If the test results show low strength or weak correlation of the instrumental variables, there may be a problem of weak instrumental variables, and it is necessary to reconsider the selection of instrumental variables or look for stronger instrumental variables. By calculating Wald's F, K-P value, it was found to be 477.770, far exceeding the critical Stock–Yogo 10% value of 16.38, which means that the instrumental variable has passed the weak instrumental variable test and has sufficient explanatory power.

Moreover, we performed over-identification tests to ensure that the number of instrumental variables is not greater than the number of endogenous variables. The over-identification test serves as a statistical assessment to evaluate the identifiability and credibility of the econometric model. The objective of the over-identification test is to check whether there are too many or redundant instrumental variables in the model to determine whether the model can provide consistent and valid estimation results. The results show that the number of instrumental variables meets the requirements of the over-identification test, which further verifies the appropriateness of the instrumental factors.

To conclude, the instrumental variables utilized in this study have been deemed suitable and effective in mitigating the endogeneity issue between ESG and financial performance. The findings of the subsequent regression analysis demonstrate a significant positive coefficient for ESG, thereby reaffirming the hypothesis of this research. These findings offer robust evidence supporting the positive influence of ESG on financial performance.

7. Robustness or Additional Analyses

The purpose of conducting robustness tests is to assess the resilience and credibility of the benchmark regression results, thereby ensuring the robustness of the research findings. By conducting a robustness test, we can check the influence of possible biased assumptions or abnormal observations in the model on the results and verify the stability of the comparative regression results.

To examine the robustness of the findings, this study takes a critical step of replacing the original explanatory variables of Tobin's Q with alternative variables and performing the regression analysis once again.

TobinQ, a measure of the relationship between a company's market capitalization and its net asset value, is often used as an alternative explanatory variable to test the robustness of research findings. Taking TobinQ as a new explained variable can compare and evaluate the stability of the original results and verify the reliability of the research conclusions.

The following are the robustness test results, and the same is presented in Table 5.5. In the robustness test, it is observed that the ESG performance has a significantly positive impact on Tobin's Q ($t = 5.0674, p < 0.001$). This indicates a positive association between enhanced ESG performance and the company's capital markets and assets. In addition, enterprise size (size) has a negative impact on TobinQ $(t = -27.3287, p < 0.001)$. The asset–liability ratio (Lev) is negatively correlated with TobinQ $(t = -13.4047, p < 0.001)$. Operating income growth (growth) has a positive impact on TobinQ $(t = 10.5710, \mathrm{p} < 0.001)$. Enterprise age has a negative impact on TobinQ $(t = -3.1728, \mathrm{p} < 0.001)$. Cashflow ratio has a positive impact on TobinQ $(t = 19.8682, \mathrm{p} < 0.001)$.

According to F statistics ($F = 76.0670, p < 0.001$) and R^2 value ($R^2 = 0.3807$), it can be seen that the regression model of the robustness test fits the fabric model well, and the explanatory power of the difference is strong. The F-statistic is an indicator used to evaluate the fit of the regression model. In our study, the value of the F-statistic is 76.0670, and the significance level of p-value is less than 0.001. This indicates that our regression model has a significant explanatory power for the

Table 5.5 Robustness or Additional Analyses

	TobinQ
Esg	0.9177***
	(5.0674)
Size	−0.3164***
	(−27.3287)
Lev	−0.9558***
	(−13.4047)
Growth	0.3077***
	(10.5710)
FirmAge	−0.1176***
	(−3.1728)
Cashflow	3.3390***
	(19.8682)
_cons	9.7489***
	(33.7395)
Industry	Yes
Year	Yes
N	11,230
F	76.0670
R^2	0.3807

Note: *, **, and *** denote statistical significance at the 10%, 5%, and 1% levels, respectively, with t-values indicated in parentheses.

sample data. The high F value indicates that the independent variables in the model have good explanatory power for each variable, and the overall model fits well. In addition, the R^2 value is used to measure the degree to which individual variables in the regression model explain the variance. In the regression model of the robustness test, the R^2 value is 0.3807. This suggests that the explanatory variables in the model can explain 38.07% of the variation. A higher R^2 value signifies a stronger explanatory power of the model and a more significant independent effect on the dependent variable.

After conducting robustness tests, our findings were found to align with previous benchmarks, indicating that ESG performance, company size, asset–liability ratio, operating income growth, and revenue are all related to business values and assets. Notably, larger companies, higher asset–liability ratios, and greater company age negatively affect Tobin's Q, while ESG performance, revenue growth, and income ratios positively influence it. This reinforces the reliability of our transformation results.

These conclusions suggest that the positive impact of ESG performance on financial outcomes applies not only to German businesses (Velte, 2017) but also to those in China. Furthermore, despite the disruptions caused by the COVID-19 pandemic, the relationship between ESG performance and financial performance remained stable, indicating that the pandemic did not positively affect this association.

The theoretical implications are significant. The robustness tests highlight ESG performance as a crucial driver of market capitalization and company assets. Strong ESG practices enhance a company's perceived value among investors, increasing opportunities for stakeholder engagement and ultimately improving market and asset values. Practically, this underscores the importance of ESG performance for market capitalization and asset value. By enhancing ESG practices, companies can build trust and recognition among investors, driving long-term growth and value creation. Companies should focus on improving ESG performance to indirectly boost financial outcomes.

To enhance ESG performance, organizations should invest in ESG initiatives. Environmentally, firms can reduce energy consumption and carbon emissions, focusing on resource management and recycling, especially in secondary industries. Socially, they should ensure a positive work environment, employee welfare, and community engagement. Governance-wise, establishing effective corporate structures that ensure compliance and transparency is essential. Moreover, company size, asset–liability ratio, operating income growth, and cash flow significantly influence market and asset values. Management should consider these factors in strategic decision-making to optimize financial performance.

This conclusion is valuable for both business managers and investors. Investors can incorporate ESG performance, company size, asset–liability ratio, operating income growth, and cash flow in their investment evaluations to mitigate risks and enhance returns. Ultimately, this research provides actionable insights for managers and investors, encouraging a focus on ESG to achieve sustainable development and promote the well-being of society and the environment (Zhu & Wang, 2024).

8. Conclusions

This research primarily examines the influence of ESG performance on financial performance, focusing specifically on Chinese firms during the COVID-19 pandemic. The study involves collecting data, categorizing it into independent and dependent variables, and conducting a thorough analysis. The main findings of this study can be summarized as follows:

1. ESG Performance and Financial Performance: ESG performance demonstrates a favourable and substantial influence on financial performance within the Chinese market.
2. Impact Post-Pandemic: Even in the aftermath of the COVID-19 pandemic, ESG performance continues to exert a positive influence on financial performance.

These findings provide valuable insights into the existing body of international research on the relationship between ESG performance and financial performance.

Prior studies, such as Velte (2017), primarily relied on data from Germany spanning the years 2010–2014. In contrast, this study leverages Chinese data covering the period from 2011 to 2021, encompassing a decade-long span. Additionally, this study includes data from the COVID-19 period, offering a comprehensive understanding of the relationship between ESG performance and financial performance during a global health crisis, an area that has not been extensively explored.

By selecting data from the Chinese market over an extended time span, this research provides a broader examination of the relationship between ESG performance and financial outcomes, enabling the application of findings to actual firms in China. This enhanced understanding of the interplay among ESG factors and financial performance offers a better decision-making framework for firms and policymakers. Moreover, the results of this study contribute new perspectives and suggestions for future research, furthering the development of ESG research in Chinese companies.

These findings may encourage companies that have not yet prioritized ESG to do so. Local governments can also promote policies and formulate relevant regulations to encourage companies to enhance their ESG performance. The beneficial influence of ESG performance on financial outcomes stems from a higher ESG score, which reflects a company's excellence in environmental compliance, customer reputation, and risk management. This implies that, in the long run, business leaders can align stakeholder satisfaction with maintaining a good reputation, thereby focusing on ensuring the firm's sustainable growth.

However, the study has some limitations. We did not analyse the impact of ESG performance on financial performance in the post-pandemic period when the situation became relatively stable. The data used in this study only extend to the end of 2021, a time when the entire workforce was battling the pandemic. By the end of 2022, the Chinese government had adopted new infection-prevention measures, transitioning from strict controls. As people began to adapt to living with the pandemic, the lack of relevant data limited the analysis of the connection between ESG performance and financial performance during the later stages of the pandemic. Future research should aim to address this gap by including data from the post-pandemic period to provide a more comprehensive understanding of this relationship.

9. References

Barros, V., Matos, P. V., Sarmento, J. M., & Vieira, P. R. (2022). M&A activity as a driver for better ESG performance. *Technological Forecasting and Social Change*, *175*, 121338.

Birindelli, G., Dell'Atti, S., Iannuzzi, A. P., & Savioli, M. (2018). Composition and activity of the board of directors: Impact on ESG performance in the banking system. *Sustainability*, *10*(12), 4699.

Cahan, S., Lam, B. M., Li, L. Z., & Rahman, M. J. (2021). Information environment and stock price synchronicity: Evidence from auditor characteristics. *International Journal of Auditing*, *25*(2), 332–350.

Chen, Z., & Xie, G. (2022). ESG disclosure and financial performance: Moderating role of ESG investors. *International Review of Financial Analysis*, *83*, 102291.

Choi, J., & Wang, H. (2009). Stakeholder relations and the persistence of corporate financial performance. *Strategic Management Journal*, *30*(8), 895–907.

Clarkson, P. M., Li, Y., Richardson, G. D., & Vasvari, F. P. (2008). Revisiting the relation between environmental performance and environmental disclosure – an empirical analysis. *Accounting, Organizations and Society, 33*(4–5), 303–327.

Díaz, V., Ibrushi, D., & Zhao, J. (2021). Reconsidering systematic factors during the COVID-19 pandemic – The rising importance of ESG. *Finance Research Letters, 38*, 101870.

Fischer, T. M., & Sawczyn, A. A. (2013). The relationship between corporate social performance and corporate financial performance and the role of innovation: Evidence from German listed firms. *Journal of Management Control, 24*, 27–52.

Freeman, R. E. (1984). *Strategic management: A stakeholder approach.* Cambridge University Press.

Garcia, A. S., Mendes-Da-Silva, W., & Orsato, R. J. (2017). Sensitive industries produce better ESG performance: Evidence from emerging markets. *Journal of Cleaner Production, 150*, 135–147.

Godfrey, P. C., Merrill, C. B., & Hansen, J. M. (2009). The relationship between corporate social responsibility and shareholder value: An empirical test of the risk management hypothesis. *Strategic Management Journal, 30*(4), 425–455.

Jensen, M. C., & Meckling, W. H. (2019). Theory of the firm: Managerial behavior, agency costs and ownership structure. In *Corporate governance* (pp. 77–132). Gower.

Kogut, B., & Zander, U. (1992). Knowledge of the firm, combinative capabilities and the replication of technology. *Organization Science, 3*(3), 383–397.

Lam, B. M., Mo, P. L. L., & Rahman, M. J. (2024). Secrecy culture, client importance, and auditor reporting behavior: An international study. *Managerial Auditing Journal, 39*(2), 113–137.

Madison, N., & Schiehll, E. (2021). The effect of financial materiality on ESG performance assessment. *Sustainability, 13*(7), 3652.

Mardini, G. H. (2022). ESG factors and corporate financial performance. *International Journal of Managerial and Financial Accounting, 14*(3), 247–264.

Orlitzky, M., & Benjamin, J. D. (2001). Corporate social performance and firm risk: A meta-analytic review. *Business & Society, 40*(4), 369–396.

Qin, X., Huang, G., Shen, H., & Fu, M. (2020). COVID-19 pandemic and firm-level cash holding – moderating effect of goodwill and goodwill impairment. *Emerging Markets Finance and Trade, 56*(10), 2243–2258.

Rahman, J., & Wu, J. (2023). M&A activity and ESG performance: Evidence from China. *Managerial Finance, 50*(1), 179–197.

Rahman, M. J., Wu, Q., & Zhu, H. (2024). Corporate social responsibility in times of social distancing: Evidence from China. *Business Ethics, the Environment & Responsibility.*

Rahman, M. J., & Zhu, H. (2024). Predicting financial distress using machine learning approaches: Evidence China. *Journal of Contemporary Accounting & Economics, 20*(1), 100403.

Rahman, M. J., Zhu, H., & Chen, S. (2023). Does CSR reduce financial distress? Moderating effect of firm characteristics, auditor characteristics, and covid-19. *International Journal of Accounting & Information Management, 31*(5), 756–784.

Rahman, M. J., Zhu, H., & Jiang, X. (2024). Family firms, client importance, and auditor reporting behavior: Evidence from China. *Meditari Accountancy Research, 32*(2), 543–578.

Rahman, M. J., Zhu, H., & Yue, L. (2024). Does the adoption of artificial intelligence by audit firms and their clients affect audit quality and efficiency? Evidence from China. *Managerial Auditing Journal, 39*(6), 668–699.

Ross, S. A. (1973). The economic theory of agency: The principal's problem. *The American Economic Review, 63*(2), 134–139.

Song, S., Zeng, Y., & Zhou, B. (2022). Information asymmetry, cross-listing, and post-M&A performance. *Journal of Business Research, 122*(2021), 447–457.

Velte, P. (2016). Women on management board and ESG performance. *Journal of Global Responsibility*, *7*(1), 98–109.

Velte, P. (2017). Does ESG performance have an impact on financial performance? Evidence from Germany. *Journal of Global Responsibility*, *8*(2), 169–178.

Waddock, S. A., & Graves, S. B. (1997). The corporate social performance – financial performance link. *Strategic Management Journal*, *18*(4), 303–319.

Yoon, B., Lee, J. H., & Byun, R. (2018). Does ESG performance enhance firm value? Evidence from Korea. *Sustainability*, *10*(10), 3635.

Zhu, H., & Rahman, M. J. (2024). Ex-ante expected changes in ESG and future stock returns based on machine learning. *The British Accounting Review*, 101457.

Zhu, B., & Wang, Y. (2024). Does social trust affect firms' ESG performance? *International Review of Financial Analysis*, *93*, 103153.

6 The Impact of ESG on Financial Performance

Md Jahidur Rahman, Tarek Rana, Hongtao Zhu, and Chenyu Mao

1. Introduction

Environmental, social, and governance (ESG) factors have become crucial for investors in their decision-making processes (Aouadi & Marsat, 2016). Originating from ethical investing in regions like the United States and Europe, ESG encompasses considerations such as corporate philanthropy, shareholder value, and societal well-being (Li et al., 2021). Investors use ESG metrics to assess corporate behaviour and predict long-term financial performance, thus determining a company's viability, risks, and managerial quality.

ESG comprises three core components: environmental, social, and governance, which together provide a comprehensive view of a company's potential for sustainable success. As concerns about the environment grow, ESG has emerged as a key investment criterion, helping investors identify risks that traditional financial metrics might overlook. High ESG performance is associated with reduced risk, lower volatility, and improved stakeholder trust, enhancing long-term value.

Investors increasingly prioritize ESG for insights into a company's profitability and risk profile. Some investors choose to invest in environmentally friendly companies even if it means lower financial returns (Starks, 2009). Positive ESG performance can enhance brand reputation, as demonstrated by Capelle-Blancard and Petit (2017), who found a link between favourable ESG news and strong corporate reputation.

ESG investing has become a popular strategy, with global ESG assets reaching $37.8 trillion by 2021, up from $22.8 trillion in 2016 (Chen & Lin, 2022). Various industries are integrating ESG into their strategies; for instance, PepsiCo has set ambitious environmental goals and invested in renewable energy, leading to significant reputational and financial gains. Similarly, the shipping industry is adopting ESG practices, aligning with the United Nations sustainable development goals (SDGs) to reduce CO_2 emissions.

In the banking sector, ESG practices have differential effects: environmental and governance measures positively influence shareholder value, while social practices may have negative impacts (Miralles-Quirós et al., 2019). The power generation sector also benefits from strong ESG ratings, enhancing return on capital employed (ROCE) and investor confidence (Zhao et al., 2018).

DOI: 10.4324/9781003488934-8

Understanding ESG's impact on financial performance is vital for stakeholders. Investors assess company value and risk using ESG metrics, while corporate leaders implement ESG strategies to enhance profitability and trust. Policymakers can develop regulations to improve ESG standards, benefiting the economy and society. This chapter investigates the relationship between ESG factors and financial performance, specifically examining whether high ESG ratings correlate with superior financial outcomes in A-share listed companies in China from 2010 to 2021.

The contributions of this chapter are significant. First, it adds to the knowledge on ESG in the Chinese market, the second-largest stock market globally (Amin & Tauseef, 2022). Second, it employs a two-way fixed effects model to analyze the overall impact of ESG on financial performance, offering a broader perspective than previous research. Third, the findings provide practical insights for investors, companies, and policymakers, emphasizing the importance of ESG in corporate strategy. Finally, the research raises awareness of ESG's significance, encouraging businesses to prioritize sustainability and ethical practices to attract investment and positively impact society.

The chapter is structured as follows: Section 2 outlines the theoretical foundation, Section 3 presents the literature review and hypotheses, Section 4 details the research design, Section 5 discusses robustness tests and empirical findings, and Section 6 concludes with implications and limitations.

2. Theoretical Framework

The relationship between ESG factors and companies' financial performance can be analysed through three main theoretical perspectives: cash flow theory (CFT), sustainable development theory (SDT), and resource-based theory (RBT). These frameworks collectively illustrate how ESG influences financial outcomes, sustainability practices, and competitive advantages.

CFT suggests a strong link between ESG factors and financial performance (Alareeni & Hamdan, 2020). It posits that higher ESG disclosure correlates positively with financial indicators like return on assets (ROA) and return on equity (ROE). Notably, governance tends to have a positive relationship with ROA, while environmental factors often show negative correlations with both ROA and ROE. Additionally, corporate governance disclosures are positively associated with ROA and Tobin's Q, while environmental and CSR disclosures are linked to Tobin's Q as well (Alareeni & Hamdan, 2020). Giese et al. (2019) differentiate between systematic risk, influenced by macroeconomic factors, and idiosyncratic risk, associated with individual company cash flows.

SDT focuses on integrating economic, social, and environmental dimensions, aligning closely with ESG principles (Shi et al., 2019). Companies adopting SDT are likely to implement eco-friendly policies, such as investing in pollution-reducing technologies. For example, PepsiCo's investments in renewable energy and fleet upgrades to reduce emissions illustrate how ESG initiatives can lead to cost reductions and operational efficiencies, promoting a balance between profitability and social responsibility.

RBT emphasizes that resources and capabilities enable companies to maintain competitive advantages (Zhou et al., 2022). Higher ESG performance often leads to better supply chain management and reduced default risks. Firms with strong ESG credentials typically demonstrate superior management practices, which contribute to competitive advantages (Giese et al., 2019). RBT suggests that leveraging ESG strengths can facilitate sustainable growth and improved financial performance.

In summary, ESG factors influence financial performance indicators like ROA, ROE, and Tobin's Q by enhancing governance and strategic risk management. The risks mitigated by ESG practices lead to more stable cash flows. ESG initiatives aligned with sustainable development foster innovation and operational efficiencies, reducing costs and improving resource use. Effective ESG strategies enhance a firm's capabilities, leading to better supply chain management and long-term competitive advantages.

These three theories – CFT, SDT, and RBT – provide a comprehensive framework for understanding the multifaceted impact of ESG on financial performance. CFT emphasizes direct financial implications, SDT highlights the broader sustainability context, and RBT underscores the role of internal resources in maintaining a competitive edge. This integrated approach lays the groundwork for further empirical research into the nuanced relationship between ESG factors and corporate financial performance.

3. Literature Review and Hypothesis Development

The influence of ESG factors on investment decision-making has gained significant attention recently (Aouadi & Marsat, 2016). Growing awareness of climate change and social issues has led to increased scrutiny of the environmental and social impacts of economic activities. While initial concerns were mainly about climate, the COVID-19 pandemic has highlighted the importance of social factors (Scatigna et al., 2021). This shift has created a demand for investment products that support environmental protection, workers' rights, and strong corporate governance, emphasizing the need for financial markets to integrate ESG considerations.

Research indicates that companies incorporating ESG factors often achieve better financial performance. Aouadi and Marsat (2016) note that firms with higher ESG ratings attract more investors, leading to increased capital inflows and potentially higher stock prices. This positive correlation is often linked to improved operational efficiencies, enhanced risk management, and stronger stakeholder relationships. Companies with robust ESG practices are perceived as better managed, providing them with a competitive edge and greater profitability (Alareeni & Hamdan, 2020).

ESG factors are also crucial for risk management. Giese et al. (2019) explained that ESG performance can mitigate systematic and idiosyncratic risks. Systematic risk affects the entire market and can lower capital costs for firms with strong ESG practices. Idiosyncratic risk, specific to individual firms, relates to future cash flows. Companies with high ESG ratings are better positioned to manage operational and reputational risks, leading to more stable financial performance.

The integration of ESG factors into investment decisions is increasingly common. According to Aich et al. (2021), ESG considerations can influence funding costs and the allocation of resources. Investors now use ESG metrics to evaluate corporate behaviour and long-term viability, recognizing that these factors can significantly affect a company's risk profile and financial performance. There is also a growing demand for standardized ESG reporting to enhance comparability and evaluation of corporate performance, as inconsistent ESG data complicate assessments (Aich et al., 2021).

The rising demand for ESG performance reporting presents both opportunities and challenges. Enhanced disclosure can offer valuable insights, but the lack of standardized metrics creates complexity in evaluating corporate performance. This highlights the need for uniform ESG reporting standards to ensure transparency and comparability. Policymakers and market participants must collaborate to develop comprehensive and consistent ESG frameworks to support the transition to a sustainable economy.

3.1 Contemporary ESG Impact on Financial Performance

The relationship between ESG factors and financial performance has garnered significant attention in recent academic research. Notably, Alareeni and Hamdan (2020) identified a nuanced correlation between ESG disclosure and corporate performance. They found that while the environmental aspect of ESG positively influences a company's Tobin's Q, indicating market valuation, it negatively affects ROA and ROE. However, for firms with high financial leverage, increased ESG disclosure is associated with improved ROA and ROE, highlighting the complexity of ESG impacts across various financial metrics.

Giese et al. (2019) further explored the economic mechanisms behind ESG impacts, introducing the cash flow channel concept. They argued that a strong ESG profile enhances competitiveness, leading to higher profitability and increased dividends for shareholders. Gregory et al. (2014) supported this view, suggesting that companies with robust ESG profiles benefit from efficient resource utilization, superior management practices, and strong long-term business relationships. These advantages enable such firms to generate higher returns, translating into greater profitability and investor dividends.

The role of ESG in risk management has also been extensively studied. Li et al. (2022) found that high ESG ratings correlate with lower credit risk, indicating a reduced likelihood of default. Their analysis of A-share listed companies in China from 2015 to 2020 revealed that ESG practices effectively reflect credit market conditions, suggesting that investors can mitigate credit risk by incorporating ESG performance into their strategies. This effect is notably stronger in non-manufacturing firms, highlighting industry-specific differences in ESG impacts.

Moreover, Giese et al. (2019) noted that companies with high ESG ratings tend to implement stringent policies and superior supply chain management, reducing unexpected credit-related issues and stabilizing stock prices. This aligns with the broader perspective that strong ESG performance enhances overall corporate stability and reduces volatility. Several studies in China also investigates the relationship between environmental accounting and firm performance (Rahman & Wu, 2023; Rahman, Wu, & Zhu, 2024; Rahman, Zhu, & Chen, 2023; Zhu & Rahman, 2024; Rahman Zhu, Zhang, & Hossain, 2024).

This hypothesis aims to empirically test the impact of ESG factors on stock prices, providing insights into how ESG performance translates into market valuation. The following sections will detail the research design and methodology for testing this hypothesis using data from A-share listed companies in China, contributing to the understanding of ESG's role in financial performance and investment decision-making. Based on the literature review, the proposed hypothesis is as follows:

H1: There is a positive relationship between ESG performance and stock price.

3.2 Existing Gaps in the Relationship between ESG and Investment Decisions

The growing literature on ESG factors and investment decisions reveals significant gaps in understanding their influence on financial choices. A key challenge is the varied impact of ESG across industries. Gholami et al. (2022) found that ESG disclosures benefit companies differently due to varying investor interests. Deng and Cheng (2019) noted that ESG performance significantly affects non-state-owned companies more than state-owned ones, especially in secondary industries.

Another challenge involves the diverse effects of ESG on different investor types. Eccles et al. (2017) highlighted that equity investors typically have longer time horizons than fixed-income investors, with regional variations in patience for outperformance. Yoon et al. (2021) indicated that younger generations are more socially conscious, necessitating ESG strategies that consider demographic and regional differences. Policymakers can promote sustainable investment by fostering regulatory environments that prioritize ESG. ESG performance's reflection in market valuations also poses challenges. While positive ESG ratings can enhance market value, Zhou et al. (2022) argued that financial performance often mediates this relationship. Nekhili et al. (2019) found that investors may react negatively to certain ESG practices, emphasizing the complexity of assessing ESG's impact on financial success.

Moreover, the rise of ESG investing faces data quality and standardization issues. Jonsdottir et al. (2022) highlighted the need for reliable ESG data, as inconsistencies hinder effective comparisons across companies. Dorfleitner et al. (2015) noted discrepancies in ESG assessments due to varying methodologies. Collaborative efforts between investors and companies are crucial for integrating ESG criteria into decision-making. This includes engaging companies to prioritize ESG and establishing industry-wide standards. Amel-Zadeh and Serafeim (2018) pointed to green bonds as a means to enhance environmental outcomes, while effective ESG data practices can attract sustainability-focused investors.

Legislation and regulatory frameworks significantly influence ESG investing. Transparency and standardization challenges, along with concerns about greenwashing, can undermine investor confidence (de Freitas Netto et al., 2020).

Yu et al. (2020) stressed the importance of regulations that promote accurate ESG reporting. This hypothesis aims to empirically test how ESG factors impact key financial performance indicators, providing insights into their influence on corporate profitability. The following sections will outline the research design and methodology for testing this hypothesis using data from A-share listed companies in China, contributing to a better understanding of ESG's role in financial performance. Based on this review, the following hypothesis is proposed:

H2: There is a positive relationship between ESG performance and ROA and ROE.

4. Research Design

4.1 Sample and Data

This study will use Wind and CSMAR databases to collect the financial data of all A-share listed companies in China from 2010 to 2021. Moreover, all the ESG ratings and indices data are from the Sino-Securities Index Information Service Company. Both financial data sources are the most comprehensive financial data sources in China. The selection of all A-share listed will ensure that the data obtained represent the whole primary market, which can reflect ESG factors and financial performance across every industry in China. By running the analysis, the study will find any positive or negative relationship between ESG factors and the company's financial performance, which provides valuable insights into how ESG information can be integrated during investment decision-making. Furthermore, the study will clean and preprocess the data collected from Wind and CSMAR databases to remove any inconsistencies, missing values, or outliers and organize the data into a structured format suitable for regression analysis. Table 6.1 depicts our data screening procedure. The preliminary dataset includes 34,434 firm-year observations. The sample is then decreased by omitting the following.

In this study, the samples from financial industries were eliminated to make the research more accurate. This is because the Chinese government has strict controls on the listed financial companies, which results in differences in accounting methods. Therefore, 789 companies from the financial industry were removed from the dataset. In addition, companies marked as ST, SST, *ST, and PT by the exchange were also removed. Those companies are considered in financial distress, which is likely to whitewash their financial statements. Therefore, 1,092 companies marked

Table 6.1 Sample Selection Criteria

Sample Selection Criteria	*No. of Firm-Year Observations*
Total number	34,434
Less: companies in the financial industry	798
Less: companies marked with ST, SST, *ST, and PT	1,092
Less: missing data or sample	2,262
Final number	30,282

with ST, SST, *ST, and PT were removed to reduce possible deviations from the research results. Finally, 2,262 observations were eliminated because of missing data or samples. As a result, there were 30,282 observations in the final dataset. The ESG data were collected from the Sino-Securities Index Information Service Company and were used to assess the relationship between ESG performance and companies' financial behaviour. All continuous variables at the enterprise level were winsorized at the yearly level of less than 1% and more than 99% to lessen the impact of outliers on the regression outcomes. In this study, data processing and analysis were primarily carried out using Stata 17.0. Finally, there are 30,282 firm-year observations. Table 6.1 provides a summary of the sample selection.

4.2 Variable Measurement

There is one dependent variable in the first hypothesis, stock price, and two dependent variables in the second hypothesis, ROA and ROE. Following Alareeni and Hamdan (2020), the study will evaluate companies' performance based on these dependent variables, which are stock price, ROA, and ROE, to find out the relationship between the study variables.

ESG is the only independent variable. This study classifies all A-share listed firms into the following grades based on ESG ratings: AAA, AA, A, BBB, BB, B, CCC, CC, and C, according to the Sino-Securities Index Information Service Company. In the regression analysis, AAA denotes a score of 9, AA a score of 8, and so on. As a result, the ESG performance is graded on a scale of 1–9.

This study has two control variables. Company size (Size) is the initial control variable, and it is calculated using the natural logarithm of total assets. Because it is tough to duplicate a huge corporation since it generally delivers economies of scale (Roberts & Dowling, 2002), we chose size as the first control variable. Additionally, we also include leverage (Lev), which is the level of debt of a company, as the second control variable because leverage can have an impact on a company's financial performance (AYDOĞMUŞ et al., 2022).

4.3 Model Specification

Borenstein et al. (2010) distinguish between two meta-analysis models: the fixed-effect model and the mixed-effect model. As a result, before the empirical regression, it is vital to pick the model to apply. Consequently, in this research, the F test was performed on the sample data first, and the results are provided in panel A in Table 6.2. The null hypothesis states that the mixed-effect model is superior to the fixed-effect model. However, because all of the F test p-values are less than 0.05, the null hypothesis is rejected. The fixed-effect model performs better than the mixed-effect model as a result. Later, the fixed-effect model and the random-effect model were compared using the Hausman test (Amini et al., 2012). Panel B in Table 6.2 displays the test findings. Hausman test's p-values are all less than 0.05, indicating that the regression analysis cannot use the random-effect model. Therefore, in this research we opted to use the fixed-effect model.

Table 6.2 Endogeneity Test

Panel A: Test results for choosing a fixed-effect model or a mixed-effect model		
Taking ROA as the explained variable	Taking ROE as the explained variable	Taking stock price as the explained variable
H_0: all u_i = 0:	H_0: all u_i = 0:	H_0: all u_i = 0:
$F(3989, 26254) = 3.08$	$F(3989, 26254) = 2.25$	$F(3989, 26254) = 14.72$
Prob > F = 0.0000	Prob > F = 0.0000	Prob > F = 0.0000
Panel B: Test results for choosing a fixed-effect model or a random-effect model		
Taking ROA as the explained variable	Taking ROE as the explained variable	Taking stock price as the explained variable
H_0: difference in coefficients not systematic	H_0: difference in coefficients not systematic	H_0: difference in coefficients not systematic
$Chi^2(39) = 1{,}773.30$	$Chi^2(38) = 1{,}829.46$	$Chi^2(39) = 1{,}652.79$
Prob > chi^2 = 0.0000	Prob > chi^2 = 0.0000	Prob > chi^2 = 0.0000

According to Amini et al. (2012), the fixed-effect model can solve the endogeneity problem caused by omitted variables. Therefore, in this study, we chose a two-way fixed-effect model of individuals and years as fixed regions to exclude the impact of the different macroeconomic environments in different years. The specific model formula is as follows.

Fixed Effects Model

$$ROA_{i,t} = \beta_0 + \beta_1 ESG_{i,t} + \sum \phi_i Controls_{i,t} + \mu_i + \mu_{year} + \varepsilon_{i,t}$$

$$Price_{i,t} = \beta_0 + \beta_1 ESG_{i,t} + \sum \phi_i Controls_{i,t} + \mu_i + \mu_{year} + \varepsilon_{i,t}$$

$$ROE_{i,t} = \beta_0 + \beta_1 ESG_{i,t} + \sum \phi_i Controls_{i,t} + \mu_i + \mu_{year} + \varepsilon_{i,t}$$

Here:

i = individual firm
t = individual year
β_0 = intercepted item
β_1 = the regression coefficient of the explanatory variable
ϕ_i = the regression coefficient of the control variable
μ_i = the fixed effect at the firm level
μ_{year} = the fixed effect at the year level
$\varepsilon_{i,t}$ = the residual item

5. Empirical Results

5.1 Descriptive Statistics

This section describes each variable's sample size, mean, standard deviation, minimum, median, and maximum in depth.

Table 6.3 shows the descriptive statistics of the entire sample selection criteria. On average, the ROA of the whole sample is 0.0352, and the standard deviation (SD) is 0.0673, while the average value of ROE is 0.0489, and the SD is 0.1740. In addition, the average stock price is 16.1891, and the SD is 19.4234. The minimum value of the stock price is 2.0500, the median is 10.9500, and the maximum value is 250.4000, which shows the wide distribution of stock prices in the sample. Additionally, the average value of ESG is 6.5095, and the standard deviation is 1.1169, indicating that the variability in ESG indicators is relatively small. Finally, for other variables, the average size of the companies is 22.2383, and the average leverage is 0.4307. The mean age for the whole sample is 2.8599, the mean growth is 0.1813, the mean Top1 is 0.3418, and the mean CFO is 0.0461. Therefore, from the results of descriptive statistics, the statistical characteristic of each variable is within a reasonable range.

5.2 Correlation Analysis

As in the descriptive statistics analysis, the sample data in Table 6.1 is rigorous and reasonable. Then, we need to find the correlation between variables and whether there is an obvious multicollinearity problem among the variables. According to Hauke and Kossowski (2011), Pearson and Spearman coefficients are used in correlation analysis to examine the correlation of each variable. In detail, the Spearman rank correlation coefficient is a distribution-free rank statistic created to assess the strength of the association between two variables, whereas the Pearson correlation coefficient quantifies the strength of a linear link between two quantitative variables. Table 6.4 displays the test findings, with the Pearson correlation coefficient on the left and the Spearman correlation left and the Spearman correlation coefficient on top.

Table 6.3 Descriptive Statistics of the Main Variables

	N	*Mean*	*SD*	*Min*	*Median*	*Max*
ROA	30282	0.0352	0.0673	−0.5451	0.0359	0.2174
ROE	30282	0.0489	0.1740	−1.9277	0.0676	0.3368
Price	30282	16.1891	19.4234	2.0500	10.9500	250.4000
ESG	30282	6.5095	1.1169	3.0000	6.0000	9.0000
Size	30282	22.2383	1.2952	19.5628	22.0538	26.5105
Lev	30282	0.4307	0.2050	0.0353	0.4250	0.9060
Age	30282	2.8599	0.3552	1.1843	2.9106	3.5765
Growth	30282	0.1813	0.4287	−0.6677	0.1147	4.3304
Top1	30282	0.3418	0.1483	0.0795	0.3200	0.7590
CFO	30282	0.0461	0.0690	−0.2218	0.0455	0.2559

From the descriptive statistics results, each variable's statistical characteristic is within a reasonable range. Variables' definitions are given in Appendix 2.1.

Table 6.4 Correlation Analysis Results among Variables

	ROA	*ROE*	*Price*	*ESG*	*Size*	*Lev*	*Age*	*Growth*	*Top1*	*CFO*
RROA	1.0000	0.9111***	0.4568***	0.1240***	-0.0535***	-0.4166***	-0.1070***	0.3237***	0.1194***	0.4263***
ROE	0.8572***	1.0000	0.3910***	0.1803***	0.1400***	-0.0857***	-0.0559***	0.3612***	0.1578***	0.3883***
Price	0.2960***	0.1968***	1.0000	0.0155***	-0.2096***	-0.2876***	-0.1817***	0.2583***	0.0511***	0.1521***
ESG	0.1608***	0.1729***	0.0318***	1.0000	0.3348***	0.0886***	0.0678***	0.0163***	0.1405***	0.0896***
Size	0.0187***	0.0905***	-0.0531***	0.3630***	1.0000	0.5033***	0.1993***	0.0355***	0.1605***	0.0684***
Lev	-0.3295***	-0.2014***	-0.1848***	0.0833***	0.4979***	1.0000	0.1448***	0.0034	0.0540***	-0.1591***
Age	-0.0927***	-0.0661***	-0.0888***	0.0506***	0.1732***	0.1578***	1.0000	-0.1101***	-0.1056***	0.0123**
Growth	0.2149***	0.2046***	0.1670***	-0.0064	0.0370***	0.0258***	-0.0599***	1.0000	0.0057	0.0552***
Top1	0.1427***	0.1378***	0.0055	0.1461***	0.2043***	0.0599***	-0.1161***	0.0064	1.0000	0.0982***
CFO	0.3697***	0.2516***	0.1619***	0.0794***	0.0685***	-0.1704***	0.0206***	0.0175***	0.0900***	1.0000

Note: *,**, and *** indicate significance at the significance level of 10%, 5%, and 1%, respectively (two-tailed test).

When the absolute value of the correlation coefficient between variables surpasses 0.75, it indicates that the correlation is significant and the multicollinearity problem is serious, resulting in some variations in the empirical results. The correlation between two variables is considered moderate when its absolute value is between 0.5 and 0.75. A better connection exists between two variables when the absolute value of the correlation coefficient falls between 0.25 and 0.5. When the absolute value of a variable's correlation coefficient is less than 0.25, the variables are either extremely weakly connected or not associated at all (Hauke & Kossowski, 2011). According to the correlation analysis results in Table 6.2, the correlation coefficient of all variables utilized in this study is less than 0.75, indicating that there is no multicollinearity problem between variables. The empirical regression model used in this study is trustworthy.

5.3 Regression Analysis and Hypothesis Testing

In Table 6.5, third column, the test result shows 0.7352, which is a positive relationship between ESG and stock price. As a result, the coefficient shows a substantial and positive correlation between ESG and stock price, supporting hypothesis *H1*. In Table 6.5, first column, the relationship between ESG and ROA is given as

Table 6.5 Regression Results

	(1) *ROA*	*(2)* *ROE*	*(3)* *Price*
ESG	0.0044*** (10.30)	0.0116*** (9.31)	0.7352*** (7.92)
Size	0.0178*** (21.85)	0.0597*** (25.12)	3.1707*** (17.98)
Lev	−0.1793*** (−56.93)	−0.4849*** (−52.64)	−9.2938*** (−13.60)
Age	0.0071 (1.57)	0.0768*** (5.78)	−7.3317*** (−7.43)
Growth	0.0277*** (37.98)	0.0698*** (32.76)	2.9178*** (18.45)
Top1	0.0670*** (12.82)	0.1730*** (11.32)	3.9716*** (3.50)
CFO	0.1807*** (33.79)	0.3257*** (20.82)	13.3657*** (11.52)
_cons	−0.3065*** (−13.58)	−1.3008*** (−19.72)	−34.0911*** (−6.96)
Industry	Yes	Yes	Yes
Year	Yes	Yes	Yes
N	30,282	30,282	30,282
R^2	0.251	0.202	0.153
adj. R^2	0.137	0.080	0.023
F	232.0019	175.2934	124.4792

Note: *, **, and *** indicate significance at the significance level of 10%, 5%, and 1%, respectively (two-tailed test). The t-test values are given in parentheses.

0.0044 and is significant at the 1% level. We explore the connection between ESG and ROE in the second column. The test's outcome reveals a positive link with a correlation coefficient of 0.0116, which is significant at the 1% level. As a result, the coefficient shows a substantial and positive correlation between ROA and ROE and ESG, supporting hypothesis *H2*.

5.4 Robustness Test

Table 6.6, first column, presents the relationship between ESG and EPS, which is 0.0367 and is significant at 1% level. Therefore, the main results remain consistent and stable even when ROA and ROE are replaced by other factors (EPS).

In Table 6.7, we use an alternative ESG score rating system, Bloomberg ESG. Then we repeated our regression analysis. The first column in the table indicates a positive relationship with a value of 0.0004, which is significant at the 1% level. The result in the second column shows a positive relationship of 0.0009 and is significant at the 1% level. The result in the third column shows a positive relationship of 0.3335 and is significant at the 1% level. Therefore, even under different datasets, ESG still has a positive relationship with the ROA, ROE, and stock price, thus supporting our main conclusions.

Table 6.6 Substituting the Regression Results for the Explained Variable

	(1) *EPS*
ESG	0.0367*** (10.22)
Size	0.2220*** (32.51)
Lev	−1.1583*** (−43.77)
Age	−0.0705* (−1.84)
Growth	0.2321*** (37.91)
Top1	0.5244*** (11.94)
CFO	1.3777*** (30.66)
_cons	−4.2099*** (−22.21)
Firm	Yes
Year	Yes
N	30282
R^2	0.196
Adj. R^2	0.073
F	168.7104

Note: *, **, and *** indicate significance at the significance level of 10%, 5%, and 1%, respectively (two-tailed test). The t-test values are given in parentheses.

Table 6.7 Substituting the Regression Results for the Explanatory Variable

	(1) *ROA*	*(2)* *ROE*	*(3)* *EPS*	*(4)* *Price*
ESG_Bloomberg	0.0004*** (3.91)	0.0009*** (2.76)	0.0082*** (6.64)	0.3335*** (8.92)
Size	0.0153*** (12.71)	0.0594*** (16.20)	0.3153*** (22.65)	6.6221*** (15.75)
Lev	−0.1852*** (−37.17)	−0.4649*** (−30.68)	−1.4580*** (−25.34)	−9.6335*** (−5.54)
Age	0.0096 (1.45)	0.0762*** (3.76)	−0.0201 (−0.26)	−3.5947 (−1.55)
Growth	0.0249*** (24.03)	0.0642*** (20.36)	0.2663*** (22.25)	3.9502*** (10.93)
Top1	0.0597*** (7.89)	0.2040*** (8.86)	0.5328*** (6.10)	−1.7623 (−0.67)
CFO	0.2061*** (26.77)	0.3957*** (16.90)	1.9672*** (22.13)	23.1634*** (8.63)
_cons	−0.3043*** (−8.98)	−1.5276*** (−14.82)	−6.7071*** (−17.14)	−130.1518*** (−11.01)
Industry	Yes	Yes	Yes	Yes
Year	Yes	Yes	Yes	Yes
N	10,768	10,768	10,768	10,768
R^2	0.277	0.202	0.222	0.144
Adj. R^2	0.167	0.081	0.104	0.015
F	99.5036	65.7246	74.0432	43.8107

Note: *, **, and *** indicate significance at the significance level of 10%, 5%, and 1%, respectively (two-tailed test). The t-test values are given in parentheses.

6. Discussion and Conclusion

6.1 Conclusion

The objective of this study is to explore the relationship between companies' financial performance and ESG factors. The quantitative analysis reveals a positive correlation between ESG ratings and financial metrics like stock price, ROA, and ROE. Specifically, higher ESG ratings are significantly associated with increased ROA and ROE, with statistical significance at the 1% level. A similar positive relationship exists between ESG ratings and stock prices, also significant at the 1% level. Robustness and substitution tests further validate these findings.

These results align with previous research indicating that ESG factors significantly impact firm performance. Alareeni and Hamdan (2020) noted that higher ESG ratings and disclosures correlate with improved ROA, ROE, and positive effects on Tobin's Q. This study supports those findings, establishing a positive link between ESG ratings and financial indicators. Additionally, ESG factors enhance non-financial aspects, adding overall value for investors. Jin (2022) suggests that integrating ESG considerations into investment strategies helps value-based investors manage risk effectively. Companies with strong ESG practices often enjoy better supply chain management, competitive advantages, and increased investor trust (Gregory et al., 2014).

However, this chapter also highlights the complexities of using ESG factors in investment decisions. The relationship between ESG ratings and financial performance is not straightforward. Zhou et al. (2022) stressed that quantifying the actual impact of ESG on market performance is challenging due to various influencing factors. While this study confirms a general positive correlation, the specific mechanisms and interactions with other variables remain unclear.

A significant challenge identified in the literature is the lack of uniform standards for ESG data, leading to varying levels of detail and accuracy across platforms (Jonsdottir et al., 2022). This study used ESG data from the Sino-Securities Index Information Service Company, a leading provider in China, and incorporated Bloomberg ESG data in robustness tests to enhance credibility. Despite the consistent finding of a positive correlation between ESG ratings and financial performance, the impact varied by data source, highlighting the need for standardized ESG metrics.

In summary, while the quantitative analysis supports the positive impact of ESG factors on financial performance, it also underscores the complexities and challenges of ESG investing. The findings emphasize the necessity for standardized ESG reporting to enable accurate evaluation of corporate performance. Further research is needed to clarify how ESG factors influence financial outcomes and to develop robust methodologies for integrating ESG considerations into investment strategies.

6.2 *Implications*

6.2.1 *Theoretical Implications*

The findings of this study strongly support CFT, which suggests that ESG factors positively correlate with a company's ROA and ROE, key indicators of profitability and capital efficiency. Alareeni and Hamdan (2020) noted that while the environmental (E) component of ESG positively affects Tobin's Q, it negatively impacts ROA and ROE. This study uses regression analysis to confirm that ESG ratings significantly influence financial metrics such as ROA, ROE, and Tobin's Q, highlighting the beneficial impact of ESG factors on financial performance.

The study also reinforces RBT, showing that higher ESG performance correlates with improved ROA and ROE, providing companies with competitive advantages (Zhou et al., 2022). The regression results indicate a positive relationship between ESG performance and stock price, suggesting that ESG investments can enhance market value.

While much literature explores the ESG–financial performance relationship, few studies address its impact across the overall market. Gholami et al. (2022) pointed out that companies in different industries reap varying benefits from ESG performance due to distinct investor interests. Deng and Cheng (2019) found ESG factors affect non-state-owned companies more than state-owned ones and have a greater impact on secondary industries compared to tertiary ones. This study mitigates industry-specific variations by analysing all A-share listed companies in China from 2010 to 2021, revealing a generally positive relationship between ESG factors and financial performance across most industries, except for financial institutions.

Overall, this study's findings align with both CFT and RBT, demonstrating that ESG performance positively influences key financial metrics. This positive impact is consistent across most industries, emphasizing the importance of integrating ESG factors into investment decisions and corporate strategies, with significant implications for investors, managers, and policymakers.

6.2.2 *Practical Implications*

With the growing influence of ESG investment and awareness (Aouadi & Marsat, 2016), global ESG assets surged from $22.8 trillion in 2016 to $37.8 trillion in 2021 (Chen & Lin, 2022). Research increasingly focuses on the relationship between ESG and companies' financial performance, revealing a positive correlation between ESG ratings and profitability. This has important implications for investors, companies, and policymakers.

For investors, recognizing that firms with better ESG performance often have higher stock prices can inform their investment strategies. Considering ESG factors allows for a more comprehensive assessment of a company's operations and financial health. Traditional financial analysis, which focuses solely on financial metrics, is no longer sufficient. Investors should incorporate ESG strategies to evaluate non-financial factors, enhancing their asset valuation during investment decisions (Aich et al., 2021). Additionally, high ESG ratings indicate lower default risks, appealing to risk-averse investors. Thus, combining traditional financial analysis with ESG considerations can improve investment returns.

For companies, adopting ESG strategies is crucial for daily operations. For example, PepsiCo's implementation of ESG practices has led to fleet upgrades and reduced fossil fuel reliance, resulting in significant cost savings and increased investor trust. By managing energy price risks, PepsiCo has also enhanced its resilience and attractiveness to investors. Furthermore, Miralles-Quirós et al. (2019) highlighted that the banking sector benefits from emphasizing environmental and governance factors, which promote shareholder value and sustainable growth. This study reinforces the strong positive relationship between ESG factors and both financial and non-financial performance, similar to PepsiCo's experience. Company leaders should recognize the correlations between ESG factors and overall performance, tailoring their strategies to fit industry-specific contexts and investor interests (Gholami et al., 2022).

For policymakers, establishing standardized ESG data and indices is essential. Currently, ESG data are sourced from various platforms, leading to low credibility and objectivity (Jonsdottir et al., 2022). The regression analysis in this study indicates that varying data sources can yield inconsistent conclusions. Additionally, the lack of strong regulations for accurate ESG data disclosure hampers investment development (Cruz & Matos, 2023). Policymakers should work towards creating uniform standards to enhance the credibility of ESG data, as well as mandate regular disclosure of ESG information from companies. A unified approach would increase investor confidence in ESG investments, fostering further growth in this area.

6.3 Limitations and Future Research

This study offers valuable insights into the relationship between ESG factors and companies' financial performance, but several limitations should be addressed. Firstly, it examines the overall relationship without isolating the impacts of individual ESG components. Future research should focus on the distinct effects of ESG factors on financial performance. This detailed analysis will help investors and corporate leaders understand the specific roles of each factor and develop targeted ESG strategies. For example, differentiating how environmental initiatives contribute to cost savings or how social policies affect employee retention and customer loyalty could lead to more effective practices.

Secondly, the chapter's regression analysis does not account for industry-specific variations. ESG factors can have different implications across sectors. For instance, Miralles-Quirós et al. (2019) found that the social component negatively impacts the banking sector while positively affecting the food industry. Future studies should investigate how ESG factors influence various industries individually, providing tailored insights for investors and company leaders.

Finally, the focus on China limits the generalizability of the findings. Conclusions drawn from Chinese A-share listed companies may not apply globally due to differing regulatory environments and cultural contexts. Future research should include ESG data from diverse countries and regions to develop more universally applicable conclusions. A global perspective would facilitate cross-country comparisons and enhance understanding of how regional differences affect the ESG–financial performance relationship.

In conclusion, while this chapter contributes significantly to understanding ESG's impact on financial performance, addressing these limitations in future studies will strengthen the findings. Disaggregating ESG into its components, considering industry variations, and incorporating global data will provide deeper insights and practical guidance for integrating ESG factors into investment and corporate strategies.

Future research should analyse the distinct impacts of ESG components on financial performance, enhancing understanding of their contributions to metrics like profitability and market valuation. Additionally, tailoring ESG evaluations to specific sectors will identify best practices relevant to each industry. Comparative studies across different regulatory and cultural contexts will improve the global applicability of ESG strategies. Longitudinal research can assess the long-term effects of consistent ESG practices on financial stability and resilience. Employing advanced methodologies, including mixed methods that integrate quantitative and qualitative data, will yield more accurate insights into the interplay between ESG factors and financial performance.

References

Aich, S., Thakur, A., Nanda, D., Tripathy, S., & Kim, H.-C. (2021). Factors affecting ESG towards impact on investment: A structural approach. *Sustainability*, *13*(19), 10868.

Alareeni, B. A., & Hamdan, A. (2020). ESG impact on performance of US S&P 500-listed firms. *Corporate Governance: The International Journal of Business in Society*, *20*(7), 1409–1428.

Amel-Zadeh, A., & Serafeim, G. (2018). Why and how investors Use ESG information: Evidence from a global survey. *Financial Analysts Journal*, *74*(3), 87–103.

Amin, N., & Tauseef, S. (2022). Does an optimal ESG score exist? Evidence from China. *Macroeconomics and Finance in Emerging Market Economies*, 1–19.

Amini, S., Delgado, M. S., Henderson, D. J., & Parmeter, C. F. (2012). Fixed vs random: The Hausman test four decades later. *Essays in Honor of Jerry Hausman*, *29*, 479–513.

Aouadi, A., & Marsat, S. (2016). Do ESG controversies matter for firm value? Evidence from international data. *Journal of Business Ethics*, *151*(4), 1027–1047.

Aydoğmuş, M., Gülay, G., & Ergun, K. (2022). Impact of ESG performance on firm value and profitability. *Borsa Istanbul Review*, *22*(2).

Borenstein, M., Hedges, L. V., Higgins, J. P. T., & Rothstein, H. R. (2010). A basic introduction to fixed-effect and random-effects models for meta-analysis. *Research Synthesis Methods*, *1*(2), 97–111.

Cahan, S., Lam, B. M., Li, L. Z., & Rahman, M. J. (2021). Information environment and stock price synchronicity: Evidence from auditor characteristics. *International Journal of Auditing*, *25*(2), 332–350.

Capelle-Blancard, G., & Petit, A. (2017). Every little helps? ESG news and stock market reaction. *Journal of Business Ethics*, *157*(2), 543–565.

Chen, Y., & Lin, B. (2022). Quantifying the extreme spillovers on worldwide ESG leaders' equity. *International Review of Financial Analysis*, *84*, 102425.

Cruz, C. A., & Matos, F. (2023). ESG maturity: A software framework for the challenges of ESG data in investment. *Sustainability*, *15*(3), 2610.

de Freitas Netto, S. V., Sobral, M. F. F., Ribeiro, A. R. B., & Soares, G. R. da L. (2020). Concepts and forms of greenwashing: A systematic review. *Environmental Sciences Europe*, *32*(1).

Deng, X., & Cheng, X. (2019). Can ESG indices improve the enterprises' stock market performance? – An empirical study from China. *Sustainability*, *11*(17), 4765.

Dorfleitner, G., Halbritter, G., & Nguyen, M. (2015). Measuring the level and risk of corporate responsibility – An empirical comparison of different ESG rating approaches. *Journal of Asset Management*, *16*(7), 450–466.

Eccles, R. G., Kastrapeli, M. D., & Potter, S. J. (2017). How to integrate ESG into investment decision-making: Results of a global survey of institutional investors. *Journal of Applied Corporate Finance*, *29*(4), 125–133.

Gholami, A., Sands, J., & Shams, S. (2022). The impact of corporate ESG performance disclosure across Australian industries. *Australasian Business, Accounting and Finance Journal*, *16*(4), 180–200.

Giese, G., Lee, L.-E., Melas, D., Nagy, Z., & Nishikawa, L. (2019). Foundations of ESG investing: How ESG affects equity valuation, risk, and performance. *The Journal of Portfolio Management*, *45*(5), 69–83.

Gregory, A., Tharyan, R., & Whittaker, J. (2014). Corporate social responsibility and firm value: Disaggregating the effects on cash flow, risk and growth. *Journal of Business Ethics*, *124*(4), 633–657.

Hauke, J., & Kossowski, T. M. (2011). Bogucki Wydawnictwo Naukowe. *Quaestiones Geographicae*, *30*(2), 87–93.

Jin, I. (2022). Systematic ESG risk and passive ESG investing. *The Journal of Portfolio Management*, *48*(5), jpm.2022.1.344.

Jonsdottir, B., Sigurjonsson, T. O., Johannsdottir, L., & Wendt, S. (2022). Barriers to using ESG data for investment decisions. *Sustainability, 14*(9), 5157.

Lam, B. M., Mo, P. L. L., & Rahman, M. J. (2024). Secrecy culture, client importance, and auditor reporting behavior: An international study. *Managerial Auditing Journal, 39*(2), 113–137.

Li, H., Zhang, X., & Zhao, Y. (2022). ESG and firm's default risk. *Finance Research Letters, 47*, 102713.

Li, T.-T., Wang, K., Sueyoshi, T., & Wang, D. D. (2021). ESG: Research progress and future prospects. *Sustainability, 13*(21), 11663.

Miralles-Quirós, M., Miralles-Quirós, J., & Redondo Hernández, J. (2019). ESG performance and shareholder value creation in the banking industry: International differences. *Sustainability, 11*(5), 1404.

Nekhili, M., Boukadhaba, A., Nagati, H., & Chtioui, T. (2019). ESG performance and market value: The moderating role of employee board representation. *The International Journal of Human Resource Management, 32*(14), 1–27.

Rahman, J., & Wu, J. (2023). M&A activity and ESG performance: Evidence from China. *Managerial Finance, 50*(1), 179–197.

Rahman, M. J., & Chen, X. (2023). CEO characteristics and firm performance: Evidence from private listed firms in China. *Corporate Governance: The International Journal of Business in Society, 23*(3), 458–477.

Rahman, M. J., Wu, Q., & Zhu, H. (2024). Corporate social responsibility in times of social distancing: Evidence from China. *Business Ethics, the Environment & Responsibility*.

Rahman, M. J., & Zhu, H. (2024). Predicting financial distress using machine learning approaches: Evidence China. *Journal of Contemporary Accounting & Economics, 20*(1), 100403

Rahman, M. J., Zhu, H., & Beiyi, S. (2023). Is COVID-19 a turning point? Evidence from CEOs' investment behavior and risk tolerance. *International Journal of Emerging Markets*.

Rahman, M. J., Zhu, H., & Chen, S. (2023). Does CSR reduce financial distress? Moderating effect of firm characteristics, auditor characteristics, and covid-19. *International Journal of Accounting & Information Management, 31*(5), 756–784.

Rahman, M. J., Zhu, H., & Jiang, X. (2024). Family firms, client importance, and auditor reporting behavior: Evidence from China. *Meditari Accountancy Research, 32*(2), 543–578.

Rahman, M. J., Zhu, H., & Yue, L. (2024). Does the adoption of artificial intelligence by audit firms and their clients affect audit quality and efficiency? Evidence from China. *Managerial Auditing Journal, 39*(6), 668–699.

Rahman, M. J., Zhu, H., Zhang, Y., & Hossain, M. M. (2024). Effect of female representation in audit committees on non-audit fees: Evidence from China. *Meditari Accountancy Research*.

Roberts, P. W., & Dowling, G. R. (2002). Corporate reputation and sustained superior financial performance. *Strategic Management Journal, 23*(12), 1077–1093.

Scatigna, M., Xia, F. D., Zabai, A., & Zulaica, O. (2021). Achievements and challenges in ESG markets. *BIS Quarterly Review*. Available online at https://www.bis.org/publ/qtrpdf/r_qt2112f.htm

Shi, L., Han, L., Yang, F., & Gao, L. (2019). The evolution of sustainable development theory: Types, goals, and research prospects. *Sustainability, 11*(24), 7158.

Starks, L. T. (2009). EFA keynote speech: "Corporate Governance and Corporate Social Responsibility: What Do Investors Care about? What Should Investors Care about?" *Financial Review, 44*(4), 461–468.

Yoon, B., Lee, J. H., & Cho, J. H. (2021). The effect of ESG performance on tax avoidance—evidence from Korea. *Sustainability, 13*(12), 6729.

Yu, E. P., Luu, B. V., & Chen, C. H. (2020). Greenwashing in environmental, social and governance disclosures. *Research in International Business and Finance*, *52*, 101192.
Zhao, C., Guo, Y., Yuan, J., Wu, M., Li, D., Zhou, Y., & Kang, J. (2018). ESG and corporate financial performance: Empirical evidence from China's listed power generation companies. *Sustainability*, *10*(8), 2607.
Zhou, G., Liu, L., & Luo, S. (2022). Sustainable development, ESG performance and company market value: Mediating effect of financial performance. *Business Strategy and the Environment*, *31*(7).
Zhu, H., & Rahman, M. J. (2024). Ex-ante expected changes in ESG and future stock returns based on machine learning. *The British Accounting Review*, 101457.

Appendix 2.1

Variable Definition and Description

Variable Type	*Variable Symbol*	*Variable Name*	*Meaning Description*	*Reference*
Explained variable	ROA	Return on assets	Net profit/total assets	Rahman, Zhu, and Beiyi (2023)
	ROE	Return on equity	Net equity/total assets	Rahman and Zhu (2024)
Explanatory variables	ESG	Environmental, social, and governance	ESG data from Sino-Securities Index Information Service Company	Zhu and Rahman (2024)
Control variable	Size	Size of the firm	Natural logarithm of total assets	Rahman, Zhu, and Yue (2024)
	Lev	Capital structure	Total debt/total assets	Rahman, Zhu, and Jiang (2024)
	Age	Age of the firm	(Statistical year – date of establishment of the enterprise)/365	Rahman Zhu, Zhang, and Hossain (2024)
	Growth	Business growth	Total operating income of the current year/total operating income of the previous year – 1	Lam et al. (2024)
	Top1	Ownership concentration	Ratio of the largest shareholder	Rahman and Chen (2023)
	CFO	Operating cash flow ratio	Net operating cash flow/total assets	Cahan et al. (2021)

7 The Impact of ESG Performance on Corporate Bankruptcy Risk

Md Jahidur Rahman, Yu Jiayi, Tarek Rana, and Hongtao Zhu

1. Introduction

Integrating environmental, social, and governance (ESG) factors into business operations has gained significant attention recently. Companies increasingly recognize the importance of addressing ESG issues for ethical and sustainable development, given their potential impact on financial performance and risk management. This research utilizes the *Z*-score model (Altman et al., 2016) to analyse corporate bankruptcy risk in China, focusing on the relationship between ESG performance and bankruptcy risk. The main questions are whether ESG performance affects the bankruptcy risk of Chinese firms and how.

Several studies in China also investigate the relationship between environmental accounting and firm performance (Rahman & Wu, 2023; Rahman, Wu, & Zhu, 2024; Rahman et al., 2023; Zhu & Rahman, 2024). Examining this relationship is crucial for several reasons. As China's green economy evolves, policies like the Green Credit Guidelines and the Environmental Protection Law (Wang & Song, 2023) are enhancing the regulatory environment. Companies are adopting sustainable practices, as ESG criteria increasingly influence financial decisions. Stricter regulations hold businesses accountable for their environmental impact, pushing them to improve ESG ratings to avoid fines and reputational damage.

Additionally, China's dynamic market presents both challenges and opportunities (McKinsey, 2021). Understanding how ESG scores relate to bankruptcy risk is vital for companies in this evolving landscape. Strong ESG practices can help manage risks, improve financial stability, and inform strategic decisions. As consumer demand for sustainable products increases, companies with high ESG performance often attract more investors and favourable financing terms, reducing their insolvency risk.

Stakeholder engagement also significantly impacts ESG ratings. Investors, customers, and employees view ESG performance as critical to a company's long-term viability (Robichaud, 2020). Companies with favourable ESG ratings are better positioned to gain investor trust, while poor ESG performance can lead to capital outflow and increased bankruptcy risk. This study contributes to understanding the financial implications of ESG practices.

DOI: 10.4324/9781003488934-9

This research employs a quantitative method to explore the correlation between ESG performance and corporate bankruptcy risk among Chinese companies. Data on financial statements, ESG ratings, *Z*-score distributions, and other relevant variables were sourced from the China Stock Market & Accounting Research (CSMAR) database. ESG indicators were selected based on their relevance to Chinese enterprises, covering ESG aspects. The study applies the *Z*-score model to assess bankruptcy risk.

Despite the growing global interest in ESG and its relation to bankruptcy risk, studies focusing on the Chinese market remain limited. This research fills that gap, providing empirical evidence on the connection between ESG performance and bankruptcy risk in China. Unique market characteristics and regulatory trends influence corporate ESG performance and bankruptcy risk (Belli-Bivar, 2019).

As the second-largest economy, China's rapid growth and evolving policies impact ESG performance and insolvency risk. The government has introduced measures to enhance corporate sustainable performance, which are expected to reduce bankruptcy risk. This study evaluates the effectiveness of these policies, offering insights for listed companies to align with low-carbon reform requirements while maintaining operations.

The study also considers stakeholder perspectives – investors, consumers, employees, and suppliers – who influence a firm's ESG performance and bankruptcy risk (Pfajfar et al., 2022). By understanding stakeholder concerns regarding ESG, companies can align with their expectations, enhancing satisfaction and reducing supply chain risks.

Investigating the link between ESG and bankruptcy helps companies appreciate ESG's role in sustainable development (Zu, 2013). As investors increasingly prioritize ESG factors, this research provides essential insights for decision-making. Strong ESG performance can enhance a company's reputation and competitiveness, ultimately reducing bankruptcy risk and fostering trust among stakeholders (Giese et al., 2019).

The remainder of this chapter is structured as follows: the next section presents a framework for comparing projected ESG and bankruptcy likelihoods. Section 3 outlines theoretical perspectives and hypotheses on bankruptcy. Section 4 describes the methodology and provides examples. Section 5 explains the results of the main tests. Sections 6 and 7 discuss endogeneity and testing. Section 8 offers a discussion, and Section 9 concludes the study.

2. Theoretical Framework

Previous research has mainly focused on US ESG data and its components, with limited investigation into the correlation between ESG and corporate bankruptcy risk in China. While extensive literature exists on financial distress related to corporate governance and bankruptcy, primarily examining board characteristics and ownership (Li et al., 2020), the specific impact of ESG on bankruptcy risk has not been thoroughly addressed. This study aims to analyse each ESG pillar – environmental, social, and governance – individually.

Agency theory suggests that conflicts between shareholders (principals) and managers (agents) can lead to decisions that harm value and increase bankruptcy risk. Strong ESG performance may align the interests of managers and shareholders, promoting sustainable practices and reducing agency costs. Research by Aydogmus et al. (2022) indicated that firms with higher ESG scores can better mitigate agency problems, thereby lowering bankruptcy risk. Additionally, findings by Friede et al. (2015) showed a favourable link between ESG performance and financial outcomes, supporting the idea that improved ESG performance can reduce bankruptcy risk.

Stakeholder theory posits that businesses have obligations to various stakeholders, including employees, customers, and society. Effective stakeholder management is crucial for long-term success, as highlighted by Stieb (2008). We hypothesize that companies with better ESG ratings are more likely to foster strong stakeholder relationships, ultimately reducing their bankruptcy risk.

3. Literature Review and Hypothesis Development

The impact of ESG grades on corporate insolvency risk has gained significant attention as companies and stakeholders recognize the importance of sustainable practices (He et al., 2023). While much research focuses on the relationship between ESG and financial success, studies examining its influence on financial failure – specifically bankruptcy risk – are limited. This literature review explores the link between ESG performance and bankruptcy risk, particularly in the Chinese context.

Several studies have highlighted the positive correlation between ESG performance and financial health. For instance, Zhao et al. (2018) found that Chinese-listed companies with strong ESG ratings also demonstrated better profitability and a lower likelihood of bankruptcy. Additionally, Li et al. (2022) reported that higher ESG scores correlate with decreased credit default risk, with Chinese firms increasingly incorporating ESG factors into their credit risk assessments (Crook et al., 2007). This suggests that ESG performance is a vital indicator of corporate creditworthiness, reflecting a company's ability to manage ESG risks.

Research also emphasizes the role of stakeholder pressure on ESG performance and bankruptcy risk. Weber (2013) found that stakeholders, including investors and consumers, significantly influence companies to adopt sustainable practices. Shareholder activism further drives improvements in ESG performance; Qian (2013) showed that companies targeted by activist shareholders typically enhance their ESG practices, potentially lowering bankruptcy risk.

Consumer awareness of sustainability also affects corporate ESG performance. Companies that align their practices with consumer preferences for social responsibility are more likely to improve their ESG scores and reduce bankruptcy risk (Geczy et al., 2020). Employees play a crucial role as well: engaged employees promote sustainable practices, and higher employee engagement correlates with better ESG performance (Kotzian, 2022). When employees identify with a company's ESG values, their motivation and engagement can lead to enhanced ESG initiatives, further reducing bankruptcy risk.

Overall, the literature indicates that companies with better ESG grades exhibit stronger financial performance and risk management, thereby decreasing their bankruptcy likelihood (Barbaric, 2021). This suggests that Chinese firms with robust ESG performance are likely to face lower bankruptcy risks. By integrating ESG factors into their operations, these companies can improve financial stability, attract investment, and ensure sustainable growth. Thus, we hypothesize a negative association between ESG performance and corporate bankruptcy risk in China.

H1: Higher ESG performance is negatively related to corporate bankruptcy risk.

Companies in China facing significant stakeholder pressure must prioritize improving their ESG performance to reduce bankruptcy risk. Stakeholder pressure can take various forms, such as demands for transparency, responsible practices, and regulatory compliance. Government regulations significantly influence how ESG performance affects bankruptcy risk. For example, environmental laws may require companies to cut carbon emissions, while governance regulations may enforce greater transparency (Do & Vo, 2023). Stricter regulations are likely to strengthen the link between ESG performance and bankruptcy risk, as companies face heightened compliance and reputational pressures. However, it is hypothesized that during certain economic periods, factors related to environmental impact, social responsibility, and governance may not significantly affect bankruptcy probability for firms in the Chinese market. Thus, ESG performance might not be a critical determinant of bankruptcy risk in the short term.

H2: In a given economic period, ESG performance does not affect the likelihood of a company going bankrupt.

4. Research Design

4.1 Sample and Data

This research studies ESG scores on the likelihood of firm insolvency using robust samples and continuous measures of ESG overall and the respective ESG pillars. Our initial model includes all listed companies in China between 2011 and 2021. All *Z*-score and financial data, such as total assets and total liabilities, are extracted from the CSMAR database. Marquis and Qian (2014) stated that CSMAR is one of the reliable databases of listed company information in China, providing various financial and non-financial data. Among them, we screened 59,921 raw data of quarterly reports of Chinese listed companies, from a total of 5,635 Chinese listed companies. Then we reduced the sample after excluding for the following factors: (1) due to the particular capital structure of China's listed companies in the financial industry, the financial industry involves complex financial products, risk management, and accounting principles. Financial data in the financial industry are unique and complex compared to that in other industries (Brav, 2009). For better research purposes, we chose to exclude the financial industry. (2) Due to missing values, especially *Z*-score and ESG scores, all data with missing values were removed, and the *Z*-scores were indented at the 1st and 99th percentiles. (3) To alleviate the effect of outliers and make the data distribution more symmetrical, natural logarithmic transformations were performed on specific variables such as total assets. (4) Special treatment (ST) companies usually have special regulatory measures in the stock market and may be subject to delisting warnings or suspension of listing. Due to these companies' special financial and regulatory situations, certain uncertainties and quality problems may exist in their data disclosure. To ensure the reliability of the data, we chose to exclude these ST companies. The final sample from 2011 to 2021 includes 1,009 Chinese listed companies and 10,732 real-year observations. Table 7.1 summarizes the data screening process.

4.2 Variable Measurements

4.2.1 Dependent Variable

The dependent variable is *Z*-score, a commonly used financial indicator to assess a company's bankruptcy risk (Altman et al., 2016). The value of the *Z*-score is obtained by calculating the data during the accounting period and standardizing the indicators. The *Z*-score is a multivariate formula that measures a company's financial health and predicts the likelihood of bankruptcy in two years. The *Z*-score combines five common business ratios to determine the likelihood of bankruptcy using a weighting system calculated by Altman et al. (2016). Scoring is based on the following formula:

$$Z\text{-score} = 1.2\,X_1 + 1.4\,X_2 + 3.3\,X_3 + 0.6\,X_4 + 1.0\,X_5$$

X_1 through X_5 represent working capital, retained earnings, earnings before interest, market capitalization, and sales, respectively, and divide all these by total assets to get the *Z* value (Altman et al., 2016). Typically, a score below 1.88 indicates that the company may be heading towards or under the weight of bankruptcy. On the contrary, companies with scores above 2.99 are less likely to go bankrupt. Scores between 2.99 and 1.88 are questionable (Habermann & Fischer, 2021).

Table 7.1 Sample Selection

Sample Selection Criteria	*No. of Companies*	*No. of Firm-Year Observations*
Total number	5,635	59,921
Less: companies in the financial industry	238	2530
Less: missing data of sample	4,281	45,522
Less: ST companies	107	1,137
Equal to = final sample	1,009	10,732

4.2.2 *Independent Variables*

ESG Combined Score (ESGScore): ESG scoring is a method used to evaluate a company's performance and performance regarding environment, society, and corporate governance. The scoring aims to quantify and measure a company's sustainability and social responsibility performance and provide helpful information for investors, stakeholders, and the public (Mathis, 2023). Independent institutions or data providers usually calculate ESG scores using a series of indicators and standards to evaluate the performance of companies in different ESG areas. These indicators may include environmental impact, carbon emissions, water resource management, labour rights, human rights, diversity, and board governance (Nordqvist, 2016).

Environmental Pillar Score (EnvPillar): Environmental factors as independent variables can be used to study the effect of environmental management and sustainable development on corporate performance and decision-making, such as air, land, and water, and complete ecosystems (Mathis, 2023). People can explore the connection among environmental management practices, environmental impact assessment and company performance, innovation ability, and market performance.

Social Pillar Score (SocPillar): As an independent variable, social factors can be used to study the influence of enterprises on society and the influence of social responsibility on enterprise performance. Researchers can explore the relationship among an enterprise's employee relations, community participation, social welfare projects, company performance, reputation, and brand image (OneTrust, 2022).

Governance Pillar Score (GovPillar): As an independent variable, corporate governance factors can be used to study the impact of corporate governance structure, decision-making process, and internal control on corporate performance and shareholder equity. People can create long-term shareholder value by exploring the relationship among company board structure, executive compensation, independent and corporate performance, shareholder returns, and risk management (Belli-Bivar, 2019).

ESGDelta: The yearly change in the ESG score, that is, (ESG score_t/ESG score_{t-1}) – 1

EnvDelta: The yearly change in the environmental score, that is, (environmental pillar score_t/environmental pillar score_{t-1}) – 1

SocDelta: The yearly change in the social score, that is, (social pillar score_t/social pillar score_{t-1}) – 1

GovDelta: The yearly change in the governance score, that is, (governance pillar score_t/governance pillar score_{t-1}) – 1

4.2.3 *Control Variables*

The study examines whether ESG scores have an impact on corporate bankruptcy risk, according to Altman et al. (2016). The role of control variables is to control or exclude possible other factors or variables. That may affect the connection between the own variable and the dependent variable. By introducing other control variables, the influence of independent variables on dependent variables can be more accurately evaluated, and interference items can be excluded (Bhandari, 2021).

Leverage: Leverage is a control variable that explains the effect of firm debt levels on the relationships studied. The degree of financial leverage of a company can be obtained by dividing total debt by total assets to exclude the influence of corporate debt levels on the association between ESG indicators and firm bankruptcy. It can help exclude the impact of financial leverage itself on the research results better to understand the impact of ESG on corporate bankruptcy risk.

Size: Size is the natural logarithm of total assets, which can eliminate the influence of company size on the relationship between ESG indicators and bankruptcy (Saraswati & Bernawati, 2020). By introducing the natural logarithm of total assets as a control variable, the interference of company size on the relationship between ESG indicators and company bankruptcy can be effectively controlled. Company size may have an impact on ESG metrics and bankruptcy risk, as many larger companies typically devote more resources to focus on and implement ESG while avoiding bankruptcy risk.

Profitability: Business performance can be achieved through understanding the profitability of the company. It can also reflect a company's ability to realize profits over a certain period of time. Profitability is a crucial indicator to measure a company's operating performance. Using profitability as a control variable, we can control for the impact of other components on the risk of bankruptcy.

Liquidity: It is calculated by dividing the after-tax income for the accounting period by the average total assets. It can reflect the company's assets and cash liquidity. This control variable considers the effect of the firm's liquidity, or availability of cash and short-term investments, on the relationship.

Ownership: Ownership can refer to different types of businesses, such as public companies, non-profit organizations, and private companies. Different types of companies with different ownership structures may have differences in ESG performance and bankruptcy risk.

Financial background: The number of people with financial backgrounds can reflect the number of employees with financial expertise and experience within the enterprise. These employees may have a relatively in-depth understanding of markets, investment, and risk management and can provide professional advice and decision support for enterprises (Mapue, 2023).

Loan balance: As a control variable, the loan balance can reflect the enterprise's financial status and debt level. If the company has a high number, this may indicate that the company is facing higher financial pressure and debt risk. However, a low loan balance may indicate a firm's financial health. At the same time, corporate borrowing may support business expansion and capital investment and borrowing heavily in response to short-term funding needs. It can also evaluate the repayment ability of the enterprise to predict the bankruptcy risk.

4.3 Model Specification

To test the impact of ESG and other variables on *Z*-score, this study employs a time-fixed effect model for correlation estimation. In Equation (1), β_0 represents the intercept term of the regression model; the coefficient of interest is β_1; $X_{i,t}$ is the core explanatory variable ESG, variable E, variable S, and variable G of this study;

$\beta_1 - \beta_8$ is an estimated parameter. If they are significantly negative, it means that variables such as leverage have a significant inhibitory effect. i represents the enterprise dimension, t is the time series dimension, θ_i represents the time-fixed effect, and $\mu_{i,t}$ denotes the error term. The base model (1) can be interpreted as follows:

$$\begin{aligned} Z\text{-}score = {} & \beta_0 + \beta_1 X_{i,t} + \beta_2 \text{Leverage}_{i,t} + \beta_3 \text{Size}_{i,t} + \beta_4 \text{Profitability}_{i,t} \\ & + \beta_5 \text{Liquidity}_{i,t} + \beta_6 \text{Ownership}_{i,t} + \beta_7 \text{Finance Background}_{i,t} \\ & + \beta_8 \text{Loan Balance} + \theta_i + \varepsilon_{i,t} \end{aligned} \tag{1}$$

Here:

- *Z-score* = *Z*-scores are calculated using fiscal period data in their models. The *Z*-score is a multivariate formula that measures a company's financial health and predicts the likelihood of bankruptcy within two years. It is to determine the probability of bankruptcy using a weighting system calculated by Altman et al. (2016). Typically, a score below 1.88 indicates that the company may be heading towards or under the weight of bankruptcy. Conversely, companies with scores above 2.99 are less likely to go bankrupt. A score between 2.99 and 1.88 is questionable (Rahman & Zhu, 2024a, 2024b).
- *ESG* = The Refinitiv ESG Composite Score is based on information reported in the ESG pillar (ESG score) and an overall company score overlaid with ESG controversies (Zhu & Rahman, 2024);
- Leverage = Total debt divided by total assets (Rahman, Zhu, & Jiang, 2024);
- Size = Natural logarithm of total assets (Rahman, Zhu, & Yue, 2024);
- Profitability = This value is calculated as the income after taxes for the fiscal period divided by the average total assets (Rahman & Zhu, 2023);
- Liquidity = Cash and short-term assets divided by total assets (Lam et al., 2024);
- Ownership = The nature of the company, such as state-owned, private, or Sino-foreign joint venture (Rahman & Zhu, 2023);
- Finance Background = The company's employees are the number of people with financial backgrounds;
- Loan Balance = The company's total loan amount.

5. Empirical Results

5.1 Descriptive Statistics

Table 7.2 demonstrates the descriptive statistics. Firstly, the dependent variable *Z*-score is calculated using the initial model data over a period of time. The *Z*-score is a multivariate formula that measures a company's financial health and predicts the likelihood of bankruptcy within two years. The *Z*-score combines five common business ratios calculated by Altman and a signal weighting system to determine the likelihood of bankruptcy. The average *Z*-score value is 5.278, which is much smaller than the median of the range of variation of this variable, indicating that the *Z*-score of this bank group is in a low state, and the average value is slightly smaller than the standard deviation, indicating that there is a particular gap

Table 7.2 Descriptive Statistics

Variable	*Number of Observations*	*Mean*	*Standard Deviation*	*Min*	*Max*
Z-score	1	5.278	15.68	−522.7	1,861
ESG	10,732	2.706	2.082	0	8
E	10,732	9.190	12.48	0	75.87
S	10,732	12.69	7.373	0	54.39
G	10,732	64.55	14.13	26.79	96.12
Leverage	10,732	0.540	0.697	−0.684	20.52
Size	10,732	22.41	1.710	14.23	29.13
Profitability	10,732	0.125	5.797	−11.34	442.3
Liquidity	10,732	3.836	30.05	−138.1	2,230
Loan balance	10,732	20.55	2.009	8.897	26.06
Finance background	10,732	2.739	3.574	1	43
Ownership	10,732	4.025	1.218	1	6

in *Z*-score among different banks. Secondly, there are four explanatory variables, and the average ESG value is 2.706, which is relatively small compared with its maximum value of 8. The mean values of variable *E*, variable *S*, and variable *G* are 9.190, 12.69, and 64.55, respectively. Finally, among the control variables, the average leverage value is slightly smaller than the standard deviation, indicating a particular gap between different banks in leverage. The average value of the natural logarithm of total assets is 22.41, similar to the maximum value of 29.13. It shows that the total asset gap of banks in these regions is relatively small, and their development levels are consistent. The heterogeneity of these variables may impact the effect of variables such as ESG on *Z*-score. After observing the value, to avoid the influence of heteroscedasticity, the total amount of borrowings is logarithmically processed to obtain the total amount of variable borrowings.

Before carrying out the following fixed-effect analysis, we first conducted a correlation test on the variables. From the test results in the above table, it can be seen that *Z*-score is significantly negatively correlated with ESG variables and *E* variables, so the assumption that the dependent variable *Z*-score has a positive impact on the independent variable ESG is preliminarily verified. Moreover, the correlation coefficient between the independent variable and the control variable in the model is small, the maximum is 0.6269, indicating that there is no serious collinearity problem between the independent variables. At the same time, it can be seen from the data test results that there is a significant positive correlation between the explanatory variables *S* and *G* and the *Z*-score, but the overall ESG index variable has a significant negative impact on the explained variable *Z*-score, indicating that in listed companies during the development period, ESG has a significant inhibitory effect on the *Z*-score of the corresponding company; that is, companies with a high ESG index have lower financial bankruptcy than companies with a low ESG index. The correlation results are shown in Table 7.3.

Table 7.3 Pearson Correlation Matrix Analysis

Variable	*Z-score*	*ESG*	*E*	*S*	*G*	*Leverage*	*Size*	*Profitability*	*Liquidity*	*Loan Balance*	*Finance Background*	*Ownership*
Z-score	1.0000											
ESG	–0.0107**	1.0000*										
E	–0.0011*	0.0087*	1.0000									
S	0.0061***	0.0242**	0.6269**	1.0000								
G	0.0181***	0.0088	0.3760**	0.2789*	1.0000							
Leverage	0.0019**	0.0175**	0 .0002	–0.0160	–0.0044**	1.0000						
Size	–0.0043**	–0.0351**	–0.0205*	0.0057***	–0.0258	0.0125**	1.0000					
Profitability	–0.0001	–0.0140*	–0.0094**	0.0003	0.0093	0.0350**	–0.0713	1.0000				
Liquidity	–0.0043**	–0.0131*	–0.0092	–0.0073	–0.0077	0.0607	–0.0567	0.0049**	1.0000			
Loan balance	–0.0179*	–0.0590***	–0.0118**	–0.0109*	–0.0528	0.0026	0.0267	0.0069	0.0002**	1.0000		
Finance background	–0.0139**	0.0127**	–0.0177*	–0.0243*	0.0387	–0.0001*	0.0085*	0.0075**	0.0116	0.0132*	1.0000	
Ownership	0.0029***	–0.0019**	0.0264***	0.0164**	0.0541*	0.0041	0.0173***	–0.0140	–0.0246**	–0.0646***	–0.0988**	1.0000

Standard errors are given in parentheses.

* $p < 0.1$, ** $p < 0.05$, *** $p < 0.01$.

5.2 Baseline Regression Results

The regression results are presented in Table 7.4. Columns 1–4 show the regression results of a single explanatory variable on the explained variable, and column 5 is the regression result of all explanatory variables on the explained variable after adding control variables.

Columns 1 and 2 show that the regression results of ESG variables and *E* variables on the *Z*-score are significantly negative, indicating that the larger the values of ESG and *E* variables, the greater the *Z*-score value. The ESG variable reflects all scores of the listed companies based on environmental information. Columns 3 and 4 show that the regression results of the *S* and *G* variables on the *Z*-score are significantly negative, and both are significant at a 5% confidence interval.

Table 7.4 Regression Results

	(1) *Z-Score*	*(2)* *Z-Score*	*(3)* *Z-Score*	*(4)* *Z-Score*	*(5)* *Z-Score*
ESG	−0.1582**				−0.1834***
	(0.1422)				(0.1918)
E		−0.0235**			−0.0466***
		(0.0187)			(0.0316)
S			0.0079**		0.0451***
			(0.0299)		(0.0507)
G				0.0021**	0.0218**
				(0.0228)	(0.0315)
Leverage					0.0740**
					(0.3947)
Size					−0.0988*
					(0.1668)
Profitability					−0.0037**
					(0.0418)
Liquidity					−0.0036*
					(0.0083)
Loan balance					−0.2870**
					(0.1400)
Finance background					−0.0965**
					(0.0793)
Ownership					−0.0581*
					(0.2330)
_cons	4.9608***	4.4023***	4.2793***	4.2866***	12.1021**
	(0.9504)	(0.8303)	(0.8678)	(1.4042)	(5.2576)
Fixed time	Yes	Yes	Yes	Yes	Yes
N	12274	12274	12274	12274	12274
Adj. R^2	0.0004	0.0004	0.0003	0.0003	0.0005

Standard errors are given in parentheses.
*$p < 0.1$, **$p < 0.05$, ***$p < 0.01$.

In Column 5, the regression results of the four explanatory variables are similar to those in the first four columns. The coefficients of the ESG and *E* variables are still negative and significant at the 1% confidence interval level, but the absolute value of the coefficient becomes more considerable. The influence of the control variable on the explained variable *Z*-score may be negative.

The regression coefficient of the control variable Leverage in the fifth column is positive and significant, suggesting that the Leverage variable has an impact on *Z*-score. Size, the regression coefficient of the natural logarithm of total assets, is negative, but the significance is not strong. Regression coefficients of the four control variables of Profitability, Liquidity, Ownership, and Loan Balance are all negative and significant. It shows that the higher the company's tax burden, the lower the ESG index of their unit; that is, when the ratio of tax surcharges to total operating income is higher, the company's ESG index will have a negative impact. Profitability, Liquidity, Loan Balance, and Finance Background significantly influence *Z*-score bankruptcy probability at 1% and 5%, respectively, and the coefficients are negative. It shows that the higher the value of variables such as Liquidity and Loan Balance, the lower the risk the company's operations face, leading to a lower *Z*-score and bankruptcy index. At the same time, it also shows that the company's effective risk avoidance tends to balance its operational risks by optimizing Liquidity and Loan Balance, which significantly impacts the *Z*-score.

6. Mitigating Endogeneity Concerns

6.1 Two-Stage Least Squares Test and Propensity Score Matching Test

In order to test the endogeneity of variables such as ESG to *Z*-score, the specific equation is given as

$$Z\text{-}score = \beta_0 + \beta_1 ESG + \varepsilon_1 \tag{2}$$

In this study, for the endogeneity test, two methods of two-stage least squares test (2SLS) and propensity score matching (PSM) were used. To address the endogeneity issue, in this study we chose the lagged one-period variable β_1 ESG of the core explanatory variable ESG as an instrumental variable. Further considering the existence of outliers in the data used and the possibility of heteroscedasticity in the benchmark model, in order to improve the estimation accuracy, this study uses the instrumental variable two-stage method (2SLS) and PMS to re-conduct the empirical analysis where the first column is the instrumental variable Regression results of the first step of the two-stage method (Mahmood, 2021). Results are shown in Table 7.5. The second column is the regression result of the second step. The coefficients of the explanatory variable ESG in the second column are all significantly positive, which aligns with the research expectations. Through the endogeneity test, it is found that variables such as ESG still have an inhibitory effect

Table 7.5 Results of the Endogeneity Test

	(1) *IV1SLS*	*(2)* *IV2SLS*	*(3)* *PSM*
ESG	−0.805**	−0.2845**	−2.528***
	(0.0051)	(0.1216)	(0.0211)
E	0.0001*	−0.0532**	−0.0003*
	(0.0013)	(0.0245)	(0.0014)
S	0.0034	0.0524*	0.0005*
	(0.0021)	(0.0358)	(0.0024)
G	−0.0004**	0.0256*	−0.0004**
	(0.0012)	(0.0146)	(0.0010)
Leverage	−0.0003**	0.0968**	0.0476*
	(0.0272)	(0.1682)	(0.0223)
Size	0.0034	−0.0955*	0.0096***
	(0.0035)	(0.0506)	(0.0082)
Profitability	0.0029*	−0.0041	−0.0111*
	(0.0011)	(0.0046)	(0.0110)
Liquidity	−0.001**	−0.0037**	0.0001**
	(0.0056)	(0.0016)	(0.0004)
Loan balance	−0.000	−0.2910**	−0.0183**
	(0.0051)	(0.1318)	(0.0068)
Finance background	−0.010*	−0.1084***	0.0007**
	(0.0232)	(0.0294)	(0.0039)
Ownership	0.0004**	−0.1021*	0.0110*
	(0.0081)	(0.1723)	(0.0113)
_cons	0.915	14.7666***	1.851***
	(0.1295)	(3.1129)	(0.017)
Fixed time	Yes	Yes	Yes
N	12,274	12,274	12,274
Adj.R_2	0.0030	0.0005	0.6250

Standard errors are given in parentheses.
$*p < 0.1$, $**p < 0.05$, $***p < 0.01$.

on *Z*-score, indicating that the larger the value of ESG variables, the more negative the effect on the improvement of *Z*-score.

The third column presents the results of the PSM method, which divides the median of the variable ESG into control and experimental groups and studies the effect of ESG and other variables on the *Z*-score. The regression coefficient of variable ESG is negative and significant at a 1% confidence interval. In summary, the endogeneity test is passed.

6.2 *Fixed-Effect Model*

The data used in this article are panel data. In order to avoid ignoring the heterogeneity of macro-individuals, an individual-effect model can be used. The model is divided into a random and fixed-effect model. Before analysing the regression

Table 7.6 Hausman Test Result

Test Suuunaty	*Chi-q. Statistic*	*Chi-Stl.d.f*	*Prob*
Random-effect model	108.01	11	0.0071

results, the Hausman test can be used to select the appropriate model. Theoretical analysis shows that the difference between the two models depends on whether there is a connection between the error term and the independent variable. When judging the model, the Hausman test further clarifies the association between the model error term and the dependent variable. The test hypotheses are given *H0*: adopt a random-effect model and *H1*: adopt a fixed-effect model. Table 7.6 shows the inspection results.

The *p*-value is $0.0071 < 0.05$. Rejecting the null hypothesis and choosing the individual fixed-effect regression model are more suitable. Based on the obtained results, it was found that the previous assumptions were overturned, so the fixed-effect model was selected, and this model was selected in the process of building the panel model.

7. Robustness Check

7.1 Robustness Test of Alternative Explanatory Variables

To ensure the reliability of the above empirical analysis findings, this study takes the explanatory variable lagging one period as the new core explanatory variable. It employs $\beta 1$ESG as the fixed model in the regression analysis, substituting the explanatory variable with the ESG measurement index. Table 7.7 reveals the regression outcomes. The first column shows that the regression result of ESG lagging one period on the *Z*-score is significantly negative, indicating that ESG lagging one period has an inhibitory effect on the *Z*-score and has a negative impact on the company's development. When considering the control variables in the second column, the regression coefficient of the ESG lagged one-period variable is still negative, and it is significant at 1% confidence interval. However, the regression coefficient becomes larger. The research results align with the previous benchmark regression results, and the robustness is established. The correlation coefficients of the control variables are basically stable and significant, and they are all significant at 1%–10% confidence interval. The research results are consistent with the previous regression results, and the robustness is established.

7.2 Multicollinearity Test

Diagnosis of collinearity in the regression model: The independent variable has a significant impact on the dependent variable; however, there may be a correlation

Table 7.7 Robustness Test of Alternative Explanatory Variables

	(1) *Z-Score*	*(2)* *Z-Score*
ESG	−0.2096**	−0.2292***
	(0.1563)	(0.2106)
E		−0.0533**
		(0.0338)
S		0.0525**
		(0.0557)
G		0.0257*
		(0.0355)
Leverage		0.0959***
		(0.4610)
Size		−0.0963**
		(0.1830)
Profitability		−0.0037*
		(0.0433)
Liquidity		−0.0037
		(0.0087)
Loan balance		−0.2881*
		(0.1541)
Finance background		−0.1084**
		(0.0875)
Ownership		−0.1023*v
		(0.2569)
_cons	5.5348***	12.5503**
	(1.0058)	(5.7639)
Fixed time	Yes	Yes
N	12,274	12,274
Adj. R^2	0.0005	0.0006

Standard errors are given in parentheses.
*$p < 0.1$, **$p < 0.05$, ***$p < 0$.

between the independent variables, that is, the problem of multicollinearity, which will affect the evaluation of the contribution rate of the independent variable. Therefore, it is necessary to diagnose the collinearity of the independent variables in the regression equation. Variance inflation factor (VIF) refers to the ratio of variance when there is multicollinearity among the independent variables to variance when there is no multicollinearity, and this value is the reciprocal of the tolerance. The larger the VIF, the more serious the multicollinearity problem. When the largest VIF does not exceed 10, the empirical rule considers that the model has no multicollinearity problem. The results in the first column show that the VIF of each variable is less than 10, and the maximum VIF of the variable inventory ratio INV is 2.48, so there is no multicollinearity in all variables. Analysis of the VIF test results shows no multicollinearity among the variables selected in this part (see Table 7.8 for details).

Table 7.8 Correlation Analysis: VIF Test Results

Variable	*VIF*	*1/VIF*
ESG	1.01	0.715
E	2.01	0.437
S	1.79	0.131
G	2.48	0.990
Leverage	1.01	0.434
Size	1.01	0.990
Profitability	1.01	0.993
Liquidity	1.01	0.984
Loan balance	1.03	0.990
Finance background	1.04	0.123
Ownership	1.01	0.442
Mean VIF	1.88	

8. Discussion

8.1 Theoretical Implications

Previous studies on ESG performance have largely focused on the United States. This research examines whether the relationship between ESG performance and bankruptcy risk holds true in the Chinese context, where rapid economic growth and an increasing emphasis on sustainability create a unique environment for analysis (Petushkova, 2022). The results confirm *H1*, revealing a negative correlation between ESG performance and corporate bankruptcy risk. This aligns with global findings that companies with strong ESG performance tend to have better financial health, risk management, and long-term sustainability.

Empirical research within the Chinese market indicates that firms with robust ESG practices are less likely to face bankruptcy. These companies prioritize environmental sustainability by minimizing pollution, managing resources efficiently, and adhering to regulations. Their commitment to social responsibility is reflected in employee welfare, community engagement, and strong stakeholder relations. Effective governance practices, such as transparency and independent boards, further enhance their resilience.

Several factors contribute to the positive link between ESG performance and reduced bankruptcy risk. Firstly, companies with strong ESG practices can adapt better to evolving regulatory environments, mitigating compliance risks amidst China's focus on environmental and social responsibility (Wang & Song, 2023). Secondly, effective governance allows companies to manage operational risks more efficiently, helping them navigate economic fluctuations and reduce bankruptcy likelihood.

Overall, this research enhances the understanding of how ESG performance influences corporate bankruptcy risk in China, indicating that higher ESG scores correlate with lower bankruptcy risk. This insight is valuable for stakeholders and policymakers aiming to support sustainable practices and bolster corporate stability.

8.2 Practical Implications

Companies must understand the strengths and limitations of evaluating the impact of ESG performance on insolvency risk in China. As suggested in *H2*, active stakeholder engagement fosters positive relationships and enhances reputation, helping to mitigate reputational risks that could lead to bankruptcy. In China, there are special provisions for enterprises nearing bankruptcy, such as high loan availability or partial loan forgiveness (Lopez, 2015). However, the sustainability of these policies must be considered, as they may offer only temporary relief and could lead to moral hazards if underlying ESG issues are not addressed.

Moreover, the specific dynamics of various Chinese industries can influence the relationship between ESG performance and bankruptcy risk. Different sectors face unique environmental and social challenges, necessitating industry-specific analysis.

Evidence indicates a positive link between ESG performance and reduced bankruptcy risk. Companies that prioritize ESG factors – like environmental sustainability, social responsibility, and effective governance – are better positioned to lower insolvency risks and enhance long-term sustainability (Robichaud, 2020). Policymakers, investors, and stakeholders should recognize ESG performance as a valuable risk management tool and encourage sustainable business practices. As awareness and data on ESG improve, further research is needed to explore the nuanced relationship between specific ESG subcategories and bankruptcy risk across different sectors in China.

9. Conclusion

This research examined the correlation between a bank's ESG performance and its bankruptcy probability index, while also testing the robustness and endogeneity of the findings. Unlike other studies, this research focused on the significance of ESG activities in actual bankruptcy events.

The benchmark regression shows that for non-financial listed companies, overall ESG performance has a significant negative effect on bankruptcy probability. Specifically, higher ESG scores correlate with a lower likelihood of bankruptcy, indicating that active participation in ESG initiatives can substantially reduce insolvency risk. While ESG-related investments grew significantly in 2019, their effects may lag and are not fully reflected in the current analysis.

Regarding control variables, the study confirms their importance in predicting bankruptcy risk. Companies with high total borrowings, substantial assets, and strong profitability tend to have lower bankruptcy risks, whereas firms with higher leverage or more financial institutional ties are at a greater risk.

The correlation coefficients for *E*, *S*, and *G* with bankruptcy probability are negative, positive, and optimistic, respectively. Environmental performance (*E*) has the most substantial impact, with sustainable practices reducing default risk. The effects of social (*S*) and governance (*G*) factors are approximately 10% of *E*'s impact, influenced by issues like omitted variables and reverse causality.

In robustness and endogeneity tests, results remain significant for bank management. The lagged ESG score shows a negative and significant relationship with bankruptcy probability at a 1% confidence level. The instrumental variable approach confirms this negative correlation, highlighting that poor financial performance and high credit risk are key factors increasing bankruptcy likelihood.

While the findings indicate that ESG activities significantly influence bankruptcy risk, future research should extend the timeframe to verify these conclusions. Additionally, the COVID-19 pandemic's impact on global economic conditions raises questions about whether regional differences might alter these results.

References

Altman, E. I., Iwanicz-Drozdowska, M., Laitinen, E. K., & Suvas, A. (2016). Financial distress prediction in an international context: A review and empirical analysis of Altman's Z- score model. *Journal of International Financial Management & Accounting, 28*(2), 131–171.

Aydogmus, M., Gulay, G., & Ergun, K. (2022). Impact of ESG performance on firm value and profitability. *Borsa Istanbul Review, 22*(2).

Barbaric, M. (2021). *ESG scores and financial performance of Swedish listed companies – Is there a link?*

Belli-Bivar, E. (2019, August 23). *Environmental, social, and governance: The ABCs of ESG*. JPT.

Bhandari, P. (2021). *Control variables | What are they and why do they matter?* Scribbr.

Brav, O. (2009). Access to capital, capital structure, and the funding of the firm. *The Journal of Finance, 64*(1), 263–308.

Crook, J. N., Edelman, D. B., & Thomas, L. C. (2007). Recent developments in consumer credit risk assessment. *European Journal of Operational Research, 183*(3), 1447–1465.

Do, T. K., & Vo, X. V. (2023). Is mandatory sustainability disclosure associated with default risk? Evidence from emerging markets. *Finance Research Letters, 55*(22), 103818.

Friede, G., Busch, T., & Bassen, A. (2015). ESG and financial performance: Aggregated evidence from more than 2000 empirical studies. *Journal of Sustainable Finance & Investment, 5*(4), 210–233.

Geczy, C. C., Guerard, J. B., & Samonov, M. (2020). Warning: SRI need not kill your sharpe and information ratios – Forecasting of earnings and efficient SRI and ESG portfolios. *The Journal of Investing, 29*(2), 110–127.

Giese, G., Lee, L.-E., Melas, D., Nagy, Z., & Nishikawa, L. (2019). Foundations of ESG investing: How ESG affects equity valuation, risk, and performance. *The Journal of Portfolio Management, 45*(5), 69–83.

Habermann, F., & Fischer, F. B. (2021). Corporate social performance and the likelihood of bankruptcy: Evidence from a period of economic upswing. *Journal of Business Ethics, 182*(04), 243–259

He, F., Ding, C., Yue, W., & Liu, G. (2023). ESG performance and corporate risk-taking: Evidence from China. *International Review of Financial Analysis, 87*(102550), 102550.

Kotzian, P. (2022). Carrots or sticks? Inferring motives of corporate CSR Engagement from empirical data. *Review of Managerial Science, 17*(8), 2921–2943.

Lam, B. M., Mo, P. L. L., & Rahman, M. J. (2024). Secrecy culture, client importance, and auditor reporting behavior: An international study. *Managerial Auditing Journal, 39*(2), 113–137.

Li, H., Zhang, X., & Zhao, Y. (2022). ESG and firm's default risk. *Finance Research Letters*, *47*(102713), 102713.
Li, Z., Crook, J., Andreeva, G., & Tang, Y. (2020). Predicting the risk of financial distress using corporate governance measures. *Pacific-Basin Finance Journal*, *68*(10), 101334.
Lopez, L. (2015, December 22). Everything just changed for Chinese companies. *Business Insider*. www.businessinsider.com/china-announces-bankruptcy-measures-2015-12
Mahmood, M. S. (2021, July 29). Heteroscedasticity in regression model. *Medium*.
Mapue, J. (2023). 27 Finance roles to know in 2020. *GoSkills.com*.
Marquis, C., & Qian, C. (2014). Corporate social responsibility reporting in China: Symbol or substance? *Organization Science*, *25*(1), 127–148.
Mathis, S. (2023, March). What is environmental, social and governance (ESG)? *WhatIs.com*.
McKinsey. (2021). *China consumer report 2021 Special edition*.
Nordqvist, C. (2016, July 19). What is ESG? Definition and . . . *Market Business News; Market Business News*.
OneTrust. (2022, June 12). ESG 101: What does social in ESG mean? *OneTrust*.
Petushkova, V. V. (2022). China's experience and prospects for sustainable development. *Herald of the Russian Academy of Sciences*, *92*(2), 207–215.
Pfajfar, G., Shoham, A., Małecka, A., & Zalaznik, M. (2022). Value of corporate social responsibility for multiple stakeholders and social impact – Relationship marketing perspective. *Journal of Business Research*, *143*, 46–61. Sciencedirect.
Qian, C. Y. (2013). *Shareholder activism in the ESG space: An analysis of the composition, success rates, and ESG score relationship of shareholder proposals from 2013–2020*. ScholarlyCommons.
Rahman, J., & Wu, J. (2023). M&A activity and ESG performance: Evidence from China. *Managerial Finance*, *50*(1), 179–197.
Rahman, M. J., Wu, Q., & Zhu, H. (2024). Corporate social responsibility in times of social distancing: Evidence from China. *Business Ethics, the Environment & Responsibility*.
Rahman, M. J., & Zhu, H. (2023). Predicting accounting fraud using imbalanced ensemble learning classifiers – evidence from China. *Accounting & Finance*, *63*(3), 3455–3486.
Rahman, M. J., & Zhu, H. (2024a). Detecting accounting fraud in family firms: Evidence from machine learning approaches. *Advances in Accounting*, *64*, 100722.
Rahman, M. J., & Zhu, H. (2024b). Predicting financial distress using machine learning approaches: Evidence China. *Journal of Contemporary Accounting & Economics*, *20*(1), 100403
Rahman, M. J., Zhu, H., & Chen, S. (2023). Does CSR reduce financial distress? Moderating effect of firm characteristics, auditor characteristics, and covid-19. *International Journal of Accounting & Information Management*, *31*(5), 756–784.
Rahman, M. J., Zhu, H., & Jiang, X. (2024). Family firms, client importance, and auditor reporting behavior: Evidence from China. *Meditari Accountancy Research*, *32*(2), 543–578.
Rahman, M. J., Zhu, H., & Yue, L. (2024). Does the adoption of artificial intelligence by audit firms and their clients affect audit quality and efficiency? Evidence from China. *Managerial Auditing Journal*, *39*(6), 668–699.
Robichaud, F. (2020, July 27). *Turn stakeholder engagement into a Higher ESG score*. Boréalis.
Saraswati, T., & Bernawati, Y. (2020). The effect of cash conversion cycle and firm size on the profitability of manufacturing companies. *International Journal of Innovation, Creativity and Change*. *Www.ijicc.net*, *11*(9).
Stieb, J. A. (2008). Assessing Freeman's stakeholder theory. *Journal of Business Ethics*, *87*(3), 401–414.
Wang, C., & Song, Z. (2023, February 8). *Green finance trends in China (1): China's green finance policy landscape*. Green Finance & Development Center.
Weber, O. (2013). Environmental, social and governance reporting in China. *Business Strategy and the Environment*, *23*(5), 303–317

Zhao, C., Guo, Y., Yuan, J., Wu, M., Li, D., Zhou, Y., & Kang, J. (2018). ESG and corporate financial performance: Empirical evidence from China's listed power generation companies. *Sustainability*, *10*(8), 2607.

Zhu, H., & Rahman, M. J. (2024). Ex-ante expected changes in ESG and future stock returns based on machine learning. *The British Accounting Review*, 101457.

Zu, L. (2013). Sustainable enterprise development. *Encyclopedia of Corporate Social Responsibility*, 2449–2458.

Part 3

Ownership Structure and ESG Ratings

8 The Impact of Enterprise Ownership Structure on ESG Rating

Md Jahidur Rahman, Tarek Rana, Hongtao Zhu, and Chong Shi

1. Introduction

Inspired by the findings of Hong and Sun (2022) on the correlation between equity concentration, share categories (e.g., state-owned enterprises, foreign enterprises, individual shares), and corporate social responsibility (a component of ESG indicators), alongside the research by Kong et al. (2014) which demonstrated a positive relationship between environmental friendliness and corporate stock performance, this chapter investigates the equity concentration of Chinese companies and the impact of different company types on ESG indicators. Given that ESG indicators are still in the popularization stage in China and lack robust data support, this exploration is both timely and necessary. Several studies in China also investigates the relationship of environmental accounting and firm performance (Rahman & Wu, 2023; Rahman, Wu, & Zhu, 2024; Rahman et al., 2023; Zhu & Rahman, 2024).

The motivations for this chapter are multifaceted. Firstly, a substantial body of literature has established a connection between ESG indicators and corporate financial performance. For instance, Luo (2022) found a significant positive correlation between the comprehensive ESG score and stock stability in the UK, with a more pronounced effect in highly liquid companies. Similarly, Capelle-Blancard and Petit (2019) identified that negative ESG performance can lead to severe economic losses for companies. High ESG indicators are associated with lower financial risks, and they mitigate the impact of negative news. Moreover, Khan et al. (2019) demonstrated that ESG performance can predict stock returns, with the top quartile of governance scores leading to superior portfolio performance compared to global benchmarks.

Secondly, there is a paucity of research exploring the impact of equity concentration on ESG indicators in Chinese companies. This study aims to fill this gap by analyzing the relationship between company equity concentration and ESG indicators, addressing the lack of data analysis in China. Since the joint release of the "Guiding Opinions on Building a Green Financial System" by seven ministries, including the People's Bank of China, in 2016, ESG elements have gained increasing recognition in Chinese society (Feng, 2019). Feng's research also underscores the significant economic impact of ESG indicators on companies. While ESG assessments are still nascent in the Chinese stock market, the trend towards

DOI: 10.4324/9781003488934-11

internationalization and growing attention to ESG performance is evident in both public and academic circles (He et al., 2023). Therefore, research on the relationship between Chinese companies and ESG indicators is both rare and crucial.

This study employs various empirical assessments grounded in theoretical analysis to understand how the equity structure of Chinese listed companies affects their ESG ratings. To measure equity structure, two criteria are identified: whether companies are State-Owned Enterprises (SOEs) and the concentration of shares. An empirical study of Chinese A-share listed companies from 2012 to 2021 is conducted. The shareholding ratio of the top shareholders and the SOE status from the CSMAR database are used to measure equity structure, while the Bloomberg ESG score serves as a proxy for ESG performance. A fixed-effects model tests the effect of equity structure on ESG ratings. To address potential endogeneity issues, explained variables are lagged by one period. Additionally, heterogeneity analysis examines the impact of regional differences on ESG performance.

The results reveal that SOEs have a significant positive impact on ESG ratings compared to non-SOEs. Furthermore, an increase in the ownership ratio of the largest shareholder positively influences ESG performance. Companies listed in eastern and central China exhibit a more pronounced positive impact on ESG ratings than those in western China.

This chapter makes several incremental contributions. It fills a gap in the literature by examining the variables that influence a firm's ESG rating, a factor often overlooked in existing studies. While much of the literature focuses on the impact and value of ESG performance to firms or investors, this study explores how firms can adjust and improve their ESG metrics. The findings suggest that SOEs and companies with high equity concentration generally achieve higher ESG ratings, providing valuable investment insights and strategies for improving ESG performance without significant expenditure. This research also highlights the benefits of corporate sustainability and stability associated with ESG indicators, offering low-risk investment options for entrepreneurs. Overall, this chapter provides new insights into how businesses and managers can effectively pursue sustainable development by demonstrating the relationship between corporate equity structure and ESG ratings.

The rest of the paper is organized as follows: Section 2 summarizes the literature review and proposed hypotheses. Section 3 explains the research design and methodology. Section 4 analyses the empirical results. Sections 5 and 6 present the endogeneity analysis and robustness test, respectively. Section 7 concludes with a summary and conclusion.

2. Literature Review and Hypothesis Development

2.1 Relationship Between Shareholding Concentration and Corporate ESG Rating

Research by Ducassy and Montandrau (2015) highlights that equity concentration, and the nature of shareholders significantly determine how well a company fulfils its social responsibility. The shareholding structure, defined as the relationship between various shareholder holdings in firms (Zhang et al., 2022), includes both shareholding concentration and the nature of the largest shareholder, whether it is a state-owned enterprise. Modern businesses often operate under a model where control and management are separated, with shareholders overseeing management based on their ownership percentage (Hong & Sun, 2022).

According to Zhang et al. (2013), CSR fulfilment often provides long-term benefits rather than short-term gains. CSR's contribution to corporate development is gradual, and its positive impact on performance lags. Consequently, CSR represents a long-term economic return. Management, driven by personal economic benefits tied to short-term performance, is typically reluctant to incur costs for fulfilling social responsibility (Qian et al., 2023). Thus, the degree of CSR fulfilment is influenced by the equity concentration or ownership percentage of shareholders. Generally, higher equity concentration strengthens the control of the majority shareholder, aligning the company's strategic decisions with the controlling shareholder's long-term interests (Liu, 2020).

Several studies have examined how equity concentration affects CSR fulfilment. Cheng et al. (2015) found that higher equity concentration enhances CSR performance. Similarly, Shi (2010) reported a positive relationship between equity concentration and CSR among companies listed on the Shanghai and Shenzhen exchanges, with firms having multiple major shareholders performing better in CSR (Zhao & Wei, 2021). However, some research indicates a negative relationship between equity concentration and CSR performance (Feng & Xi, 2019).

Low equity concentration, where shareholding is fragmented, often leads to a lack of incentive for shareholders to monitor management, resulting in a "free-rider" phenomenon (Hong & Sun, 2022). Without sufficient motivation to oversee CSR fulfilment, there is inadequate monitoring. Higher environmental protection costs, which reduce short-term economic benefits, further discourage management from prioritizing CSR. Consequently, low equity concentration is not conducive to CSR fulfilment. Conversely, when equity concentration is high, the interests of the largest shareholder align closely with the company's long-term interests, prompting greater willingness to monitor management and support CSR (Hong & Sun, 2022).

Based on this reasoning, the following hypothesis is proposed:

H1. There is a positive relationship between shareholding concentration and corporate ESG rating.

2.2 The Relationship Between SOE and Corporate ESG Rating

SOEs typically exhibit a heightened awareness of the regulations enacted by their shareholders, primarily the government. Companies with a significant proportion of government holdings are more likely to demonstrate robust corporate governance practices. Consequently, SOEs may be more inclined to issue reports on Corporate Social Responsibility (CSR) to meet accountability requirements and gain stakeholder trust (Habbash, 2016).

Extensive research has investigated the impact of state ownership on corporate social responsibility practices. Cheung et al. (2014) posits that SOEs engage in less CSR activity compared to non-SOEs because they are less susceptible to external stakeholder influence due to ongoing financial support from the Chinese government. Contrarily, Abdullah et al. (2011) argue that there is no direct relationship between being an SOE and the extent of social responsibility undertaken by the firm. Nonetheless, research by Khan et al. (2019) suggests that state ownership positively influences CSR performance, indicating that a reduction in state ownership percentage could negatively affect CSR outcomes. Guo et al. (2019) also confirm that state ownership enhances CSR disclosure, with this relationship becoming more pronounced as the proportion of state ownership increases.

From a stakeholder perspective, SOEs are owned by a diverse group of stakeholders, including the general public in addition to the government (Ghazali, 2007). To enhance public perception of their legitimacy and improve their ESG ratings, SOEs are often required to engage in more socially responsible activities and provide relevant disclosures. This discussion leads to the following hypothesis:

H2. There is a positive relationship between state ownership (SOE) and corporate ESG rating

3. Research Design

3.1 Data Acquisition

The data collection for this study, which is restricted to non-financial enterprises registered on the Chinese stock exchange, mostly ignores companies in the financial sector. This is largely caused by the highly different ways that financial sector corporations use accounting principles compared to non-financial sector organizations, as well as the fact that they have various disclosure obligations and norms (Fadli et al., 2022). ST businesses are also not included. Firms that have lost money for two years in a row are cautioned by Chinese stock market rules that they run the prospect of being delisted, therefore ST companies are the same as financially troubled companies (Qin et al., 2020).

These firms' statistics are taken from the CSMAR database. Marquis and Qian (2014) claim that CSMAR, which offers a variety of financial and non-financial data, is one of the trustworthy sources for information on Chinese listed businesses. The period of the study is from 2012 to 2021, and some companies that went public after 2012 and those with significant missing relevant variables were excluded from the sample. A 1% bilateral tail reduction was performed on all continuous variables to mitigate the effects of outliers. The final 1134 companies met the study selection criteria and the identification process for this sample is shown in Table 8.1

3.2 Variable Measurements

3.2.1 Dependent Variable

The dependent variable in this study is the ESG rating, which stands for environmental, social, and governance. ESG evaluation standards, which are quickly evolving internationally, gauge a company's total performance based on its operational

Table 8.1 Study Population

Study Population Summary	*No. of Listed Companies in China*
Total number listed companies in China on December 31, 2021	3,341
Lees: financial companies & ST	78
Less: companies that were not listed for the entire study period	877
Less: companies with severely missing relevant variables	1,252
Total number of companies in this study	1,134

Source: CSMAR database

stability and long-term economic value in three dimensions: corporate governance, social responsibility, and the environment. Yang and Shen (2022) assert that the environmental criterion in ESG examines how well a company adapts to the environment, the social criterion looks at how the company manages its relationships with employees, suppliers, and clients, and the governance is primarily reflected in the company's financial performance. The governance criteria focus on management, executive remuneration, audit, internal control, and shareholder rights while the social criterion evaluates how the firm handles its relationships with employees, suppliers, and consumers. ESG standards focus on social considerations, which are different from the traditional financial metrics of public companies around earnings. Overall, ESG standards provide a more comprehensive, systematic, quantifiable, and applicable measure of a company's value.

Numerous studies have employed rankings (scores) from independent organizations to measure the ESG performance of businesses (Eliwa & Aboud, 2021; Gillan et al., 2021; Xie et al., 2019). These groups build various indicator systems, give these indications varying weights, and then put them all up to provide ESG ratings for various corporations. As an illustration, consider the ESG rating data offered by Shanghai Huazheng Index Information Service Company (hereafter referred to as Huazheng Index, accessible in the WIND database), which grades all A-share listed companies based on four criteria: overall rating, environmental performance, social responsibility, and governance performance. The grades are AAA, AA, A, BBB, BB, B, CCC, CC, and C. The ESG rating data released by Bloomberg, one of the top news sources for business and financial information, is preferred by researchers. Bloomberg ESG ratings include a 3-part scale of E, S, and G, ranging from 0 to 100, with 100 being the best score a company can receive. The ESG data they use for the E & S score includes voluntary disclosures obtained from direct (primary) sources, to guarantee authenticity and consistency with the original business information, check sources including sustainability reports published by corporations, annual filings, proxy statements, corporate governance reports, supplementary news releases, and company websites (MSCI Inc., 2023).

The ESG performance of listed companies is reflected in this study using Bloomberg's ESG ratings, which are based on the requirements of research and

Table 8.2 Bloomberg ESG Scoring System

Pillar (Weight)	*Topic*	*Weight*
Environmental (33%)	Air Quality	4.78%
	Climate Change	4.70%
	Ecological & Biodiversity Impacts	4.79%
	Energy	4.73%
	Materials & Waste	4.74%
	Supply Chain	4.79%
	Water	4.79%
Social (33%)	Community & Customers	5.53%
	Diversity	5.49%
	Ethics & Compliance	5.57%
	Health & Safety	5.58%
	Human Capital	5.55%
	Supply Chain	5.54%
Governance (33%)	Audit Risk & Oversight	4.17%
	Board Composition	4.16%
	Compensation	4.16%
	Diversity	4.17%
	Independence	4.18%
	Nominations & Governance Oversight	4.18%
	Sustainability Governance	4.18%
	Tenure	4.18%

Note: The company ESG score is the weighted average of the environmental, social, and governance ratings.

data accessibility. For robustness testing, ESG rating information from Huazheng is also employed. Table 8.2 displays the precise Bloomberg assessment framework.

3.2.2 Independent Variables

Many researchers measure the equity structure of a company by two factors, whether it is a state-owned enterprise (SOE) and the Top1 shareholding (Top1) (Zhang, 2022; Qin & Zhang, 2022; Wei & Wang, 2023).

State-Owned Enterprise

Enterprises that are under the jurisdiction of the national government are known as state-owned enterprises (SOEs). The government's intentions impact how SOEs act. Therefore, the differential in ESG performance between SOEs and non-SOEs may be a result of governmental obligations for environmental control and CSR (Khalid et al., 2021). If a company is a state-owned business, SOE assigns a value of 1, otherwise a value of 0.

Top1 shareholding

The selection of the management and majority shareholder shareholdings reflects the features of the firm's ownership structure (Ren et al., 2023). The composition of a company's decision-makers may be revealed by the ownership structure, which also has a big influence on the company's ESG performance (Cucari et al., 2018). The number of shares held by the top shareholder divided by the total number of shares is known as the top 1 shareholding (Top 1).

3.2.3 Control Variables

This study considers some of the firm's attributes and management style as control variables that may affect ESG performance. Therefore, the model incorporates firm attributes such as the presence of CEO duality, firm size, equity checks and balances, firm age, and operating income growth rate. The specific measures are shown in Table 8.3 below.

Model Specification

In this study, the optimal estimation model was determined by the Hausman test, and the test chi-square value was 394.33 with a p-value of 0.0000, so a fixed effects model should be used instead of a random effects model. The Hausman Test results are tabulated in Table 8.4 below.

Based on the above research hypotheses, this study uses a fixed-effects model for benchmark regressions to examine the relationship between the equity structure of listed companies and their ESG scores. The benchmark model is set up as follows:

$$\begin{aligned} BloombergESG_{i,t} \\ &= \alpha_0 + \alpha_1 Top1_{i,t} + \alpha_2 Size_{i,t} + \alpha_3 Balance1_{i,t} \\ &+ \alpha_4 Growth_{i,t} + \alpha_5 Dual_{i,t} \\ &+ \alpha_6 FirmAge_{i,t} + Industry + Year + \varepsilon_{i,t} \end{aligned}$$

Table 8.3 Measures of Control Variables

Company	*Size*	*Natural Logarithm of Total Assets Size = ln (Total Assets)*	*Rahman, Zhu, and Yue (2024)*
Equity Checks and Balances	Balance1	Balance1 = 1/Z Index	Rahman and Zhu (2024)
Operating income growth rate	Growth	Current year's operating income/ Previous year's operating income- 1	Lam et al. (2024)
Duality	Dual	The chairman and general manager are the same person as 1, otherwise, it is 0	Rahman, Zhu, and Zhang (2024)
Company Age	FirmAge	ln(current year – year of incorporation + 1)	Rahman, Zhu, and Jiang (2024)

Table 8.4 Hausman Test

Inspection method	*Chi2()*	*Prob>Chi2()*
Hausman Test	394.33	0.00

$$
\begin{aligned}
BloombergESG_{i,t} &= \alpha_0 + \alpha_1 SOE_{i,t} + \alpha_2 Size_{i,t} + \alpha_3 Balance1_{i,t} \\
&+ \alpha_4 Growth_{i,t} + \alpha_5 Dual_{i,t} \\
&+ \alpha_6 FirmAge_{i,t} + Industry + Year + \varepsilon_{i,t}
\end{aligned}
$$

α_0 is a constant term, $\alpha_1, \alpha_2, \alpha_3, \alpha_4, \alpha_5$ are coefficients corresponding to each variable.

Year: Fixed year effect
Industry: Industry fixed effects
$\varepsilon_{i,t}$: Random Error term

4. Empirical Results

4.1 Descriptive Statistics

Table 8.5 below shows the outcomes of descriptive statistics for all variables. The vast range of maximum and minimum ESG score values among them shows that the environmental, social, and governance performance of various organizations varies significantly. In varied degrees, other control variables also change. Overall, the statistical results show that the data are homogeneous and that no significant outliers exist.

4.2 Correlation Analysis

The correlation coefficients for the main variables of interest in this study are listed in the following Table 8.6 along with their magnitude and significance levels. The findings demonstrate that practically all correlation coefficients are substantially lower than 0.5, showing that there is no significant connection and preventing estimating mistakes caused by multicollinearity. ESG is tentatively found to be positively correlated with the first largest shareholder's shareholding, state-owned businesses, enterprise size, equity checks and balances, and enterprise age, and negatively correlated with the operating income growth rate and the integration of

Table 8.5 Summary Statistics

VarName	*Obs*	*Mean*	*SD*	*Min*	*Median*	*Max*
ESG Bloomberg	9342	28.35	8.874	6.1983	27.452	68.9166
ESG Huazheng	9342	4.41	1.140	1	4	8
Top1	9342	0.37	0.158	.081265	.354383	.757786
SOE	9342	0.52	0.499	0	1	1
Size	9342	23.26	1.286	19.55112	23.1683	26.42972
Balance1	9342	0.34	0.284	.0062452	.244236	1
Growth	9342	0.16	0.415	−.659698	.0993695	4.330351
Dual	9342	0.19	0.395	0	0	1
Firm Age	9342	2.96	0.321	1.609438	2.995732	3.610918

Table 8.6 Correlation Coefficient

	ESG Bloomberg	*ESG Huazheng*	*Top1*	*SOE*	*Size*	*Balance1*	*Growth*	*Dual*	*FirmAge*
ESG Bloomberg	1								
ESG Huazheng	0.161***	1							
Top1	0.052***	0.091***	1						
SOE	0.099***	0.140***	0.321***	1					
Size	0.390***	0.204***	0.214***	0.248***	1				
Balance1	0.106***	–0.026**	–0.607***	–0.216***	0.026**	1			
Growth	–0.027**	–0.034***	–0.010	–0.093***	0.028***	0.041***	1		
Dual	–0.022**	–0.059***	–0.118***	–0.279***	–0.085***	0.074***	0.049***	1	
FirmAge	0.181***	0.004	–0.152***	0.124***	0.170***	0.037***	–0.036***	–0.065***	1

two offices based on the correlation coefficients between ESG and each variable. However, further research is required to determine the precise causal link between ownership structure and ESG performance.

4.3 Baseline Regression Results

The empirical findings based on models (1) and (2) are summarized in Table 8.7 below, where column (1) evaluates the impact of Top1 ownership (Top1) on the ESG Bloomberg index without considering the control variables. Without taking into account the control variables, Column 3 investigates the impact of the firm's status as a state-owned company (SOE) on the ESG Bloomberg index. The results of the control variables regression are displayed in columns (2) and (4). According to the results, the more concentrated the shareholding (the higher the shareholding of the first largest shareholder) the higher the ESG score of listed companies. State Owned Enterprises (SOEs) have a significant and positive impact on ESG rating compared to non-state-owned enterprises. And companies with state capital are more concerned about environmental sustainability than individual investors or common shareholders, so they may be more willing to invest more in the environment and society in their corporate decisions (Ren et al., 2023).

Table 8.7 Baseline Regression Results

	(1)	*(2)*	*(3)*	*(4)*
	ESG Bloomberg	*ESG Bloomberg*	*ESG Bloomberg*	*ESG Bloomberg*
Top1	4.414***	6.508***		
	(9.39)	(11.35)		
SOE			1.581***	0.921***
			(10.53)	(6.12)
Size		2.138***		2.252***
		(36.14)		(38.62)
Balance1		4.439***		2.617***
		(14.91)		(11.03)
Growth		–0.239		–0.126
		(–1.51)		(–0.79)
Dual		0.038		0.177
		(0.23)		(1.02)
FirmAge		0.880***		0.200
		(3.59)		(0.82)
_cons	26.728***	–27.828***	27.518***	–25.995***
	(143.55)	(–18.53)	(260.68)	(–16.98)
Year	Yes	Yes	Yes	Yes
Industry	Yes	Yes	Yes	Yes
N	9,342	9,342	9,342	9,342
Adj. R^2	0.410	0.506	0.411	0.501

5. Endogeneity Tests

The method of lagging the explained variable by one period as a test of endogeneity is commonly used in studying the relationship between ESG rating and other variables (Tao et al., 2023; Xu & Liu, 2023; Tang, 2022). In this paper, the explained variable (ESG Bloomberg) is lagging for one period to alleviate the endogeneity problem.

According to the results in columns (1) and (2) of Table 8.8, the coefficients of the dependent variable (F.ESG Bloomberg) in the previous period are 6.107 and 0.844, respectively, which are significantly positive at the 1% level. And since the results were consistent with the fixed effects model, the statistics did not indicate any serious endogeneity problems. The test result is shown in Table 8 below.

$$\begin{aligned} Bloomberg\,ESG\_(i,t+1) &= \alpha\_0+\alpha\_1\,Top1\_(i,t)+\alpha\_2\,Size\_(i,t) \\ &\quad +\alpha\_3[\![Balance1]\!]\_(i,t)+\alpha\_4\,Growth\_(i,t) \\ &\quad +\alpha\_5[\![Dual]\!]\_(i,t)+\alpha\_6\,FirmAge\_(i,t) \\ &\quad +Industry+Year+\varepsilon\_(i,t) \end{aligned}$$

Table 8.8 Endogeneity Tests Result: Explained Variable Lags for One Period

	(1)	*(2)*
	F.ESG Bloomberg	*F.ESG Bloomberg*
Top1	6.107***	
	(9.62)	
SOE		0.844***
		(5.05)
Size	2.239***	2.344***
	(33.86)	(35.89)
Balance1	4.241***	2.521***
	(12.81)	(9.55)
Growth	−0.390**	−0.272
	(−2.25)	(−1.55)
Dual	−0.012	0.113
	(−0.06)	(0.59)
FirmAge	0.757***	0.105
	(2.84)	(0.40)
_cons	−28.603***	−26.777***
	(−17.18)	(−15.78)
Year	Yes	Yes
Industry	Yes	Yes
N	8,001	8,001
Adj. R^2	0.476	0.472

$$
\begin{aligned}
Bloomberg\,ESG\_(i,t+1) &= \alpha\_0+\alpha\_1SOE\_(i,t)+\alpha\_2\,Size\_(i,t)\\
&\quad+\alpha\_3[\![Balance1]\!]\_(i,t)+\alpha\_4Growth\_(i,t)\\
&\quad+\alpha\_5[\![Dual]\!]\_(i,t)+\alpha\_6\,FirmAge\_(i,t)\\
&\quad+Industry+Year+\varepsilon\_(i,t)
\end{aligned}
$$

α_0 is a constant term, α_1, α_2, α_3, α_4, $\alpha_{5,}$, α_6 are coefficients corresponding to each variable.

Year: Fixed year effect

Industry: Industry fixed effects

$\varepsilon_{i,t}$: Random Error term

6. Robustness Tests

Robustness Tests replace the explanatory variables. Bloomberg's ESG ratings are used in the benchmark regression to gauge corporate ESG performance. Using Huazheng's ESG ratings for public corporations runs a robustness test. The ESG ratings of the Huazheng are used as a substitute proxy variable for the dependent variables. Based on four criteria – comprehensive rating, environmental performance, social responsibility, and governance performance – this rating specifically classifies all A-share listed firms into nine groups (AAA, AA, A, BBB, BB, B, CCC, CC, and C). The results show that the equity structure of a listed firm can still significantly affect the ESG performance of that firm. The test result is shown in Table 8.9 below.

$$
\begin{aligned}
Huazheng\,ESG\_(i,t) &= \alpha\_0+\alpha\_1Top1\_(i,t)+\alpha\_2\,Size\_(i,t)\\
&\quad+\alpha\_3[\![Balance1]\!]\_(i,t)+\alpha\_4Growth\_(i,t)\\
&\quad+\alpha\_5[\![Dual]\!]\_(i,t)+\alpha\_6\,FirmAge\_(i,t)\\
&\quad+Industry+Year+\varepsilon\_(i,t)
\end{aligned}
$$

$$
\begin{aligned}
Huazheng\,ESG\_(i,t) &= \alpha\_0+\alpha\_1SOE\_(i,t)+\alpha\_2\,Size\_(i,t)\\
&\quad+\alpha\_3[\![Balance1]\!]\_(i,t)+\alpha\_4Growth\_(i,t)\\
&\quad+\alpha\_5[\![Dual]\!]\_(i,t)+\alpha\_6\,FirmAge\_(i,t)\\
&\quad+Industry+Year+\varepsilon\_(i,t)
\end{aligned}
$$

6.1 Heterogeneity Analysis

Due to the vast territory of China, the impact of corporate equity structure on different ESG scores may vary significantly due to the vast differences in physical geography and economic development levels in different regions. Based on

Table 8.9 Robustness Tests Result: Replace the Dependent Variable

	(1)	(2)
	ESG Huazheng	*ESG Huazheng*
Top1	0.342***	
	(3.45)	
SOE		0.273***
		(10.62)
Size	0.190***	0.179***
	(18.58)	(17.96)
Balance1	−0.005	−0.024
	(−0.11)	(−0.59)
Growth	−0.112***	−0.089***
	(−4.11)	(−3.26)
Dual	−0.109***	−0.044
	(−3.78)	(−1.49)
FirmAge	−0.160***	−0.246***
	(−3.78)	(−5.88)
_cons	0.381	0.860***
	(1.47)	(3.29)
Year	Yes	Yes
Industry	Yes	Yes
N	9,342	9,342
Adj. R^2	0.106	0.115

the geographic locations of listed firms, this research separates companies into Eastern, Central, and Western corporations since the eastern portion of China (East) has much greater levels of economic development and digital finance than the central and western areas (Cent & West). This study can better support the sustainable growth of organizations by examining the association between ESG ratings and the equity structure of enterprises in greater detail using heterogeneity analysis.

The eastern and central areas, but not the western region, have a more prominent effect of corporate equity structure on ESG ratings, according to heterogeneity analysis. The following details can be used to explain this outcome: The middle and western areas' economies are developing more slowly than the eastern regions. In the eastern region, the main industries are high-end industries with low energy consumption and high value added (Yu et al., 2023), which can increase ESG investment. In contrast, the economy of the central and western regions is generally less developed, and the industrial structure is mainly primary and secondary industries (Yu et al., 2023). Therefore, listed companies in the more backward regions should make efforts to establish ESG systems and strive to improve ESG performance. The test result is shown in Table 8.10 below.

Table 8.10 Heterogeneity Analysis Result: In Terms of Geographical Location

	Eastern	*Central*	*Western*	*Eastern*	*Central*	*Western*
	ESG Bloomberg	*ESG Bloomberg*	*ESG Bloomberg*	*ESG Bloomberg*	*ESG Bloomberg*	*ESG Bloomberg*
Top1	6.794***	5.910***	0.334			
	(9.52)	(4.61)	(0.23)			
SOE				1.494***	-0.086	-0.584
				(7.91)	(-0.25)	(-1.59)
Size	2.408***	1.516***	1.462***	2.481***	1.663***	1.497***
	(32.88)	(10.46)	(10.01)	(34.40)	(11.65)	(10.27)
Balance1	4.753***	4.843***	−0.687	2.974***	3.038***	−1.015*
	(12.71)	(7.28)	(−0.94)	(10.16)	(5.50)	(−1.74)
Growth	−0.474**	0.236	0.398	−0.316	0.274	0.345
	(−2.40)	(0.68)	(1.06)	(−1.60)	(0.79)	(0.92)
Dual	0.008	0.000	−0.685	0.268	−0.161	−0.889*
	(0.04)	(0.00)	(−1.41)	(1.31)	(−0.40)	(−1.78)
FirmAge	1.255***	0.587	−0.775	0.443	0.154	−0.782
	(4.38)	(0.84)	(−1.11)	(1.54)	(0.22)	(−1.14)
_cons	−35.176***	−13.051***	−3.579	−32.180***	−12.324***	−3.784
	(−19.06)	(−3.52)	(−0.91)	(−16.98)	(−3.31)	(−0.97)
Year	Yes	Yes	Yes	Yes	Yes	Yes
Industry	Yes	Yes	Yes	Yes	Yes	Yes
N	6305	1803	1233	6305	1803	1233
Adj. R^2	0.523	0.476	0.548	0.521	0.470	0.548

7. Discussion

7.1 Relationship with Previous Literature

To the best of our knowledge, most previous studies have primarily focused on the impact of ESG indicators on stock risk. Studies such as those by Sun et al. (2024) have examined the influence of a firm's equity structure on social responsibility. However, these studies tend to be limited in scope, often covering only one aspect of ESG indicators. Sun et al. (2024) concluded that there is a significant relationship between equity structure and social responsibility, but their analysis was restricted to social responsibility alone. Similarly, Kong et al. (2014) reported positive feedback regarding the relationship between corporate stock and environmental friendliness, indicating a beneficial link between environmental practices and stock performance.

This study aims to extend and confirm these previous findings by exploring the broader relationship between equity structure and ESG indicators, encompassing environmental, social, and governance aspects. It is based on the premise that ESG indicators contribute to stability and benefits for investors and entrepreneurs. By investigating how a company's contributions to ESG performance influence its external relations, this research provides a comprehensive extension of existing studies. Furthermore, Khan et al. (2019) found a significant positive correlation between CSR and state ownership, highlighting that state-owned companies are more likely to engage in socially responsible activities. Since CSR indicators are similar to ESG indicators in measuring social contributions, this study also serves to confirm and extend Khan et al.'s (2019) findings. The positive relationship between state ownership and ESG performance observed in this study aligns with and supports the existing literature, offering additional empirical evidence and validation of the beneficial impact of state ownership on corporate ESG ratings.

7.2 Theoretical Contribution

This study makes significant theoretical contributions by validating and extending existing theories on the relationship between equity concentration, state ownership, and ESG indicators. The findings of this research confirm that high equity concentration is positively correlated with enhanced ESG performance. This result supports the premise that firms with high equity concentration are more likely to engage in non-profit activities and focus on matters that extend beyond immediate financial returns. This aligns with the findings of Hong and Sun (2022) and Kong et al. (2014), who identified a strong association between high equity concentration and elevated levels of social responsibility.

Moreover, this study contributes to the literature by highlighting the positive correlation between state ownership and ESG indicators. The analysis reveals that State-Owned Enterprises (SOEs) consistently demonstrate higher ESG performance compared to other types of firms. This finding underscores the willingness of SOEs to invest in non-profit activities, particularly environmental protection initiatives, as indicated by Ren et al. (2023). These results provide empirical support for legitimacy theory, suggesting that SOEs, due to their unique ownership structure and regulatory oversight, are more motivated to comply with societal expectations and enhance their legitimacy through robust ESG practices.

Additionally, the positive relationship between state ownership and ESG performance aligns with stakeholder theory. SOEs, being accountable to a broad spectrum of stakeholders, including the government and the public, are more likely to engage in socially responsible activities to maintain and enhance their legitimacy and stakeholder trust. This finding also corroborates the research by Khan et al. (2019), which demonstrated a significant positive correlation between CSR and state ownership.

This chapter contributes to the theoretical understanding of how equity concentration and state ownership influence ESG performance. By integrating legitimacy and stakeholder theories, the research provides a comprehensive framework for analyzing the motivations behind corporate engagement in ESG activities. This extension of existing theories offers valuable insights for policymakers, regulators, and corporate managers aiming to improve ESG performance and achieve sustainable development.

7.3 Practical Implications

This study provides practical insights that can help investors make safer investment decisions, guide entrepreneurs in risk reduction and corporate governance, and assist policymakers in fostering an environment that promotes high ESG performance and stability within the corporate sector. The findings of this study have several significant practical implications, particularly for investors, entrepreneurs, and policymakers.

Firstly, the positive correlation between high equity concentration and elevated ESG indicators suggests that companies with concentrated equity are generally more stable and present lower stock risk. This information is invaluable for investors, as it highlights that investments in such companies are likely to involve manageable risks, leading to smoother and more predictable returns. This insight can guide investors in making more informed decisions, particularly in markets where risk management is paramount.

Secondly, the study reveals that state-owned enterprises (SOEs) exhibit higher ESG performance compared to non-state-owned companies. This indicates that Chinese SOEs demonstrate greater social responsibility and stability. For investors, this provides a critical insight into the comparative advantages of investing in SOEs, suggesting that these companies are more likely to adhere to social ethics and exhibit reliable performance. Therefore, investments in SOEs can be considered safer and more aligned with sustainable investment strategies.

For entrepreneurs, the study underscores the importance of equity concentration in achieving higher ESG performance and reducing corporate risk. Entrepreneurs should consider strategies to concentrate equity ownership to enhance their companies' ESG indicators. Higher ESG performance not only reflects positively on the company's social and environmental commitments but also significantly reduces operational risks, thus contributing to the overall stability and attractiveness of the company to investors.

Policymakers can also draw practical implications from these findings. Encouraging practices that lead to higher equity concentration could be a strategic move to improve the overall ESG performance of firms within the country. Additionally, policies that support the unique structure of SOEs and their commitment to social responsibility could further stabilize and enhance the economic environment.

8. Conclusion

In recent years, corporate social responsibility awareness has become an increasingly important determinant of investment decisions due to climate and environmental issues (Krueger et al., 2020). Additionally, the current Chinese market climate has raised the bar for business ESG performance. With the 2015 amendment to the Environmental Protection Law, which further increases environmental fees and taxes, and the gradual establishment of green credit systems by major Chinese commercial banks and financial institutions, which will result in stricter access to high-pollution and high-emission industries, Chinese companies are now under regulatory and policy pressure to improve their ESG performance (Ren et al., 2023).

Therefore, it has become a common issue for both industry and academics to figure out how to encourage the market to spend more on green sectors and how to get businesses to intentionally boost their sustainable growth.

This study investigated whether equity structure affects the ESG rating of Chinese-listed companies by empirically testing 1134 listed Chinese companies from 2012–2021. Specifically, this study used a linear regression with a fixed effects model, using ESG ratings issued by Bloomberg agencies as a proxy for ESG performance. In the empirical test analysis, endogeneity and robustness tests were conducted to further validate the findings and make them more reliable. The results show that companies with higher SOE and equity concentration have a significant and positive impact on ESG rating, and the results of qualitative analysis also indicate that company equity structure has a more significant positive effect on ESG rating for companies listed in the eastern and central regions of China.

Regarding the practical repercussions, policymakers, regulators, businesses, and investors should increase public understanding of how an organization's ownership structure impacts its ESG rating. Companies that better uphold their social obligations not only benefit from government and community support, but also obtain preference under some laws and regulations, such as those governing financing options, etc. Therefore, investigating corporate social responsibility may aid in the peaceful growth of businesses and society, benefiting both the national environment and the corporations themselves.

The following policy conclusions are reached in light of the aforementioned findings: (1) Businesses should appropriately acknowledge the value of ESG investments and concentrate on the cooperative growth of the environment, society, and government. They ought to take advantage of this chance to set up a reliable method for disclosing ESG information. (2) Regulators can create a suitable mechanism for mandated ESG information disclosure and can include ESG performance in the regulatory framework. Encourage companies to employ environmentally friendly funding and investment strategies, and act as financial institutions for the advancement of sustainable development. Regulators and financial institutions, on the other hand, must concentrate on the system's growth as well as the importance of ESG inside enterprises in less economically developed regions like western China. (3) When making investment selections, investors should give the ESG performance of the company due consideration. A company's investment risk may be decreased by concentrating on its environmental performance, and sustainable corporate growth is a dependable strategy to guarantee long-term profits for investors.

The following discussion addresses the limitations of the study. The scale of this study in terms of the available data is the first constraint. This article examines ownership structure and corporate ESG performance of Chinese listed firms, although it has limits since there is a dearth of ESG data for many of these organizations and because ESG disclosure is still in its infancy. The second drawback is that this study only covers listed firms that are involved in industries other than finance. The focus of future study may include ownership arrangements in the banking industry. The third drawback is that although the influence of internal corporate governance measures, such as board independence, on corporate ESG performance is absent, only the impact of various ownership arrangements on ESG performance is evaluated. Future research should thoroughly examine each of these difficulties.

References

Abdullah, S. N., Mohamad, N. R., & Mokhtar, M. Z. (2011). Board independence, ownership, and CSR of Malaysian large firms. *Corporate Ownership and Control*, *8*(3), 417–435.

Capelle-Blancard, G., & Petit, A. (2019). Every little helps? ESG news and stock market reaction. *Journal of Business Ethics*, *157*, 543–565.

Cheng, P., Xiao, W., & Deng, C. (2015). Research on the relationship between equity structure and corporate social responsibility of listed companies. *Qiu Suo*, *2015*(7), 101–105.

Cheung, Y.-L., Kong, D., Tan, W., & Wang, W. (2014). Being good when being international in an emerging economy: The case of China. *Journal of Business Ethics*, *130*, 805–817.

Cucari, N., De Falco, S. E., & Orlando, B. (2018). Diversity of board of directors and environmental social governance: Evidence from Italian listed companies. *Corporate Social Responsibility and Environmental Management*, *25*(3), 250–266.

Ducassy, I., & Montandrau, S. (2015). Corporate social performance, ownership structure, and corporate governance in France. *Research in International Business and Finance*, *34*, 383–396.

Eliwa, Y., & Aboud, A. (2021). ESG practices and the cost of debt: Evidence from EU countries. *Critical Perspectives on Accounting*, *79*, 102097. https://doi.org/10.1016/j.cpa.2019.102097

Fadli, A. A., Sands, J., Jones, G., Beattie, C., & Pensiero, D. (2022). The influence of ownership structure on the extent of CSR reporting: An emerging market study. *Business and Society Review*, *127*(3), 725–754.

Feng, L., & Xi, J. (2019). Equity concentration, executive tenure and corporate social responsibility performance. *Journal of Guangxi University of Finance and Economics*, *32*(3), 106–115.

Ghazali, N. A. (2007). Ownership structure and corporate social responsibility disclosure: Some Malaysian evidence. *Corporate Governance: The International Journal of Business in Society*, *7*(3), 251–266.

Gillan, S. L., Koch, A., & Starks, L. T. (2021). Firms and social responsibility: A review of ESG and CSR research in corporate finance. *Journal of Corporate Finance*, *66*, 101889. https://doi.org/10.1016/j.jcorpfin.2021.101889

Guo, M., Hu, Y., Zhang, Y., & Tian, F. (2019). State-owned shareholding and CSR: Do multiple financing methods matter?-Evidence from China. *Sustainability*, *11*, 1292.

Habbash, M. (2016). Corporate governance and corporate social responsibility disclosure: Evidence from Saudi Arabia. *Social Responsibility Journal*, *12*(4), 740–754.

He, F., Ding, C., Yue, W., & Liu, G. (2023). ESG performance and corporate risk-taking: Evidence from China. *International Review of Financial Analysis*, *87*, 102550.

Hong, X., & Sun, Y. (2022). Research on the impact of equity concentration on social responsibility. *Frontiers of Social Science*, *11*(8), 3571–3578.

Khalid, F., Sun, J., Huang, G., & Su, C. (2021). Environmental, social and governance performance of Chinese multinationals: A comparison of state- and non-state-owned enterprises. *Sustainability*, *13*(7), 4020.

Khan, F. U., Zhang, J., Usman, M., Badulescu, A., & Sial, M. S. (2019). Ownership reduction in state-owned enterprises and corporate social responsibility: Perspective from secondary privatization in China. *Sustainability*, *11*, 1008.

Kong, D., Liu, S., & Dai, Y. (2014). Environmental policy, company environment protection, and stock market performance: Evidence from China. *Corporate Social Responsibility and Environmental Management*, *21*(2), 100–112.

Krueger, P., Sautner, Z., & Starks, L. T. (2020). The importance of climate risks for institutional investors. *The Review of Financial Studies*, *33*(3), 1067–1111.
Lam, B. M., Mo, P. L. L., & Rahman, M. J. (2024). Secrecy culture, client importance, and auditor reporting behavior: An international study. *Managerial Auditing Journal*, *39*(2), 113–137
Liu, S. (2020). Equity concentration and corporate social responsibility: Moderating effects based on executive incentive methods. *Green Accounting*, *2020*(10), 52–56.
Luo, D. (2022). ESG, liquidity, and stock returns. *Journal of International Financial Markets, Institutions and Money*, *78*, 101526.
Marquis, C., & Qian, C. (2014). Corporate social responsibility reporting in China: Symbol or substance? *Organization Science*, *25*(1), 127–148.
MSCI Inc. (2023). *ESG ratings: A benchmark for performance*. www.knowesg.com/featured-article/esg-ratings-a-benchmark-for-performance
Qian, K., Liang, X., & Liu, X. (2023). Managerial ability, managerial risk taking and innovation performance. *Finance Research Letters*, *57*, 104193.
Qin, C., Zhou, L., Hu, Z., Zhang, S., Yang, S., Tao, Y., Xie, C., Ma, K., Shang, K., Wang, W., & Tian, D. S. (2020). Dysregulation of immune response in patients with coronavirus 2019 (COVID-19) in Wuhan, China. *Clinical Infectious Diseases*, *71*(15), 762–768.
Qin, X., & Zhang, K. (2022). Research on optimizing the performance of mining listed companies: A multidimensional perspective based on the company's equity structure. *Accounting*, *2022*(8), 28–31
Rahman, J., & Wu, J. (2023). M&A activity and ESG performance: Evidence from China. *Managerial Finance*, *50*(1), 179–197.
Rahman, M. J., Wu, Q., & Zhu, H. (2024). Corporate social responsibility in times of social distancing: Evidence from China. *Business Ethics, the Environment & Responsibility*.
Rahman, M. J., & Zhu, H. (2024). Predicting financial distress using machine learning approaches: Evidence China. *Journal of Contemporary Accounting & Economics*, *20*(1), 100403.
Rahman, M. J., Zhu, H., & Chen, S. (2023). Does CSR reduce financial distress? Moderating effect of firm characteristics, auditor characteristics, and covid-19. *International Journal of Accounting & Information Management*, *31*(5), 756–784.
Rahman, M. J., Zhu, H., & Jiang, X. (2024). Family firms, client importance, and auditor reporting behavior: Evidence from China. *Meditari Accountancy Research*, *32*(2), 543–578.
Rahman, M. J., Zhu, H., & Yue, L. (2024). Does the adoption of artificial intelligence by audit firms and their clients affect audit quality and efficiency? Evidence from China. *Managerial Auditing Journal*, *39*(6), 668–699.
Rahman, M. J., Zhu, H., Zhang, Y., & Hossain, M. M. (2024). Effect of female representation in audit committees on non-audit fees: Evidence from China. *Meditari Accountancy Research*.
Ren, X., Zeng, G., & Zhao, Y. (2023). Digital finance and corporate ESG performance: Empirical evidence from listed companies in China. *Pacific-Basin Finance Journal*, *79*, 102019.
Shi, M. (2010). Empirical study on the impact of equity structure on corporate social responsibility. *Northern Economy*, *2010*(10), 13–15.
Sun, Q., Li, Y., & Hong, A. (2024). Integrating ESG into corporate strategy: Unveiling the moderating effect of digital transformation on green innovation through employee insights. *Systems*, *12*(5), 148.
Tang, H. (2022). The effect of ESG performance on corporate innovation in China: The mediating role of financial constraints and agency cost. *Sustainability*, *14*(7), 3769.
Tao, C., Chen, X., & Li, C. (2023). ESG rating, media attention, and audit fees. *Friends of Accounting*, *2023*.
Wei, R., & Wang, S. (2023). The impact of equity structure on financial performance of enterprises: A study based on the Monetary and Financial Services Industry. *Contemporary Economics*, *40*(5), 9.

Xie, J., Nozawa, W., Yagi, M., Fujii, H., & Managi, S. (2019). Do environmental, social, and governance activities improve corporate financial performance? *Business Strategy and the Environment*, *28*(2), 286–300.

Xu, X., & Liu, Z. (2023). ESG, cultural distance and corporate profitability: Evidence from Chinese multinationals. *Sustainability*, *15*(8), 6771.

Yang, J., & Shen, D. (2022). Environmental, social, and governance ratings and firm performance: Evidence from the Chinese stock market.

Yu, S., Pu, Y., Shi, L., Yu, H., & Huang, Y. (2023). Regional difference and dynamic evolution of development quality of power industry in China. *Chinese Journal of Population, Resources and Environment*, *21*(1), 1–12.

Zhang, X. (2022). Research on the impact of equity structure on the risk level and profitability of rural cooperative institutions. *Financial Regulation Research*, *2022*(3), 71–84. https://doi.org/10.3969/j.issn.2095-3291.2022.03.005

Zhang, Z., Jin, X., & Li, G. (2013). Empirical study on the intertemporal impact of the interaction between corporate social responsibility and financial performance. *Accounting Research*, *2013*(8), 32–39+96.

Zhang, Z., Wei, M., & Shi, C. (2022). IPO overraising and corporate growth: An empirical study based on the adjustment of equity structure. *Finance and Economics*, *2022*(7), 11–20.

Zhao, G., & Wei, S. (2021). Governance and corporate social responsibility of multiple major shareholders. *Economic and Management Review*, *37*(5), 150–160.

Zhu, H., & Rahman, M. J. (2024). Ex-ante expected changes in ESG and future stock returns based on machine learning. *The British Accounting Review*, 101457.

9 The Relationship between ESG Disclosure, Financial Reporting Quality, and Investment Efficiency

Md Jahidur Rahman, Tarek Rana, Hongtao Zhu, and Lingna Zhuge

1. Introduction

Environmental, social, and governance (ESG) dimensions serve as a crucial framework for evaluating corporate social responsibility (CSR) (Şeker & Şengür, 2021). From an environmental perspective, ESG investments focus on resource consumption, climate change, pollution emissions, and related issues. Socially, ESG considerations include employee relations, working conditions, and other pertinent social factors (Malik, 2015). Governance within ESG pertains to the structure of the board of directors, taxation policies, and other governance-related matters (Cheng et al., 2014). Collectively, ESG plays an instrumental role in assessing a company's commitment to social responsibility (Palazuelos et al., 2018). Companies must be cognizant of their ESG responsibilities while advancing economic objectives, thereby contributing to sustainable societal development, and reflecting their social value (Wang et al., 2022).

The increasing influx of foreign investment into Chinese companies has spurred heightened attention to ESG disclosure (Cheng et al., 2014). Since the early 21st century, China has progressively established an ESG regulatory framework to promote ESG disclosure among enterprises. Notably, in 2016, seven Chinese ministries and commissions introduced the "Guidance on Building a Green Financial System," explicitly supporting green investments and the development of green financial products (Wang et al., 2022). However, ESG development in China remains nascent, with a significant gap relative to international standards.

In recent years, ESG disclosure has garnered increased attention from companies, stakeholders, and investors alike. Financial regulators and rating agencies evaluate ESG performance based on company disclosures, aiding investors in making informed decisions (Ellili, 2022). Stakeholders' information needs have evolved beyond financial data, now demanding comprehensive reports on ESG impacts, which can influence stakeholder behaviour and build trust in corporate practices (Zhang et al., 2020; Fan & Wong, 2005). Consequently, accurate and transparent ESG disclosures are pivotal in earning stakeholders' trust and enhancing corporate reputation. Several studies in China also investigate the relationship between environmental accounting and firm performance

DOI: 10.4324/9781003488934-12

(Rahman & Wu, 2023; Rahman, Wu, et al., 2024; Rahman et al., 2023; Zhu & Rahman, 2024).

This study aims to explore the effects of ESG disclosure on investment efficiency, the influence of financial reporting quality (FRQ) on investment efficiency, and the interrelationships among ESG disclosure, FRQ, and investment efficiency within the context of Chinese A-share listed companies from 2018 to 2022. Specifically, the research seeks to address two primary questions: (1) what is the relationship between ESG disclosure and investment efficiency? (2) What is the relationship between FRQ and investment efficiency?

Several factors motivate this research. Firstly, while foreign companies have long practised ESG disclosure, leading to its recognition as a critical decision-making tool, ESG disclosure remains a relatively new concept in China. Studying ESG disclosure in China can enhance the understanding of the interplay among national ESG practices and motivate more companies to adopt and improve ESG disclosures (Zhang et al., 2020). Additionally, examining ESG reports can help companies implement emerging green and open development concepts, promoting sustainable economic and high-quality corporate development.

Previous studies have demonstrated a strong correlation between FRQ and investment efficiency, with higher FRQ leading to improved investment outcomes (Biddle et al., 2009; Xue, 2023). Financial quality reports are crucial for understanding investment projects, providing reliable information to decision-makers, and reducing investment risks (Martínez-Ferrero, 2014). Despite various studies on ESG and investment efficiency, there remains a lack of definitive conclusions, particularly within the Chinese context (Wang et al., 2022). This research addresses this gap by focusing on ESG disclosure and its impact on investment efficiency in China, providing valuable insights for future studies.

The study employs regression analysis on data from all A-share listed companies in China from 2018 to 2022, with ESG scores sourced from the Wind database. Two models, Dechow and Dichev's (DD; 2002) model and Kasznik's (KA; 1999) model, are used to calculate the FRQ variable, investigating the effects of ESG and FRQ on investment efficiency. The results indicate a positive correlation among FRQ, ESG disclosure, and investment efficiency, suggesting that high-quality ESG and FRQ disclosures enhance firms' investment efficiency (Martínez-Ferrero et al., 2015). These findings can help companies make better decisions, reduce investment risks, and maximize benefits, ultimately fostering long-term sustainable development (Sharma et al., 2020).

This study contributes to the existing literature in several ways. Firstly, it utilizes comprehensive data from all A-share listed companies in China, enhancing the study's accuracy and reliability. Secondly, it not only examines overall ESG disclosure but also disaggregates ESG into its ESG components, providing a nuanced analysis. Thirdly, it enriches the relatively sparse literature on ESG disclosure and investment efficiency in China. Lastly, it explores the role of FRQ in investment efficiency, offering valuable references for corporate decision-making.

The chapter is organized as follows: Section 2 presents the literature review and hypothesis development. Section 3 describes the research design. Section 4 discusses the empirical results. Section 5 concludes the study.

2. Literature Review and Hypothesis Development

Dhaliwal et al. (2012) conducted a comprehensive study examining the relationship between non-financial reporting and financial analysts' forecasts, utilizing data from firms in 31 countries. Their findings indicated that CSR reporting was not significantly associated with financial analysts' forecast bias. However, this relationship was notably significant in countries where CSR levels impacted the company's financial performance. The study further revealed that a higher level of non-financial information disclosure led to a reduction in the cost of equity capital and decreased information asymmetry and the cost of debt capital (Orens et al., 2010). These findings underscore the critical role of corporate transparency and disclosure for investors and stakeholders (Al-Hiyari et al., 2023).

Satisfying stakeholder needs and maximizing their interests are essential for securing long-term support for the company's operations (Al-Hiyari et al., 2023). Increased corporate transparency and disclosure allow investors to assess the risk and return of their investments, thereby enhancing investment efficiency (Fung, 2014) more accurately. Consequently, improving the transparency in non-financial information disclosure, bolstering insider trust, and enhancing the quality of financial reporting can collectively lead to improved investment efficiency (Sharma et al., 2020; Bushman & Smith, 2001). Building on these arguments, the following hypotheses are proposed:

H1: ESG disclosure is positively correlated with investment efficiency.

Prior research on the FRQ of US firms indicates a significant relationship between FRQ and investment efficiency, particularly among large firms. Higher quality financial reporting is associated with greater investment efficiency (Chen et al., 2011). Improved FRQ enables firms to increase their dividend payouts, effectively mitigating issues related to corporate dividend underpayments (Koo et al., 2017). Biddle and Hilary (2006) found that superior accounting information quality reduces information bias between internal managers and external suppliers, leading to more efficient investment decisions.

The quality of a company's financial reports also significantly impacts its overall performance. Enhanced FRQ leads to better future performance, as markets are more inclined to positively evaluate companies that provide transparent and reliable information for stakeholders and investors, thereby reducing information asymmetry (Martínez-Ferrero, 2014).

Moreover, Costello and Wittenberg-Moerman (2011) argued that FRQ influences the terms of debt contracts and that lower quality financial reporting results in stricter lending terms. Their findings also indicate that high-quality financial reports mitigate the problem of corporate over-investment. Additionally, short-term debt can enhance investment efficiency by reducing the likelihood of under-investment or over-investment (Gomariz & Ballesta, 2014). Biddle et al. (2009) observed that higher FRQ helps under-invested firms increase their investment levels while reducing over-investment in firms. Based on these insights, the following hypothesis is proposed:

H2: FRQ disclosure is positively correlated with investment efficiency.

3. Research Design and Methodology

3.1 Sample and Data

This study reviews the correlation between ESG disclosure and FRQ in A-share listed companies in China during 2018–2022. In 2016, China officially released a study on the ESG rating system of Chinese listed companies, and an increasing number of listed companies were found to voluntarily disclose ESG information (Wang et al., 2022). The data used are from the China Stock Market & Accounting Research (CSMAR) database. ESG scores and other related data are from the Wind and Bloomberg databases. Excluding financial institutions (Ullah et al., 2022) and companies for which data are not available, the sample consists of 5,207 companies from 19 industries. Four sets of variable data are used in this study, which contain ESG disclosure variables, FRQ variables, investment efficiency variables, and control variables. All the variables are presented in Table 9.1.

3.2 ESG Variables

ESG is a measure of the sustainability of business operations and the ability to create long-term value through three dimensions: environmental, social, and governance (Şeker & Şengür, 2021). This study provides ESG scores, along with separate environmental, social, and governance scores, and explores their impact on investment efficiency. These data were obtained from databases such as Refinitiv, Bloomberg, and Wind (Dorfleitner et al., 2015; El Ghoul et al., 2011). In calculating Wind's ESG score, the environmental and social scores account for 40%, respectively, and the governance score accounts for 20%. The composition of the Wind ESG system includes the assessment of management practices (total score of 7) and controversial events (total score of 3), and it is categorized into seven ratings of "AAA-CCC.". Companies with higher ESG scores have stronger profitability and are more likely to get investment opportunities from investors (Şeker & Şengür, 2021). More and more international brand parties are asking Chinese companies to participate in ESG disclosure, and they will only agree to cooperate when their ESG disclosure reports meet the requirements of international brand parties (Sharma et al., 2020). Therefore, good ESG disclosure reports can help companies gain more customer groups and promote cooperation among companies.

Table 9.1 Definition of Variables

Variable	*Sign*	*Definition*	*Reference*
ESG score	ESG	Environmental, social and governance information. ESG score calculated by Wind	Zhu and Rahman (2024)
Environment score	ES	Firms concerned with resource consumption, climate change, pollution emissions, and so on. ES score calculated by Wind	Zhu and Rahman (2024)
Social score	SS	Firms concerned with employee relations, working conditions, and so on. SS score calculated by Wind	Zhu and Rahman (2024)
Government score	GS	Firms concerned with the structure of the board of directors, taxation, and so on. GS score calculated by Wind	Zhu and Rahman (2024)
Financial resources	SLACK	Calculated by dividing cash by fixed assets	Rahman and Zhu (2024a, 2024b)
Corporation age	AGE	Age of the company	Rahman, Zhu, and Jiang (2024)
Corporation size	SIZE	Obtained from logarithm (total assets)	Lam et al. (2024)
Corporation performance	ROA	Obtained by dividing net income by total assets	Rahman and Chen (2023)
Financial leverage	LEV	Calculated by dividing total liabilities by total assets	Rahman, Zhu, and Yue (2024)
Asset tangibility	TANG	Calculated by dividing fixed assets by total assets	Rahman and Zhu (2024a, 2024b)
FRQ variable	FRQ-DD	Derived from the DD (2002) model of the absolute value of residuals multiplied by −1	Rahman and Zhu (2023)

3.3 *FRQ Variables*

In this study, FRQ is another variable that reflects the truthfulness and integrity of financial reports and enhances investors' understanding and knowledge of financial reports. According to Chen et al.'s (2011) previous research, FRQ variables are calculated using two models. The first one is the DD (2002) model, presented as FRQ-DD in the following section, which is derived from the DD (2002) model of the absolute value of residuals multiplied by −1. The DD model (2002) is given as

$$WCA_{i,t} = \beta_0 + \beta_1 CFO_{i,t-1} + \beta_2 CFO_{i,t} + \beta_3 CFO_{i,t+1} + \in_t \quad (1)$$

Here, *WCA* represents working capital accruals, which indicates the expected recognition of realized cash flows plus an adjustment for the estimation error term, and the accruals are negatively correlated with current cash flows, and the higher result shows the higher financial report quality.

The second one is based on Kasznik (1999), presented as FRQ-KA in the following section, where FRQ is obtained by multiplying the absolute value of the residuals of total accruals (TA) by −1.

$$TA_{I,t} = \beta_0 + \beta_1 \Delta Sales_{i,t} + \beta_2 PPE_{i,t} + \beta_3 \Delta CFO_{i,t-1} + \in_t \quad (2)$$

Here, *TA* stands for total accruals; $\Delta Sales$ represents change in sales; *PPE* is property, plant, and equipment; and ΔCFO stands for change in cash flow, and the higher result represents a higher FRQ.

3.4 Investment Efficiency

From a previous study by Zhong and Gao (2017), investment efficiency (INVEFF) is derived by subjecting the model of Biddle et al. (2009) to the absolute value of the residuals. A review of the previous (Biddle et al., 2009; Chen et al., 2011) literature reveals that we can use the numerical deviation between timing investment and expected investment as a functional model to estimate the efficiency of the investment. Inefficient investment includes over-investment and under-investment, while under-investment is the negative deviation of actual investment from expected investment (Chen et al., 2011). When the residuals are negative, it indicates that the firm is under-invested, and when the residuals are positive, it indicates that the firm is over-invested. The calculated absolute value is multiplied by −1. The higher the absolute value the better, and it indicates better investment efficiency. This model is used to test *H1* and *H2*. They argue that sales growth or sales decline has an impact on investment. Therefore, they added an NEG variable to this model.

$$INV_{i,t} = \beta_0 + \beta_1 NEG_{i.t-1} + \beta_2 GROWTH_{i,t-1} + \beta_3 NEG_{i,t-1} * GOWTH_{i,t-1} + \in_{I,t} \quad (3)$$

Here, *INV* is calculated by dividing investment expenses by the beginning value of the assets and multiplying by 100.

NEG is referred to as a dummy variable indicating negative sales growth when its value is 1, and it will take the value of 0 when sales growth is positive (Biddle et al., 2009).

GROWTH is calculated by dividing the difference between year-end sales and beginning-of- year sales by the beginning value of sales and multiplying by 100.

3.5 Control Variables

According to a previous study by Şeker & Şengür (2021) and Bates (2005), some variables may have an impact on FRQ. These include companies' financial resources (*SLACK*), leverage (*LEV*), asset tangibility (*TANG*), size (*SIZE*), age (*AGE*), and performance (*ROA*) (Ellili, 2022). Financial resources are divided into internal and external financial resources, which are the funds provided by the enterprise for the activities and investment projects they hold, financial resources that companies rely on to maintain their operations (Broadbent & Cullen, 2012), and it is calculated by dividing cash by fixed assets. Asset tangibility is the company's assets in physical form (Almeida & Campello, 2007) and is calculated by dividing fixed assets by total assets. Leverage is the company's use of borrowed funds to purchase assets and expand its business. It can also be used to measure the degree of risk resistance of a company (Long & Malitz, 1985) and is calculated by dividing total liabilities by total assets. Size is obtained from logarithm (total assets). Age is the age of the company, and ROA measures the efficiency of a company in generating profits from its assets. The higher the ROA, the more efficient the company's assets are (Jewell & Mankin, 2011), and this is obtained by dividing net income by total assets.

This study focuses on the correlation of ESG and FRQ with efficiency of investment. The following is the required model:

$$\begin{aligned} INVEFF_{i,t} &= \beta_0 + \beta_1 ESG_{i,t} + \beta_2 FRQ_{i,t-1} + \beta_3 SLACK_{i,t-1} + \beta_4 TANG_{i,t-1} \\ &+ \beta_5 LEV_{i,t-1} + \beta_6 SIZE_{i,t-1} + \beta_7 AGE_{i,t-1} + \beta_8 ROA_{i,t-1} \\ &+ Industry\ Dummies + \epsilon_{I,t} \end{aligned} \tag{4}$$

4. Empirical Results

4.1 Descriptive Statistics

The ESG disclosures, FRQ, efficiency of investment, and descriptive statistics of control variables are shown in Table 9.2. According to the table, it is known that the government disclosure has the highest score, and it has a mean of 7.1320. From 2019, the China Securities Regulatory Commission (CSRC) requires listed companies to disclose ESG information, and ESG is included in the disclosure rating. Next, the company's investment efficiency percentage is 5.18%, which shows that

Table 9.2 Descriptive Statistics for Variables

Variable	*Mean*	*Standard Deviation*	*Min*	*Max*
SLACK	0.1905	0.1392	0.0001	0.9779
TANG	0.1843	0.1497	0.0000	0.9542
LEV	0.4429	1.3589	0.0084	178.3455
SIZE	22.2656	1.5722	16.4123	31.3101
AGE	9.9276	8.8335	–4.0000	32.0000
ROA	0.0233	0.3617	–30.6882	7.4461
ESG	6.0427	0.8498	2.6600	9.0400
ES	1.4285	1.7383	0.0000	9.5600
SS	3.8933	1.6734	0.0000	9.2200
GS	7.1320	0.6696	2.8600	9.7000
INVEFF	0.0518	0.0415	0.0007	0.2133
FRQ1	1.5716	0.3628	0.0000	20.5982
FRQ2	1.0428	0.1529	0.0000	20.1472

Source: Created by author

the efficiency of investment of China's A-share listed companies is not high. The average value of the FRQ variable calculated by the two models, the DD (2002) and KA (1999) models, is 1.5716 and 1.0428, respectively. From the statistics, the slack level of sample companies is relatively high at 0.1905, asset tangibility is low at 0.1843, and leverage is relatively high at 0.4429. The level of ROA is 0.0233, which indicates that the profitability of the enterprises is low.

Table 9.3 shows the correlation coefficients between ESG, FRQ, and other control variables. From the table, it can be concluded that ESG disclosure is positively correlated with the second calculation criterion FRQ-KA, and ESG disclosure is negatively correlated with asset tangibility (TANG), implying that high-quality ESG disclosure decreases the firm's asset tangibility (TANG). However, ESG disclosure is positively correlated with performance (ROA), leverage (LEV), and the company's financial resources (SLACK), so high-quality ESG disclosure will increase the company's performance (ROA), leverage (LEV), and the company's financial resources (SLACK) accordingly. From these data, it can be found that ESG can discipline internal management and reduce agency costs, thus improving investment efficiency. Moreover, there is no multicollinearity problem because the correlation coefficients of other variables are not high.

4.2 Relationship among ESG Disclosure, FRQ, and Investment Disclosure

Models (1) and (2) investigate the effect of ESG disclosure and FRQ on investment efficiency using two different calculation methods, FRQ-DD and FRQ-KA, respectively. Models (3) and (4) investigate the effect of other control variables on efficiency of investment. Table 9.4 shows the results of the study.

Models (1) and (2) show that ESG disclosure and FRQ have a positive correlation with efficiency of investment. These research findings correspond with the results of Biddle et al. (2009) and Makosa et al. (2020), which confirms that high-quality ESG disclosure and FRQ are effective in increasing firms' efficiency of investment, decreases information bias between internal managers and outsiders and reduces agency costs, and helps investors make the right investment decisions. High-quality ESG and FRQ will increase the trust of insiders and other stakeholders, which will enhance investment efficiency.

The results of models (3) and (4) show that governance disclosure is positively correlated with corporate investment efficiency. The correlation between corporate environment and society and investment efficiency is not significant, and companies need to pay attention to governance disclosure to reduce the risk of over-investment and under-investment and improve firm efficiency of investment. The control variables that are positively correlated with investment efficiency are company performance (ROA), age, asset tangibility (TANG), and financial resources (SLACK), while the control variables that are negatively correlated with investment efficiency are leverage (LEV) and size. This means that the more asset tangibility (TANG) and financial resources (SLACK) a firm has and the higher the company performance (ROA), the higher the investment efficiency; however, the higher the leverage and the larger the size of a firm, the lower the investment efficiency.

Table 9.3 Pearson Correlation Coefficients

Variable	*ESG*	*ES*	*SS*	*GS*	*INVEFF*	*FRQ-DD*	*FRQ-KA*	*SLACK*	*TANG*	*LEV*	*SIZE*	*AGE*	*ROA*
ESG	1												
ES	4.2300*	1											
SS	1.5521*	0.3669*	1										
GS	0.8473*	0.2003*	0.5459*	1									
INVEFF	–0.0637	–0.0326	–0.0271	0.0219*	1								
FRQ-DD	3.8449	0.9090	2.4773	4.5380	0.0330	1							
FRQ-KA	5.7946*	1.3699	3.7335*	–6.8393	0.0497	1.5071	1						
SLACK	31.7197*	7.4987*	20.4369	37.4379	0.2719	8.2498	5.4740	1					
TANG	–32.7817*	–7.7498*	–21.1212*	38.6914	–0.2810	8.5260	5.6572	1.0335	1				
LEV	13.6449*	3.2257*	8.7914*	16.1047*	–0.1170	–3.5488	2.3547	0.4302	0.4162	1			
SIZE	0.2714*	0.0642*	0.1749*	0.3203*	0.0023	0.0706	0.0468	0.0086	0.0083	0.0199	1		

Source: Table created by the author

Notes: *denotes significance at the 5% level.

Table 9.4 Effect of ESG Disclosure and FRQ on Investment Efficiency

Variable	*1)*	*2)*	*3)*	*4)*
ESG	0.0692***(1.1549)	0.0835***(0.5721)		
ES			0.0053(0.1542)	0.0082(0.1830)
SS			0.0047(0.1862)	0.0071(0.1927)
GS			0.0072*(0.1962)	0.0065***(0.1760)
FRQ- DD	0.0019**(0.2790)		0.0087***(0.1621)	
FRQ- KA		0.0359*(0.1692)		0.0079*(0.4901)
SLACK	0.0531*(0.4028)	0.0882**(0.5903)	0.0570**(0.4017)	0.0392***(0.3805)
TANG	0.1596***(0.1200)	0.3701***(0.1831)	0.3951***(0.2921)	0.5296***(0.3771)
LEV	–0.7815***(–0.2869)	–0.8203***(–0.1960)	–0.8507**(–0.1068)	–0.7092***(–0.1029)
SIZE	–0.0969***(–0.1692)	–0.0614***(–0.0528)	–0.1591**(–0.0468)	–0.1884***(–0.0372)
AGE	0.0059**(0.2907)	0.0039*(0.2866)	0.0062***(0.3851)	0.0053**(0.2830)
ROA	0.0196***(0.5264)	0.0268*(0.8629)	0.0187***(0.7620)	0.0396*(0.6341)
Industry dummies	Yes	Yes	Yes	Yes
Prob> *F*	0.0001	0.0001	0.0005	0.0002

Notes

* denotes significant at the 10% level.
** denotes significant at the 5% level.
*** denotes significant at the 1% level.Source: Created by the author

5. Discussion

5.1 Relationship with Prior Studies

Previous studies have shown many different findings regarding the relationship between the level of profitability and information disclosure of firms (Mallin, 2013; Taliento et al., 2019). The study by Galani et al. (2012) showed that there is little relationship between profitability of the companies and information disclosure. However, the study by Sharma et al. (2020) showed that there is a strong relationship between the level of profitability and information disclosure of firms. Moreover, stakeholder trust is crucial for a firm (Liu et al., 2021). ESG disclosure can enhance stakeholders' trust and gain their support to maximize stakeholders' interests, which can help the company obtain more capital and attract more investors, thus improving investment efficiency and enabling the company to operate in the long run (Liu et al., 2021).

Review of prior literature revealed that corporate ESG disclosure can enhance investment efficiency in three ways (Matten & Moon, 2008). Firstly, public disclosure of financial information of listed firms can alleviate the agency problem between internal managers and external investors and reduce the information bias between them (Ellili, 2022), and it also makes an important contribution to the economic performance of the firm, thus providing more investors with investment opportunities and enhancing the investment efficiency of the firm, and obtaining more capital gains (Bushman & Smith, 2001). Secondly, voluntary disclosure of non-financial information by firms provides more information to investors, and the more foreign investors that firms have, the more information they disclose (Sharma et al., 2020), and good reporting of non-financial information enables investors to make better choices, and investors' investment risk is thus reduced, thus improving investment efficiency (Cheynel, 2013). Thirdly, companies with high-quality non-financial information can reduce the impact of information bias on investment efficiency (Herath & Albarqi, 2017), and high transparency of corporate disclosure enables managers to make the right investment decisions and improve investment efficiency (Samet & Jarboui, 2017; Matten & Moon, 2008). Therefore, ESG disclosure of firms is positively correlated with investment efficiency.

FRQ is a financial statement that reflects the accurate financial position of a company and provides fair and unbiased financial information to external investors (Herath & Albarqi, 2017; Bushman et al., 2004). High-quality financial reports reduce conflicts between corporate managers and external investors as well as reduce information bias and help better management of corporate activities (Hope & Thomas, 2008; Bushman & Smith, 2001). In addition, the credibility of financial reporting reduces the information bias of companies, makes managers more accountable for the quality of corporate financial reporting, and provides investors with truly valuable and transparent accounting data about the company that helps them make scientific investment decisions (Bushman & Smith, 2001).

The connection between FRQ and firms' investment efficiency can be tested in two ways. According to Verdi (2006), firms' investment efficiency is related to firms' over-investment and under-investment and is negatively correlated. Leuz & Verrecchia (2000) argued that an increase in the level of information disclosure of the company reduces the information inequality between internal and external potential buyers or sellers of the company, managers are not able to change the sale price of shares at will (Shahzad et al., 2019), and shares are sold at a fair price (Myers & Majluf, 1984). Thus, high-quality FRQs enhance the efficiency of firms' investments by reducing moral hazard (Shahzad et al., 2019). Secondly, there is a positive relationship between FRQ and the measurement of executive compensation, which is designed based on profitability criteria, and it has become an important tool for shareholders of the firm to regulate the managers of the firm (Li & Wang, 2010; Martínez-Ferrero et al., 2015). Thus, firms are able to control managers through financial information in compensation contracts (Ellili, 2022).

5.2 Theoretical Implications

The results of this study support the stakeholder theory that corporate disclosure of ESG and FRQ provides reliable information to stakeholders and satisfies stakeholders' needs for financial and non-financial information within the company, rather than just maximizing shareholders' interests (Wijnberg, 2000), which is consistent with the stakeholder theory. Firms put stakeholders' interests in the first place and gain their trust and support so that they can cooperate with the firm in the long run (Wijnberg, 2000), which leads to long-term development and further improves the efficiency of the firm's investment.

The research results also support the legitimacy theory. By voluntarily disclosing ESG information and FRQ, the company can let more people inside and outside the company know about its business activities and show the public and stakeholders that the company's development is consistent with its social values, thus maintaining and increasing the legitimacy of the company (Gray et al., 1988). As a result, the company can grow in the long term, gain more recognition and support from stakeholders and external investors, and improve the efficiency of the company's investment.

5.3 Practical Implications

This study provides insights for corporate stakeholders and external investors. The results show that, firstly, a more detailed ESG disclosure of a company will enhance the investment efficiency of the company. In addition, the improvement of FRQ also enhances the investment efficiency of a firm, and their three relationships are positively correlated.

Firstly, for a company to improve ESG performance, they need to improve their environmental, social, and corporate governance performance, which also requires companies to have a deeper knowledge of the environment, interconnect their development with green development and sustainable development (Liu et al., 2021), and take the protection of environment and resources as the basis of their development. Secondly, companies need to pay attention to social issues, and their development should be in line with social values and conform to social norms. Companies also need to meet the needs and expectations of their stakeholders and fulfil their obligations (Ellili, 2022). The long-term development of enterprises cannot be achieved without the help and support of stakeholders. ESG disclosure enhances the transparency of enterprises, reduces the illegitimacy of companies (Hai et al., 2022), strengthens the trust of internal and external personnel, and improves the efficiency of enterprises' investment.

Secondly, high-quality financial reporting can reduce the information bias between internal managers and external investors, and if the accounting data of enterprises are more transparent, it can reduce agency costs and can also help better supervise the managers of the enterprises, prompting them to better perform their duties and be responsible for the company (Biddle et al., 2009). FRQ can also reduce the risk of financial loss caused by over-investment and under-investment of enterprises.

6. Conclusion

This study used a research sample of all A-share listed companies in China for the period 2018–2022. The relationship among ESG disclosure, FRQ, and investment efficiency of firms was examined using empirical data. The results of the study show that, firstly, the high-quality ESG disclosure of firms is positively correlated with investment efficiency, and the more data on ESG disclosure, the higher the investment efficiency of firms. Secondly, we not only studied the overall ESG disclosure but also split it into three parts: environmental disclosure, social disclosure, and corporate governance disclosure, and found that investment efficiency increases with higher governance disclosure. Therefore, governance disclosure is the most important part of ESG disclosure, and companies should pay more attention to their governance disclosure, and thus improve overall ESG performance (Zeng et al., 2019). Thirdly, the control variables of the firm show that the variable that affects corporate investment efficiency is corporate performance, which means when corporate performance increases, the investment efficiency will also increase; the second is asset tangibility, which indicates that corporate investment efficiency increases with the increase in asset tangibility; and the third variable is financial is financial resources, wherein the higher the financial resources of the company, the higher the investment efficiency of the company. On the other hand, high-quality ESG disclosure and FRQ can reduce the information difference between internal managers and outsiders and make the company's data and information more transparent to the outside world, which can attract more investors and long-term support from stakeholders, thus improving investment efficiency.

This study contributes to the current literature on ESG in China. Firstly, while most of the existing literature on ESG is focused on foreign listed companies and unilaterally considers the impact of only one factor (Castelló-Taliani et al., 2021; Bostian et al., 2016), ESG, on investment efficiency, this study subdivides ESG into three additional components and investigates the impact of each component on corporate investment efficiency, which can provide a new perspective for companies to think about how to improve investment efficiency and enable them to readjust and improve their internal disclosure information to maintain the long-term operation of the firm.

Secondly, this study combines ESG disclosure, FRQ, and investment efficiency, so that companies can break away from the traditional concept of information disclosure, which emphasizes the company's profitability and cash flow (Herath & Albarqi, 2017), and use a disclosure report that combines financial and non-financial information to analyse the company's operations and possible risks (Şeker & Şengür, 2021) more comprehensively. This is used to determine whether the company is able to achieve its sustainability goals and whether it is worth investing in the long term. The results show that the relationship among ESG disclosure, FRQ, and investment efficiency is positively correlated, which provides a new understanding of the literature related to ESG, FRQ, and investment efficiency.

Since the Chinese market is not mature enough for ESG disclosure and is still in the developing stage, it will face many challenges. Firstly, the proportion of ESG disclosure varies among different types of companies. ESG disclosure in China does not cover all enterprises, with a higher proportion of ESG disclosure in the financial sector and energy-intensive enterprises (Li et al., 2023), and the data collection systems of other enterprises are not consistent and comprehensive enough. Secondly, data from financial and non-financial departments need to be linked and harmonized to make the data more complete and more systematic (Cui, 2022). Thirdly, the data disclosure reports of many Chinese companies are not standardized enough to meet international rating standards, and companies have different disclosure standards for the same subject matter, making it impossible to compare data between different companies (Li et al., 2023).

There is still much room for improvement in ESG disclosure by Chinese companies. Firstly, enterprises of all types and sizes should actively participate in ESG disclosure, make ESG disclosure a part of corporate culture and development, carry out more public welfare activities, establish good awareness and image of sustainable development, improve the company's reputation, attract more investors, get the support of stakeholders, and promote the long-term development of the enterprise economy. Secondly, the government should establish a unified ESG disclosure system and propose more specific indicators for enterprises to refer to, enrich the content of ESG disclosure reports, effectively improve the quality of ESG reports, show the unique competitive advantages of enterprises, and make correct financial decisions. The government should impose severe penalties on those enterprises that make false ESG disclosure. Thirdly, companies should consider not only financial information reports but also non-financial information reports when making investment decisions and include environmental, social, and corporate governance into the consideration of investment decisions, so as to break the traditional reference content of investment decisions and achieve scientific investment decisions.

There are limitations in this study. Firstly, our study sample includes only all A-share listed companies in China, which does not cover all Chinese companies and is limited to only one country. In future studies, the study sample should be expanded to include more countries. Secondly, since ESG disclosure reports in China are still in the development stage, there is no unified rating and scoring standard, so the collected data are imperfect and lack comparability. In the future, China's ESG disclosure system will become more and more perfect, more and more companies will join the ranks of ESG disclosure, and future research on ESG disclosure in China will become more informative. In addition, there are more factors affecting the investment efficiency of companies besides ESG and FRQ disclosure, which can be studied in the future, and companies will continue to develop in new directions.

References

Al-Hiyari, A., Ismail, A. I., Kolsi, M. C., & Kehinde, O. H. (2023). Environmental, social and governance performance (ESG) and firm investment efficiency in emerging markets: The interaction effect of board cultural diversity. *Corporate Governance: The International Journal of Business in Society*, *23*(3), 650–673.

Almeida, H., & Campello, M. (2007). Financial constraints, asset tangibility, and corporate investment. *The Review of Financial Studies*, *20*(5), 1429–1460.

Bates, T. W. (2005). Asset sales, investment opportunities, and the use of proceeds. *The Journal of Finance*, *60*(1), 105–135.

Biddle, G. C., & Hilary, G. (2006). Accounting quality and firm-level capital investment. *The Accounting Review*, *81*(5), 963–982.

Biddle, G. C., Hilary, G., & Verdi, R. S. (2009). How does financial reporting quality relate to investment efficiency? *Journal of Accounting and Economics*, *48*(2–3), 112–131.

Bostian, M., Färe, R., Grosskopf, S., & Lundgren, T. (2016). Environmental investment and firm performance: A network approach. *Energy Economics*, *57*, 243–255.

Broadbent, M., & Cullen, J. (2012). *Managing financial resources*. Routledge.

Bushman, R., Chen, Q., Engel, E., & Smith, A. (2004). Financial accounting information, organizational complexity and corporate governance systems. *Journal of Accounting and Economics*, *37*(2), 167–201.

Bushman, R. M., & Smith, A. J. (2001). Financial accounting information and corporate governance. *Journal of Accounting and Economics*, *32*(1–3), 237–333.

Castelló-Taliani, E., Giralt Escobar, S., & da Rosa, F. S. (2021). Environmental disclosure: Study on efficiency and alignment with environmental priorities of Spanish ports. *Sustainability*, *13*(4), 1791.

Chen, F., Hope, O. K., Li, Q., & Wang, X. (2011). Financial reporting quality and investment efficiency of private firms in emerging markets. *The Accounting Review*, *86*(4), 1255–1288.

Cheng, B., Ioannou, I., & Serafeim, G. (2014). Corporate social responsibility and access to finance. *Strategic Management Journal*, *35*(1), 1–23.

Cheynel, E. (2013). A theory of voluntary disclosure and cost of capital. *Review of Accounting Studies*, *18*, 987–1020.

Costello, A. M., & Wittenberg-Moerman*, R. E. G. I. N. A. (2011). The impact of financial reporting quality on debt contracting: Evidence from internal control weakness reports. *Journal of Accounting Research*, *49*(1), 97–136.

Cui, C. (2022, December). Status, challenges and strategic direction of the ESG development in China. In *2022 international conference on economics, smart finance and contemporary trade (ESFCT 2022)* (pp. 96–104). Atlantis Press.

Dechow, P. M., & Dichev, I. D. (2002). The quality of accruals and earnings: The role of accrual estimation errors. *The Accounting Review*, *77*(s–1), 35–59.

Dhaliwal, D. S., Radhakrishnan, S., Tsang, A., & Yang, Y. G. (2012). Nonfinancial disclosure and analyst forecast accuracy: International evidence on corporate social responsibility disclosure. *The Accounting Review*, *87*(3), 723–759.

Dorfleitner, G., Halbritter, G., & Nguyen, M. (2015). Measuring the level and risk of corporate responsibility – An empirical comparison of different ESG rating approaches. *Journal of Asset Management*, *16*, 450–466.

El Ghoul, S., Guedhami, O., Kwok, C. C., & Mishra, D. R. (2011). Does corporate social responsibility affect the cost of capital? *Journal of Banking & Finance*, *35*(9), 2388–2406.

Ellili, N. O. D. (2022). Impact of ESG disclosure and financial reporting quality on investment efficiency. *Corporate Governance: The International Journal of Business in Society*, *22*(5), 1094–1111.

Fan, J. P., & Wong, T. J. (2005). Do external auditors perform a corporate governance role in emerging markets? Evidence from East Asia. *Journal of Accounting Research*, *43*(1), 35–72.

Fung, B. (2014). The demand and need for transparency and disclosure in corporate governance. *Universal Journal of Management*, *2*(2), 72–80.

Galani, D., Gravas, E., & Stavropoulos, A. (2012). Company characteristics and environmental policy. *Business Strategy and the Environment*, *21*(4), 236–247.

Gomariz, M. F. C., & Ballesta, J. P. S. (2014). Financial reporting quality, debt maturity and investment efficiency. *Journal of Banking & Finance*, *40*, 494–506.

Gray, R., Owen, D., & Maunders, K. (1988). Corporate social reporting: Emerging trends in accountability and the social contract. *Accounting, Auditing & Accountability Journal*, *1*(1), 6–20.

Hai, M., Fang, Z., & Li, Z. (2022). Does business group's conscious of social responsibility enhance its investment efficiency? Evidence from ESG disclosure of China's listed companies. *Sustainability*, *14*(8), 4817.

Herath, S. K., & Albarqi, N. (2017). Financial reporting quality: A literature review. *International Journal of Business Management and Commerce*, *2*(2), 1–14.

Hope, O. K., & Thomas, W. B. (2008). Managerial empire building and firm disclosure. *Journal of Accounting Research*, *46*(3), 591–626.

Jewell, J. J., & Mankin, J. A. (2011). What is your ROA? An investigation of the many formulas for calculating return on assets. *Academy of Educational Leadership Journal*, *15*, 79–91.

Kasznik, R. (1999). On the association between voluntary disclosure and earnings management. *Journal of Accounting Research*, *37*(1), 57–81.

Koo, D. S., Ramalingegowda, S., & Yu, Y. (2017). The effect of financial reporting quality on corporate dividend policy. *Review of Accounting Studies*, *22*, 753–790.

Lam, B. M., Mo, P. L. L., & Rahman, M. J. (2024). Secrecy culture, client importance, and auditor reporting behavior: An international study. *Managerial Auditing Journal*, *39*(2), 113–137.

Leuz, C., & Verrecchia, R. E. (2000). The economic consequences of increased disclosure. *Journal of Accounting Research*, 91–124.

Li, H., & Li, D. (2023). ESG investment in China: Current situation and future prospects. *World Scientific Research Journal*, *9*(4), 17–21.

Li, Q., & Wang, T. (2010). Financial reporting quality and corporate investment efficiency: Chinese experience. *Nankai Business Review International*, *1*(2), 197–213.

Liu, Z., Li, W., Hao, C., & Liu, H. (2021). Corporate environmental performance and financing constraints: An empirical study in the Chinese context. *Corporate Social Responsibility and Environmental Management*, *28*(2), 616–629.

Long, M. S., & Malitz, I. B. (1985). Investment patterns and financial leverage. In *Corporate capital structures in the United States* (pp. 325–352). University of Chicago Press.

Makosa, L., Yang, J., Sitsha, L., & Jachi, M. (2020). Mandatory CSR disclosure and firm investment behavior: Evidence from a quasi-natural experiment in China. *Journal of Corporate Accounting & Finance*, *31*(4), 33–47.

Malik, M. (2015). Value-enhancing capabilities of CSR: A brief review of contemporary literature. *Journal of Business Ethics*, *127*, 419–438

Mallin, C. (2013). International journal of disclosure and governance. *International Journal of Disclosure and Governance*, *10*, 193–194.

Martínez-Ferrero, J. (2014). Consequences of financial reporting quality on corporate performance: Evidence at the international level. *Estudios de economía*, *41*(1), 49–88.
Martínez-Ferrero, J., Garcia-Sanchez, I. M., & Cuadrado-Ballesteros, B. (2015). Effect of financial reporting quality on sustainability information disclosure. *Corporate Social Responsibility and Environmental Management*, *22*(1), 45–64.
Matten, D., & Moon, J. (2008). "Implicit" and "explicit" CSR: A conceptual framework for a comparative understanding of corporate social responsibility. *Academy of Management Review*, *33*(2), 404–424.
Myers, S. C., & Majluf, N. S. (1984). Corporate financing and investment decisions when firms have information that investors do not have. *Journal of Financial Economics*, *13*(2), 187–221.
Orens, R., Aerts, W., & Cormier, D. (2010). Web-based non-financial disclosure and cost of finance. *Journal of Business Finance & Accounting*, *37*(9–10), 1057–1093.
Palazuelos, E., Crespo, Á. H., & del Corte, J. M. (2018). Accounting information quality and trust as determinants of credit granting to SMEs: The role of external audit. *Small Business Economics*, *51*, 861–877.
Rahman, J., & Wu, J. (2023). M&A activity and ESG performance: Evidence from China. *Managerial Finance*, *50*(1), 179–197.
Rahman, M. J., & Chen, X. (2023). CEO characteristics and firm performance: Evidence from private listed firms in China. *Corporate Governance: The International Journal of Business in Society*, *23*(3), 458–477
Rahman, M. J., Wu, Q., & Zhu, H. (2024). Corporate social responsibility in times of social distancing: Evidence from China. *Business Ethics, the Environment & Responsibility*.
Rahman, M. J., & Zhu, H. (2023). Predicting accounting fraud using imbalanced ensemble learning classifiers – evidence from China. *Accounting & Finance*, *63*(3), 3455–3486.
Rahman, M. J., & Zhu, H. (2024a). Detecting accounting fraud in family firms: Evidence from machine learning approaches. *Advances in Accounting*, *64*, 100722.
Rahman, M. J., & Zhu, H. (2024b). Predicting financial distress using machine learning approaches: Evidence China. *Journal of Contemporary Accounting & Economics*, *20*(1), 100403
Rahman, M. J., Zhu, H., & Chen, S. (2023). Does CSR reduce financial distress? Moderating effect of firm characteristics, auditor characteristics, and covid-19. *International Journal of Accounting & Information Management*, *31*(5), 756–784.
Rahman, M. J., Zhu, H., & Jiang, X. (2024). Family firms, client importance, and auditor reporting behavior: Evidence from China. *Meditari Accountancy Research*, *32*(2), 543–578.
Rahman, M. J., Zhu, H., & Yue, L. (2024). Does the adoption of artificial intelligence by audit firms and their clients affect audit quality and efficiency? Evidence from China. *Managerial Auditing Journal*, *39*(6), 668–699.
Samet, M., & Jarboui, A. (2017). How does corporate social responsibility contribute to investment efficiency? *Journal of Multinational Financial Management*, *40*, 33–46.
Şeker, Y., & Şengür, E. D. (2021). The impact of environmental, social, and governance (ESG) performance on financial reporting quality: International evidence. *Ekonomika*, *100*(2), 190–212.
Shahzad, F., Rehman, I. U., Hanif, W., Asim, G. A., & Baig, M. H. (2019). The influence of financial reporting quality and audit quality on investment efficiency: Evidence from Pakistan. *International Journal of Accounting & Information Management*, *27*(4), 600–614.
Sharma, P., Panday, P., & Dangwal, R. C. (2020). Determinants of environmental, social and corporate governance (ESG) disclosure: A study of Indian companies. *International Journal of Disclosure and Governance*, *17*, 208–217.
Taliento, M., Favino, C., & Netti, A. (2019). Impact of environmental, social, and governance information on economic performance: Evidence of a corporate 'sustainability advantage' from Europe. *Sustainability*, *11*(6), 1738.
Ullah, I., Zhao, Q., Zeb, A., Iqbal, A., & Khan, M. A. (2022). Board diversity and financial reporting quality: Evidence from China. *Economic Research-Ekonomska Istraživanja*, 1–19.

Verdi, R. S. (2006). Information Environment and the Cost of Equity Capital (July 7, 2005). Available at SSRN: https://ssrn.com/abstract=757966 or http://dx.doi.org/10.2139/ssrn.7579660

Wang, W., Yu, Y., & Li, X. (2022). ESG performance, auditing quality, and investment efficiency: Empirical evidence from China. *Frontiers in Psychology*, *13*, 948674.

Wijnberg, N. M. (2000). Normative stakeholder theory and Aristotle: The link between ethics and politics. *Journal of Business Ethics*, *25*, 329–342.

Xue, H. (2023). ESG disclosure, market forces, and investment efficiency. *Available at SSRN 4344253.*

Zeng, S., Qin, Y., & Zeng, G. (2019). Impact of corporate environmental responsibility on investment efficiency: The moderating roles of the institutional environment and consumer environmental awareness. *Sustainability*, *11*(17), 4512.

Zhang, Q., Loh, L., & Wu, W. (2020). How do environmental, social and governance initiatives affect innovative performance for corporate sustainability? *Sustainability*, *12*(8), 3380.

Zhong, M., & Gao, L. (2017). Does corporate social responsibility disclosure improve firm investment efficiency? Evidence from China. *Review of Accounting and Finance*, *16*(3), 348–365.

Zhu, H., & Rahman, M. J. (2024). Ex-ante expected changes in ESG and future stock returns based on machine learning. *The British Accounting Review*, 101457.

10 ESG, Financial Constraints, and Family Firm Performance

Md Jahidur Rahman, Tarek Rana, Hongtao Zhu, and Binqing Lu

1. Introduction

Globalization and economic advancement owe significantly to the contributions of family enterprises. The world's largest 500 family-owned businesses, particularly in the United States and China, generated $7.28 trillion in sales in 2021 (Espinosa-Méndez et al., 2023). This study investigates the relationship among environmental, social, and governance (ESG) factors, financial constraints, and the overall performance of Chinese family-owned businesses. The research objectives are to determine (1) whether family-owned firms experience greater performance gains from ESG adoption compared to their non-family counterparts, and (2) the extent of this effect. Additionally, this study explores (3) the impact of differing philosophies between founders and second-generation members on the success of family enterprises, and (4) the evolution and significance of ESG in Chinese family businesses over time. The primary variables under examination include ESG factors, firm size, growth potential, operational capability, and temporal aspects, all in relation to their positive association with the success of Chinese family firms.

There are several compelling reasons to pursue this research. Family businesses play a crucial role in the contemporary economy, comprising 85.4% of China's private sector, generating 75% of new jobs, and contributing over 50% of GDP (Kong, 2023). The strong connections between family businesses and their local communities and governments imply that the ESG performance of family enterprises has significant implications for their surrounding environment. Berrone et al. (2010) posited that family-owned firms are better equipped to balance the interests of diverse stakeholders. Moreover, Kotlar and de Massis (2013) contended that the ESG performance and related ethical behaviours of family businesses are influenced by a combination of economic and non-economic objectives, distinguishing them from non-family enterprises. These findings present conflicting perspectives on the relationship between family enterprises and ESG factors, thus necessitating empirical investigation. Several studies in China also investigate the relationship between environmental accounting and firm performance (Rahman & Wu, 2023; Rahman, Wu, et al., 2024; Rahman et al., 2023; Zhu & Rahman, 2024).

ESG research has emerged as a prominent area of study, particularly regarding the impact of ESG performance on firm value (Hoepner et al., 2020; Martin &

DOI: 10.4324/9781003488934-13

Moser, 2016; Pekovic et al., 2018). Several studies have explored the effects of ESG performance at the environmental, social responsibility, and corporate governance levels (Albuquerque et al., 2019; Mishra & Modi, 2013). Most recent works have concentrated on the influence of ESG's three dimensions on firms. In examining the effect of ESG on family enterprises, this research adjusts for variations in firm size, growth and operational capabilities, and time. Notably, the adoption of ESG principles in China initially lagged but has since accelerated. The number of listed Chinese firms disclosing ESG data (Luo et al., 2023) and those focusing on ESG quality is increasing annually. Moreover, there is a paucity of research investigating the impact of ESG performance on debt financing costs. This study seeks to address whether strong ESG performance in family firms leads to more favourable loan conditions from financial institutions, as this is a critical concern for family businesses. Consequently, this research will examine the effects of ESG performance on liquidity challenges within family enterprises.

Additionally, this study explores the influence of ESG mediating mechanisms on the financing constraints and performance of family-owned businesses. To examine the impact of ESG on family firms, we propose investigating the mediation effect. Zhuo et al. (2022) introduced a novel intermediary variable – financial performance – to better understand the influence of ESG performance on the market value of publicly traded firms. Given that financial constraints pose a significant challenge for family businesses and substantially affect their growth and operations, this study employs financing constraints as a proxy for family business success.

Tobin's Q is the primary focus of this research due to its ability to detect shifts in family business performance caused by ESG. It is widely regarded as a reliable indicator of a company's future profitability and worth. This study empirically investigates questions about China's economy and society from 2012 to 2021. The dependent variable comprises an environmental indicator (*E*), a social index (*S*), and a governance index (*G*). Our findings reveal strong associations between Tobin's Q and four environmental, social, and governance factors. We employed a two-stage least squares (2SLS) model with regression using the generalized method of moments (GMM) technique, mediation analysis, and fixed-effect models to address the issue of endogeneity in the selection of family enterprises. The research indicates that ESG has a favourable relationship with company success and a negative relationship with financial constraints faced by family-owned businesses.

This research makes significant contributions to both theory and practice. It advances the literature on ESG and auditing by analysing how ESG affects family businesses. The increasing global focus on ESG practices, spurred by the COVID-19 pandemic and government publications, underscores the relevance of this study. By focusing on family companies, this research addresses a gap in the literature, demonstrating that ESG performance can alleviate financial burdens on family businesses, leading to enhanced performance. These results provide new metrics for creditors to use in evaluating corporations and encourage businesses to develop more ESG-compliant practices.

The findings also suggest that the involvement of second-generation children is linked to the influence of ESG on firms, broadening the literature on the operations and performance of family enterprises. Professionals working in family enterprises and similar organizations will find these data valuable. This study further indicates that ESG has a more pronounced effect on family businesses compared to non-family businesses, demonstrating that family businesses have distinct structures and objectives.

Theoretical and practical questions are raised by this research. Our findings offer a theoretical basis for modelling the impact of ESG on businesses using fixed effects and mediation effects. The stability and endogeneity test outcomes were positively correlated. The study's findings on funding limitations in family enterprises have important policy implications. We also demonstrate that the second generation of a family significantly impacts the ESG performance of a company.

The chapter is structured as follows: the subsequent section provides the historical context for the study of ESG institutions and Chinese family businesses. Section 3 outlines the theoretical stances on ESG performance of family firms. The hypotheses are presented in Section 4. Section 5 describes our methodology and dataset. Section 6 presents the results of the primary tests. Sections 7 and 8 cover the endogeneity and robustness tests, respectively. The findings are discussed in Section 9, with the conclusion in Section 10.

2. Background

2.1 ESG Institutional Setting in China (2012–2021)

The concept of ESG emerged from the broader framework of socially responsible investing (SRI), which has its origins in the 1960s. In the aftermath of World War II, as the industrial economies of Europe and the United States experienced rapid growth, a host of environmental and social issues surfaced, leading to the development of ESG principles (Ge et al., 2022). With the swift expansion of China's economy in recent years, the Chinese government has increasingly prioritized the establishment and enhancement of ESG frameworks. China's current ESG rating system is progressively aligning with international standards, aiming to "promote the transformation of the quality, efficiency, and driving force of economic development, and improve the total factor productivity," as articulated in the report of the 19th National Congress of the Communist Party of China (Ge et al., 2022).

Despite these efforts, there remain significant challenges in integrating China's ESG rating system with global norms, primarily due to philosophical and cultural differences, particularly in the context of family enterprises (Tan & Zhu, 2022). In response to these challenges, SynTao Green Finance, an independent Chinese agency, introduced the nation's first ESG ratings in 2015 (SynTao Green Finance & UK PACT, 2019). The Chinese government's commitment to ESG was further underscored by the introduction of the "dual-carbon" strategy in September 2020, aimed at achieving carbon neutrality and carbon peaking. This strategy highlights the centrality of ESG considerations in China's future economic development (Ge et al., 2022).

The institutional setting for ESG in China has thus evolved significantly over the past decade. The government's proactive stance, combined with increasing alignment with international standards and the establishment of independent rating agencies, marks a notable progression in the country's approach to ESG. This evolving landscape provides a crucial context for understanding the dynamics of ESG adoption and its impact on family-owned businesses in China.

2.2 Family Firms in China

Since the 1992 reform of China's economic system, which marked the transition from a planned economy to a socialist market economy, Chinese family companies have experienced significant growth (Cheng, 2014). These family-owned enterprises have a profound impact on their local communities and are becoming prominent players in the country's capital market. However, Chinese family businesses face challenges related to succession and the broader economic environment, which in turn affect their ESG performance and overall viability (Tang et al., 2022).

One of the critical challenges for Chinese family firms is succession. Given the one-child policy that was in effect from 1980 to 2015, there is typically only one potential successor to take over the family business (Cao et al., 2015). This limitation complicates the succession process and often results in the sale of family enterprises upon the passing of the first generation of owners (Bennedsen et al., 2015; Tang, 2022). However, the recent changes in China's birth policy may influence the dynamics of business succession in the future.

The economic environment in China also presents significant hurdles for family-owned enterprises. The country's evolving ESG rating system, which still grapples with standardization issues, further complicates the sustainable development of these firms. Despite these challenges, there have been efforts to standardize ESG practices. The 2015 publication of the "Environmental, Social, and Governance Reporting Guidelines" and the 2018 revision of the "Listed Company Governance Guidelines" by relevant Chinese government departments and regulatory agencies represent significant steps towards improved ESG supervision for Chinese family businesses (Ge et al., 2022).

These developments indicate that while Chinese family firms have shown resilience and growth, they must navigate complex succession issues and a challenging economic environment. Additionally, the evolving regulatory landscape surrounding ESG practices will continue to shape the future of these enterprises. As China enhances its ESG frameworks to align more closely with international standards, the impact on family-owned businesses will be a crucial area of focus for both researchers and practitioners.

3. Theoretical Perspectives on ESG Performance and Financial Constraints

Most prior research on the subject of family businesses' social responsibility has either concentrated on the correlation between corporate social responsibility (CSR) and family engagement or the effect of CSR on family firm (FF) performance (Mariani et al., 2021). However, as the capital market has evolved, the basic CSR idea has become inadequate; creditors and stakeholders now want more in-depth approaches to assessing businesses. This study analyses the financial limitations of family businesses via the lens of ESG. Managers of family firms have an edge in the information department as compared to creditors. Managers and creditors suffer from adverse selection and moral hazard due to a lack of transparency (Huang & Liu, 2020). Creditors need additional data to accurately assess the funding capacities of family businesses. When evaluating and forecasting a company's success, ESG performance is more complete than information like financial statements. The information gap between enterprises and creditors may be greatly narrowed by implementing ESG, as discovered by Yang et al. (2018). According to Hamrouni et al. (2019), fund providers can be attracted, financing constraints can be loosened, and debt financing can be made easier all because of ESG disclosure, which can provide useful financial information that is not included in financial statements and accurately reflect ESG performance. To explain the relationship between ESG performance and Tobin's Q, we include financial limitations as a mediator. There are also competing theories on the importance of firms' ESG disclosure. The first school of thought contends that the voluntary incorporation of ESG problems into business operation choices by firms is the foundation of ESG disclosure. That the company follows the norms of public opinion is shown by the disclosure (Kim et al., 2012; Campopiano & De Massis, 2015). The second theory is that managers engage in ESG disclosure as a kind of defensive action meant to safeguard their interests (Borralho et al., 2022). According to the signalling theory, companies can improve transparency and stakeholder participation and reduce corporate opportunistic behaviour and creditor financing constraints by disclosing non-financial information (such as ESG performance) to the market. External investors of the firm experience substantial information asymmetry and are frequently unable to endure the high risk of business investment due to the intricate connection inside the family business, where a lot of information is not given as business secrets. Therefore, the ESG performance of family businesses may be discussed using knowledge asymmetry theory. Businesses with strong ESG performance benefit from fewer funding hurdles, increasing their value and productivity (H. Tang, 2022).

4. Literature Review and Hypothesis Development

4.1 ESG Performance and Financial Constraints

This study investigates the impact of ESG actions on family businesses' access to capital and overall profitability. While family companies are increasingly recognized for their importance in the global economy (Agostino & Ruberto, 2021), the relationship between ESG performance and the value of family businesses remains underexplored. Modern corporate finance theory posits that the cost of external financing exceeds that of internal financing due to information asymmetry and agency costs (Tang, 2022). The disclosure of ESG performance aligns with signalling theory and information asymmetry theory, facilitating a reduction in information asymmetry between companies, creditors, and stakeholders. By demonstrating a commitment to CSR, companies can enhance their credibility with stakeholders, improve their creditworthiness and valuation, and mitigate investors' risk perceptions (Zhang et al., 2019). This, in turn, can lead to increased investment (El Ghoul et al., 2017; Shi & Liu, 2015) and an expanded array of financing options.

ESG performance can significantly influence a company's financial performance. We posit that corporate disclosure of robust ESG performance can bolster investor confidence, thereby elevating investment levels and stock prices. Conversely, poor ESG performance can engender investor scepticism, leading to increased restrictions or even withdrawal of investment. ESG performance serves as a crucial reference point for financing institutions; creditors utilize these metrics to assess a company's performance and future potential. Deficiencies in an enterprise's ESG practices can diminish its competitiveness relative to peers. Strong ESG performance can enhance an enterprise's market competitiveness, thereby facilitating easier access to financing. Based on these considerations, we hypothesize the following:

H1: ESG performance can reduce financing constraints for family businesses.

The hypothesis reflects the anticipated positive correlation between strong ESG performance and the alleviation of financial constraints in family businesses. This research aims to empirically validate this hypothesis by examining the effects of ESG actions on the financial flexibility and overall profitability of family-owned enterprises. By doing so, it contributes to the broader understanding of how sustainable business practices influence financial outcomes in family businesses.

4.2 The Mediating Role of Financial Constraints

ESG practices can yield positive outcomes such as sending positive signals to the capital market, gaining stakeholder buy-in, reducing information asymmetry among creditors, and alleviating financing constraints for businesses (Qiu & Yin, 2019). Family firms with strong ESG performance in the areas of environment, society, and governance tend to achieve higher credit ratings, encounter fewer financing obstacles, and have easier access to capital. Consequently, these firms often see an increase in their value and efficiency. The relationship between ESG outcomes and stock price is mediated by cash flow issues.

Financing constraints significantly impact corporate performance by limiting a company's investment capabilities, thereby hindering the completion of planned expansions or investments. These constraints also influence corporate investment decisions, often leading to more conservative investment strategies. Additionally, financing constraints can raise investor concerns about the company's performance, subsequently affecting stock prices. This study hypothesizes the following:

H2: Financing constraints mediate the relationship between ESG performance and firm performance.

This hypothesis posits that the impact of ESG performance on firm performance is mediated by the level of financial constraints faced by the company. High ESG performance can mitigate financing constraints, thereby enabling the company to pursue more aggressive investment strategies and improve overall performance. Conversely, poor ESG performance may exacerbate financial constraints, leading to reduced investment capabilities and lower firm performance.

The mediating role of financial constraints highlights the importance of ESG practices not only in enhancing a firm's market reputation and stakeholder trust but also in improving its financial flexibility and operational capabilities. By examining this mediating effect, this research aims to provide a comprehensive understanding of how ESG performance influences firm performance through the channel of financial constraints. This insight is crucial for family businesses seeking to enhance their financial health and strategic positioning in the market.

4.3 ESG Performance and Family Firm Value

There are differing perspectives regarding the correlation between the performance of family businesses and their ESG performance. According to the Socioemotional Wealth (SEW) framework proposed by Espinosa-Méndez et al. (2023), it is suggested that family businesses prioritize the interests of stakeholders to safeguard their reputation. Family businesses often emphasize non-financial objectives to enhance stakeholder welfare and establish a strong reputation (Zellweger et al., 2013; Berrone et al., 2012). Stewardship theory posits that family ownership is positively correlated with ESG factors, as family members are likely to act as stewards who prioritize the long-term success and sustainability of the business (Davis et al., 1997).

Espinosa-Méndez et al. (2023) found that business managers in family firms prioritize the continuity of the family business and are responsible for its development and succession to future generations. However, it is also common for family businesses to prioritize economic interests, leading to the argument that there may not be a straightforward relationship between ESG performance and the value of family businesses.

On the other hand, ESG factors encompass elements related to corporate image and have significant implications for various aspects of corporate operations, including financing. A positive correlation exists between the corporate performance of many family businesses and their ESG performance. Family businesses that demonstrate strong ESG performance can benefit from enhanced corporate reputation, improved stakeholder relationships, and reduced financing constraints. This, in turn, can lead to increased investment and better overall performance.

The impact of ESG performance on family business value is also influenced by the age of the firm. In recent years, Chinese family businesses have increasingly focused on ESG considerations due to the delayed establishment of the country's ESG evaluation system. As stakeholders pay more attention to ESG issues, companies with strong ESG performance are likely to face fewer financing restrictions and attract more investment.

Based on these considerations, the following hypothesis is proposed:

H3: The firm performance of family businesses is positively correlated with ESG performance.

This hypothesis posits that strong ESG performance is associated with improved firm performance in family businesses. By addressing ESG factors, family businesses can enhance their market competitiveness, attract investment, and achieve sustainable growth. This research aims to empirically validate this hypothesis by examining the relationship between ESG performance and the value of family-owned enterprises, contributing to a deeper understanding of how sustainable business practices influence the success of family firms.

5. Research Design

5.1 Sample and Data

From 2012 through 2021, all firms trading on Shanghai and Shenzhen's stock exchanges will serve as the first sample. Data on ESG factors come from the Bloomberg database, the SA index, the CSMAR database for information on family businesses, and the Choice database for everything else. Financial and non-financial data about Chinese listed businesses may be obtained reliably through CSMAR, as stated by Marquis and Qian (2014). Bloomberg is the biggest supplier of financial information services in the world, and as such, it is a leading source of news and data on the business and financial sectors throughout the globe. This hub provides users with real-time and past financial market data, quotations, prices, trade data, news, and an array of communication options. The Chinese company Oriental Fortune Securities owns the Choice database. Information about stocks, bonds, futures, options, US stocks, Hong Kong stocks, and other financial instruments listed in Shanghai and Shenzhen may be found in the Choice database. It provides a wealth of background data on these things. Users may get professional information, such as financial announcements and statistics, via a variety of ways of transmission.

The preliminary dataset includes 15,751 observations of company-year pairs, derived from a sample of 2,981 family businesses. The sample size was reduced by excluding the following factors: the financial industry data were omitted. The financial industry possesses distinct characteristics that set it apart from other industries. The business model, financial indicators, and market performance of this entity are distinct. Excluding the financial industry from research on the laws of the general economy or industry can prevent the specific characteristics of the financial industry from influencing the results. Address the issue of missing data in samples. This study examines the disclosure of ESG data by a limited number of companies. Due to missing values in certain variables, the author opted to exclude samples with missing data when conducting regression analysis using Stata software. Special treatment (ST) companies were excluded due to multiple reasons. In

Table 10.1 Sample Selection

	Number of Companies	*Number of Firm-Year Observations*
Total number	2,981	15,751
Less: ST companies	105	683
Less: companies in the financial industry	13	85
Less: missing sample data	2,264	11,726
Final holdout sample	599	3,257

accordance with Chinese stock market regulations, companies that have incurred consecutive losses for two years are subject to ST, which includes a warning of potential delisting risks (Qin et al., 2020). Ultimately, a total of 3,257 firm-years were observed. Table 10.1 presents an overview of the sample selection process.

5.2 *Variable Measurements*

5.2.1 *Dependent Variable*

Tobin's Q is widely recognized as a reliable metric due to its prospective nature and comparability across various industries (Anderson et al., 2004). The numerator of the ratio, which represents the firm's market value, is influenced by the mediating effect of both the firm's ESG scores and SA index. Since the denominator of the ratio is simply the asset's replacement cost expressed in present value, a firm's Tobin's Q ratio is strongly linked to financing constraints under ESG influences. However, Tobin's Q will also have certain errors. The results provided by Gregory (2020) show that pollutants that cause externalities cause the Q ratio to deviate from its true value, which depends on the ability of the firm to influence prices, firm size, tax rates, and capital costs. In this study, through the screening of samples and use of control variables, the influence of relevant factors on Tobin's Q is minimized.

5.2.2 *Independent Variables*

The environmental index (*E*), social index (*S*), and governance index (*G*) make up the independent variables that make up the ESG comprehensive index (ESG). ESG is a business paradigm that assesses how a company operates in terms of environmental and social responsibility. In order to give information on ESG indicators to stakeholders, sustainability rating agencies (SRAs) are evaluating an increasing number of businesses (Clementino & Perkins, 2021).

According to the definition provided by SustainAbility (2018, p. 4), an ESG rating is "a comparison of a company's performance across environmental, social, and governance indicators." According to Avetisyan and Hockerts (2017), the SRA assess businesses and provide data on a wide range of *E*, *S*, and *G* factors, such as pollution output, respect for human rights, and corporate transparency. Some organizations provide all-encompassing assessments of business operations by combining data on many ESG factors into a single composite score. In addition, several organizations compile lists of businesses that meet certain ESG standards, known as "ESG indices" or "sustainability indices" (Clementino & Perkins, 2021). The ESG assessment method was first used by China Guoxin in 2023. The assessment system has 122 indicators at the fourth level, including 11 at the second level that focus on the environment, society, and government. More than 400 underlying data items are successfully captured by these indicators. This article makes use of ESG data from Bloomberg Labs.

5.2.3 Intermediary Variables

Following C. H. Hadlock and J. R. Pierce (2010), we use the SA index as the intermediary variables. In the appropriate size range, according to the correlation analysis of the SA index formula and enterprise assets, we find that the relationship is negative, that is, the larger the asset scale, the smaller the SA value. As the scale of assets increases, enterprises experience reduced financing constraints. This study utilizes the absolute value of the SA index as a metric for assessing the financing constraints faced by enterprises. The SA index categorizes the level of financing constraints faced by enterprises into four tiers, with one-quarter of enterprises experiencing significant constraints. From quarter to three quarters, the financing constraints gradually weaken. At the same time, the financing constraint state of the same enterprise may change during the observation time.

$SA = -0.737 * Size + 0.043 * size - 0.040 * age$
Size: the natural logarithm of the company's total assets
Age: business year = observation year (current statistics end date) – establishment time of the enterprise (year)
If any indicator is empty, the calculation result is empty.

5.2.4 Control Variables

The control variables in our study include enterprise size (size), development capability (growth), operating capability (turnover), and year of control (year). The company's size has a moderate impact on its ESG score. In relation to the environment, structural equation modelling (SEM) suggests that companies with a larger scale exhibit higher ESG scores. Contrary to popular belief, the size of a company does not inherently make it more sustainable than smaller companies in terms of achieving climate change mitigation goals, even if they have higher environmental and ESG scores (Drempetic et al., 2020). ESG can effectively demonstrate the company's development capabilities, particularly in sustainable development. The company's operational capabilities are interconnected with the three elements of ESG. Year control is an important factor in determining the ESG performance of Chinese family businesses. China's commitment to the Paris Agreement led to the inclusion of carbon peaking and carbon neutrality goals in the government work report. These goals aim to achieve carbon peaking by 2030 and carbon neutrality by 2060 and are part of the broader plan for ecological civilization construction (Zhang et al., 2024). Government attention also impacted enterprises. The focus on ESG factors has experienced a notable rise.

5.3 Model Specification

Based on the hypothesis on the impact of ESG on Tobin's Q and financing constraints, the benchmark model is constructed as follows:

$tbqit = \beta esgit + \gamma\ 1sizeit + \gamma\ 2growthit + \gamma\ 3turnoverit + c + ui + vt + \varepsilon\ it$

The mediation effect, proposed by Wen Zhonglin, involves a three-step method for examining this effect. The specific model is constructed in the following manner.

The initial procedure involves conducting a regression analysis between the explanatory variable and the calculated variable. The objective is to assess the significance of the coefficient associated with the explanatory variable.

$tbqit = \beta 1esgit + \gamma\ 1sizeit + \gamma\ 2growthit + \gamma\ 3turnoverit + c + ui + vt + \varepsilon it$

The second step is to regress the explanatory variable and the mediator variable and observe the significance of the explanatory variable, as follows:

$sait = \beta 2esgit + \gamma\ 1sizeit + \gamma\ 2growthit + \gamma\ 3turnoverit + c + ui + vt + \varepsilon\ it$

The third step is to regress the explanatory variable, mediator variable, and explained variable at the same time and observe the significance of the mediator variable, as follows:

$tbqit = \beta 3esgit + \gamma\ 1sizeit + \gamma\ 2growthit + \gamma\ 3turnoverit + c + ui + vt + \varepsilon\ it$

In the above model, *i* represents the individual enterprise; *t* represents the year and time; β, γ, and ε are the fitting coefficients of the variables, the model intercept item, the model individual-fixed effect, the year control effect, and the random error item.

Here, tbq is Tobin's Q ratio, which is the market worth of a company as compared to the cost to replace its assets. It shows how two assessments of a company's worth compare to one another. The market value of the firm is used as the numerator, while the replacement cost of the business serves as the denominator in the "basic value" formula (Rahman & Zhu, 2023).

esg denotes organizations in the for-profit and non-profit sectors that have developed something called an ESG rating to determine how well a firm is doing in terms of contributing to the United Nations' sustainable development goals. The Bloomberg ESG metrics are used in this piece (Zhu & Rahman, 2024).

Size represents extra-large, big, medium, small, and micro-sized businesses, which are the most common classifications. Enterprises may be categorized by their scale based on their production and operational spheres. Indicators such as headcount, operational income, and total assets, in addition to sector-specific factors, inform the development of these detailed criteria (Rahman & Zhu, 2024).

Growth denotes that a company's operational circumstances and market share, as well as its future growth tendency, may be gauged by looking at its operating income growth rate. If the index is larger than zero, it indicates that the company's operational income has grown. A higher index value indicates a more rapidly expanding company with brighter market prospects (Rahman, Zhu, & Jiang, 2024).

Turnover shows how asset utilization compares to the revenue generated by a company. The greater the rate of return on total assets, the more robust the enterprise's operational capacity and the more efficient its operations (Rahman, Zhu, & Yue, 2024).

6. Empirical Results

6.1. *Descriptive Statistics*

We focus on A-share listed family firms between 2012 and 2021, excluding information from the finance sector and adjusting for missing data to arrive at a sample size of 3,257. The esg data are from the Bloomberg database, the SA index is from the CSMAR database, and family business identification data are from the Choice database. According to the literature on the topic, a firm is considered to be family-owned if its members own 10% or more of the company's shares, or if they have seats on the company's board of directors. Firstly, we provide the variables' descriptive statistics. The data are excellent for modelling analysis since the mean of all the variables is 3,257, the data are rather consistent in magnitude, and there are no extreme values. Descriptive data are shown in Table 10.2.

6.2. *Baseline Regression Results*

Table 10.3 displays the results of a Tobin Q regression demonstrating the effect of ESG on Tobin Q measures of business value. Below are the univariate regression benchmark findings for family firms. The esg variable's fitting coefficient of 0.019 is statistically significant at the 1% level, as shown. This demonstrates how a high esg score may substantially raise a company's worth. The significance tests for the fitting coefficients of the environmental (e), social (s), and governance (g) indices all pass at the 1%, 1%, and 5% levels of authority, respectively. As can be seen, raising the environmental and social index raises the value of a company, whereas

Table 10.2 Descriptive Statistics

Variable	*Obs*	*Mean*	*SD*	*Min*	*Median*	*Max*
tbq	3257	2.384	1.630	0.818	1.798	8.971
esg	3257	28.242	8.243	10.744	27.150	66.251
e	3257	8.893	12.286	0.000	1.933	73.815
s	3257	12.282	6.967	0.000	9.250	51.391
g	3257	64.375	13.061	27.273	69.296	89.855
sa	3257	3.793	0.239	2.974	3.791	4.398
Size	3257	22.810	1.107	20.555	22.738	27.011
Growth	3257	19.999	32.129	–49.118	14.966	144.061
Turnover	3257	0.668	0.397	0.085	0.586	2.731

raising the governance index lowers its worth. The Tobin Q regression is presented in Table 10.3.

The preceding univariate regression findings were further investigated by including control variables. All four indicators (esg, *e*, *s*, and *g*) passed the significance test, and the signs of the fitting coefficients agree with the prior findings. Consistent inferences may be made as a result. Tobin Q predicts that an increase in the governance index would decrease the value of a business, while an increase in the environment and social indices will enhance the value of an organization, provided that the control variables size, growth, turnover, and year are also included. The Tobin Q regression and control variables are shown in Table 10.4.

6.3 Subsample Discussion

6.3.1 Family Firm vs Non-Family Firm

Next, we comparatively study the impact of esg of non-family firms on firm performance. It can be seen that in non-family enterprises, the fitting results of esg, *e*, and *s* indicators are also significantly positive. But we compare the fitting coefficients. In family enterprises, the fitting coefficients of esg, *e*, and *s* factors are 0.019, 0.014, and 0.033, respectively; in non-family enterprises, the fitting coefficients of esg, *e*, and *s* factors are 0.012, 0.005, and 0.015, respectively. Through comparison, we can clearly see that compared with non-family businesses, esg is more capable of improving performance for family businesses. Table 10.5 shows the Tobin Q regression of non-family firms.

Table 10.3 Baseline Regression Results

	(1)	*(2)*	*(3)*	*(4)*
	tbq	*tbq*	*tbq*	*tbq*
esg	0.019*** (3.730)			
e		0.014*** (5.238)		
s			0.033*** (6.216)	
g				−0.008** (−2.267)
_cons	1.664*** (13.175)	2.007*** (27.550)	1.741*** (19.878)	2.425*** (13.393)
Year	Yes	Yes	Yes	Yes
N	3,257	3,257	3,257	3,257
R^2	0.205	0.209	0.212	0.202

t statistics are given in parentheses.
* $p < 0.1$, ** $p < 0.05$, *** $p < 0.01$.

Table 10.4 Univariate Regression Results with Control Variables

	(1)	*(2)*	*(3)*	*(4)*
	tbq	*tbq*	*tbq*	*tbq*
esg	0.019***			
	(3.716)			
e		0.014***		
		(5.245)		
s			0.035***	
			(6.545)	
g				−0.008**
				(−2.418)
Size	−0.155***	−0.174***	−0.196***	−0.120**
	(−2.718)	(−3.062)	(−3.446)	(−2.137)
Growth	0.003***	0.003***	0.003***	0.003***
	(4.750)	(4.740)	(4.944)	(4.864)
Turnover	0.796***	0.784***	0.773***	0.808***
	(6.968)	(6.881)	(6.804)	(7.070)
_cons	4.377***	5.156***	5.367***	4.376***
	(3.500)	(4.081)	(4.268)	(3.471)
Year	Yes	Yes	Yes	Yes
N	3,257	3,257	3,257	3,257
1	0.238	0.242	0.247	0.236

t statistics are given in parentheses.
* $p < 0.1$, ** $p < 0.05$, *** $p < 0.01$.

6.3.2 Whether the Second-Generation Children of the Family Business Participate In

It can be seen that in companies where only the first-generation founders participate, the esg, *e*, and *s* variable fits are significantly positive, and the *g* variable fit is not significant. The variable fit is significantly positive, and the *g* variable fit is significantly negative. This shows that the participation of the second generation will lead to an increase in the governance index and inhibit corporate performance. In this case, the author believes that there may be differences in management concepts between the children and the founders, which in turn leads to reduced efficiency. Table 10.6 shows the Tobin Q regression of first- and second-generation firms.

6.3.3 Differences between Years

Next, the author divides the year into the first 5 years and the next 5 years, namely, 2012–2016 and 2017–2021. It can be seen that during 2012–2016, only the fitting coefficients of ESG and the three basic indicators were negative, with ESG, S, and G passing the significance test. In the 2017–2021 period, ESG, E, and S passed the significance test, and the fitting coefficients were positive.

We have seen that with the development of esg in China, its impact on corporate performance has also undergone fundamental changes. Table 10.7 shows the Tobin Q regression in different years.

Table 10.5 Benchmark Regression Results for Non-Family Businesses

	(1)	(2)	(3)	(4)
	tbq	*tbq*	*tbq*	*tbq*
esg	0.012***			
	(4.678)			
e		0.005***		
		(4.163)		
s			0.015***	
			(5.760)	
g				0.001
				(0.908)
Size	−0.370***	−0.366***	−0.378***	−0.356***
	(−12.232)	(−12.106)	(−12.465)	(−11.806)
Growth	0.002***	0.002***	0.002***	0.002***
	(5.927)	(5.906)	(5.921)	(5.975)
Turnover	0.309***	0.309***	0.309***	0.308***
	(6.040)	(6.041)	(6.042)	(6.014)
_cons	9.687***	9.816***	9.969***	9.542***
	(13.901)	(14.049)	(14.266)	(13.596)
Year	Yes	Yes	Yes	Yes
N	6,790	6,790	6,790	6,790
R^2	0.136	0.135	0.138	0.133

t statistics are given in parentheses.
* $p < 0.1$, ** $p < 0.05$, *** $p < 0.01$.

6.4 *Research on Intermediary Mechanism*

The author then moves on to investigate the role played by the middleman. That is to say, esg impacts corporate finance limitations, and in turn, corporate performance is impacted by esg. Three out of the four groups below passed the mediation effect test based on the regression findings, while the fourth group did not. At the 1% level, the esg variable in the first group has a fitting coefficient of −0.002 (indicating that esg helps relieve the financial responsibilities of the firm), whereas at the 10% level, the sa variable has a fitting value of −1.196. Examining the likelihood of success with and without sufficient funding to draw conclusions about the impact on a business. A comprehensive analysis shows that esg improves business performance by removing constraints on corporate financing. The centre ground is similarly obvious in the last two sets. *E*/*s* improves productivity since it allows companies to use previously unavailable funds. Table 10.8 displays the results of ESG's role as a mediator in the face of budgetary constraints.

7. Endogeneity Tests

By looking for instrumental variables, the author adopts the 2SLS model and uses the GMM method for regression. The author adopts two instrumental variables, respectively, and implements two mediation effect tests.

Table 10.6 Distinguish Whether the Second-Generation Participates

	First Generation				*Second Generation and Above Participate*			
	tbq	*tbq*	*tbq*	*tbq*	*tbq*	*tbq*	*tbq*	*tbq*
esg	0.020***				0.013			
	(2.928)				(1.409)			
e		0.014***				0.013**		
		(3.760)				(2.550)		
s			0.038***				0.027***	
			(5.510)				(2.602)	
g				−0.006				−0.017**
				(−1.393)				(−2.549)
Size	−0.182**	−0.201***	−0.226***	−0.137*	0.050	0.018	0.012	0.084
	(−2.485)	(−2.742)	(−3.098)	(−1.910)	(0.367)	(0.133)	(0.089)	(0.623)
Growth	0.004***	0.004***	0.004***	0.004***	0.001	0.001	0.001	0.001
	(4.274)	(4.194)	(4.423)	(4.292)	(0.613)	(0.715)	(0.700)	(0.773)
Turnover	0.695***	0.694***	0.670***	0.739***	1.005***	1.005***	0.980***	0.917***
	(4.725)	(4.727)	(4.586)	(5.026)	(3.732)	(3.752)	(3.662)	(3.413)
_cons	5.025***	5.808***	6.051***	4.688***	−0.190	0.756	0.660	0.204
	(3.154)	(3.584)	(3.788)	(2.938)	(-0.062)	(0.243)	(0.213)	(0.066)
Year	Yes	Yes	Yes	Yes	Yes	Yes	Yes	Yes
N	2,227	2,227	2,227	2,227	735	735	735	735
R^2	0.241	0.243	0.250	0.238	0.206	0.212	0.212	0.212

t statistics in parentheses.
* $p < 0.1$, ** $p < 0.05$, *** $p < 0.01$.

Table 10.7 Differences between Years of Exploration

	2017–2021				*2012–2016*			
	tbq	*tbq*	*tbq*	*tbq*	*tbq*	*tbq*	*tbq*	*tbq*
Esg	0.022**				−−0.031***			
	(2.438)				(−3.525)			
e		0.010**				−0.012		
		(2.398)				(−1.392)		
s			0.047***				−0.018*	
			(5.537)				(−1.789)	
g				−0.006				−0.011***
				(−0.677)				(−3.057)
Size	0.427***	0.442***	0.376***	0.479***	−0.802***	−0.812***	−0.803***	−0.815***
	(3.521)	(3.670)	(3.139)	(3.992)	(−8.170)	(−8.232)	(−8.119)	(−8.302)
Growth	0.004***	0.004***	0.004***	0.004***	−0.000	−0.000	−0.000	−0.000
	(3.395)	(3.351)	(3.463)	(3.351)	(−0.341)	(−0.337)	(−0.365)	(−0.294)
Turnover	0.906***	0.912***	0.908***	0.928***	1.152***	1.178***	1.176***	1.136***
	(4.100)	(4.126)	(4.156)	(4.186)	(5.942)	(6.036)	(6.033)	(5.841)
_cons	−9.417***	−9.200***	−8.093***	−9.513***	19.241***	18.879***	18.830***	19.448***
	(−3.420)	(−3.331)	(−2.960)	(−3.384)	(8.764)	(8.553)	(8.535)	(8.828)
Year	Yes	Yes	Yes	Yes	Yes	Yes	Yes	Yes
N	1,536	1,536	1,536	1,536	1,386	1,386	1,386	1,386
R^2	0.246	0.246	0.263	0.242	0.379	0.372	0.373	0.377

t statistics in parentheses.
* $p < 0.1$, ** $p < 0.05$, *** $p < 0.01$.

Table 10.8 Research on Intermediary Mechanism

	Group I Intermediaries		*Group II Intermediaries*		*Group III Intermediaries*		*Group IV Intermediaries*	
	sa	*tbq*	*sa*	*tbq*	*sa*	*tbq*	*sa*	*tbq*
esg	−0.002***	0.016**						
	(−3.960)	(2.257)						
E			−0.001***	0.013***				
			(−4.213)	(4.715)				
S					−0.002***	0.033***		
					(−7.673)	(6.096)		
G							−0.000	−0.008**
							(−1.624)	(−2.536)
Sa		−1.196*		−1.088***		−1.054***		−1.451***
		(−1.707)		(−2.669)		(−2.602)		(−3.598)
Size	−0.041***	−0.204*	−0.041***	−0.218***	−0.041***	−0.239***	−0.045***	−0.186***
	(−4.233)	(−1.854)	(−4.208)	(−3.689)	(−14.915)	(−4.038)	(−16.799)	(−3.153)
Growth	0.000	0.003***	0.000	0.003***	0.000	0.003***	0.000	0.003***
	(0.276)	(3.559)	(0.271)	(4.768)	(0.169)	(4.958)	(0.331)	(4.899)
Turnover	0.017	0.816***	0.017	0.803***	0.017***	0.791***	0.015***	0.830***
	(1.304)	(4.349)	(1.321)	(7.038)	(3.111)	(6.956)	(2.661)	(7.263)
_cons	4.552***	9.823**	4.504***	10.058***	4.523***	10.134***	4.620***	11.077***
	(21.164)	(2.110)	(20.743)	(4.514)	(75.020)	(4.562)	(76.143)	(4.929)
Year	Yes	Yes	Yes	Yes	Yes	Yes	Yes	Yes
N	3,257	3,257	3,257	3,257	3,257	3,257	3,257	3,257
R^2	0.750	0.241	0.750	0.244	0.748	0.249	0.743	0.240

t statistics in parentheses.* $p < 0.1$, ** $p < 0.05$, *** $p < 0.01$.

7.1 First-Stage Results

To begin, when the Dibo Internal Control Index is used as an instrumental variable in a regression, we find that the esg of a business is positively correlated with its degree of internal control. There is a correlation between an enterprise's internal control and its esg, with a greater esg corresponding to a higher internal control. However, there is some degree of independence between the internal control level and the financial metrics of the firm because of this. Below are the results of the regression analysis. In the table below, we can see that the LM, Wald, *F*, and *t* statistics all passed the test, except for formula (4), which did not. The outcomes of the second phase of the two-stage regression are shown in the table below. The favourable match between esg, *e*, and *s* is readily apparent. Table 10.9 displays the preliminary endogeneity test findings.

7.2 Second-Stage Results

The author once again used the lagged one-period data of the esg indicator as an instrumental variable to construct a 2SLS regression model. There is a significant correlation between the lagged variable and the current variable, and the correlation between the lagged variable and other variables in the current period is significantly weakened, which meets the independence requirement. Therefore, generally speaking, lagged variables are better instrumental variables. The following endogeneity

Table 10.9 Mitigating Endogeneity Concerns with the Dibo Internal Control Index

	(1)	(2)	(3)	(4)
	tbq	*tbq*	*tbq*	*tbq*
esg	0.052*** (4.302)			
e		0.027*** (4.106)		
s			0.053*** (3.347)	
g				0.012 (0.977)
Size	−0.234** (−2.385)	−0.239** (−2.402)	−0.246** (−2.457)	−0.108 (−1.134)
Growth	0.002** (2.509)	0.002** (2.465)	0.002*** (2.805)	0.002** (2.449)
Turnover	1.002*** (5.109)	1.014*** (5.238)	0.990*** (5.137)	1.073*** (5.531)
Year	Yes	Yes	Yes	Yes
N	2,544	2,544	2,544	2,544
LM	133.897	115.167	92.924	74.281
Wald	291.325	271.936	146.144	82.497
F of one-stage	326.70	111.78	48.12	242.06
t of one-stage L.esg	17.07	16.49	12.09	9.08

t statistics in parentheses.
* $p < 0.1$, ** $p < 0.05$, *** $p < 0.01$.

test results show that formulas (1), (2), and (3) still passed the test, but formula (4) did not. The result is consistent with the result of the Dibo Internal Control Index. Table 10.10 shows the second-stage results of the endogeneity test.

8. Robustness Check

Considering that there is a certain lag period between the enterprise's esg transmission and corporate value, the author uses the lag period esg and the three sub-indices of the lag period to replace the current indicators, respectively, and constructs a model for regression to construct robustness check. Consistent with the findings of the benchmark model, the following results show that the fitting coefficients of the three variables L.esg, L.e, and L.s are all positive and have passed the significance test. Nonetheless, the L.g variable does not seem to be statistically significant, since the fitting coefficient is positive, and the sign of the coefficient does not match that of the aforementioned reference model. Therefore, through the robustness test, the author believes that the esg comprehensive index, the *e* index, and the *s* index have all increased the value of the enterprise, but the *g* index has no significant impact on the enterprise. Table 10.11 shows the second-stage results of robustness check.

Table 10.10 Mitigating Endogeneity Concerns with the 2SLS Models

	(1)	*(2)*	*(3)*	*(4)*
	tbq	*tbq*	*tbq*	*tbq*
esg	0.371**			
	(2.364)			
e		0.174***		
		(2.653)		
s			0.327***	
			(2.663)	
g				1.358
				(0.451)
Size	−0.794**	−0.767***	−0.829***	0.604
	(−2.507)	(−2.786)	(−2.835)	(0.371)
Growth	0.002	0.002*	0.003***	−0.005
	(1.470)	(1.858)	(3.318)	(−0.258)
Turnover	0.545*	0.525**	0.512**	1.520
	(1.910)	(2.164)	(2.007)	(0.848)
Year	Yes	Yes	Yes	Yes
N	3,139	3,139	3,139	3,139
LM	7.025	8.786	9.588	0.212
Wald	7.044	9.050	9.922	0.211
F of one-stage	236.14	69.39	40.36	267.93
t of one-stage isi	2.65	3.01	3.15	0.646

t statistics in parentheses.
* $p < 0.1$, ** $p < 0.05$, *** $p < 0.01$.

Table 10.11 Robustness Tests for Substitution of Explanatory Variables

	(1)	(2)	(3)	(4)
	tbq	*tbq*	*tbq*	*tbq*
L.esg	0.029***			
	(4.929)			
L.e		0.016***		
		(4.977)		
L.s			0.023***	
			(3.922)	
L.g				0.003
				(0.943)
Size	−0.163**	−0.175***	−0.168**	−0.110
	(−2.412)	(−2.584)	(−2.457)	(−1.640)
Growth	0.002***	0.002***	0.002***	0.002***
	(2.786)	(2.792)	(2.988)	(2.748)
Turnover	1.040***	1.038***	1.033***	1.070***
	(7.769)	(7.748)	(7.687)	(7.955)
_cons	4.702***	5.516***	5.186***	3.914**
	(3.135)	(3.625)	(3.405)	(2.577)
Year	Yes	Yes	Yes	Yes
N	2,595	2,595	2,595	2,595
R^2	0.214	0.214	0.211	0.205

t statistics in parentheses.
* $p < 0.1$, ** $p < 0.05$, *** $p < 0.01$.

9. Discussion

9.1 Relationship with Previous Literature

The ESG performance of Chinese family enterprises and the associated limitations of their access to capital have not been extensively studied. This research demonstrates that ESG performance significantly influences the performance and financing constraints of Chinese family enterprises, with a stronger effect observed compared to non-family firms. Similar results have been identified in other contexts, although prior research has not specifically focused on Chinese family businesses. For example, Borralho et al. (2022) analysed ESG disclosures of state-to-family and family enterprises in Spain and France, both operating under Roman law or legal systems. Their findings indicate that family-owned businesses benefit more from ESG transparency in managing their profits. Espinosa-Méndez et al. (2023) also found a positive correlation between total ESG scores and corporate value using a sample of 254 businesses from the world's top 500 family-owned enterprises from 2015 to 2021. Their research, which encompasses large-scale family-owned organizations, reinforces the importance of ESG performance. Furthermore, Ge et al. (2022) suggested that strong ESG performance fosters high-quality organizational growth through the intermediate impact of innovation input.

9.2 Theoretical Implications

This research supports the information asymmetry hypothesis and signalling theory. ESG disclosure can mitigate corporate opportunism and creditor financing restrictions while enhancing transparency, stakeholder engagement, and the dissemination of ESG information (Bénabou & Tirole, 2010). Conversely, a lack of attention to or disclosure of ESG factors may increase creditors' mistrust of family companies, exacerbating financing constraints and impacting business operations. Using the SEW framework and management theory, this research explores the varied connections between ESG performance and family companies. Family firms often prioritize non-financial objectives, such as stakeholder satisfaction and brand enhancement, over short-term profits (Zellweger et al., 2013; Berrone et al., 2012). However, family firms that pursue economic objectives also tend to excel in terms of their ESG performance.

9.3 Practical Implications

Policymakers and other stakeholders can derive substantial insights from this study's conclusions. One key finding is that ESG performance exerts a more substantial influence on Chinese family enterprises than on non-family ones. Additionally, the involvement of the next generation in a family firm is associated with a decline in operational efficiency and impacts the company's ESG performance. These results may encourage further research into the effects of various family business objectives and practices on ESG, addressing the paucity of prior work in this area. This study fills gaps left by previous research by incorporating control variables such as company size, development, operations, and year. Our analysis indicates that good ESG performance is associated with lower financing limitations and higher profitability for Chinese family businesses. Practitioners and policymakers in China and elsewhere can use these insights to shape ESG policies. This research employs a combination of fixed effects and mediating effects to investigate ESG concerns in Chinese family companies, with financing issues serving as a moderating factor. Future research on company value and profits could incorporate various intermediaries, such as the adoption of new ideas from other stakeholders in the family company.

10. Conclusion

This study investigates the implications of ESG performance on the financial constraints and overall effectiveness of Chinese family enterprises. The findings shed light on the influence of ESG factors on controlled and mediating variables within these businesses. Our initial sample comprises all firms listed on the Shanghai and Shenzhen stock exchanges in China from 2012 to 2021. We found that ESG performance is positively correlated with corporate success in family firms where economic interests are the primary focus, a trend that has become more pronounced in recent years.

These results contribute to several areas of ESG and family business research. Firstly, we employed the mediation effect to examine various types of family businesses, aligning our findings with signalling theory and information asymmetry theory. Additionally, we explored the impact of second-generation family business owners on ESG factors. This differentiation provided deeper insights into how the involvement of the next generation affects firm performance and ESG outcomes. Finally, our analysis of different years highlighted significant shifts in ESG performance among Chinese family firms, offering an understanding of temporal changes in this area.

Despite the contributions of this study, there are certain limitations. We did not extrapolate the effects of individual organizations' ESG practices on broader business outcomes. There remain research gaps, particularly concerning the evaluation of ESG impacts on business value and performance through the lens of financing constraints. While our data and samples have been rigorously vetted, there is room for improvement in classifying family companies. This study focuses on Chinese family enterprises from 2012 to 2022; future research could expand to include data from other countries and economies.

While this study provides valuable insights into the relationship between ESG performance and the financial constraints of Chinese family enterprises, several areas warrant further investigation. Future research could expand on the following directions to deepen our understanding and address existing gaps in the literature: Future studies could explore the impact of ESG performance on family businesses across different countries and cultural contexts. By comparing data from various economies, researchers can identify whether the observed trends in Chinese family firms hold true internationally or if there are significant regional differences. Extending the temporal scope of the analysis beyond 2021 could provide a more comprehensive view of how ESG performance evolves over time and its long-term effects on family business success. Longitudinal studies could help understand the sustained impact of ESG practices on financial performance and operational efficiency. Investigating the effects of ESG performance within specific industries or sectors could reveal nuanced insights. Different sectors may face unique ESG challenges, and understanding these can help tailor ESG strategies to industry-specific needs. Future research could disaggregate the ESG factors and examine the individual impact of ESG components on family firm performance. This approach would provide a more detailed understanding of which specific aspects of ESG are most beneficial to family businesses. Exploring the role of different governance structures within family firms, such as board composition, ownership distribution, and management practices, could elucidate how these factors interact with ESG performance. Such studies could offer insights into the optimal governance configurations for enhancing ESG outcomes. Investigating additional mediating and moderating variables that influence the relationship between ESG performance and family firm success could provide a more comprehensive understanding. Factors such as innovation capacity, corporate culture, and external economic conditions might play significant roles. Further research could explore the policy implications of ESG performance in family firms, providing recommendations for policymakers to support sustainable business practices. Understanding the regulatory and institutional frameworks that facilitate or hinder ESG adoption can inform more effective policy interventions. By pursuing these future research directions, scholars can contribute to a more comprehensive and nuanced understanding of the interplay between ESG performance and family business success, ultimately promoting sustainable development in the global business landscape.

To this end, this research provides a comprehensive analysis of the role of ESG performance in mitigating financial constraints and enhancing the success of family businesses in China. The findings underscore the importance of ESG factors in family enterprises and highlight the need for further research to explore these dynamics in different contexts and over more extended periods. The insights gained from this study can inform policymakers, practitioners, and academics as they seek to understand and leverage ESG practices to promote sustainable growth in family businesses.

References

Agostino, M., & Ruberto, S. (2021). Environment-friendly practices: Family versus non-family firms. *Journal of Cleaner Production, 329*, 129689.

Albuquerque, R., Koskinen, Y., & Zhang, C. (2019). Corporate social responsibility and firm risk: Theory and empirical evidence. *Management Science, 65*(10), 4451–4469.

Anderson, E. W., Fornell, C., & Mazvancheryl, S. K. (2004). Customer satisfaction and shareholder value. *Journal of Marketing, 68*(4), 172–185.

Avetisyan, E., & Hockerts, K. (2017). The consolidation of the ESG rating industry as an enactment of institutional retrogression. *Business Strategy and the Environment, 26*(3), 316–330.

Bénabou, R., & Tirole, J. (2010). Individual and corporate social responsibility. *Economica, 77*, 1–19.

Bennedsen, M., Fan, J. P., Jian, M., & Yeh, Y. H. (2015). The family business map: Framework, selective survey, and evidence from Chinese family firm succession. *Journal of Corporate Finance, 33*, 212–226.

Berrone, P., Cruz, C., & Gomez-Mejia, L. R. (2012). Socioemotional wealth in family firms: Theoretical dimensions, assessment approaches, and agenda for future research. *Family Business Review, 25*, 258–279.

Berrone, P., Cruz, C., Gomez-Mejia, L. R., & Larraza-Kintana, M. (2010). Socioemotional wealth and corporate responses to institutional pressures: Do family-controlled firms pollute less? *Administrative Science Quarterly, 55*(1), 82–113.

Borralho, J. M., Hernández-Linares, R., Gallardo-Vázquez, D., & de Sousa Paiva, I. C. (2022). Environmental, social and governance disclosure's impacts on earnings management: Family versus non-family firms. *Journal of Cleaner Production, 379*, 134603.

Campopiano, G., & De Massis, A. (2015). Corporate social responsibility reporting: A content analysis in family and non-family firms. *Journal of Business Ethics, 129*, 511–534.

Cao, J., Cumming, D., & Wang, X. (2015). One-child policy and family firms in China. *Journal of Corporate Finance, 33*, 317–329.

Cheng, Q. (2014). Family firm research – a review. *China Journal of Accounting Research, 7*(3), 149–163.

Clementino, E., & Perkins, R. (2021). How do companies respond to environmental, social and governance (ESG) ratings? Evidence from Italy. *Journal of Business Ethics, 171*, 379–397.

Davis, J. H., Schoorman, F. D., & Donaldson, L. (1997). Toward a stewardship theory of management. *Academy of Management Review, 22*, 20–47.

Drempetic, S., Klein, C., & Zwergel, B. (2020). The influence of firm size on the ESG score: Corporate sustainability ratings under review. *Journal of Business Ethics*, *167*, 333–360.

El Ghoul, S., Guedhami, O., & Kim, Y. (2017). Country-level institutions, firm value, and the role of corporate social responsibility initiatives. *Journal of International Business Studies*, *48*, 360–385.

Espinosa-Méndez, C., Maquieira, C. P., & Arias, J. T. (2023). The impact of ESG performance on the value of family firms: The moderating role of financial constraints and agency problems. *Sustainability*, *15*(7), 6176.

Ge, G., Xiao, X., Li, Z., & Dai, Q. (2022). Does ESG performance promote high-quality development of enterprises in China? The mediating role of innovation input. *Sustainability*, *14*(7), 3843.

Gregory, R. P. (2020). *Measuring the effect of sustainability on Tobin's Q*. Available at SSRN 3586537.

Hadlock, C. J., & Pierce, J. R. (2010). New evidence on measuring financial constraints: Moving beyond the KZ index. *The Review of Financial Studies*, *23*(5), 1909–1940.

Hamrouni, A., Boussaada, R., & Toumi, N. B. F. (2019). Corporate social responsibility disclosure and debt financing. *Journal of Applied Accounting Research*, *20*(4), 394–415.

Hoepner, A., Cojoianu, T., Ascui, F., Clark, G., & Wojcik, D. (2020). Does the fossil fuel divestment movement impact new oil & gas fundraising. *Journal of Economic Geography*, *21*, 1–33.

Huang, J. R., & Liu, Y. M. (2020). Media attention on the cost of corporate debt financing impact study: Mediator effect test based on accounting robustness. *Review of Investment Studies*, *39*(2), 113–133.

Kim, Y., Park, M. S., & Wier, B. (2012). Is earnings quality associated with corporate social responsibility? *The Accounting Review*, *87*(3), 761–796.

Kong, W. (2023). The impact of ESG performance on debt financing costs: Evidence from Chinese family business. *Finance Research Letters*, 103949.

Kotlar, J., & De Massis, A. (2013). Goal setting in family firms: Goal diversity, social interactions, and collective commitment to family-centered goals. *Entrepreneurship Theory and Practice*, *37*(6), 1263–1288.

Luo, C., Wei, D., & He, F. (2023). Corporate ESG performance and trade credit financing – Evidence from China. *International Review of Economics & Finance*, *85*, 337–351.

Mariani, M. M., Al-Sultan, K., & De Massis, A. (2021). Corporate social responsibility in family firms: A systematic literature review. *Journal of Small Business Management*, 1–55.

Marquis, C., & Qian, C. (2014). Corporate social responsibility reporting in China: Symbol or substance? *Organization Science*, *25*(1), 127–148.

Martin, P. R., & Moser, D. V. (2016). Managers' green investment disclosures and investors' reaction. *Journal of Accounting and Economics*, *61*(1), 239–254.

Mishra, S., & Modi, S. (2013). Positive and negative corporate social responsibility, financial leverage, and idiosyncratic risk. *Journal of Business Ethics*, *117*(2), 431–448.

Pekovic, S., Grolleau, G., & Mzoughi, N. (2018). Environmental investments: Too much of a good thing? *International Journal of Production Economics*, *3*(197), 297–302.

Qin, X., Huang, G., Shen, H., & Fu, M. (2020). COVID-19 pandemic and firm-level cash holding – moderating effect of goodwill and goodwill impairment. *Emerging Markets Finance and Trade*, *56*(10), 2243–2258.

Qiu, M. Y., & Yin, H. (2019). Analysis of enterprises' ESG performance and financing costs under the background of ecological civilization construction. *The Journal of Quantitative & Technical Economics*, *3*, 108–123.

Rahman, M. J., & Wu, J. (2023). M&A activity and ESG performance: Evidence from China. *Managerial Finance*, *50*(1), 179–197.

Rahman, M. J., Wu, Q., & Zhu, H. (2024). Corporate social responsibility in times of social distancing: Evidence from China. *Business Ethics, the Environment & Responsibility*. https://doi.org/10.1111/beer.12651

Rahman, M. J., & Zhu, H. (2023). Predicting accounting fraud using imbalanced ensemble learning classifiers – evidence from China. *Accounting & Finance*, *63*(3), 3455–3486.
Rahman, M. J., & Zhu, H. (2024). Detecting accounting fraud in family firms: Evidence from machine learning approaches. *Advances in Accounting*, *64*, 100722.
Rahman, M. J., Zhu, H., & Chen, S. (2023). Does CSR reduce financial distress? Moderating effect of firm characteristics, auditor characteristics, and covid-19. *International Journal of Accounting & Information Management*, *31*(5), 756–784.
Rahman, M. J., Zhu, H., & Jiang, X. (2024). Family firms, client importance, and auditor reporting behavior: Evidence from China. *Meditari Accountancy Research*, *32*(2), 543–578.
Rahman, M. J., Zhu, H., & Yue, L. (2024). Does the adoption of artificial intelligence by audit firms and their clients affect audit quality and efficiency? Evidence from China. *Managerial Auditing Journal*, *39*(6), 668–699.
Shi, Y., & Liu, L. G. (2015). Study on the differences of influencing factors of corporate social responsibility. *Future Development*, *12*, 81–87.
SustainAbility. (2018). *Rate the raters 2018: Ratings revisited*. SustainAbility.
SynTao Green Finance, & UK PACT. (2019). *ESG data in China: Recommendations for primary ESG indicators*. UNEP Finance Initiative.
Tan, Y., & Zhu, Z. (2022). The effect of ESG rating events on corporate green innovation in China: The mediating role of financial constraints and managers' environmental awareness. *Technology in Society*, *68*, 101906.
Tang, H. (2022). The effect of ESG performance on corporate innovation in China: The mediating role of financial constraints and agency cost. *Sustainability*, *14*(7), 3769.
Tang, J., Osmer, E., & Zheng, Y. (2022). Do married couples make better family firm leaders: Evidence from China. *Journal of Economics and Business*, *118*, 106030.
Yang, S., He, F., Zhu, Q., 2018. How does corporate social responsibility change capital structure? *Asia-Pacific Journal of Accounting & Economics*, *25*(3–4), 352–387.
Zellweger, T., Nason, R., Nordqvist, M., & Brush, C. (2013). Why do family firms strive for nonfinancial goals? An organizational identity perspective. *Entrepreneurship Theory and Practice*, *37*, 229–248.
Zhang, J. X., Cai, Y. D., & Ni, G. Q. (2019). The effect of disclosure tone of corporate social responsibility and disclosure integrity of financial information on investors' perceived fulfillment of corporate social responsibility: An experimental research. *Nankai Business Review*, *22*, 206–212.
Zhang, Q., Jie, D., Li, J., & Zhou, J. (2024). Carbon compensation cost in Jing-Jin-Ji region under the carbon neutrality goal: Considering emission responsibility and carbon abatement cost. *Journal of Cleaner Production*, *467*, 142950.
Zhou, G., Liu, L., & Luo, S. (2022). Sustainable development, ESG performance and company market value: Mediating effect of financial performance. *Business Strategy and the Environment*, *31*(7), 3371–3387.
Zhu, H., & Rahman, M. J. (2024). Ex-ante expected changes in ESG and future stock returns based on machine learning. *The British Accounting Review*, 101457.

Part 4

ESG and Auditing

11 ESG, Dividend Payout Policy, and the Moderating Role of Audit Quality

Md Jahidur Rahman, Tarek Rana, Hongtao Zhu, and Wang Xinyi

1. Introduction

Dividends represent a direct source of appeal for shareholders, and safeguarding their interests is a fundamental objective of corporate governance. The formulation of dividend policy directly influences the distribution of dividends. Numerous studies and theories have examined the drivers and influencing factors of dividends (Saravanakumar, 2011). As environmental, social, and governance (ESG) considerations increasingly shape corporate decision-making and investor preferences, a re-evaluation by both management and investors has been triggered. Research indicates that firms with robust ESG performance tend to exhibit more stable overall performance (Di Tommaso & Mazzuca, 2023). Nevertheless, two key contradictions persist regarding ESG practices and stakeholder interests: (1) whether a firm's ESG efforts attract more investors and (2) whether the pursuit of sustainable development justifies potential sacrifices in shareholder value. There can be inherent financial conflicts between a firm's commitment to ESG initiatives and its capacity to distribute dividends.

While these issues have garnered international attention, studies examining the impact of ESG objectives on corporate dividend payments have yielded inconsistent results (Limkriangkrai et al., 2017; Saldi et al., 2023; Benlemlih, 2019). The relationship between ESG practices and dividend payments may vary by geographical context, underscoring the necessity for focused research within specific regions, such as China. Concurrently, the increasing investor preference for ESG considerations is compelling Chinese firms to prioritize ESG policies and reporting. As an emerging market, China is actively engaging in the ESG movement, reflected in the diversification of domestic ESG rating agencies (Li et al., 2022) and the frequent issuance of ESG-related corporate governance regulations by the Chinese government. These measures are fostering the development of a robust ESG framework in China and elevating the ESG awareness among enterprises and investors. The primary objective of this study is to ascertain the interaction between ESG practices and dividend payout ratios in Chinese listed companies.

The influence of corporate governance elements, such as board size, on the ESG–dividend relationship cannot be overlooked (Cheung et al., 2018). Previous research (Zahid et al., 2022) has highlighted the significant role of mediating factors, necessitating their consideration. This study employs audit quality as a moderating variable, positing that enhanced audit quality can mitigate information

DOI: 10.4324/9781003488934-15

asymmetry and thereby influence the dividend payout ratio (Imen & Anis, 2020). Moreover, audit quality is impacted by ESG disclosure (Zahid et al., 2022). Several studies in China also investigate the relationship between environmental accounting and firm performance (Rahman & Wu, 2023; Rahman, Wu, et al., 2024; Rahman et al., 2023; Zhu & Rahman, 2024).

Extant research has demonstrated that corporate ESG practices can lead to improved corporate performance (Friede et al., 2015), with ESG disclosures helping overcome information barriers. However, existing literature has yet to fully address the impact of ESG practices on dividend distribution and the sustainability of audit reports. Studies have shown that auditor experience influences corporate management decisions and audit opinions (Wang et al., 2023). The secondary objective of this research is to evaluate how both financial and non-financial audit quality affect the relationship between ESG practices and dividend payments.

To address potential endogeneity issues, this study utilizes data from Chinese listed companies between 2011 and 2019, employing ESG scores from the Bloomberg database. The ordinary least squares (OLS) regression analysis method is used to assess the effect of ESG scores on dividend payments. An adjustment effect model is developed to examine the moderating role of Big Four audits and their interaction with dividend payments. Hypotheses are tested using a panel dataset, with empirical validation indicating a positive correlation between ESG practices and dividend payout ratios. However, the adoption of Big Four audits is found to negatively impact the dividend payout ratio.

This study offers several key contributions: firstly, it provides novel insights into the interplay between corporate ESG practices and dividend payments, the moderating effects of audit quality, and their underlying mechanisms, thereby contributing to the discourse on corporate ESG practices and investor decision-making. Current ESG research in China predominantly focuses on the validity of ESG scores and their impact on corporate performance. This study's findings offer valuable insights into the outcomes of ESG practices in developing nations, considering both financial and non-financial information. Secondly, by incorporating audit quality and corporate social responsibility (CSR) or non-financial reporting assurance, this research broadens the scope of ESG practice studies, accounting for a wider array of influencing factors and enhancing the understanding of the relationship between ESG practices and dividend policy. Thirdly, this study provides new empirical evidence from China. As an emerging market active in the international arena, China must respond promptly to international investors, particularly those from developed countries influenced by ESG concepts, to ensure steady market share growth. Additionally, this research serves as a reference for investors, elucidating the impact of investment directions in Chinese companies on dividend payments.

2. Literature Review and Hypothesis Development

2.1 Relationship between ESG and Dividend Payments

Evidence from earlier studies suggests a positive correlation between CSR and dividend payments. Benlemlih (2019) demonstrated that sustainability practices are linked to more consistent dividend policies. Similarly, Samet and Jarboui (2017) found that high CSR scores correlate with increased earnings by improving stakeholder relationships, particularly for non-financial firms. Cheung et al. (2018) also asserted that improved stakeholder relationships due to high CSR scores enhance earnings, especially for non-financial businesses. Rakotomavo (2012), examining US corporations prior to the 2007 financial crisis, hypothesized that CSR initiatives and dividend increases often coincide. Therefore, social and sustainable actions do not diminish investors' expectations for dividends.

However, achieving the anticipated increase in profitability from ESG practices may require significant time and investment. Duque-Grisales and Aguilera-Caracuel (2021) argued that the high cost of ESG investments negatively impacts businesses' cash flow and profitability in the short term. Despite these costs, Starks et al. (2017) noted that long-term investors prefer companies with higher ESG performance, recognizing the potential long-term benefits.

Agency theory is pertinent in this context, as it posits that effective ESG disclosure mitigates information asymmetry, thereby fostering investor confidence in a company's financial performance and dividend payments. Improved information symmetry reduces external financing costs, enabling the company to allocate sufficient funds for dividends. Thus, if the assumptions of agency theory hold, there should be a positive relationship between ESG practices and dividend payments. Consequently, the study proposes the following hypothesis:

H1: The association between ESG practices and dividend payouts is substantial.

2.2 Moderating Role of Audit Quality in ESG Dividend Payment Decision

Improving audit quality is crucial for enhancing the accuracy of financial statements, reducing financing costs, and mitigating opportunistic management practices (Rahman & Ziru, 2022). Rahman, Zhu, and Yue (2024) found a positive correlation between the engagement of Big Four audit firms and high-quality audit performance. Higher audit quality leads to greater transparency and reduced information asymmetry. Research by Rahman, Zhu, and Jiang (2024) and Lam et al. (2024) indicated that Big Four-affiliated audit firms have a significant and favourable influence on dividend policy. Conversely, Rahman, Zhu, and Hossain (2023) demonstrated that poor audit quality results in higher information asymmetry and lower dividend payments to shareholders.

Agency theory posits that information symmetry is a solution to agency problems. Jensen and Meckling (1976) argued that higher audit quality reduces information asymmetry. Enhanced information transparency also addresses the challenges of ESG information disclosure. According to signalling theory, providing investors with additional information effectively communicates the steps taken by corporate management to enhance performance, engage in social responsibility, and pay dividends (Zhong et al., 2022). Studies suggest that experienced auditors are more likely to produce comprehensive audit reports. The quality of these audit reports reflects the quality of information that companies convey to investors. High-quality signals are more likely to attract investor interest and support.

Audit quality thus contributes significantly to ESG information disclosure and influences dividend payments. Financial auditors, through implicit training in ESG practices and strategies, can help businesses improve their procedures and reduce reputational risks, thereby preventing corporate misconduct (Asante-Appiah & Lambert, 2023). Enhanced audit quality positively impacts ESG practices, dividend policies, and overall corporate financial performance. Moreover, it can prevent financial fraud and other actions that threaten a company's sustainable growth. The second hypothesis of the study is therefore proposed as follows:

H2: The association between ESG rankings and dividend payouts is strongly moderated by audit quality.

Non-financial reporting assurances play a critical role in influencing ESG dividend decisions. The inclusion of ESG practices in audit quality may have a less pronounced impact on dividend payment policies, as Big Four auditors, due to their reputation and expertise, can engage in ESG practices and thereby reduce capital costs (Martínez-Ferrero & García-Sánchez, 2017). These cost savings lead to improved retained earnings and increased dividend payments. Enhanced audit quality provided by Big Four auditors offers additional credit assurance to firms (Bacha et al., 2020), facilitating trust from banks in handling both financial and non-financial information. This, in turn, results in higher loans at lower costs.

As previously discussed, signalling theory suggests that additional information disclosure can effectively capture investors' attention. Assurance of ESG disclosure demonstrates a company's commitment to ESG practices. Sherry and Hatab (2022) found that auditors trained in ESG auditing place greater emphasis on a company's sustainability report information. Significant discrepancies exist between ESG information in audited and unaudited financial reports (Del Giudice & Rigamonti, 2020). The non-financial disclosure information in audit reports broadens the scope of information disclosure. Consequently, audit quality can serve as a moderating variable, while the audit quality of non-financial disclosures can act as an intermediary variable to narrow the scope of moderating variables. The third research hypothesis is thus proposed as follows:

H3: The association between ESG scores and dividends is strongly moderated by the audit quality of non-financial disclosures.

3. Research Design

3.1 Data Description and Sample Selection

Based on calculated ESG scores from the Bloomberg database, we identify organizations engaging in ESG activities. Bloomberg's ESG data are derived from company reports, news on company websites, and other relevant sources. The ESG score is based on a rigorous quantitative analysis of key performance indicators, as calculated by Bloomberg analysts. Consequently, we included only Chinese listed businesses whose ESG scores were accessible in the Bloomberg database between 2010 and 2019, a period unaffected by the economic shock of COVID-19 and thus representative of the financial crisis recovery. Our sample consists of Chinese A-listed companies, excluding (1) enterprises in the finance sector, (2) firms that received special treatment or specialized transfers, and (3) firms with missing data. The total number of observations in the sample is 5,309. The sample selection process is summarized in Table 11.1.

3.2 *Variable Measurements*

3.2.1 *Dependent Variable*

The dividend payout ratio is used to determine the dividend payout policies. The dividend payout ratio is calculated as the ratio of dividends paid to total assets, according to Benlemlih (2019). Corporate assets have been added to reduce the effect of firm size on dividend distributions. The following equations reflect the various measurements for our dependent variable:

$$\text{Div}_{\text{Payout}} = \left(\frac{\text{Dividend Paid}}{\text{Total Assets}}\right) * 100$$

3.2.2 *Moderating and Independent Variables*

The Bloomberg database's yearly ESG score serves as our main independent variable. The objective ESG scores from Bloomberg are obtained from corporate CSR/sustainability reports or other publicly accessible sources. Compared to other ESG ratings, Bloomberg's ESG data coverage is broader and more convincing (Eshleman & Guo, 2014). The data for audit quality were obtained from the China Securities Market & Accounting Research (CSMAR) database. The audit quality was measured by establishing two dummy variables. The four auditor variables reflect the moderating effects of auditors and audit quality (Li et al., 2022). If the company chooses a Big Four accounting firm as the audit unit, the value is 1. For non-Big Four auditors, it is 0. Additionally, the variable CSR Four Auditors has a value of 1 for businesses that have received a CSR or non-financial information assurance

Table 11.1 Sample Selection

	Number of Observations
Initial sample	30,007
Excluded financial companies	11,587
Excluded special treatment and particular transfer firms	6,579
Companies with missing data	6,532
Final sample	5,309

report from one of the Big Four external auditors for sustainability, and it has a value of 0 for businesses that do not (Zahid et al., 2023).

3.2.3 Control Variables

Numerous factors influence dividend payments, as evidenced by primary literature and recent empirical studies on the determinants of dividends (Saravanakumar, 2011; Dhaka et al., 2022). To isolate the effects of ESG and audit quality on dividend policy, adjustments were made for various corporate and corporate governance aspects (Benlemlih, 2019) and ESG practices (Suttipun, 2021) that could impact a company's dividend policy.

Corporate governance factors significantly affect corporate decision-making, necessitating their inclusion as control variables. The study's control variables include the size of the board of directors, the total number of directors, CEO duality, and board independence. Board size (BSize) is calculated by the total number of directors on a company's board (Liao et al., 2018). CEO duality (CEOD) is a dummy variable indicating whether the CEO also serves as a board member, coded as 1 if true and 0 otherwise. Board independence (BInde) is the percentage of independent directors relative to the total number of board members, representing the ties between the board and management (Kim & Lu, 2011).

Company size is another determinant of dividend payments. Benlemlih (2019) found a positive correlation between the dividend payout ratio and firm size. The natural logarithm of total assets is used to measure firm size (SizeTA), as larger companies typically have more free cash flow available for dividends. However, financial leverage can negatively affect dividend payments when lenders restrict managers to protect their interests (Adjaoud & Ben-Amar, 2010). Financial leverage (FL) is measured as the ratio of total liabilities to total assets, influencing dividend payments and the potential for ESG investments.

Free cash flow (FCF), a measure of cash availability, and return on assets (ROA), a measure of profitability, also affect a company's ability to pay dividends. Productive businesses are expected to generate more FCF and pay higher dividends (Benlemlih, 2019). ROA is calculated by dividing net income before extraordinary items by total assets. FCF is determined by the cash available for payments at the end of the reporting period.

According to the firm life-cycle hypothesis, companies with robust growth potential should retain profits for reinvestment, supporting economic growth. Conversely, companies with less promising growth prospects should distribute higher dividends from cash flow (Adjaoud & Ben-Amar, 2010). Growth potential is evaluated using sales growth (SG), calculated as the percentage change in sales from the previous year.

Elim (2019) noted that tax and retained earnings significantly impact dividend policy. Elton and Gruber (1970) detailed how taxes affect corporate dividend policy. Earnings play a crucial role in determining US dividend policy, according to Baker et al. (1985). The natural logarithm of retained earnings (RE) and the effective tax rate (iTax), calculated by dividing the amount of taxes paid by profits before interest and taxes (EBIT), are also considered in this study.

3.2.4 Econometric Model

We estimate the following models (Zahid et al., 2023) to test the proposed links between ESG, audit quality, and corporate dividend payment choices:

$$\begin{aligned}Div = \alpha &+ \beta_1 ESG_{it} + \beta_2 BSize_{it} + \beta_3 BInde_{it} + \beta_4 CEOD_{it} + \beta_5 FL_{it} \\ &+ \beta_6 Size(TA)_{it} + \beta_7 SG_{it} + \beta_8 ROA_{it} + \beta_9 RE_{it} + \beta_{10} FCF_{it} \\ &+ \beta_{11} iTax_{it} + \sum_{i=1}^{n} \beta_n Country\_Dummies_{it} \\ &+ \sum_{i=1}^{n} \beta_n Industry\_Dummies_{it} + \sum_{i=1}^{n} \beta_n Year\_Dummies_{it} + \varepsilon_{it}\end{aligned}$$

Here:

i is the firm, and *t* is the time (fiscal year).
Div is the dividend paid, alternatively measured by Div Payout.
ESG refers to the ESG total score.
BSize refers to the total number of directors on corporate boards.
BInde is the number of independent directors on corporate boards.
CEOD depicts the dual role of the CEO as a director of the board.
FL is financial leverage, measured as the ratio of total debt to total assets.
Size(TA) is the natural logarithm of the total assets of the firm.
SG is sales growth.
ROA is the return on assets.
RE is the natural logarithm of retained earnings.
FCF is the natural logarithm of free cash flows available.
iTax is the effective income tax rate.
ε is the error term.

The moderating impact of audit quality on the relationship between ESG and dividend distribution is seen in the following equation. Firstly, Big4 x ESG is an interaction term used to measure how the Big Four financial audit moderating influence. Secondly, the Big4CSR x ESG interaction term measures the impact of the Big Four firms' guarantee of sustainability reporting. The remaining variables are identical to those in the base model.

$$\begin{aligned}Div = \alpha &+ \beta_1 ESG_{it} + \beta_2 Big4_{it} + \beta_3 Big4_{it} \times ESG_{it} \\ &+ \beta_4 BSize_{it} \times + \beta_5 BInde_{it} \times + \beta_6 CEOD_{it} + \beta_7 FL_{it} + \beta_8 Size(TA)_{it} \\ &+ \beta_9 SG_{it} + \beta_{10} ROA_{it} + \beta_{11} RE_{it} + \beta_{12} FCF_{it} + \beta_{13} iTax_{it} \\ &+ \sum_{i=1}^{n} * \beta_n Country\_Dummies_{it} + \sum_{i=1}^{n} \beta_n Industry\_Dummies_{it} \\ &+ \sum_{i=1}^{n} \beta_n Year\_Dummies_{it} + \varepsilon_{it}\end{aligned}$$

$$\begin{aligned} Div = {} & \alpha + \beta_1 ESG_{it} + \beta_2 Big4CSR_{it} + \beta_3 Big4CSR_{it} \times ESG_{it} \\ & + \beta_4 BSize_{it} \times + \beta_5 BInde_{it} \times + \beta_6 CEOD_{it} + \beta_7 FL_{it} + \beta_8 Size(TA)_{it} \\ & + \beta_9 SG_{it} + \beta_{10} ROA_{it} + \beta_{11} RE_{it} + \beta_{12} FCF_{it} + \beta_{13} iTax_{it} \\ & + \sum_{i=1}^{n} * \beta_n Country - Dummies_{it} + \sum_{i=1}^{n} \beta_n Industry - Dummies_{it} \\ & + \sum_{i=1}^{n} \beta_n Year - Dummies_{it} + \varepsilon_{it} \end{aligned}$$

4. Empirical Results and Discussion

4.1 Descriptive Statistics

According to Table 11.2, the standard deviation of the average dividend payout ratio, which is 31.2% on average with a standard error of 1.184, is rather low. The mean of the ESG score is 26.567, the standard deviation is 7.285, and the deviation between its components is slightly higher. The adjustment variables Big4CSR and Big4 are dummy variables. A mean Big4 of 0.93 indicates that most companies' financial statements are reviewed by the Big Four auditors. There were 0–19, with an average of 9, and the average level of board independence was 37.434%. CEOs of companies appearing to be board members make up about 27.1%.

Table 11.3 shows the results of the correlation analysis between the main independent factors and the dependent variables. A multicollinearity issue between these variables is less likely because the correlation coefficient between all variables is less than 0.8. From the perspective of explanatory variable ESG, the correlation coefficient between it and the explained variable Div_Payout is positive and can pass the significance test. However, since correlation analysis is only a one-to-one correlation coefficient analysis of variables, and no other variables are

Table 11.2 Descriptive Statistics

Variable	*Obs*	*Mean*	*Std. Dev.*	*Min*	*Max*
Div_Payout	12372	.312	1.184	0	107.409
ESG	4387	26.567	7.285	7.851	59.099
Big4CSR	12563	.991	.094	0	1
Big4	12563	.93	.255	0	1
BSize	12582	8.671	1.859	0	19
BInde	12580	37.434	5.468	20	80
FL	15013	1.483	10.44	−44.908	856.607
SizeTA	12369	22.098	1.51	18.496	30.952
ROA	11328	11.256	9.082	−35.668	130.247
SG	11484	18.066	46.361	−88.17	1976.512
iTax	11307	16.693	34.527	−2986.899	669.105
lnFCF	11475	18.742	1.899	9.901	27.552
lnRE	11575	19.967	1.611	12.09	27.945
CEOD	28106	.271	.444	0	1

Table 11.3 Correlation of the Key Variables

Variable	*Div_Payout*	*ESG*	*BSize*	*BInde*	*FL*	*SizeTA*	*ROA*	*SG*	*iTax*	*lnFCF*	*lnRE*	*CEOD*
Div_Payout	1.000											
ESG	0.025*	1.000										
BSize	0.008	0.208***	1.000									
BInde	–0.016*	0.037**	–0.462***	1.000								
FL	0.000	0.012	0.003	0.012	1.000							
SizeTA	–0.021**	0.538***	0.389***	0.002	0.013	1.000						
ROA	0.006	–0.046**	0.000	–0.007	–0.033***	–0.072***	1.000					
SG	–0.032***	–0.012	–0.052***	0.027**	–0.004	–0.052***	0.217***	1.000				
iTax	–0.030***	0.030*	0.016	0.016	0.004	0.056***	–0.021**	–0.008	1.000			
lnFCF	–0.010	0.476***	0.330***	0.017	0.001	0.789***	–0.132***	–0.014	0.048***	1.000		
lnRE	–0.019*	0.564***	0.367***	0.005	–0.002	0.866***	–0.173***	–0.066***	0.040***	0.731***	1.000	
CEOD	0.027***	–0.019	–0.179***	0.107***	–0.012	–0.213***	0.062***	0.041***	–0.046***	–0.159***	–0.173***	1.000

*** $p < 0.01$, ** $p < 0.05$, * $p < 0.1$.

added for analysis, the results of the correlation analysis can only be a preliminary judgement of the correlation relationship between variables. To see the factors affecting the explained variable Div_Payout, further analysis should be carried out in combination with the subsequent model regression results.

4.2 ESG and Dividend Payout

We built a fixed-effect model comprising fixed industry, individual, and period for an empirical study to confirm the association between ESG and dividend payout. According to the results of the regression analysis shown in Table 11.4 below, the dividend payout ratio is significantly positively impacted by the ESG score. The coefficient for this relationship is 0.0461, and the test at the significance level of 1% shows that an increase in ESG score can also promote an increase in the dividend payout

Table 11.4 Baseline Regression Results

	Div_Payout
ESG	0.00461***
	(4.01)
BSize	−0.00329
	(−0.72)
BInde	−0.00267**
	(−2.20)
FL	−0.00266
	(−0.95)
SizeTA	−0.0405**
	(−2.11)
ROA	−0.00435***
	(−3.87)
SG	−0.000510***
	(−3.83)
iTax	0.000246
	(0.88)
lnFCF	0.00380
	(1.18)
lnRE	−0.0107
	(−0.66)
CEOD	0.00843
	(0.54)
_cons	1.357***
	(3.85)
Year	Included
Firm	Included
Industry	Included
N	2,424
R^2	0.087

t statistics in parentheses.
* $p < 0.1$, ** $p < 0.05$, *** $p < 0.01$.

ratio. Verify that ESG standards do not impact shareholder profits and that China prioritizes dividend distributions. To calculate the dividend payout ratio, which reflects the relationship between shareholder remuneration and company size, our research emphasizes and examines dividend payout capacity from the perspective of the internal company. Financial leverage prevents dividend payments, and company size has a detrimental effect on payouts. As a result, businesses that invest more in ESG initiatives typically pay lower dividends. Only board independence, out of the specific governance factors considered by the model, significantly affects the dividend payout ratio. Dividend payout is constrained by more independent boards.

4.3 ESG and Dividend Payouts: The Moderating Role of Audit Quality

We build a comparable moderating effect model for analysis to examine if the four major auditors moderate the influence of ESG scores on dividend payments. Table 11.5 shows the results. The results in the second column are based on the baseline regression of the first column, with the addition of the Big Four auditors and the interaction term ESG_Big4 between the regulatory variable and the independent variable ESG. The significance level for the continued positive and significant impact of ESG on the dividend payment ratio is 1%. With a coefficient of −0.0031 and a passing test at a significance level of 5%, the interaction term ESG_Big4 hurts the dividend payout ratio. This suggests that the regulating variable Big4 negatively impacts the explanatory variable ESG's influence on dividend payout. If Big4 is 1, the positive promotion effect of ESG practice on dividend payout will be weakened.

The regression results in the third column presents the moderating effect of Big4CSR. According to the regression results, the interaction term ESG_Big4CSR between Big4CSR and ESG has a negative influence on dividend payout, with a coefficient of −0.00778, and the test at the significance level of 10% indicates that the regulating variable Big4CSR also plays a negative regulating role. If Big4CSR is 1, it will weaken the positive promoting effect of ESG practice on dividend payout. The regression results in the third column present the moderating effect of Big4CSR. According to the regression results, the interaction term ESG_Big4CSR between Big4CSR and ESG has a negative influence on dividend payout, with a coefficient of −0.00778, and the test at the significance level of 10% indicates that the regulating variable Big4CSR also plays a negative holding role. If Big4CSR is 1, it will weaken the positive promoting effect of ESG practice on dividend payout.

It is impossible to isolate the relationship between ESG and dividend distribution from the assurance of non-financial disclosure. A company's dividend policy is significantly impacted by the non-financial guarantee of ESG data, suggesting that auditor engagement is related to trust and reliability in a company's ESG policies.

4.4 Sensitivity Analysis

The results of the main empirical study may suffer from endogeneity problems of omitted variables and reverse causality, such as unknown industry or company-specific factors affecting the results. This study used an instrumental

Table 11.5 Moderating Role of Audit Quality in ESG–Dividend Policy Nexus

	Div_Payout	*Div_Payout*	*Div_Payout*
ESG	0.00461***	0.00367***	0.00464***
	(4.01)	(2.97)	(4.03)
Big4		0.0198	
		(0.62)	
ESG_Big4		−0.00331**	
		(−2.15)	
Big4CSR			0.0235
			(0.51)
ESG_Big4CSR			−0.00778*
			(−1.83)
Bsize	−0.00329	−0.00253	−0.00318
	(−0.72)	(−0.55)	(−0.70)
BInde	−0.00267**	−0.00263**	−0.00263**
	(−2.20)	(−2.17)	(−2.17)
FL	−0.00266	−0.00273	−0.00266
	(−0.95)	(−0.98)	(−0.96)
SizeTA	−0.0405**	−0.0385**	−0.0399**
	(−2.11)	(−2.00)	(−2.08)
ROA	−0.00435***	−0.00434***	−0.00432***
	(−3.87)	(−3.87)	(−3.84)
SG	−0.000510***	−0.000510***	−0.000516***
	(−3.83)	(−3.83)	(−3.87)
iTax	0.000246	0.000264	0.000237
	(0.88)	(0.94)	(0.85)
lnFCF	0.00380	0.00392	0.00396
	(1.18)	(1.22)	(1.23)
lnRE	−0.0107	−0.00994	−0.0110
	(−0.66)	(−0.61)	(−0.68)
CEOD	0.00843	0.00891	0.00954
	(0.54)	(0.58)	(0.62)
_cons	1.357***	1.291***	1.320***
	(3.85)	(3.58)	(3.70)
Year	Included	Included	Included
Firm	Included	Included	Included
Industry	Included	Included	Included
N	2,424	2,424	2,424
R^2	0.087	0.090	0.089

t statistics in parentheses.
* $p < 0.1$, ** $p < 0.05$, *** $p < 0.01$.

variable approach to determine the association between ESG scores and dividend payouts to lessen the bias brought on by endogenous issues. We employed an instrumental variable called "Mean," representing the average ESG score for the same industry and year. This instrumental variable is related to the critical, independent variable called the ESG score but not to the dependent variable called dividend payment. The correlation and exclusion requirements of legitimate instruments were satisfied by the study's instrumental variables. The outcomes of the 2SLS regression estimates are displayed in Table 11.6. Using the model's explanatory factors, we performed a regression analysis on the ESG score and its constituent parts. From the first-stage regression results, it is clear that the choice of Mean and the one-lag ESG score as instrumental variables passed the test for weak instrumental variables because their effects on the independent variable ESG

Table 11.6 2SLS Regression Results

Variable	*First Stage*	*Second Stage*
	ESG	*Div_Payout*
Mean	0.288***	
	(10.87)	
L.ESG	0.702***	
	(35.20)	
ESG		0.00759***
		(8.72)
BSize	0.0530	0.00906***
	(1.03)	(3.86)
BInde	0.0186	−0.00221**
	(1.05)	(−2.48)
FL	0.283***	−0.0120***
	(3.97)	(−3.57)
SizeTA	0.350*	−0.0339**
	(1.71)	(−2.47)
ROA	0.0112	0.00497***
	(0.58)	(3.63)
SG	0.00358	−0.000919***
	(1.13)	(−3.75)
iTax	0.00430	0.000507
	(0.76)	(0.94)
lnFCF	−0.0348	0.00957**
	(−0.40)	(2.27)
lnRE	0.407**	−0.0101
	(2.16)	(−0.76)
CEOD	0.301	−0.0209
	(1.20)	(−1.24)
_cons	−16.73***	0.904***
	(−8.39)	(7.89)
Year	Included	Included
Firm	Included	Included
Industry	Included	Included
N	1,196	1,196
R^2	0.767	0.129

t statistics in parentheses.
* $p < 0.1$, ** $p < 0.05$, *** $p < 0.01$.

score can pass the significance test. The influence of the ESG score on the dividend payout ratio is positively associated, as can be seen from the regression findings of the second stage. The research findings are consistent and in line with the underlying model after accounting for any potential endogenous issues.

4.5 Robustness Tests

The robustness test in this study was performed using the regression approach with lagged independent variables. Although associated endogenous issues are excluded by the instrumental variable approach, there can be a delay in the effect of ESG policies on dividend payment ratios. Regression in this study uses the independent variable ESG with a one-period lag. The coefficient estimates of the dividend payout ratio using the one-period lagged ESG score are still highly positive at the 1% level, as shown in the third row of the second column of Table 11.6, and the outcome has not changed. It demonstrates that the conclusion drawn from the prior regression analysis can pass the robustness test.

5. Discussion

5.1 Relationship with Prior Literature

The relationship between ESG practices and dividend payout policy has been examined in a number of research. No substantial correlation has been found between overall ESG scores and business dividend payments, according to Australian studies (Limkriangkrai et al., 2017). Studies from South Korea (Jung & Kim, 2022) and Indonesia (Saldi et al., 2023) show a favourable correlation between ESG policies and dividend payments. Meanwhile, data from the United Arab Emirates (Ellili, 2022) demonstrate a negative correlation between ESG and dividend payments. ESG principles can supplement the existing literature on the variables influencing dividend payout policies and are becoming increasingly important considerations for investors and policymakers.

However, there are currently no empirical studies that look at how audit quality affects the relationship between dividend distributions and ESG practices in the Chinese setting. To our knowledge, only one study in Western Europe (Zahid et al., 2023) has examined the moderating effect of audit quality on dividend distributions and ESG practices. According to Zahid et al. (2023), more excellent ESG ratings for public companies in Western Europe result in higher dividend payouts. Still, our findings are consistent with improved audit quality reducing dividend payments. This may be because Western European and Chinese businesses and governments have given ESG concepts considerable consideration.

5.2 Theoretical Contribution

This study contributes to the theoretical advancement by demonstrating how ESG practices influence dividend payment policies through the lenses of agency theory, stakeholder theory, life-cycle theory, and signalling theory. It highlights the critical role of ESG disclosures in reducing information asymmetry, aligning stakeholder interests, and signalling corporate commitment to sustainability, thereby promoting higher dividend payouts. Additionally, it underscores the importance of maintaining high audit quality to support these theoretical frameworks and enhance overall corporate governance.

The study's findings reveal a strong positive correlation between ESG practices and dividend payout policies, supporting the tenets of agency theory. By enhancing ESG disclosures, companies reduce information asymmetry between management and shareholders, thereby mitigating agency problems. This transparency fosters investor confidence, leading to lower external financing costs and higher dividend payouts. Thus, our research extends agency theory by highlighting the role of ESG disclosures in promoting transparent and effective corporate governance.

The results underscore the importance of stakeholder theory, demonstrating that high ESG scores, reflecting a firm's commitment to social responsibility, correlate with more substantial dividend payouts. This alignment suggests that companies engaging in robust ESG practices not only fulfil their ethical obligations to stakeholders but also enhance their financial performance, thereby satisfying shareholder expectations. This integration of stakeholder interests with financial outcomes extends the applicability of stakeholder theory in the context of ESG practices.

While life-cycle theory posits that firms with growth potential should retain earnings for reinvestment, our study reveals that ESG practices can coexist with dividend payments, particularly in mature firms. Although the impact of life-cycle theory is less pronounced compared to that of agency and stakeholder theories, our findings suggest that ESG initiatives do not necessarily preclude dividend distributions. This extension of life-cycle theory includes the consideration of ESG disclosures as part of the firm's strategic life-cycle management.

The positive correlation between ESG scores and dividend payouts also supports signalling theory. Enhanced ESG disclosures serve as a signal to investors of a firm's commitment to sustainable practices and robust financial health. This signalling effect helps attract investor support and trust, thereby facilitating higher dividend payments. Our research reinforces signalling theory by demonstrating how ESG disclosures can act as a credible signal of corporate performance and governance quality.

The study also reveals that while improved audit quality may temporarily negatively impact dividend payment decisions, it remains crucial for managers to prioritize audit quality. High audit quality enhances the credibility of ESG disclosures, which, in turn, strengthens the positive effects of agency, stakeholder, and signalling theories on dividend policy. This finding suggests that the temporary costs associated with higher audit quality are outweighed by the long-term benefits of increased transparency and investor trust.

5.3 Practical Implications

Our findings have important implications for companies, investors, auditors, and policymakers. Companies should recognize the positive correlation between higher ESG scores and dividend payments. By adopting ESG practices to improve ESG scores, companies can enhance their attractiveness to investors looking for sustainable investment opportunities. For investors, ESG factors should be factored into investment decisions, as companies with higher ESG scores are more likely to offer sustainable and higher dividend payments. Investors should consider not only a company's financial performance but also a company's ESG score to make informed investment decisions. Auditors should strive to enhance their understanding of ESG frameworks, metrics, and reporting standards. This indicates their ability to assess the ESG practices of the audited companies effectively. Auditors can also actively work with companies to ensure that audits accurately reflect a company's commitment to sustainability by understanding the impact of ESG practices on dividend policies. Finally, for policymakers, it should ensure that the quality of corporate audits improves. Policymakers should encourage companies to employ auditors with ESG knowledge and expertise, which, while resulting in a temporary negative performance in dividend payment policies, can significantly impact a company's ESG practices.

6. Conclusion

The absence of empirical data on the influence of ESG on dividend payment choices and the moderating effect of audit quality on the ESG–dividend relationship in the Chinese context are the driving forces behind this effort. The literature in this area demonstrates various research outcomes in many places. Therefore, general conclusions may not be applicable. It also aims to broaden the field's national and geographic breadth. By analysing data from Chinese listed businesses from 2011 to 2019, our research complements the current research agenda in the Chinese environment. The association between ESG score and the dividend payout ratio is supported theoretically and empirically in this study. The analysis found that Big Four auditors have a significant, unfavourable impact on the relationship between ESG and dividend payout ratios. The Big Four auditors produce high-quality audits, but their use results in reduced dividend payment rates.

One implication of this research is that companies can gain investor attention through ESG practices. Shareholder concerns motivate company management to improve the financial or non-financial characteristics of the company's ESG performance. The impact of stakeholders' knowledge of a company's ESG performance can be substantial, giving investors' interest and confidence to invest. The study suggests that shareholders who want to get more returns under the company's dividend policy consider the company's investment direction.

A final caveat is that this study was conducted in a Chinese context and needs to be rethought before being generalized to other countries or regions. Because China, as an emerging market, is rapidly following the development direction of the international market, the Chinese government also regards ESG goals such as "carbon neutrality" as important issues. So Chinese companies may be more responsible than companies in other developing countries but still lag behind some developed countries. Further research should not ignore the impact of national policies and market characteristics on corporate ESG performance and financial decision-making.

References

Adjaoud, F., & Ben-Amar, W. (2010). Corporate governance and dividend policy: Shareholders' protection or expropriation? *Journal of Business Finance & Accounting*, *37*(5–6), 648–667.

Asante-Appiah, B., & Lambert, T. A. (2023). The role of the external auditor in managing environmental, social, and governance (ESG) reputation risk. *Review of Accounting Studies*, *28*(4), 2589–2641.

Bacha, S., Ajina, A., & Ben Saad, S. (2020). CSR performance and the cost of debt: Does audit quality matter? *Corporate Governance: The International Journal of Business in Society*, *21*(1), 137–158.

Baker, H. K., Farrelly, G. E., & Edelman, R. B. (1985). A survey of management views on dividend policy. *Financial Management*, *14*(3), 78-84.

Benlemlih, M. (2019). Corporate social responsibility and dividend policy. *Research in International Business and Finance*, *47*, 114–138.

Cheung, A. W., Hu, M., & Schwiebert, J. (2018). Corporate social responsibility and dividend policy. *Accounting & Finance*, *58*(3), 787–816.

Del Giudice, A., & Rigamonti, S. (2020). Does audit improve the quality of ESG scores? Evidence from corporate misconduct. *Sustainability*, *12*(14), 5670.

Dhaka, V., Singh, S., Anil, A. G., Sunil Kumar Naik, T. S., Garg, S., Samuel, J., Kumar, M., Ramamurthy, P. C., & Singh, J. (2022). Occurrence, toxicity and remediation of polyethylene terephthalate plastics. A review. *Environmental Chemistry Letters*, *20*, 1777–1800.

Di Tommaso, C., & Mazzuca, M. (2023). The stock price of European insurance companies: What is the role of ESG factors? *Finance Research Letters*, *56*, 104071.

Duque-Grisales, E., & Aguilera-Caracuel, J. (2021). Environmental, social and governance (ESG) scores and financial performance of multilatinas: Moderating effects of geographic international diversification and financial slack. *Journal of Business Ethics*, *168*(2), 315–334.

Elim, J. (2019). Model of firm value – Indonesian stock exchange case. *International Journal of Economics and Financial Issues*, *9*(3), 154–162.

Ellili, N. O. D. (2022). Impact of environmental, social and governance disclosure on dividend policy: What is the role of corporate governance? Evidence from an emerging market. *Corporate Social Responsibility and Environmental Management*, *29*(5), 1396–1413.

Elton, E. J., & Gruber, M. J. (1970). Homogeneous groups and the testing of economic hypotheses. *Journal of Financial and Quantitative Analysis*, *4*(5), 581–602.

Eshleman, J. D., & Guo, P. (2014). Do big 4 auditors provide higher audit quality after controlling for the endogenous choice of auditor? *Auditing: A Journal of Practice & Theory*, *33*(4), 197–219.

Friede, G., Busch, T., & Bassen, A. (2015). ESG and financial performance: Aggregated evidence from more than 2000 empirical studies. *Journal of Sustainable Finance & Investment*, *5*(4), 210–233.

Imen, F., & Anis, J. (2020). The moderating role of audit quality on the relationship between auditor reporting and earnings management: Empirical evidence from Tunisia. *EuroMed Journal of Business*, *16*(4), 416–430.

Jensen, M. C., & Meckling, W. H. (1976). Theory of the firm: Managerial behavior, agency costs and ownership structure. *Journal of Financial Economics*, *3*(4), 305–360.

Jung, S.-C., & Kim, Y.-H. (2022). ESG activities and dividend policy in Korean firms. *Asian Review of Financial Research, 35*(2), 107–145.

Kim, E. H., & Lu, Y. (2011). *The independent board requirement and CEO connectedness.* Available at SSRN 1970591.

Lam, B. M., Mo, P. L. L., & Rahman, M. J. (2024). Secrecy culture, client importance, and auditor reporting behavior: An international study. *Managerial Auditing Journal, 39*(2), 113–137.

Li, S., Yin, P., & Liu, S. (2022). Evaluation of ESG ratings for Chinese listed companies from the perspective of stock price crash risk. *Frontiers in Environmental Science, 10*, 933639.

Liao, L., Lin, T. P., & Zhang, Y. (2018). Corporate board and corporate social responsibility assurance: Evidence from China. *Journal of Business Ethics, 150*(1), 211–225.

Limkriangkrai, M., Koh, S., & Durand, R. B. (2017). Environmental, social, and governance (ESG) profiles, stock returns, and financial policy: Australian evidence. *International Review of Finance, 17*(3), 461–471.

Martínez-Ferrero, J., & García-Sánchez, I.-M. (2017). Sustainability assurance and cost of capital: Does assurance impact on credibility of corporate social responsibility information? *Business Ethics: A European Review, 26*(3), 223–239.

Rahman, M. J., & Wu, J. (2023). M&A activity and ESG performance: Evidence from China. *Managerial Finance, 50*(1), 179–197.

Rahman, M. J., Wu, Q., & Zhu, H. (2024). Corporate social responsibility in times of social distancing: Evidence from China. *Business Ethics, the Environment & Responsibility.*

Rahman, M. J., Zhu, H., & Chen, S. (2023). Does CSR reduce financial distress? Moderating effect of firm characteristics, auditor characteristics, and covid-19. *International Journal of Accounting & Information Management, 31*(5), 756–784.

Rahman, M. J., Zhu, H., & Hossain, M. M. (2023). Auditor choice and audit fees through the lens of agency theory: Evidence from Chinese family firms. *Journal of Family Business Management, 13*(4), 1248–1276.

Rahman, M. J., Zhu, H., & Jiang, X. (2024). Family firms, client importance, and auditor reporting behavior: Evidence from China. *Meditari Accountancy Research, 32*(2), 543–578.

Rahman, M. J., Zhu, H., & Yue, L. (2024). Does the adoption of artificial intelligence by audit firms and their clients affect audit quality and efficiency? Evidence from China. *Managerial Auditing Journal, 39*(6), 668–699.

Rahman, M. J., & Ziru, A. (2022). Clients' digitalization, audit firms' digital expertise, and audit quality: Evidence from China. *International Journal of Accounting & Information Management, 31*(2), 221–246.

Rakotomavo, M. T. J. (2012). Corporate investment in social responsibility versus dividends? *Social Responsibility Journal, 8*(2), 199–207.

Saldi, W. A. I., Adrianto, F., & Hamidi, M. (2023). ESG and dividend policy in Indonesia. *Journal of Social Research, 2*(3), 724–734.

Samet, M., & Jarboui, A. (2017). How does corporate social responsibility contribute to investment efficiency? *Journal of Multinational Financial Management, 40*, 33–46.

Saravanakumar, S. (2011). Determinants of corporate dividend policy. *Asia Pacific Business Review, 7*(2), 25–36.

Sherry, H., & Hatab, E. (2022). ESG audit training perspective in Asia. *International Journal of Computer Auditing, 4*(1), 28–35.

Smith, A. (1776). *The wealth of nations.*

Starks, L. T., Venkat, P., & Zhu, Q. (2017). *Corporate ESG profiles and investor horizons.* Available at SSRN 3049943.

Suttipun, M. (2021). The influence of board composition on environmental, social and governance (ESG) disclosure of Thai listed companies. *International Journal of Disclosure and Governance, 18*(4), 391–402.

Wang, X., Song, X., & Sun, M. (2023). How does a company's ESG performance affect the issuance of an audit opinion? The moderating role of auditor experience. *International Journal of Environmental Research and Public Health, 20*(5), 3878.

Zahid, R. M. A., Khan, M. K., Anwar, W., & Maqsood, U. S. (2022). The role of audit quality in the ESG-corporate financial performance nexus: Empirical evidence from Western European companies. *Borsa Istanbul Review*, *22*, S200–S212.

Zahid, R. M. A., Taran, A., Khan, M. K., & Chersan, I.-C. (2023). ESG, dividend payout policy and the moderating role of audit quality: Empirical evidence from Western Europe. *Borsa Istanbul Review*, *23*(2), 350–367.

Zhong, X., Chen, W., & Ren, G. (2022). The impact of corporate social irresponsibility on emerging-economy firms' long-term performance: An explanation based on signal theory. *Journal of Business Research*, *144*, 345–357.

Zhu, H., & Rahman, M. J. (2024). Ex-ante expected changes in ESG and future stock returns based on machine learning. *The British Accounting Review*, 101457.

12 Does ESG Performance Reduce Financial Distress? Moderating Effect of Firm Characteristics

Md Jahidur Rahman, Tarek Rana, Hongtao Zhu, and Wang Yujing

1. Introduction

This study seeks to elucidate the relationship among environmental, social, and governance (ESG) factors and financial distress in China, addressing the paucity of research on ESG's directional impact within the global financial domain, particularly concerning Chinese data. To achieve these objectives, we first collected ESG and financial data from Chinese A-share companies using the Wind and China Stock Market & Accounting Research (CSMAR) databases. The ESG Composite score from the Wind database was utilized to measure ESG performance.

To enhance the robustness of our research, we incorporated the *Z*-score (standard score) and *O*-score (operating performance score) as predictive measures of financial distress, following the established literature. These quantifiable models can forecast financial distress by identifying potential risks in advance. The *Z*-score, specifically, employs preset thresholds to assess a company's financial status, providing a risk value for reference by investors and managers. This aids in financial planning and strategic adjustments to mitigate business risks. Edward Altman, one of the pioneers of the *Z*-score model, demonstrated its superior efficacy over other financial models in predicting enterprise risk (Altman, 1968). Similarly, the *Z*-score has shown greater predictive accuracy and reliability for financial distress in British companies compared to other models (Taffler, 1984). As an alternative measure, the *O*-score was also employed to assess financial distress.

ESG is an investment philosophy and evaluation criterion emphasizing external consequences and governance levels over financial performance. With societal development, corporate investors increasingly consider non-financial indicators, such as positive external effects, alongside traditional financial metrics. This shift has driven the rapid emergence of ESG investment. ESG is now a critical area of study within financial academia, with diversified and in-depth research underscoring its positive correlation with corporate culture and financial performance, contributing to sustainable enterprise development (Eccles et al., 2011). ESG data significantly impact corporate financial performance (CFP) and can be used to assess a company's potential value and risks (Kotsantonis & Serafeim, 2019). Moreover, ESG data provide timely information, aiding investors and managers in making informed corporate decisions (Khan et al., 2016).

DOI: 10.4324/9781003488934-16

Despite growing recognition of ESG's pivotal role in financial markets globally, significant gaps remain in the research, particularly regarding its impact on financial distress. Prior studies have shown that sustainable practices can enhance financial advantages and that corporate social responsibility (CSR), conceptually akin to ESG, correlates with lower financing costs (Cheng et al., 2014). ESG performance also positively influences corporate capital flows (Hartzmark & Sussman, 2017). Several studies in China also investigate the relationship between environmental accounting and firm performance (Rahman & Wu, 2023; Rahman, et al., 2024, 2023; Zhu & Rahman, 2024).

Financial distress is a critical concern within financial academia due to its potential to disrupt business operations and precipitate bankruptcy. Previous research has highlighted the effectiveness of financial ratios in predicting corporate bankruptcy (Beaver, 1966) and the broader economic implications of financial distress, such as market imbalances and unemployment (Ben-Ner & Jones, 1995). Identifying financial distress is thus essential for sustainable enterprise development.

This study is motivated by several factors. Firstly, Chinese listed companies, many of which evolved from state-owned enterprises (SOEs), exhibit unique characteristics. Delisting and bankruptcy are rare outcomes, partly due to government interventions that maintain financial stability (Allen et al., 2005). Consequently, financial distress has not been a major focus within the Chinese financial market. Furthermore, traditional Chinese business culture, which emphasizes stability and conservatism, often leads to the concealment of financial distress data to preserve corporate and societal image (Redding, 1995).

Secondly, ESG awareness and implementation are still developing in China and many Asian countries. Traditional cultural values often prioritize economic development and profit maximization over sustainable practices (Huang et al., 2019). Consequently, ESG disclosure and reporting standards remain underdeveloped.

Thirdly, the relationship between ESG and corporate financial outcomes is a burgeoning area of international academic research. Prior studies in other contexts have demonstrated that ESG practices can enhance corporate transparency and reduce bankruptcy risks (Hoepner et al., 2016). However, the applicability of these findings to the Chinese market, which operates under different economic and cultural conditions, remains to be explored.

Fourthly, while recent studies have examined the relationship between CSR (akin to ESG) and financial distress, most have focused on US companies (Boubaker et al., 2020; Antunes et al., 2023). Exploring this relationship within the Chinese context could yield novel insights and contribute to a more comprehensive understanding of ESG's global implications.

This study makes significant contributions to the existing literature. It is the first to investigate the relationship between ESG and financial distress based on data from Chinese listed companies. It provides valuable data for understanding the financial difficulties of the Chinese market and informs global economic and financial stability. Additionally, this research offers practical insights for investors, shareholders, and corporate stakeholders regarding the importance of ESG performance in mitigating financial distress and enhancing sustainable development.

The remainder of this chapter is structured as follows. Section 2 presents the theoretical framework. Section 3 discusses the literature review and hypothesis development. The research design is outlined in Section 4. Empirical findings are presented in Section 5. Endogeneity and robustness tests are covered in Sections 6 and 7, respectively. Conclusions are drawn in Section 8.

2. Theoretical Framework

ESG factors have long been a strategic concern for businesses globally due to the growing attention from investors and customers. In recent years, an increasing number of companies worldwide have published sustainability reports detailing their ESG performance. By disclosing ESG data, these companies aim to demonstrate transparency to investors and shareholders, thereby gaining their trust and enhancing enterprise value. The World Economic Forum's 2019 data underscored the significance and influence of ESG in the global investment landscape, providing evidence from investors, businesses, and governments that ESG has become a crucial strategic concern for businesses worldwide (World Economic Forum, 2019). Ioannou and Serafeim (2014) provided extensive data showing that companies have integrated ESG performance into their investment decisions, thereby attracting investor interest.

Many countries have implemented legal and regulatory measures requiring companies to disclose real ESG data and adhere to ESG standards. For instance, the European Union's "Non-Financial Reporting Directive" of 2018 mandates listed companies to report their ESG performance to ensure compliance with EU standards (Kotsantonis & Serafeim, 2019). Similarly, the UK's "Corporate Governance Act" requires large companies to disclose ESG performance, and the Financial Market Regulator has established ESG reporting requirements for listed companies (Zhu & Rahman, 2024). In Asia, Japan's Financial Services Authority introduced the Stewardship Code in 2014, encouraging institutional investors to incorporate ESG factors in their investment processes to promote sustainable growth and enterprise value (Mōri et al., 2022).

The concept of ESG, which evolved from the broader framework of CSR, first emerged in the 20th century (Jamali et al., 2019). In the United States, the Securities and Exchange Commission (SEC) has consistently focused on ESG disclosure, even establishing a dedicated ESG team in 2021 to update ESG disclosure requirements (Wirth, 2023). However, China's approach to ESG varies across industries, and compared to other developed countries, China is still in the early stages of ESG development. The concept and practice of ESG are less recognized in China's corporate and business markets largely because the country prioritizes rapid economic growth.

The Chinese government emphasizes economic growth promotion, and Chinese companies rarely engage in ESG reporting due to a lack of professional expertise and resources. Despite its relatively recent development, ESG has become integral to many Chinese companies, especially listed ones. Morgan Stanley Capital International (MSCI) reported that since 2010, ESG investment in Chinese companies has increased more than fivefold, driven by growing investor attention to sustainable development and ESG performance (MSCI, 2019). The Chinese government has also updated its economic policies, becoming increasingly sensitive to corporate ESG reporting to achieve key green economic objectives (Zhang, 2022).

In 2018, the China Securities Regulatory Commission (CSRC) revised the "Code of Corporate Governance for Listed Companies," mandating ESG information disclosure by listed companies (Government of the People's Republic of China, 2018). The People's Bank of China issued guidelines for pilot environmental information disclosure by financial institutions in 2020, and in 2021, the CSRC updated the format standards for annual and semi-annual reports of listed companies, emphasizing environmental protection and social responsibility. "Measures for Enterprises to Disclose Environmental Information According to Law," implemented in 2022, require five types of enterprises to disclose environmental information.

As China strives for a greener economy and improved social equity, the importance of ESG for businesses and governments will only grow. China aims to peak carbon emissions by 2030 and achieve carbon neutrality by 2060, necessitating a shift to low-carbon business models. Since launching its green financial system in 2016, China's ESG concept has rapidly developed, driven by national carbon peaking and neutrality goals (Li, 2016). Policy incentives and regulations largely drive ESG development in China (Huld, 2022). According to JP Morgan Chase, larger Chinese companies have increasingly released ESG information, with 86% of the 300 largest A-share companies publishing ESG reports in 2020, a 49% increase from 2010 (JP Morgan, 2023).

From a financial perspective, "financial distress" has become a significant concern in banking, commercial markets, and the financial industry due to its close relationship with creditors (Chu, 2021). Financial distress is highly regarded in academic and financial practice, although delisting and bankruptcy are rare in China's government-supported market (He et al., 2019). Nonetheless, Chinese companies still face financial difficulties, as evidenced by cases like Haier's financial crisis in 2016, Huawei's challenges due to US sanctions, and CITIC Group's financial difficulties during the 2015 financial crisis (Zhong et al., 2022; Kharpal, 2023; Fang et al., 2018).

Many researchers have examined the link between ESG and corporate financial distress. Our goal is to investigate this relationship within the context of the current Chinese economic situation, a challenging and in-depth research area. ESG has the potential to reduce business risk (Eccles & Serafeim, 2013), which can adversely affect financial distress risk (FDR) (Boubaker et al., 2020). Thus, we aim to determine whether these relationships hold true for listed companies in China.

3. Literature Review and Hypothesis Development

3.1 ESG and Financial Distress

Numerous studies have concluded that ESG factors can mitigate the likelihood of corporate bankruptcy. Some stakeholders posit that investing in CSR can generate moral capital and goodwill, which serve as protective mechanisms that help reduce corporate risks (Marks, 2017). For instance, Sun and Stuebs examined the relationship between CSR and firm productivity within the US chemical industry, finding that CSR positively impacts firm competitiveness through learning and innovation cycles (Kapelko, 2022). Similarly, Cohena's analysis of the S&P 500 Index stocks indicated that higher environmental and social risks diminish financial stability and elevate default risk (Cohen, 2023). Additionally, Buallay (2021) empirically demonstrated that ESG reporting can enhance company value.

Further evidence comes from a meta-analysis of 2,200 studies, which identified a positive relationship between ESG reporting and CFP (Friede et al., 2015). In Malaysia, research has shown that companies providing ESG reports are more valuable and favoured by investors compared to those that do not (Harymawan et al., 2020). In Indonesia, researchers found that ESG performance alleviates financial distress among listed companies (Sumarno et al., 2023). Australian studies also corroborate these findings, with data from 651 listed companies over the past decade revealing a negative correlation between ESG and financial distress (Al-Hadi et al., 2017).

From the extant literature, it is evident that there is generally an inverse relationship between ESG and financial distress. However, most of these findings are derived from data specific to Western or other Asian countries and may not be directly applicable to China. This study seeks to extend these insights by examining whether the same relationship holds true within the Chinese context using data from 2009 to 2022. Accordingly, the first hypothesis of this research is formulated as follows:

H1: ESG performance is negatively related to financial distress in China.

3.2 ESG and Financial Distress in SOE Firms

The majority of listed companies in China have their origins in SOEs, and SOEs continue to dominate a significant portion of the Chinese market (Chu, 2021). While ESG principles are broadly applicable across different types of companies, the unique characteristics of SOEs warrant separate consideration (Li et al., 2021). SOEs in China have a distinct status within the commercial market, characterized by closer ties to the government compared to non-SOEs. This relationship provides SOEs with substantial financing advantages.

Given the special status of SOEs and their governmental connections, the impact of ESG performance on financial distress may differ between SOEs and non-SOEs. SOEs' financing advantages could mitigate the risks associated with financial distress, potentially weakening the observed relationship between ESG performance and financial stability. Therefore, this study proposes the following hypothesis:

H2: The relationship between ESG performance and financial distress is weaker in SOEs than in non-SOEs.

4. Research Design

4.1 Sample Composition

We obtained corporate ESG data from the Wind database. Financial data were obtained from the CSMAR database. We focus on China's A-share listed companies to construct our samples, merge the two databases, then clean the variables in the study, delete missing values, and finally include 31,373 samples in the analysis. Table 12.1 shows the number of initial and final samples. The data before cleaning are presented in Table 12.2.

4.2 Measuring ESG

China's ESG rating system is developed through internationally accepted information disclosure standards. At present, China uses professional research institutions, market institutions, and experts and scholars to build an ESG rating system (2023). Huazheng ESG rating system has created a three-tier index system in accordance with the norms of China's domestic market based on the foundational and developmental experience of ESG. Huazeng Index has created an algorithm-driven big data engine to quantify the ESG level of listed Chinese firms on a non-annual basis using both conventional and alternative data sources. Huazheng ESG rating covers all A-share companies, dating back to 2009 at the earliest, and is currently the ESG

Table 12.1 Sample Selection Step

Sample Selection Procedure	*Firm-Year Observations*
Initial sample	42,195
Exclude: firm-year lack of variables	10,822
Final sample	31,373

Table 12.2 Original Variable Situation Description

Variable	*Obs*	*Mean*	*Std. Dev.*	*Min*	*Max*
Year	42,195	2016.761	3.927364	2009	2022
Composite score	42,195	72.94367	5.540398	36.62	92.93
Z-score	40,824	5.220057	15.21088	−700.877	1860.963
O-Score	36,020	−8.22048	13.50205	−356.397	1277.342
MTB	37,099	8.102153	150.2199	−4792.95	19509.4
VOL	37,015	3.21765	3.312382	0.324873	182.8675
SLACK	37,080	16.82689	13.90014	−16.4788	100
TANG	37,069	20.77407	16.61067	0.000786	295.9932
Total annual cumulative div	26,527	4.42E+08	3.26E+09	181500	1.05E+11
DIV	37,097				
Ending cash	37,080	4.64E+09	4.40E+10	1386.5	1.98E+12
Total assets (yuan)	37,097	6.47E+10	8.33E+11	84823.6	3.52E+13
Fixed assets (yuan)	37,069	3.88E+09	2.24E+10	1335.4	7.33E+11

grading system in China's domestic market with the longest retrospective period. Since we have to conduct data research for more than ten years, we decided to use Huazheng ESG rating data. We decided to use the ESG Composite Score as a measurement tool for ESG.

4.3 Measuring Financial Distress

For the assessment of financial distress, we used FDR in this study. We found a variety of methods for estimating FDR. Since this study is based on accounting and business markets, after comprehensive analysis, it was decided to use the strategy provided by Altman et al. to measure financial distress. Because this approach is dependent on accounting data (Altman et al., 2017; Tykvová & Borell, 2012), we will use two accounting-based metrics to calculate FDR: *Z*-score (Altman, 1968; Equation 1) and *O*-score (Ohlson, 1980; Equation 2). A high *O*-score is linked to a high FDR, whereas a high *Z*-score is linked to a low FDR, based on Boubaker et al. (2020).

Working capital is represented by WC, total assets by TA, retained earnings by retEARNINGS, profits before interest and taxes by EBIT, market value of equity by MV, total liabilities by TL, sales by SAL, current liabilities by CL, and current assets by CA. When TL surpasses TA, TLdummy has a value of 1; otherwise, it has a value of 0. A dummy variable named NLdummy has a value of 1 if the company has reported a net loss over the preceding two years, and 0 otherwise. Funds from operations are represented by FFO, whereas net income is denoted by NI (Boubaker et al., 2020).

4.4 Empirical Model

4.4.1. ESG and FDR

In this study, the fundamental OLS regression approach is first used to evaluate Hypothesis 1. The effects of variables that are omitted but do not change over time are then taken into account using the fixed-effect (FE) technique.

Control refers to a set of control variables:

A) The market-to-book (MTB) ratio evaluates the difference between the equity's book and market values. From previous literature studies, we know that corporate investors are more willing to invest in companies with high growth prospects than companies with low growth prospects (Hsu et al., 2015). This study predicts a negative relationship between business risk and MTB.
B) The word volatility (VOL) is used to define the annualized standard deviation of monthly stock returns. This study suggests that VOL has a strong link with financial trouble, which is why investors respect this indicator.
C) Financial slack (SLACK) is the amount of cash and cash equivalents in relation to total assets. The pecking order theory states that companies with better financial flexibility tend to depend less on outside financing and have lower debt

levels (Verwijmeren & Derwall, 2010). This study predicts a negative relationship between idling and financial distress.

D) SIZE stands for the natural logarithm of the total assets. The possibility of insolvency is increased due to the greater likelihood and ratio of indebtedness of large corporations (Hsu et al., 2015). This study predicts a positive relationship between variable size and financial distress.

E) Asset tangibility (TANG) is defined as the proportion of total fixed assets to total assets. According to Sharpe and Stadnik (2007), real assets can enhance the company's ability to obtain financing and allow the company to obtain more debt financing. This study predicts a positive relationship between TANG and financial distress.

F) To ascertain if a corporation pays dividends in the current year (DIV), a dummy variable is utilized. Generally speaking, companies that pay dividends have easier access to external financing than their rivals who don't. As a result, it makes sense to assume that companies that pay dividends rely less on debt financing (Verwijmeren & Derwall, 2010). This study expected a negative relationship between DIV and financial problems.

For Equation (4), this research mainly focuses on the regression coefficient of ESG. If the variable FDR adopts the *Z*-score, then the regression coefficient is significantly positive; the higher the comprehensive ESG score, the lower the risk of corporate financial distress, that is, the two are negatively correlated. If FDR adopts the *O*-score, then the regression coefficient is significantly negative; the higher the ESG comprehensive score, the lower the risk of corporate financial distress, that is, the two are negatively correlated. Both results support our first hypothesis.

4.4.2. Moderating Effect of Firm Characteristics

For test Hypothesis 2, we added SOE and ESG vs. CSR × SOE as dummy variables to the previous test. SOE is a dummy variable for the nature of the firm, which is 1 for SOE and 0 otherwise. Other variables were the same as in the above tests. If the regression coefficient is negative when FDR is used as the *Z*-score, or the regression coefficient is positive when FDR is used as the *O*-score, it means that the social responsibility of SOEs has little effect on alleviating financial distress.

5. Empirical Findings

5.1 Summary Statistics

Table 12.3 reports the sample distribution by year. The sample size from 2009 to 2012 was less than 2,000 because the Wind database started rating data in 2015. Although it dates back to 2009, it is still incomplete due to insufficient data. We can observe that the overall ESG comprehensive score from 2009 to 2021 is relatively average, and the score has not increased because of the emphasis. However, it can be clearly seen that the FDR of Chinese companies has increased significantly in

Table 12.3 Distribution of ESG and Z-Score in Different Years

Year	*Freq.*	*Percent*	*Mean*		*Median*	
			ESG	*Z-score*	*ESG*	*Z-score*
2009	1,386	4.42	72.78	4.323	72.89	2.823
2010	1,430	4.56	71.95	5.448	72.14	3.038
2011	1,583	5.05	72.72	4.163	72.86	2.585
2012	1,934	6.16	73.1	3.837	73.47	2.588
2013	2,173	6.93	72.96	4.563	73.26	2.824
2014	2,267	7.23	72.65	5.576	72.95	3.271
2015	2,271	7.24	72.19	8.266	72.52	4.279
2016	2,423	7.72	71.94	6.76	72.53	3.643
2017	2,609	8.32	72.43	5.079	72.79	3.001
2018	2,944	9.38	73.07	3.778	73.45	2.447
2019	3,318	10.58	72.61	4.416	73.28	2.792
2020	3,410	10.87	72.5	4.789	73.22	2.924
2021	3,625	11.55	72.5	5.205	73.1	3.139
Total	31,373	100	72.57	5.091	72.98	2.955

2015–2016. In 2015, China was facing a dual crisis both domestically and internationally (Financial Information, 2022). This reason may be responsible for the high financial risk at this time.

Table 12.4 provides the descriptive statistics of the variables. It clearly shows that the mean and standard deviation of the *Z*-scores are 5.091 and 10.94, respectively. The average ESG comprehensive score of the sample companies is 72.57. The MTB ratio is not low (7.425), the volatility is low (2.821), and the scale ratio is 22.25.

For the purpose of identifying issues with multicollinearity between independent variables, Table 12.5 presents Pearson pairwise correlations. The results in Table 12.4 show a moderate correlation coefficient between the two indicators of financial distress. The correlation coefficient of *Z*-score and *O*-score is −0.4342, indicating that their correlation is extremely low. Compared with ESG scores, the correlation coefficients of the above two financial distress indicators are 0.0169 and −0.0792, respectively, which cannot preliminarily prove Hypothesis 1. The *Z*- and *O*-scores of the two indicators of financial distress are, respectively, −0.0843 and 0.020 compared with the ESG*SOE scores; both *Z*-scores and *O*-scores can prove Hypothesis 2.

5.2 Regression Results

5.2.1 ESR and FDR

This study investigates the link between corporate ESG and financial difficulty in corporations. The ESG score, which we are interested in, employs the dependent variables Ohlson's (1980) *O*-score and Altman's (1968) *Z*-score to reflect FDR

Table 12.4 Descriptive Statistics

Variable	*N*	*Mean*	*SD*	*Min*	*p1*	*p25*	*p50*	p75	p99	Max
ESG	*31,373*	*72.57*	*5.774*	*36.62*	*55.43*	*69.41*	*72.98*	76.42	84.18	92.93
Z-score	31,373	5.091	10.94	−522.7	−0.694	1.709	2.955	5.399	38.04	419.8
O-score	31,373	−8.326	11.03	−356.4	−16.11	−9.645	−8.247	−7.064	−2.576	1277
MTB	31,373	7.425	159.4	−4793	0.574	1.925	3.117	5.356	44.95	19509
VOL	31,373	2.821	1.189	0.325	1.270	2.242	2.700	3.246	5.185	80.42
SLACK	31,373	15.16	11.95	−5.983	0.814	6.843	11.94	19.90	57.23	99.27
TANG	31,373	21.94	16.86	0.00100	0.160	8.794	18.49	31.42	70.86	296.0
SIZE	31,373	22.25	1.354	15.42	19.57	21.32	22.07	22.99	26.24	28.64
DIV	31,373	0.682	0.466	0	0	0	1	1	1	1
SIZE	31,373	22.25	1.354	15.42	19.57	21.32	22.07	22.99	26.24	28.64
SOE	31,373	0.425	0.494	0	0	0	0	1	1	1
SOExESG	31,373	31.13	36.36	0	0	0	0	72.34	83.22	92.93

and correct for standard errors in the regression. OLS regression yields the results for the association between ESG and FDR, which are presented in Table 12.6, while FE regression results are shown in Table 12.7. We adjust for various business variables, such as price-to-book ratio, firm volatility, stock return, firm size, and TANG, which may have an impact on financial reporting, based on prior research (Hsu et al., 2015).

We can see from the table that *Z*-score shows a positive correlation in both OLS and FE regression, which indicates that it is suitable for measuring China's FDR. This shows that *O*-score has problems when measuring China's FDR. But in the above analysis, and also in the next research, we will pay more attention to the *Z*-score. We study the forecast because the net income in the financial data of the enterprise will be used when calculating the *O*-score, and the net income data will not be used in the calculation process of the *Z*-score. Therefore, the discrepancy in net income data may be one of the reasons for the above problems.

Table 12.6 shows the results of the OLS regression of the *Z*-scores against the ESG composite score and other control variables. The regression coefficient

Table 12.5 Pearson Correlation Coefficients between Regression Variables

	ESG	*Z-Score*	*O-Score*	*MTB*	*VOL*	*SLACK*	*TANG*
ESG	*1*						
Z-score	0.0169*	1					
O-score	−0.0792*	−0.4342*	1				
MTB	−0.0328*	0.0210*	0.00360	1			
VOL	−0.0961*	0.0782*	0.00490	0.0398*	1		
SLACK	0.1005*	0.2222*	−0.0624*	0.0143	0.0211*	1	
TANG	−0.0394*	−0.0835*	0.00730	−0.0100	−0.0552*	−0.2877*	1
SIZE	0.2786*	−0.2057*	−0.0403*	−0.0268*	−0.1537*	−0.1863*	0.0585*
DIV	0.3353*	0.0437*	−0.1072*	−0.0291*	−0.0876*	0.1513*	−0.0649*
SIZE	0.2786*	−0.2057*	−0.0403*	−0.0268*	−0.1537*	−0.1863*	0.0585*
SOE	0.0911*	−0.0843*	0.0208*	0.00120	−0.0830*	−0.0314*	0.1622*
SOExESG	0.1536*	−0.0842*	0.0176*	−0.00220	−0.0890*	−0.0261*	0.1556*
	SIZE	DIV	SIZE	SOE	SOExESG		
SIZE	1						
DIV	0.2061*	1					
SIZE	1.0000*	0.2061*	1				
SOE	0.2828*	−0.0146*	0.2828*	1			
SOExESG	0.3051*	0.00660	0.3051*	0.9950*	1		

Table 12.6 OLS Regression of ESG and FDR

	Z-Score	*O-Score*
ESG	0.0772***	−0.0791***
	(6.87)	(−6.73)
MTB	0.000961**	0.0000209
	(2.59)	(0.05)
VOL	0.484***	−0.0869
	(9.58)	(−1.65)
SLACK	0.156***	−0.0498***
	(29.10)	(−8.87)
TANG	−0.0103**	−0.00939*
	(−2.82)	(−2.45)
SIZE	−1.498***	−0.183***
	(−31.48)	(−3.67)
DIV	1.091***	−1.949***
	(7.92)	(−13.53)
SIZE	0	0
	(0)	(0)
_cons	28.55***	4.011**
	(23.92)	(3.22)
N	31,373	31,373
R^2	0.084	0.016
Adj. R^2	0.0845	0.0160

Table 12.7 FE Regression of ESG and FDR

	Z-Score	*O-Score*
ESG	0.0834***	−0.0780***
	(6.16)	(−4.70)
MTB	0.000965**	−0.000284
	(2.92)	(−0.70)
VOL	0.523***	−0.101
	(11.51)	(−1.81)
SLACK	0.0974***	−0.0276***
	(14.90)	(−3.45)
TANG	−0.0211**	−0.0206*
	(−3.12)	(−2.49)
DIV	0.537***	−1.041***
	(3.54)	(−5.59)
SIZE	−0.983***	−1.603***
	(−11.13)	(−14.81)
_cons	18.05***	34.87***
	(8.30)	(13.09)
N	31,373	31,373
R^2	0.024	0.012

between *Z*-score (FDR) and ESG is positive, indicating a positive correlation. This supports our Hypothesis 1. The data results show that companies with high ESG scores are less likely to encounter financial distress than other companies.

The findings of the fixed-effect regression of *Z*-scores versus the ESG composite score and additional control factors are presented in Table 12.7. The regression coefficients for *Z*-score and ESG score are very similar to that mentioned in Table 12.6 (OLS regression). The regression coefficient is positive, which further supports Hypothesis 1.

5.2.2 Moderating Effect of Firm Characteristics

Similar to Tables 12.6 and 12.7, we added dummy variables SOE and ESG*SOE in Tables 12.8 and 12.9. We mainly focus on OLS and FE regression of the *Z*-score and ESG*SOE.

Table 12.8 shows the results of the OLS regression of *Z*-scores against ESG*SOE and other control variables. Table 12.9 shows the results of FE regression of *Z*-scores against ESG*SOE and other control variables. According to the results of the OLS regression, there is a negative connection between FDR and ESG*SOE, which suggests that the ESG of privately held companies contributes significantly to reducing financial distress. This conclusion supports Hypothesis 2. According to Table 12.9, the regression coefficients of the FE regression between *Z*-score and ESG were found to be very similar to those in the OLS regression. This partly supports Hypothesis 2.

Table 12.8 Regression of ESG*SOE and FDR (OLS)

	Z-Score	*O-Score*
ESG	0.0820***	−0.125***
	(5.89)	(−8.59)
MTB	0.000975**	0.0000305
	(2.63)	(0.08)
VOL	0.476***	−0.0758
	(9.41)	(−1.44)
SLACK	0.158***	−0.0522***
	(29.37)	(−9.29)
TANG	−0.00769*	−0.0122**
	(−2.07)	(−3.15)
SIZE	−1.436***	−0.290***
	(−28.86)	(−5.58)
DIV	1.035***	−1.861***
	(7.48)	(−12.88)
SIZE	0	0
	(0)	(0)
SOE	0.00909	−7.387***
	(0.01)	(−4.59)
SOExESG	−0.00792	0.112***
	(−0.37)	(5.07)
_cons	27.04***	9.375***
	(19.15)	(6.36)
N	31,373	31,373
R^2	0.085	0.018
Adj. R^2	0.0848	0.0177

6. Endogeneity Test

Additional tests were carried out in this study to determine whether our results were influenced by factors that were overlooked. To address possible endogeneity difficulties, we performed 2SLS regression analysis, and the data are presented in Table 12.10 Panel A. Our second-stage regression results show that the coefficient for CSR is positive, indicating that endogeneity does not appear to drive our conclusions.

Also, in Table 12.10 Panel B, we use the system GMM approach to estimate our model. Our model is a dynamic panel data model with one year of trailing *Z* values in the regression. The findings revealed a positive correlation between ESG scores and *Z*-scores. After accounting for endogeneity issues, these empirical results show no qualitative change in our conclusions.

7. Robustness Test (*Multicollinearity Test)*

Variance inflation factors (VIFs) were utilized in this work to test for multicollinearity. Senaviratna and Cooray (2019) stated that multicollinearity is typically regarded

Table 12.9 Regression of ESG*SOE and FDR (FE)

	Z-Score	*O-Score*
ESG	0.0975***	−0.134***
	(5.66)	(−6.35)
MTB	0.000952**	−0.000230
	(2.88)	(−0.57)
VOL	0.524***	−0.102
	(11.52)	(−1.83)
SLACK	0.0972***	−0.0270***
	(14.87)	(−3.37)
TANG	−0.0212**	−0.0203*
	(−3.13)	(−2.45)
DIV	0.536***	−1.035***
	(3.53)	(−5.56)
SIZE	−0.976***	−1.631***
	(−11.03)	(−15.05)
SOE	0	0
	(0)	(0)
SOExESG	−0.0359	0.143***
	(−1.32)	(4.29)
_cons	17.99***	35.09***
	(8.28)	(13.17)
N	31,373	31,373
R^2	0.024	0.012

as VIF values more than 10. Table 12.11 demonstrates that each variable's VIF value in this study was less than 10. Multicollinearity is therefore not a problem.

8. Discussion

8.1 Relationship with Prior Literature

The findings of this study align with those of previous related literature, which demonstrate an inverse relationship between ESG and financial distress. Notable studies with similar conclusions include those by Al-Hadi et al. (2017), Sumarno et al. (2023), and Friede et al. (2015). However, the distinguishing feature of this study is its use of data from listed companies in China, which sets it apart from prior research predominantly based on data from Western or other Asian countries. This study reveals that in the Chinese context, ESG performance is indeed related to financial health, with ESG initiatives helping alleviate financial distress in businesses. Additionally, this research delves deeper into the characteristics of companies, concluding that the negative correlation between ESG performance and financial distress is less pronounced in SOEs than in non-SOEs.

Table 12.10 Panel A 2SLS Regression

	ESG	*ESG*
Z-score	0.0347***	0.0403***
	(6.04)	(6.62)
MTB	−0.00154**	−0.00143**
	(−3.22)	(−2.74)
VOL	−0.407***	−0.440***
	(−10.03)	(−10.23)
SLACK	0.0429***	0.0432***
	(13.44)	(12.33)
TANG	−0.00300	−0.00218
	(−1.51)	(−1.02)
DIV	3.280***	3.343***
	(45.22)	(42.38)
SIZE	1.127***	1.195***
	(41.92)	(40.85)
_cons	45.50***	43.89***
	(72.02)	(63.86)
N	27,461	23,802
R^2	0.182	0.193

t statistics in parentheses.
* $p < 0.05$, ** $p < 0.01$, *** $p < 0.001$.

Table 12.10 Panel B 2SLS Regression

ESG	0.0772***
	(5.26)
MTB	0.000961
	(1.40)
VOL	0.484***
	(4.16)
SLACK	0.156***
	(13.14)
TANG	−0.0103**
	(−3.07)
DIV	1.091***
	(6.51)
SIZE	−1.498***
	(−18.16)
_cons	28.55***
	(11.08)
N	31,373
R^2	0.261

Table 12.11 Multicollinearity Test

Variable	*VIF*	
ESG	0.830	1.205
MTB	0.997	1.003
VOL	0.968	1.034
SLACK	0.849	1.178
TANG	0.914	1.094
DEP	0.849	1.177
Size	0.842	1.188
是、SOE Soe	1.000	1.000

8.2 Theoretical Contribution

This study makes a significant theoretical contribution to the existing body of research. It is based on the latest data from listed companies in China and, for the first time, examines the relationship between ESG performance and financial distress within this context, while also considering the moderating effect of company characteristics. The results indicate that ESG can mitigate financial distress in enterprises and that this relationship is particularly strong in non-SOEs. This adds a nuanced understanding to the existing literature by highlighting the differential impact of ESG on financial distress across different types of firms in China.

8.3 Practical Implication

The implications of this study could potentially alter the current landscape of the Chinese commercial market. Comparatively, the Chinese market has not prioritized ESG to the same extent as the markets in the United States, Europe, and other parts of Asia. The findings suggest that ESG will garner more attention in the future from shareholders, business managers, and scholars. This research can facilitate the promotion of ESG in the Chinese commercial market and encourage enterprises, particularly non-SOEs, to increase their investment in ESG initiatives. Furthermore, the results could drive Chinese listed companies to engage larger audit firms, thereby improving audit quality and reducing the sensitivity of the relationship between ESG and financial distress. This could, in turn, enhance the overall corporate governance and financial stability of Chinese companies.

9. Conclusions

This study used a sample of 31,373 Chinese listed companies for data analysis. During the period 2009–2022, we investigated the relationship between ESG scores and financial distress of Chinese companies. We used *Z*-score as a proxy for FDR and found that FDR decreases with an increase in ESG through data research. This result confirms our hypothesis that there is a negative correlation between ESG and FDR. In addition, we used the dummy variable SOE to examine the factors affecting the relationship between ESG and FDR. The research results showed that the negative correlation between ESG reporting and financial reporting is more significant in non-SOEs. These findings are robust to matched samples (2SLS and GMM).

The findings show that the higher the ESG score, the lower the risk of financial distress, and the better the corporate ESG realization, the lower the corporate risk. Therefore, a company can reduce its financial distress and corporate risk by adopting ESG-centred behaviours, thereby increasing the financial stability of the company and increasing the risk resistance of the company's economy. This research has many applications. For policymakers, the findings recommend continuing to encourage companies to adopt better ESG-scoring behaviours, as this can reduce corporate risk, guide companies into better investment environments, and reduce the likelihood of bankruptcy. For business managers, this study provides them with better suggestions. For example, managers should also pay attention to the ESG of enterprises in addition to social benefits because companies with high ESG scores can reap economic benefits.

This study also has some limitations. Firstly, the *O*-scores did not show the expected results, and the reasons for this were not very clear. Secondly, this study did not discuss in depth which aspects of ESG can affect financial distress, which may lead to companies not knowing which part of ESG should be improved to reduce financial distress. So in conclusion, in the future, it is possible to study the factors that lead to *O*-score outliers when China measures FDR, and which part of ESG reduces China's FDR. These will be very interesting topics.

References

Al-Hadi, A., Hasan, M. M., Taylor, G., Hossain, M., & Richardson, G. (2017). Market risk disclosures and investment efficiency: International evidence from the Gulf Cooperation Council financial firms. *Journal of International Financial Management & Accounting*, *28*(3), 349–393.

Allen, F., Qian, J., & Qian, M. (2005). Law, finance, and economic growth in China. *Journal of Financial Economics*, *77*(1), 57–116.

Altman, E. I. (1968). Financial ratios, discriminant analysis and the prediction of corporate bankruptcy. *The Journal of Finance*, *23*(4), 589–609.

Altman, E. I., Iwanicz-Drozdowska, M., Laitinen, E. K., & Suvas, A. (2017). Financial distress prediction in an international context: A review and empirical analysis of Altman's Z-score model. *Journal of International Financial Management & Accounting*, *28*(2), 131–171.

Antunes, J., Wanke, P., Fonseca, T., & Tan, Y. (2023). Do ESG risk scores influence financial distress? Evidence from a dynamic NDEA approach. *Sustainability*, *15*(9), 7560. https://doi.org/10.3390/su15097560

Beaver, W. H. (1966). Financial ratios as predictors of failure. *Journal of Accounting Research*, *4*(3), 71–111.

Ben-Ner, A., & Jones, D. C. (1995). Employee participation, ownership, and productivity: A theoretical framework. *Industrial Relations*, *34*(4), 532–554.

Boubaker, S., Cellier, A., Manita, R., & Saeed, A. (2020). Does corporate social responsibility reduce financial distress risk? *Economic Modelling*, *91*, 835–851.

Buallay, A. (2021). Sustainability reporting and agriculture industries' performance: Worldwide evidence. *Journal of Agribusiness in Developing and Emerging Economies*. www.scopus.com/inward/record.uri?eid=2-s2.0-85108600111&doi=10.1108%2FJADEE-10-2020-0247&partnerID=40&md5=45c0d3599d81e24e6052263744746761

Cheng, B., Ioannou, I., & Serafeim, G. (2014). Corporate social responsibility and access to finance. *Strategic Management Journal*, *35*(1), 1–23.

Chu, X. (2021). The application of corporate social responsibility in mitigating the risk of financial distress. *Jiangsu Business*, *9*, 113–116, 126. https://doi.org/10.13395/j.cnki.issn.1009-0061.2021.09.031

Cohen, G. (2023). ESG risks and corporate survival. *Environment Systems and Decisions*, 16–21.

Detailed Description of Mainstream ESG Rating System for A-Share Listed Companies-CIH. (2023, March 20). Retrieved June 28, 2023, from http://cncih.org/newsinfo/5695388.html

Eccles, R. G., Ioannou, I., & Serafeim, G. (2011). The impact of a corporate culture of sustainability on corporate behavior and performance. *SSRN Electronic Journal*, *17950*(1).

Eccles, R. G., & Serafeim, G. (2013). The performance frontier: Innovating for a sustainable strategy. *Harvard Business Review*, *91*(5), 50–60.

Fang, L., Sun, B., Li, H., & Yu, H. (2018). Systemic risk network of Chinese financial institutions. *Emerging Markets Review*, *35*, 190–206. https://doi.org/10.1016/j.ememar.2018.02.003

Financial Information. (2022). *What are the economic crises experienced by my country (how does China get out of previous crises): Extreme time and space*. https://daiyo.cc/news/12483.html.

Friede, G., Busch, T., & Bassen, A. (2015). ESG and financial performance: Aggregated evidence from more than 2000 empirical studies. *Journal of Sustainable Finance & Investment*, *5*, 210–233.

Hartzmark, S. M., & Sussman, A. B. (2017). Do investors value sustainability? A natural experiment examining ranking and fund flows. *SSRN Electronic Journal*, *74*(6).

Harymawan, I., Nasih, M., Salsabilla, A., & Putra, F. K. G. (2020). External assurance on sustainability report disclosure and firm value: Evidence from Indonesia and Malaysia. *Entrepreneurship and Sustainability Issues*, *7*(3), 1500–1512. https://doi.org/10.9770/jesi.2020.7.3(5)

He, Y., Xu, L., & McIver, R. P. (2019). How does political connection affect firm financial distress and resolution in China? *Applied Economics*, *51*(26), 2770–2792.

Hoepner, A. G. F., Oikonomou, I., Sautner, Z., Starks, L. T., & Zhou, X. (2016). ESG shareholder engagement and downside risk. *SSRN Electronic Journal*, 52–71. https://doi.org/10.2139/ssrn.2874252

Hsu, P. H., Lee, H. H., Liu, A. Z., & Zhang, Z. (2015). Corporate innovation, default risk, and bond pricing. *Journal of Corporate Finance*, *35*, 329–344.

Huang, Q., Liu, X., & Li, J. (2019). Contextualization of Chinese entrepreneurship research: An overview and some future research directions. *Entrepreneurship & Regional Development*, 1–17. https://doi.org/10.1080/08985626.2019.1640437

Huld, A. (2022, February 23). *China ESG reporting – disclosing enterprise environmental information.* www.china-briefing.com/news/china-esg-reporting-disclosing-enterprise-environmental-information/

Ioannou, I., & Serafeim, G. (2014). The impact of corporate social responsibility on investment recommendations: Analysts' perceptions and shifting institutional logics. *Strategic Management Journal*, *36*(7), 1053–1081. https://doi.org/10.1002/smj.2268

Jamali, D., Ngwu, F. N., & Osuji, O. (Eds.). (2019). *CSR and sustainable development cross-country studies*. Retrieved June 28, 2023, from www.cambridge.org/core/books/abs/corporate-social-responsibility-in-developing-and-emerging-markets/csr-and-sustainable-development-crosscountry-studies/229DA12FB07D30C5C372F454449B7F87

JP Morgan. (2023, April). *JPMorgan China: A research enhanced index equity (ESG) UCITS ETF USD (acc) | JRCE | IE00BMDV7578*. Retrieved June 28, 2023, from www.justetf.com/uk/etf-profile.html?isin=IE00BMDV7578

Kapelko, M. (2022). Environmental inefficiency of the world construction industry. In *Current perspectives and new directions in mechanics, modelling and design of structural systems* (pp. 1578–1582). CRC Press.

Khan, M., Serafeim, G., & Yoon, A. (2016). Corporate sustainability: First evidence on materiality. *The Accounting Review, SSRN Electronic Journal*, *91*(6), 1697–1724. https://doi.org/10.2139/ssrn.2575912

Kharpal, A. (2023). *Huawei reports biggest profit decline ever as U.S. sanctions, pandemic controls hit Chinese giant*. www.cnbc.com/2023/03/31/huawei-earnings-2022-biggest-profit-decline-since-2011-revenue-flat.html

Kotsantonis, S., & Serafeim, G. (2019). *Four things no one will tell you about ESG data*. www.hbs.edu/faculty/Pages/item.aspx?num=56372

Li, M. (2016, August 31). *Seven ministries issued the "guiding opinions on building a green financial system"*. www.scio.gov.cn/32344/32345/35889/36819/xgzc36825/Document/1555348/1555348.htm

Li, Z., Crook, J., Andreeva, G., & Tang, Y. (2021). Predicting the risk of financial distress using corporate governance measures. *Pacific-Basin Finance Journal*, *68*, 101334.

Marks, J. (2017). *Human biodiversity: Genes, race, and history*. Routledge.

Mōri, A., Miyake, T.-A., & Adachi, O. (2022, August 22). *At a glance: ESG and investing in Japan*. Retrieved June 28, 2023, from www.lexology.com/library/detail.aspx?g=114c011f-7793-4b56-b3d7-5efb06757839

MSCI. (2019). *MSCI China ESG leaders index (USD)*. www.msci.com/documents/10199/78514cc5-a16d-493a-9774-af1012aa0420

Ohlson, J. A. (1980). Financial ratios and the probabilistic prediction of bankruptcy. *Journal of Accounting Research*, 109–131.

Rahman, M. J., & Wu, J. (2023). M&A activity and ESG performance: Evidence from China. *Managerial Finance*, *50*(1), 179–197.

Rahman, M. J., Wu, Q., & Zhu, H. (2024). Corporate social responsibility in times of social distancing: Evidence from China. *Business Ethics, the Environment & Responsibility*.

Rahman, M. J., Zhu, H., & Chen, S. (2023). Does CSR reduce financial distress? Moderating effect of firm characteristics, auditor characteristics, and covid-19. *International Journal of Accounting & Information Management*, *31*(5), 756–784.

Redding, G. (1995). Overseas Chinese networks: Understanding the enigma. *Long Range Planning*, *28*(1), 61–69.

SEC.gov | SEC Response to Climate and ESG Risks and Opportunities. (n.d.). www.sec.gov/sec-response-climate-and-esg-risks-and-opportunities

Senaviratna, N. A. M. R., & A Cooray, T. M. J. (2019). Diagnosing multicollinearity of logistic regression model. *Asian Journal of Probability and Statistics*, *5*(2), 1–9.

Sharpe, I. G., & Stadnik, A. (2007). Financial distress in Australian general insurers. *Journal of Risk and Insurance*, *74*(2), 377–399.

Sumarno, D. C., Andayani, W., & Prihatiningtias, Y. W. (2023). The effect of environmental, social and governance (ESG) assessment on firm value with profitability as a mediating variable. *APMBA (Asia Pacific Management and Business Application)*, *12*(1), 55–64.

Taffler, R. J. (1984). Empirical models for the monitoring of UK corporations. *Journal of Banking & Finance*, *8*(2), 199–227.

Tykvová, T., & Borell, M. (2012). Do private equity owners increase risk of financial distress and bankruptcy? *Journal of Corporate Finance*, *18*(1), 138–150.

Verwijmeren, P., & Derwall, J. (2010). Employee well-being, firm leverage, and bankruptcy risk. *Journal of Banking & Finance*, *34*(5), 956–964.

Wirth, G. (2023, May 19). *SEC makes ESG issues a top concern in examinations, even before it finalizes new disclosure rules*. Retrieved June 28, 2023, from www.thomsonreuters.com/en-us/posts/government/sec-exams-esg-concerns/

World Economic Forum. (2019). *Seeking return on ESG advancing the reporting ecosystem to unlock impact for business and society*. Produced in collaboration with Allianz SE and Boston Consulting Group. https://www3.weforum.org/docs/WEF_ESG_Report_digital_pages.pdf

Zhang, Z. (2022, January 13). *ESG reporting in China: Trends, challenges, and outlook*. www.china-briefing.com/news/what-is-esg-reporting-and-why-is-it-gaining-traction-in-china/

Zhong, B., Soh, W. N., Ong, T. S., Muhammad, H. B., & He, C. X. (2022). Risk assessment of Haier group's overseas investment under international financial reporting standards. *Frontiers in Psychology*, *13*.

Zhu, H., & Rahman, M. J. (2024). Ex-ante expected changes in ESG and future stock returns based on machine learning. *The British Accounting Review*, *56*(6), 101457.

13 The Relationship between ESG and Corporate Financial Performance and the Role of Audit Quality

Md Jahidur Rahman, Tarek Rana, Hongtao Zhu, and Yuxin Song

1. Introduction

This study examines the relationship between environmental, social, and governance (ESG) factors and corporate financial performance (CFP), with a particular focus on the moderating effect of audit quality (AQ) in the Chinese context. Specifically, it explores whether ESG scores impact corporate financial reports and how AQ mediates the link between ESG and CFP. Zahid et al. (2022) found that ESG ratings negatively affect CFP in Western European markets. This study extends the inquiry to the Chinese market, examining whether ESG impacts corporate financial reporting similarly and whether AQ has a comparable moderating effect under the Chinese system.

Several motivations drive this study. Firstly, the growing emphasis on ESG factors has heightened the importance of transparency regarding businesses' sustainability actions, encapsulated in ESG scores (Broadstock et al., 2020). Companies are increasingly integrating sustainable development practices into their strategies to enhance long-term value and reduce risk. Consequently, stakeholders demand greater corporate transparency, including comprehensive ESG performance reporting, to assess financial performance. The rise in independent sustainability reports reflects stakeholders' growing interest in environmental and social issues, including employees, consumers, regulators, governmental organizations, and socially responsible investors (Qiu et al., 2016).

Secondly, a substantial body of research, including over 2,100 empirical studies, demonstrates a positive correlation between ESG and firm financial performance (Friede et al., 2015; Aydoğmuş et al., 2022). However, some studies argue that assessing ESG's impact on financial performance is challenging due to the small and arbitrary sample of businesses considered (Galant & Cadez, 2017). This study aims to address these gaps by examining the effects of various ESG concerns on financial performance, particularly in non-US contexts (Aouadi & Marsat, 2016).

Thirdly, Zahid et al. (2022) highlighted the significant implications of ESG for managers and decision-makers in European nations. However, the relevance for developing countries like China, where the number of firms reporting ESG data has increased dramatically, remains underexplored (He et al., 2023). This study seeks to fill this gap by investigating the relationship between ESG and corporate financial reporting in China, a rapidly growing market with evolving corporate governance standards.

DOI: 10.4324/9781003488934-17

This study adopts a comprehensive approach to analysing the effects of ESG on CFP, incorporating the ESG composite score and sub-item scores for ESG dimensions. This method allows for a more nuanced understanding of the relationship between different ESG indicators and financial reports, aiding corporate managers and regulators in better comprehending the impact of ESG on financial reporting.

Previous research on the relationship between corporate social responsibility (CSR) and financial success often overlooks moderating factors such as AQ (Zahid et al., 2022). This study addresses this gap by incorporating AQ as a moderating variable, providing a more comprehensive understanding of the ESG–CFP relationship. Independent external audits play a crucial role in corporate governance, particularly in firms where management and ownership are separate (Francis, 2004). Thus, including AQ in the research enhances the analysis of ESG's impact on financial performance.

This empirical study focuses on A-share listed companies in Shanghai and Shenzhen, China, from 2009 to 2022. Return on assets (ROA) serves as the proxy variable for CFP, with return on equity (ROE) as a secondary measure. To address endogeneity issues, a two-stage least squares (2SLS) regression model is employed. The results show a significant positive correlation between ESG and ROA, indicating that ESG positively impacts CFP. However, for companies audited by Big Four firms, the relationship between ESG performance and ROA is inversely correlated, suggesting that higher AQ may negatively affect the financial health of ESG-related firms. These findings are consistent with robustness and endogeneity tests.

The study makes several contributions to the literature and practice. Firstly, it expands the body of knowledge on the ESG–CFP relationship by examining the role of AQ. The use of a larger sample size enhances the accuracy, representativeness, and generalizability of the findings. Secondly, it highlights the mediating role of AQ, a critical factor in the audit process (Watkins et al., 2004). Thirdly, it offers empirical evidence and practical insights for Chinese businesses and investors, helping guide sustainable development strategies and inform regulatory policies.

The remainder of this study is structured as follows: Section 2 reviews the literature and develops hypotheses; Section 3 describes the research methodology; Section 4 discusses the empirical findings; Sections 5 and 6 address endogeneity and robustness tests, respectively; Section 7 discusses the results; and Section 8 concludes the research.

2. Literature Review and Hypothesis Development

2.1 ESG and Corporate Financial Performance

Integrating the perspectives of stakeholder theory and the resource-based view, it becomes evident that sustainable development is essential for the long-term success of enterprises. The participation of stakeholders is crucial in strengthening company environmental policies and promoting sustainable development (Lokuwaduge & Heenetigala, 2016).

Research by Velte (2017) demonstrated that ESG positively impacts the value (Tobin's Q) and profitability (ROA) of German enterprises. Governance, in particular, has a significant effect on financial performance. Academic exploration of the relationship between ESG standards and corporate financial success dates back to the 1970s (Friede et al., 2015). ESG metrics can be used to assess and quantify corporate performance, much like traditional financial metrics, indicating that ESG is intrinsically linked to business performance (Kay et al., 2020).

ESG has been found to play a regulatory role in enhancing the positive effects of enterprise risk management on financial performance and company value. This underscores the growing demand for ESG from businesses and investors. Companies must increasingly integrate ESG into their operations to achieve strong performance, while investors can leverage ESG awareness in their investment decisions (Chairani & Siregar, 2021). Several studies in China also investigate the relationship between environmental accounting and firm performance (Rahman & Wu, 2023; Rahman et al., 2023, 2024; Zhu & Rahman, 2024).

However, not all studies have found a consistent link between ESG and financial performance. For instance, research by Aggarwal (2013) found no significant relationship between governance standards and financial success, measured by various financial ratios such as ROE, ROA, market-to-book value, price–earnings ratio, and reward yield. Sustainable development remains critical for companies, especially those managing limited resources. For example, the profitability of banking organizations is significantly influenced by staff productivity. Although staff productivity has a considerable impact on financial success, the association with CSR was not found to be significant in this context (Tunio et al., 2021).

The relationship between ESG and financial performance is complex and varies across studies. Whelan et al. (2021) reported that only 58% of the publications reviewed found a positive link between ESG and financial success, while 8% found a negative association, 13% found no association, and 21% reported mixed results. This indicates that the evidence connecting ESG to corporate financial performance is not conclusive and can vary depending on the market and profitability metrics used (Zahid et al., 2022).

Given the inconclusive nature of existing research on the impact of ESG on corporate financial performance, particularly in the Chinese context, this study aims to fill this gap through empirical investigation. Based on the theoretical justifications and empirical data discussed above, the following hypothesis is proposed:

H1: ESG and its components positively influence CFP.

2.2 AQ in the ESG and CFR

According to the theories of legitimacy and stakeholders, auditing ensures that information is equal, accurate, and reliable; complies with legal and regulatory requirements; and is accepted by society. Furthermore, it protects the rights and interests of stakeholders. Higher AQ can prevent errors or illegal activities in the audit process and provide valuable insights (Dewi & Monalisa, 2016).

Firms certified by high-quality auditors show a more significant reduction in the cost of debt due to CSR initiatives. High-quality auditors and CSR performance, according to creditors and financial institutions, can increase business value and prevent resource misallocation. Enhanced AQ by the Big Four auditors gives banks more confidence in managing both financial and non-financial information when making loan decisions (Bacha et al., 2021). By adhering to high-quality auditing standards, accredited audit firms help ensure that the financial accounts of audited companies are reliable, understandable, and useful. Rigorous auditing supports effective corporate governance and internal controls, potentially enhancing financial performance. Due to their desire to maintain their reputations, the Big Four are less likely to compromise on accepted audit standards (Ado et al., 2020).

However, audit firms with a solid reputation for quality audits typically demand higher fees (Zahid et al., 2022). These increased audit fees could potentially impact CFP negatively. Therefore, incorporating AQ into the research model is crucial to understand its moderating effect on the relationship between ESG and CFP in the Chinese context. Based on the theoretical justifications and empirical data discussed above, the following hypothesis is proposed:

H2: Improvements in AQ *enhance the positive relationship between ESG and CFP.*

3. Research Design

3.1 Sample and Data

Between 2009 and 2022, we performed a preliminary sample screening of all the companies listed on A-shares in Shanghai and Shenzhen, China. The two other audit indicators (Big Four businesses audits and audit fees) and the financial data for the ESG ratings were sourced from the China Stock Market & Accounting Research (CSMAR) database and the Wind database, respectively. In the preliminary data collection stage, we selected 42,009 observations as a sample. However, the sample size was reduced after some factors were excluded. Firstly, some companies were excluded due to the risk of delisting; secondly, financial industry companies were also excluded. Finally, after review, 37,573 observations were selected as data sources. Table 13.1 shows the sample selection procedure.

Table 13.1 Sample Selection

Sample Selection Criterion	*No. of Observations*
Total number	42,009
Less: companies in the financial industry	969
Less: missing sample data	1,317
Less: ST companies	2,150
Equal to = final sample	37,573

Source: Table created by authors

Note: Final sample after screening is presented.

3.2 Variable Measurements

3.2.1 Dependent Variable

To quantify CFP, as the variable of dependence, we used ROA as a proxy variable. The proportion of net income to total assets, or ROA, is a metric that is generally used to evaluate a company's profitability about the value of its entire assets. We assessed utilizing the parameters of ROA and CFP (Zahid et al., 2022).

3.2.2 Independent Variable

Based on the ESG score of the Wind database, we can use multiple ESG indicators and data sources to evaluate and calculate the ESG performance of enterprises systematically. These indicators include three aspects: environment, society, and governance. Enhancing openness about businesses' sustainability actions and condensing them into a single number, called the ESG score, is made possible in large part by ESG ratings and rating organizations (Broadstock et al., 2020).

In this study, we used the ESG score as a comprehensive independent variable to measure the sustainable development performance of enterprises. Specifically, we focused on ESG scores and their components, incorporating governance, socio-economic, and environmental scores. These results reflect how the company performed in many ESG areas, thus providing a comprehensive indicator to evaluate the ESG performance level of the company. Through our analysis of the ESG score and its components, we can determine which financial performance of the company (CFR) is mostly influenced by the component. As separate factors, we used ESG ratings as well as component scores for governance, social, and environmental issues. ESG scores are an index that combines both financial and non-financial data into a composite score. It assesses how well a firm performs in terms of its commitment to social responsibility, environmental sustainability, and governance principles (Zahid et al., 2022).

3.2.3 Moderating Variable

The study used AQ as a moderating variable, which is a dummy variable used to reflect whether the Big Four audit firms have examined the company's financial accounts. If the financial statements are audited with one of the Big Four audit firms, the quality of the audit variable has a value of 1; alternatively, it has a value of 0. As a moderator variable, it can help us gain insight into the mechanism of ESG's impact on CFR and explore how AQ fits within this connection. We take AQ into account as a moderating variable. The Big Four organizations, with their well-known and recognized brand names, are especially motivated to provide excellent audit services. They have a stake in maintaining their reputation and have a greater incentive to make sure that they offer excellent auditing services as a result (Zahid et al., 2022).

3.2.4 Control Variable

In order to achieve a more accurate and thorough investigation of the connection between ESG with CFP, we completely took into account many control variables: firm size, financial leverage, dividend payments, and net market capitalization. They show the potential effects on the ESG-CFP relationship of business size, financial adaptability, profitability, and firm growth. When assessing the impact of ESG on CFP, we take into account a variety of control factors determined by prior studies, dimensions, liquidity, payouts paid, and price-to-book value (Zahid et al., 2022).

Firstly, we consider firm size as a control variable. With the association between business size and financial performance, the company's size is viewed as a control variable (Zahid et al., 2022). One of the key markers of corporate activity is considered to be the size of the firm, which may have an impact on the relationship between ESG and CFP. Larger companies typically have more resources and capabilities, are better able to fulfil ESG responsibilities, and achieve more significant results in terms of financial performance.

Secondly, financial leverage is considered another control variable. Financial leverage measures the debt level of a company and may have an impact on the relationship between ESG and CFP. High financial leverage may increase the financial risk of the company and reduce the priority of ESG performance, which may have a negative impact on CFP. Leverage in finance and a business's financial performance are inversely associated (Naseem et al., 2019).

To measure business profitability, we also add dividend payments as a control variable. One of the most important metrics for assessing a company's financial performance is profitability, which can interact with CFP and ESG performance. Companies that pay out significant dividends are considered to have great financial performance, and we analyse this using the proportion of dividends payable to the amount of assets (Benlemlih, 2019).

Finally, Companies that pay out significant dividends are considered to have great financial performance, and we analyse this using the proportion of dividends payable to the number of assets. We can more accurately evaluate the effect of ESG on CFP and prevent it from being overwhelmed by business growth considerations by controlling the net market value. Net assets will be utilized as a key metric for assessing the company's market worth (Abdolmohammadi, 2005). We can more accurately evaluate the effect of ESG on CFP and prevent it from being overwhelmed by business growth considerations by controlling the net market value. Net assets will be utilized as a key metric for assessing the company's market worth. This analysis method helps eliminate the potential interference of other factors on the relationship between ESG and CFP and provides more comprehensive and reliable conclusions to completely understand the intricate connection between ESG and company financial success.

3.2.5 Model Specification

Examining whether ESG has a beneficial effect on corporate financial reporting was our first premise. Following Zahid et al. (2022), our first premise was to investigate if ESG had a positive impact on corporate financial reporting:

$$\begin{aligned} Fin\_Perf\_ = {} & \alpha + \beta_1 ESG_{it} + \beta_2\, Size_{it} + \beta_3 FL_{it} + \beta_4\, Div\_payout_{it} + \beta_5 PTB_{it} \\ & + \sum_{i=1}^{n} \beta_n\, Industry\_Dummies_{it} \\ & + \sum_{i=1}^{n} \beta_n\, Year\_\_Dummies_{it} + \varepsilon_{it} \end{aligned} \tag{1}$$

Here:

Fin_Perf	=	financial performance
ESG	=	Scores for the governance, social, and environment
Size	=	logarithm of the company's total assets
FL	=	financial leveraging
DP	=	dividend payout
PTB	=	price-to-book ratio
Industry	=	industry-specific fixed effect
Year	=	year-specific fixed effect (2009–2022)
$\mathcal{E}$	=	error term
I	=	firm
T	=	year

On the basis of Model 1, we added an interaction term, Big×ESG, which explores which ESG, and its components interact with the items that the Big Four accounting firms audit. The goal is to investigate the moderating effects of AQ further. Equation (2) represents the model.

$$\begin{aligned} Fin\_Perf\_ = {} & \alpha + \beta_1 ESG_{it} + \beta_2 Big4_{it} + \beta_3 Big4_{it} \times ESG_{it} \\ & + \beta_4 Div\_Payout_{it} + \beta_3 FL_{it} + \beta_4 ROA_{it} + \beta_5 PTB_{it} \\ & + \sum_{i=1}^{n} \beta_n\, Industry\_Dummies_{it} \\ & + \sum_{i=1}^{n} \beta_n\, Year\_Dummies_{it}\, \varepsilon_{it} \end{aligned} \tag{2}$$

In this modified model, all variables are held constant from Equation (1) except for the inclusion of the connection phrase Big4×ESG. By using this improved model, the moderating impact of AQ on the association between ESG and CFR was assessed. The Big4×ESG interaction phrase describes how AQ has a moderating influence (Zahid et al., 2022).

4. Empirical Results

4.1 Descriptive Statistics

Table 13.2 presents the descriptive data of the whole sample of A shares of Chinese listed businesses in Shanghai and Shenzhen from 2009 to 2022. The standard deviation of ROA is 6.542, and its average value is 4.352. The ESG score on average is 73.129. The ESG score standard deviation is 5.148. The governance score has the highest average value of the three ESG factors, at 79.27, and the standard deviation of the governance score is also the smallest among these three indicators, which is 6.91. It can be seen that the performance of governance is better than that of other aspects, and it has governance practical stability. At the same time, it can be observed that the average FL and PTB of the companies in the sample are relatively low. This means that these companies have adopted a relatively conservative strategy in terms of financial risk and valuation. In addition, the data show that only 0.057 proportion of companies choose Big4_Auditor (four major accounting firms) for auditing.

4.2 ESG and CFP Correlation Analysis

Table 13.3 shows the relevance of analysing ESG for CFP. The fixed-effect approach was utilized for regression evaluation to account for the endogenous issues brought on by industry impacts and temporal effects.

In regression model 1, at the 1% level of significance, the dependent variable ROA and the primary explanatory variable ESG have a significant positive connection with a coefficient of 0.106, which means that for every 1 unit

Table 13.2 Descriptive Statistics

Variable	*Obs*	*Mean*	*SD*	*Min*	*Median*	*Max*
ROA	37573	4.352	6.542	−36.234	4.100	25.633
ROE	37573	6.819	13.305	−121.159	7.519	47.651
ESG	37573	73.129	5.148	54.520	73.430	85.480
Environment	37573	60.312	7.452	43.200	60.060	84.580
Social	37573	74.139	9.773	36.890	74.790	100.000
Governance	37573	79.270	6.910	45.470	80.730	93.730
Size	37573	22.153	1.278	19.267	21.968	26.403
FL	37573	41.781	20.602	2.828	40.982	92.527
PTB	37573	3.989	3.835	0.615	2.903	51.225
DP	37573	1.419	1.955	0.000	0.737	12.233
Age	37573	10.866	7.649	1.000	9.000	30.000
Audit_fee	37573	13.667	0.641	12.101	13.592	16.058
Big4_Auditor	37573	0.057	0.232	0.000	0.000	1.000

Note: See notes to Model 1.

Table 13.3 ESG and CFP

Variable	*ROA*	*ROA*	*ROA*	*ROA*
ESG	0.106*** (0.007)			
Environment		−0.000 (0.004)		
Social			0.044*** (0.003)	
Governance				0.086*** (0.005)
Size	1.222*** (0.033)	1.382*** (0.033)	1.302*** (0.033)	1.269*** (0.033)
FL	−0.099*** (0.002)	−0.104*** (0.002)	−0.104*** (0.002)	−0.095*** (0.002)
PTB	0.258*** (0.014)	0.254*** (0.014)	0.257*** (0.014)	0.253*** (0.014)
DP	1.410*** (0.018)	1.445*** (0.018)	1.431*** (0.018)	1.407*** (0.018)
Age	−0.055*** (0.004)	−0.067*** (0.004)	−0.057*** (0.004)	−0.060*** (0.004)
Constant	−28.783*** (0.759)	−24.215*** (0.685)	−25.861*** (0.693)	−29.009*** (0.773)
Observations	37,573	37,573	37,573	37,573
R^2	0.407	0.402	0.405	0.408
Industry	Yes	Yes	Yes	Yes
Year	Yes	Yes	Yes	Yes

increase in ESG, ROA increases by an average of 0.106 when other conditions remain an unchanged unit. In regression model 2, we observe that the moderating variable's value is not essential. On further analysis, in regression models 3 and 4, we found that *S* (social) and *G* (governance) as control variables had a significant positive effect on CFP. It indicates that in our research sample, ESG significantly improved the organizations' CFP. In addition, the model fitting effect is better, the explanatory power is larger, and the R^2 of the equation is likewise over 0.4.

4.3 *ESG and Corporate Financial Report Correlation Analysis: Moderating Effect of AQ*

The regression findings presented in Table 13.4 indicate that at the 1% level of significance, the statistics of the relationship term across Big Four with ESG is negative, which is opposite to the sign of the adjusted variable ESG, indicating that there is a weakened moderating effect. Under the condition of controlling other variables, when the company chooses to be audited by the Big Four accounting

Table 13.4 Moderating Effect of AQ

Variable	*ROA*	*ROA*	*ROA*	*ROA*
ESG	0.114***			
	(0.007)			
ESG_big4	−0.130***			
	(0.019)			
Environment		0.001		
		(0.004)		
Environment_big4		−0.017		
		(0.014)		
Social			0.045***	
			(0.003)	
Social_big4			−0.021**	
			(0.008)	
Governance				0.092***
				(0.006)
Governance_big4				−0.116***
				(0.016)
Big4	8.904***	0.254	0.849	8.547***
	(1.463)	(0.871)	(0.646)	(1.291)
Size	1.289***	1.441***	1.358***	1.340***
	(0.035)	(0.035)	(0.034)	(0.034)
FL	−0.100***	−0.105***	−0.105***	−0.095***
	(0.002)	(0.002)	(0.002)	(0.002)
PTB	0.265***	0.258***	0.261***	0.260***
	(0.014)	(0.014)	(0.014)	(0.014)
DP	1.410***	1.446***	1.432***	1.407***
	(0.018)	(0.018)	(0.018)	(0.018)
Age	−0.056***	−0.068***	−0.059***	−0.062***
	(0.004)	(0.004)	(0.004)	(0.004)
Constant	−30.755***	−25.510***	−27.089***	−30.996***
	(0.805)	(0.724)	(0.727)	(0.820)
Observations	37,573	37,573	37,573	37,573
R^2	0.408	0.402	0.405	0.410
Industry	Yes	Yes	Yes	Yes
Year	Yes	Yes	Yes	Yes

Note: See notes to model 1. Robust standard errors in parentheses.
*** $p < 0.01$, ** $p < 0.05$, * $p < 0.1$.

firm (Big4 = 1), the positive relationship between ESG performance and the rate of return (ROA) of the companies in the sample is weaker. The adjustment variable represented by esg_big4 has a negative coefficient. When only considering the companies served by Big Four auditors, the regression findings demonstrate that the esg_big4 variable significantly lowers ROA. (The coefficient is −0.130, the standard error is 0.019, $p < 0.001$). This shows that when other control variables remain constant, among the companies served by Big Four auditors, the regression findings demonstrate that the esg_big4 variable significantly lowers ROA. This result can be interpreted as the audit by the Big Four accounting firm playing a moderating role in improving the company's ESG performance. In the presence of a Big Four audit, the financial performance of businesses will benefit more significantly from the incorporation of ESG elements.

5. Endogeneity Tests

Endogeneity issues arise when there is an underlying correlation between ROA and possible error terms in a regression model, so we use a 2SLS method to alleviate it. Following the different stages in this regression model,

$$Fin\_Perf\_ = \alpha + \beta_1 ESG_{it} + \beta_2 Size_{it} + \beta_3 FL_{it} + \beta_4 Div\_payout_{it} + \beta_5 PTB_{it}$$
$$+ \sum_{i=1}^{n} \beta_n Industry\_Dummies_{it}$$
$$+ \sum_{i=1}^{n} \beta_n Year\_\_Dummies_{it} + \varepsilon_{it}$$

5.1 *First-Stage Results*

In the first four columns of Table 13.5 (labelled "Stage I"), the first stage of the regression using 2SLS shows the effect of ESG on the instrumental variable (Δ ESG), and the results are all positive and significant coefficients, where instrumental variables increase by 0.476 for every unit increase in ESG.

5.2 *Second-Stage Results*

In the last four columns of Table 13.5 (labelled "Stage II"), Δ ESG variables are highly and positively connected with ROA, as seen by the correlation value of 0.078 between ESG variables and ROA. In addition, the statistics of the weak instrumental variable test are significant at the 1% level, and the instrumental variable (Δ ESG) is valid.

Table 13.5 presents the results of bias correction for endogenous variables using instrumental variables. In order to solve the possible endogenous problems in the regression model, this study adopts the 2SLS model for regression. The first-order difference (Δ ESG) is selected as the instrumental variable. Considering that there is a strong correlation between the difference between Δ ESG and ESG, the weak instrumental variable test and unidentified test findings both significantly reject the null hypothesis, showing that the instrumental variables were chosen effectively and that they meet the exogenous criteria. At the 1% level of significance, the core independent variable has a substantial positive correlation with the dependent variable, which is in line with earlier findings. This suggests that the adopted 2SLS model effectively addresses the endogeneity issue and increases the degree to which the link between the primary variables and their dependents is estimated.

Table 13.5 Relationship between ESG and CFR by Using 2SLS

	stage I	*stage I*	*stage I*	*stage I*	*stage II*	*stage II*	*stage II*	*stage II*
Variable	ESG	E	S	G	ROA	ROA	ROA	ROA
ESG	0.476***							
	(0.007)							
Environment		0.468***						
		(0.006)						
Social			0.472***					
			(0.006)					
Governance				0.485***				
				(0.009)				
ESG					0.078***			
					(0.018)			
Environment						−0.015		
						(0.011)		
Social							0.046***	
							(0.008)	
Governance								0.057***
								(0.013)
Size	1.539***	1.553***	1.862***	1.341***	1.333***	1.481***	1.371***	1.378***
	(0.027)	(0.038)	(0.047)	(0.036)	(0.044)	(0.040)	(0.038)	(0.039)
FL	−0.047***	0.013***	−0.003	−0.106***	−0.100***	−0.104***	−0.104***	−0.097***
	(0.002)	(0.002)	(0.003)	(0.002)	(0.002)	(0.002)	(0.002)	(0.003)
PTB	−0.048***	−0.134***	−0.056***	−0.001	0.253***	0.248***	0.251***	0.249***
	(0.008)	(0.011)	(0.013)	(0.011)	(0.015)	(0.015)	(0.015)	(0.015)
DP	0.309***	0.119***	0.294***	0.417***	1.444***	1.471***	1.455***	1.444***
	(0.015)	(0.022)	(0.025)	(0.019)	(0.021)	(0.020)	(0.020)	(0.021)

(*Continued*)

Table 13.5 (Continued)

	stage I	*stage I*	*stage I*	*stage I*	*stage II*	*stage II*	*stage II*	*stage II*
Age	−0.113***	−0.050***	−0.241***	−0.072***	−0.042***	−0.050***	−0.038***	−0.047***
	(0.004)	(0.005)	(0.006)	(0.005)	(0.005)	(0.005)	(0.005)	(0.005)
Under identification test					2471.215***	3243.234***	2287.528***	1412.745***
Weak identification test					6566.319***	5400.349***	8193.477***	7586.059****
Observations	32,666	32,666	32,666	32,666	32,666	32,666	32,666	32,666
R^2	0.341	0.317	0.440	0.351	0.366	0.361	0.365	0.367
Industry	Yes	Yes	Yes	Yes	Yes	Yes	Yes	Yes
year	Yes	Yes	Yes	Yes	Yes	Yes	Yes	Yes

Note: See notes to model 1. Robust standard errors in parentheses.
*** $p < 0.01$, ** $p < 0.05$, * $p < 0.1$.

6. Robustness Tests

6.1 Alternative Dependent Variable

In order to remove the bias in the selection of the proxy variables from having an impact on the regression findings, this study uses the substitution variable method for robustness testing. We replaced the original proxy variable ROA with the approximate indicator ROE and rerun the regression analysis. Table 13.6 shows the results of regression with the proxy variable ROA replaced by ROE. The findings demonstrate the surrogate variables' continued significance and agreement with the earlier findings, showing the reliability of the regression findings. The robustness of the study is increased by the use of such surrogate variables, which also aid in confirming the accuracy of the primary data. To ensure the robustness of our primary and moderating models, we computed them and replaced the important dependent variables with ROE, a different way to assess CFP (Zahid et al., 2022).

6.2 Alternative Moderator Variable about AQ

We substituted the audit fee logarithm for the moderating impact within the same framework and used AQ to quantify audit fee as an alternative to the Big Four auditors. By dividing the audit charge by G, it is possible to calculate the impact of AQ on ESG and the connection between CFP (Zahid et al., 2022). By performing regression analysis again, we observed that the significance and sign direction of the interaction term in the results were consistent with those of previous studies, which indicated the robustness and reliability of the results. Table 13.7 presents the findings.

7. Discussion

7.1 Relationship with Previous Literature

The results of this study are consistent with some previous literature, which showed that ESG plays a positive role in CFP, such as Velte (2017), Friede et al. (2015), and Chairani and Siregar (2021). The data used in this study come from China, which is different from some previous literature data. Additionally, when examining the impact of ESG on business financial performance, the majority of extant literature studies do not properly take other adjusting factors into account. The AQ is thought to be a potential surrogate moderating factor in this study, which also fills in any gaps in the literature.

On the basis of previous studies, this study used a large sample to investigate in the context of China, and the results were consistent with Zahid et al. (2022). It demonstrates that the association between ESG and company performance measures is negatively moderated by AQ.

Table 13.6 ESG–CFP and Alternative Dependent Variable (ROE)

Variable	*ROE*	*ROE*	*ROE*	*ROE*	*ROE*	*ROE*	*ROE*	*ROE*
ESG	0.211***				0.224***			
	(0.016)				(0.016)			
Environment		−0.006				−0.004		
		(0.009)				(0.010)		
Social			0.091***				0.091***	
			(0.008)				(0.008)	
Governance				0.165***				0.176***
				(0.013)				(0.014)
ESG_big4					−0.229***			
					(0.045)			
Environment_big4						−0.033		
						(0.029)		
Social_big4							−0.022	
							(0.020)	
Governance_big4								−0.241***
								(0.040)
Big4					16.088***	1.032	0.713	18.351***
					(3.425)	(1.837)	(1.540)	(3.310)
Size	2.656***	2.981***	2.810***	2.758***	2.751***	3.060***	2.882***	2.863***
	(0.086)	(0.086)	(0.085)	(0.085)	(0.091)	(0.091)	(0.090)	(0.089)
FL	−0.125***	−0.135***	−0.135***	−0.117***	−0.126***	−0.136***	−0.136***	−0.118***
	(0.006)	(0.006)	(0.006)	(0.006)	(0.006)	(0.006)	(0.006)	(0.006)
PTB	0.244***	0.235***	0.241***	0.235***	0.254***	0.242***	0.247***	0.245***
	(0.047)	(0.047)	(0.047)	(0.047)	(0.047)	(0.047)	(0.047)	(0.047)
DP	2.161***	2.230***	2.202***	2.157***	2.160***	2.232***	2.204***	2.157***
	(0.034)	(0.034)	(0.034)	(0.034)	(0.034)	(0.034)	(0.034)	(0.034)

(*Continued*)

Table 13.6 (Continued)

Variable	*ROE*	*ROE*	*ROE*	*ROE*	*ROE*	*ROE*	*ROE*	*ROE*
Age	−0.098***	−0.122***	−0.102***	−0.108***	−0.099***	−0.124***	−0.103***	−0.110***
	(0.010)	(0.010)	(0.010)	(0.010)	(0.010)	(0.010)	(0.010)	(0.010)
Constant	−65.201***	−56.005***	−59.497***	−65.276***	−68.165***	−57.790***	−61.052***	−68.415***
	(1.948)	(1.794)	(1.800)	(1.979)	(2.084)	(1.913)	(1.904)	(2.117)
Observations	37,573	37,573	37,573	37,573	37,573	37,573	37,573	37,573
R^2	0.232	0.227	0.230	0.233	0.233	0.227	0.230	0.234
Industry	Yes	Yes	Yes	Yes	Yes	Yes	Yes	Yes
Year	Yes	Yes	Yes	Yes	Yes	Yes	Yes	Yes

Note: See notes to model 1. Robust standard errors in parentheses.
*** $p < 0.01$, ** $p < 0.05$, * $p < 0.1$.

Table 13.7 ESG–CFP and Alternative Moderating Variables for AQ (Audit Fee)

Variable	*ROA*	*ROA*	*ROA*	*ROA*
ESG	0.496***			
	(0.123)			
ESG_audit	−0.029***			
	(0.009)			
Environment		0.240***		
		(0.071)		
Environment_audit		−0.017***		
		(0.005)		
Social			0.328***	
			(0.053)	
Social_audit			−0.021***	
			(0.004)	
Governance				−0.081
				(0.106)
Governance_audit				0.012
				(0.008)
Audit	0.910	-0.215	0.269	−2.083***
	(0.681)	(0.333)	(0.304)	(0.638)
Size	1.714***	1.887***	1.809***	1.726***
	(0.046)	(0.047)	(0.047)	(0.046)
FL	−0.099***	−0.104***	−0.104***	−0.095***
	(0.002)	(0.002)	(0.002)	(0.002)
PTB	0.275***	0.271***	0.274***	0.265***
	(0.014)	(0.014)	(0.014)	(0.014)
PD	1.398***	1.430***	1.416***	1.399***
	(0.018)	(0.018)	(0.018)	(0.018)
Age	−0.063***	−0.075***	−0.065***	−0.068***
	(0.004)	(0.004)	(0.004)	(0.004)
Constant	−51.776***	−32.543***	−40.707***	−9.844
	(9.319)	(4.560)	(4.149)	(8.681)
Observations	37,573	37,573	37,573	37,573
R^2	0.413	0.408	0.412	0.414
Industry	Yes	Yes	Yes	Yes
Year	Yes	Yes	Yes	Yes

Note: See notes to model 1. Robust standard errors in parentheses.
*** $p < 0.01$, ** $p < 0.05$, * $p < 0.1$.

7.2 Theoretical Implications

From a theoretical perspective, research results support stakeholder theory (Freeman, 1984) and resource-based theory, and improvement in ESG rating can help a company improve its financial performance, which reflects the mutual benefit of the two. Allocation of resources also affects the company's activities, and improvement in ESG can drive resource availability, sustainable development, and improved utilization of resources (Zhu & Rahman, 2024). The ESG rating of a company can also reflect the value of the company from the side. The research results also support the theory of legitimacy. The operation of enterprises needs the support of society. At present, various countries are beginning to pay more attention to ESG. Therefore, a company with a high ESG rating is what society needs, along with social recognition. It can help enterprises develop, and improvement in ESG also plays a positive role in CFP.

7.3 Practical Implications

The results of this study provide important insights for managers, policymakers, and practitioners of Chinese enterprises. Improvement in ESG can help improve the performance of enterprises. In addition, it also reflects the role of AQ. It guides investors who can better understand the positive role ESG can play in corporate financial reporting. Managers can apply these findings to corporate decision-making to better face and deal with ESG-related risks and opportunities. For policymakers, the research results can be used to encourage companies to enhance ESG ratings and promote sustainable development. And for practitioners, for example, accounting firms can refer to the results of this study to provide companies with better ESG reporting and auditing services.

8. Conclusion

This study aimed to explore the impact of ESG on corporate financial reporting and the changes with the adjustment of AQ. Our initial sample included A-share listed companies in Shanghai and Shenzhen, China, from 2009 to 2022. The final survey results found that under the same conditions, changes in ESG have a significant positive correlation with ROA. This also illustrates that ESG has a negative impact on a company's historical financial performance. When the AQ increases, it plays a negative role in regulating the financial report of the company. When the AQ is the four major audits, there is a positive relationship with ROA, that is, a positive impact. This shows that strict auditing can help companies improve financial performance.

These findings have contributed to the literature on ESG and corporate financial reports. Firstly, we selected a larger sample size for this research. In order to ensure that the research results are more accurate and representative, empirical evidence was added to the literature. The conclusion can be more widely applicable to different types of enterprises and markets. Secondly, in the sample selection of this study, relevant data of listed companies in China were selected, and references for the country's development in improving ESG were added. The results have great implications for managers and practitioners of Chinese enterprises. Finally, the study introduced AQ as an adjustment variable to better reflect the relationship between the dependent variable and independent variables, making the empirical results more accurate and rigorous. In-depth analysis by controlling AQ is also lacking in the current literature on ESG and corporate financial reporting. It broadens new ideas and reference value for subsequent scholarly research in this area.

There are also some limitations in this study. Firstly, development of ESG in China is still in its infancy, so disclosure of ESG is not perfect in fact, which will lead to relatively low reliability and transparency of data. Secondly, ESG ratings given by different institutions do not have a unified evaluation standard, so there are differences in the analysis of data. The same is true for ESG ratings among different countries, so only empirical analysis in the Chinese environment was conducted in this study. Finally, the assessment of audit quality (AQ) is currently limited to the Big Four audit firms, as well as those firms that are not part of the Big Four. To provide a more comprehensive analysis, it may be useful to consider the Big Eight or even the Big Ten audit firms, which could help better understand the role of moderating variables.

References

Abdolmohammadi, M. J. (2005). Intellectual capital disclosure and market capitalization. *Journal of Intellectual Capital*, *6*(3), 397–416.

Ado, A. B., Rashid, N., Mustapha, U. A., & Ademola, L. S. (2020). The impact of audit quality on the financial performance of listed companies Nigeria. *Journal of Critical Reviews*, *7*(9), 37–42.

Aggarwal, P. (2013). Impact of corporate governance on corporate financial performance. *IOSR Journal of Business and Management*, *13*(3), 1–5.

Aouadi, A., & Marsat, S. (2016). Do ESG controversies matter for firm value? Evidence from international data. *Journal of Business Ethics*, *151*(4), 1027–1047.

Aydoğmuş, M., Gülay, G., & Ergun, K. (2022). Impact of ESG performance on firm value and profitability. *Borsa Istanbul Review*, *22*(2).

Bacha, S., Ajina, A., & Ben Saad, S. (2021). CSR performance and the cost of debt: Does audit quality matter? *Corporate Governance: The International Journal of Business in Society*, *21*(1), 137–158.

Benlemlih, M. (2019). Corporate social responsibility and dividend policy. *Research in International Business and Finance*, *47*, 114–138.

Broadstock, D. C., Matousek, R., Meyer, M., & Tzeremes, N. G. (2020). Does corporate social responsibility impact firms' innovation capacity? The indirect link between environmental & social governance implementation and innovation performance. *Journal of Business Research*, *119*, 99–110.

Chairani, C., & Siregar, S. V. (2021). The effect of enterprise risk management on financial performance and firm value: The role of environmental, social and governance performance. *Meditari Accountancy Research*, *29*(3), 647–670.

Dewi, K., & Monalisa, M. (2016). Effect of corporate social responsibility disclosure on financial performance with audit quality as a moderating variable. *Binus Business Review*, *7*(2), 149–155.

Francis, J. R. (2004). What do we know about audit quality? *The British Accounting Review*, *36*(4), 345–368.

Friede, G., Busch, T., & Bassen, A. (2015). ESG and financial performance: Aggregated evidence from more than 2000 empirical studies. *Journal of Sustainable Finance & Investment*, *5*(4), 210–233.

Freeman, R. B. (1984). Longitudinal analyses of the effects of trade unions. *Journal of labor Economics*, *2*(1), 1–26.

Galant, A., & Cadez, S. (2017). Corporate social responsibility and financial performance relationship: A review of measurement approaches. *Economic Research-Ekonomska Istraživanja*, *30*(1), 676–693.

He, F., Ding, C., Yue, W., & Liu, G. (2023). ESG performance and corporate risk-taking: Evidence from China. *International Review of Financial Analysis*, *87*.

Kay, I., Brindisi, M., & Martin, B. (2020). *The stakeholder model and ESG*. Harvard Law School Forum.

Lokuwaduge, C. S. D. S., & Heenetigala, K. (2016). Integrating environmental, social and governance (ESG) disclosure for a sustainable development: An Australian study. *Business Strategy and the Environment*, *26*(4), 438–450.

Naseem, T., Shahzad, F., Asim, G. A., Rehman, I. U., & Nawaz, F. (2019). Corporate social responsibility engagement and firm performance in Asia Pacific: The role of enterprise risk management. *Corporate Social Responsibility and Environmental Management*, *27*(2).

Qiu, Y., Shaukat, A., & Tharyan, R. (2016). Environmental and social disclosures: Link with corporate financial performance. *The British Accounting Review*, *48*(1), 102–116.

Rahman, M. J., & Wu, J. (2023). M&A activity and ESG performance: Evidence from China. *Managerial Finance*, *50*(1), 179–197.

Rahman, M. J., Zhu, H., & Chen, S. (2023). Does CSR reduce financial distress? Moderating effect of firm characteristics, auditor characteristics, and covid-19. *International Journal of Accounting & Information Management*, *31*(5), 756–784.

Rahman, M. J., Zhu, H., Zhang, Y. & Hossain, M. M. (2024), "Effect of female representation in audit committees on non-audit fees: evidence from China", *Meditari Accountancy Research*, *32*(4), 1258–1290. https://doi.org/10.1108/MEDAR-05-2023-1996

Tunio, R. A., Jamali, R. H., Mirani, A. A., Das, G., Laghari, M. A., & Xiao, J. (2021). The relationship between corporate social responsibility disclosures and financial performance: A mediating role of employee productivity. *Environmental Science and Pollution Research*, *28*, 10661–10677.

Velte, P. (2017). Does ESG performance have an impact on financial performance? Evidence from Germany. *Journal of Global Responsibility*, *8*(2), 169–178.

Watkins, A. L., Hillison, W., & Morecroft, S. E. (2004). Audit quality: A synthesis of theory and empirical evidence. *Journal of Accounting Literature*, *23*, 153.

Whelan, T., Atz, U., Van Holt, T., & Clark, C. (2021). *ESG and financial performance: Uncovering the relationship by aggregating evidence from 1,000 plus studies published between 2015–2020*. NYU Stern Center for Sustainable Business.

Zahid, R. A., Khan, M. K., Anwar, W., & Maqsood, U. S. (2022). The role of audit quality in the ESG-corporate financial performance nexus: Empirical evidence from Western European companies. *Borsa Istanbul Review*, *22*.

Zhu, H., & Rahman, M. J. (2024). Ex-ante expected changes in ESG and future stock returns based on machine learning. *The British Accounting Review*, *56*(6), 101457.

Part 5

ESG Disclosure and Capital Markets

14 ESG Factors, Firm Value, and Company Size

Md Jahidur Rahman, Tarek Rana, Hongtao Zhu, and Zhang Tianyu

1. Introduction

Deeper market changes have prompted investors to prioritize corporate sustainability in light of the rise of a green mindset and global climate investment awareness. Companies need to improve their environmental, social, and governance (ESG) reporting in non-financial ways, such as by adopting stricter guidelines and being more forthcoming with information (Baid & Jayaraman, 2022; Luke, 2022). It is important to note that Chinese enterprises, in contrast to their foreign counterparts, are driven by regulations rather than the market (Rahman, Zhu, & Jiang, 2024). As a result, for the benefit of all parties involved and in reaction to the changing market environment, companies need to take the next step towards making changes under strict supervision. ESG factors may affect the long-term growth and continuity of an organization's internal governance (Varvara & Victoria, 2022). Organizations that are inspired by ESG factors may create value and attract sustainable investments by prioritizing environmental preservation and development, high social standards, and socially responsible corporate operations. Environmental sustainability, social responsibility, and sound corporate governance are the three pillars upon which the ESG rating framework rests, and they are all crucial to attracting outside capital. The influence of ESG factors on the success of businesses of varying sizes remains unclear, however, and more research is required.

We were prompted to investigate this topic in the Chinese context by a dearth of information on how ESG factors into the success of companies of varied sizes. Our interest in this area was further piqued by the work of Bissoondoyal-Bheenick et al. (2023). This study examines the overall ESG score and the impact of different latitudes on the performance of Chinese organizations of varying sizes by analysing ESG data from all Chinese A-share listed businesses from 2011 to 2021. According to the findings of Shah et al. (2022), larger corporations are more likely to engage in ESG-related investments and activities, and they also tend to receive higher ESG ratings overall. Therefore, from a stakeholder theory point of view, businesses stand to gain by cutting expenses, which boosts both performance and value. By devoting more resources to ESG concerns, businesses can reduce or eliminate risks such as labour disputes, social badland threats due to pollution and emissions, legal challenges, and threats to the firm's social image and reputation (Shah et al., 2022).

DOI: 10.4324/9781003488934-19

Therefore, businesses face both advantages and disadvantages when evaluating ESG factors. This research aims to quantify the connection between environmental (*E*), social (*S*), and governance (*G*) variables that make up ESG grading and the attainment of business goals in order to better understand the effect that ESG has on the profitability of businesses of varying sizes.

We also examined the literature's depiction of the connection between ESG and business performance. Based on our research, ESG may help businesses not only create value but also increase that value for their stakeholders (Zhong et al., 2022). However, ESG places additional strain on the internal operations of the organization (e.g., more work items and procedures) due to the rising requirement for openness and accountability. Costs for items like environmental upkeep, social good, and corporate employee benefits increase, while risks associated with corporate governance decrease, according to Zhong et al. (2022). There has been a flurry of new books and articles in this field in recent years, which may indicate that ESG is gaining traction within corporations and that companies are beginning to understand the value of prioritizing the interests of all of their stakeholders rather than just shareholders. This demonstrates that ESG is gaining acceptance within organizations and that companies are beginning to see the value in putting an emphasis on ESG. Although ESG aids in maximizing short-term shareholder value, it does not, according to Shah et al. (2022), aid in the firm's long-term growth. This is in stark contrast to conventional approaches to corporate governance, which have focused narrowly on benefits to the company's owners (the shareholders). To some extent, stakeholder theory can be seen as an expansion of ESG, given that the development of ESG prioritizes the value not only to shareholders but also to the community, the government, and the workers inside an organization. Therefore, a company's performance over its whole lifespan depends on its adoption of ESG efforts (Freeman, 1994).

Since most data imply that ESG is predominantly impacted by stakeholders, we take *E*, *S*, and *G* to imply varying degrees of significance in their effect on business performance (Friedman & Miles, 2002). There may be a wide range of approaches because companies of different sizes have varied priorities. One criterion to evaluate ESG of a firm is data from independent assessment systems offered by professional organizations, which is crucial from a financial perspective if a company needs to obtain capital and attract investors. Because different ESG aspects are given different levels of importance, a company's size can be used as a stand-in for its effectiveness in this area. For instance, studies have shown that local communities and social responsibility are less important to smaller enterprises (Ali et al., 2022). More importantly, the different weightings mean that *E*, *S*, and *G* serve different purposes when evaluating businesses of different sizes. Investors place more weight on *S* and *G* ratings than other criteria (such as the internal structure of the organization); therefore, companies in high-risk industries, for example, would prioritize improving these scores.

While our major interest is in a company's bottom line, we do take into account ESG factors including social responsibility and environmental sustainability. Firstly, we have mostly considered the potential impacts of enterprises when considering environmental impact (*E*), that is, carbon emission reduction and chemical pollution prevention on one side and green thinking and long-term growth on the other (Ning et al., 2023). Secondly, we apply social criteria (*S*) to the company's evaluation, taking into account the positive and negative effects it has on society. Nguyen (2022) listed several instances of projects that transcend outside the traditional boundaries of business, including those that promote gender equality, racial equality, cultural equality, religious equality, employee care, and social good.

Finally, the governance (*G*) part examines the changes in the company's internal governance structure through time, focusing on the role of management as the principal agent of change and the changing dynamic between shareholders and management. Examples include resolving disputes over proxy voting, encouraging a diverse and engaged workforce, and striking a balance between the interests of shareholders and executives by allocating authority through salary and stock. We also look at how *E*, *S*, and *G* work in large, medium, and small businesses. Many studies (Henisz et al., 2019; Pástor et al., 2021; Di Tommaso & Thornton, 2020) have found that ESG equities are more likely to perform well and attract investors. These stocks have a longer-term future. Businesses with higher ESG ratings are risk-averse and mitigated, according to research by Chava (2014) and Bae et al. (2018). This leads to stronger bank credit ratings and faster loan approvals, a finding supported by research from other groups (Giese et al., 2019; Jang et al., 2020). Both studies observed similar results.

Even among companies of the same size in the same country, the effect of ESG on company performance can vary widely depending on the industry (Bissoondoyal-Bheenick et al., 2023), indicating that ESG is a contentious topic. Companies' overall effectiveness is measured by their ESG scores. Recent studies and published works have produced important new insights and advancements. Documents and research like these examine the good and negative implications of ESG aspects on business results. The bulk of studies (90%) show a favourable correlation between ESG elements and corporate performance, as shown by Friede et al. (2015). Sixty-two percent of the research conducted by Van Beurden and Gössling (2008) indicated a favourable and statistically significant association between CSR and firm performance. Twenty-seven percent of the research found no relationship between the two variables. Although the vast majority of academic studies have found that ESG variables improve business performance, there is still a sizable group of researchers who are agnostic and unable to draw a causal link. According to Brooks and Oikonomou (2018), there may be no correlation between ESG and business value because empirical research have not revealed evidence of a negative association between the two, even if there are no prior negative connotations.

This investigation makes use of experimental testing to learn new things about ESG factors. The return on assets (ROA) model was used to analyse how ESG issues affected the performance of companies. The study found a significant link between ESG parameters and company performance even after controlling for other variables. ESG score was used for the analysis because of its emphasis on profitability. In order to deal with endogeneity in model estimate, the propensity score matching (PSM) approach along with the two-stage least squares (2SLS) method is used in this investigation. As a proxy for the industry as a whole, average ESG scores of competing businesses are used. Sequentially applying assessments across three ESG dimensions, the findings are categorized as large, medium, or small (Chen & Xie, 2022). In this study, ESG and business performance metrics are substituted for verification purposes. According to our research, bigger companies have better ESG scores than smaller ones.

This chapter's remaining sections are structured as follows. Section 2 details the development of China's ESG policies and the country's progress in this area from 2011 to 2022. In Section 3, we review the various theoretical stances on how ESG variables affect a company's bottom line. In Section 4, we examine the hypothesis, and in Section 5, we detail the methodology and sample selection for the empirical analysis. Primary examination results are presented in Section 6. Sections 7 and 8 focus on endogeneity and robustness analysis, respectively. The literature review, theoretical framework, and experimental findings are presented in Section 9, while the conclusion is given in Section 10.

2. Background

2.1 ESG Institutional Setting in China (2011–2021)

Since 2011, China has strictly restricted the expansion of businesses. Since 2011, businesses have had to fulfil higher environmental management requirements, and environmental laws and regulations have been modified on a regular basis. Air pollution was prohibited in January 2016, followed by water pollution in January 2018, solid waste pollution in 2020, and noise pollution on June 5, 2022. In 2015, five laws were passed. On June 5, 2022, the Noise Pollution Prevention and Control Law was put into force (He et al., 2013; Rahman, Zhu, & Beiyi, 2023; Zhang, 2013, 2016). Since 2011, nine resource protection laws have been revised and expanded: the Forestry Law, Grassland Law, Fisheries Law, Agriculture Law, Mineral Resources Law, Land Management Law, Water Law, Soil and Water Conservation Law, Wildlife Protection Law, and Coal Management Law (Boxer, 1989; Li et al., 2019).

Meanwhile, businesses have started to place more emphasis on social responsibility since 2011 when they were allowed to get state tax deductions for social donations. Donations to the Asian Sand Conference, enterprises producing and assembling specialized goods for the disabled, and the announcement of the first batch of goods eligible for pre-tax deductibility of public welfare donations in 2011 were all made public in 2011 (Yang, 2014; Chen et al., 2010; Zhou et al., 2012). Meanwhile, China implemented changes to improve corporate governance; safeguard the rights of enterprises, shareholders, and creditors; keep the economy running smoothly; and advance the socialist market economy. The Company Law was last revised in 2013 and again in 2018. The People's Republic of China's most recent Labour Law went into effect in 2018, while the Securities Law was replaced on March 1, 2020. Both the Trademark Law (last updated in 2013) and the Copyright Law (last updated on November 11, 2020) demonstrate China's commitment to the standardised functioning of firms and the preservation and regulation of intellectual property rights.

2.2 ESG Development in China

Environmental, social, and corporate governance may have various features depending on the country or place (Bissoondoyal-Bheenick et al., 2023) owing to disparities in development level, culture, and social governance. China is self-aware and expanding. ESG goals are replacing sustainable development. China pioneered ESG in the 1980s, and ESG has matured in China. After opening to the world, China's environmental laws were widely supported (He, 2012; Zhang, 2021). China has enacted several environmental regulations, and several studies in China also investigate the relationship between environmental accounting and firm performance (Rahman & Wu, 2023; Rahman, Wu, et al., 2024; Rahman, Zhu, & Chen, 2023; Zhu & Rahman, 2024).

The government enacted five control laws and nine resource control legislation to enhance corporate environmental management. He et al. (2012) argued that China's ISO14001 environmental management system and green supply chain management have played a crucial role in promoting environmental protection and improving business management practices. This is highly beneficial. The 2001 legislation pertaining to company governance brought about significant reforms. Subsequently, the Code of Governance for Listed Companies was implemented.

Bissoondoyal-Bheenick et al. (2023) state that the ESG disclosure system mandates companies to integrate ESG considerations into product development, ensuring the inclusion of economic and social benefits from the outset. China has established a social responsibility bureau to implement the new development concept and investigate the development of a comprehensive ESG system. The bureau aims to encourage more listed companies, particularly those holding central enterprises, to disclose ESG reports. The ultimate objective is to achieve "full coverage" by the year 2023 (Chen et al., 2015). The bureau aims to achieve comprehensive disclosure of ESG report by 2023.

Nonetheless, there are still some issues. Firstly, standardization of ESG agencies faces challenges such as the fact that investors may be influenced by the varying ratings provided by various rating agencies (Bissoondoyal-Bheenick et al., 2023). Secondly, China lacks a framework that is in line with current market development, including the building of ESG market infrastructure, further improvement of government laws and regulations, and the time needed to harmonize between investor rating agencies and data providers (He et al., 2012). Sustainable development and corporate social responsibility (CSR) have benefited greatly from China's ESG development, which has progressed from its infancy to full maturity.

3. Theoretical Perspectives on ESG and Firm Value

Freeman (1994) argued that the two most important theoretical frameworks for considering the effect of ESG factors on firm performance are the shareholder and stakeholder theories. Relationships between stakeholders and shareholders are emphasized in both systems. The bottom line is all that matters to shareholders. Stakeholder theory suggests that external stakeholders, such as investors and customers, should be given more importance than internal ones. Stakeholder theory (Phillips et al., 2003; Zhang, 2011; Parmar et al., 2010) suggests that individuals' and groups' needs should be prioritized over those of businesses. Zhang (2011) and Parmar et al. (2010) made contributions to it. According to the stakeholder hypothesis, a company's performance can improve if it demonstrates strong social responsibility and corporate governance (Donaldson & Preston, 1995; Friedman & Miles, 2002). Two separate studies on this, one by Donaldson and Preston and another by Friedman and Miles, have been published.

The expanding corporation, on the other hand, now integrates shareholder theory. According to shareholder theory, in order to maximize value, a firm must first increase shareholder shares (Freeman, 2010). This is required under shareholder theory. ESG measures, according to a 2020 Cornell and Damodaran study, are problematic and always cost more. Because ESG gains take years to materialize, some research imply that ESG practices may reduce a company's value (Cornell, 2021).

The stakeholder paradigm supports the approach to ESG. Because it rates and influences firm performance, ESG is more practical than CSR (Park et al., 2023). CSR is more theoretical than ESG. ESG is more useful than CSR. According to Cini and Ricci (2018), CSR promotes ESG performance endogenously. According to the evidence, CSR promotes ESG performance. Baraibar-Diez et al. (2019) found more evidence that CSR boosts ESG performance.

4. Literature Review and Hypothesis Development

4.1 ESG Factor and Firm Value

CSR reports provide insight into how ESG factors impact enterprises. The debate on whether ESG factors influence firm performance is contentious. Some scholars argue that CSR does not have a direct impact on economic success. Friedman (1970) was a notable opponent of CSR, advocating for direct capitalism and economic freedom. According to Friedman, socially responsible firms limit shareholder economic freedom, positing that CSR represents a distorted view of capitalism that ultimately harms both the company and the broader economy (Freeman & Liedtka, 1991). Additionally, CSR is considered outdated due to agency issues (Beaudoin, 2008; Liang & Renneboog, 2018; Barnea & Rubin, 2010). These authors suggest that CSR should be abandoned.

Conversely, other scholars posit that stakeholders significantly influence business performance through ESG issues (Huang, 2021; Rodrigue et al., 2013;

Barnett, 2007). Carroll (2004) argued that corporations must consider a range of stakeholder groups to meet their expectations. Stakeholder theory suggests that by fostering positive stakeholder–firm relationships, ESG can address stakeholder concerns and enhance financial performance (Cornell & Shapiro, 1987; Neville et al., 2005; Scholtens & Zhou, 2008). This perspective implies that ESG initiatives can lead to improved business performance by expanding the influence of enterprise stakeholders.

H1: ESG can expand the influence range of enterprise stakeholders, thereby affecting enterprise performance and increasing enterprise value.

4.2 Stakeholders in Different Corporate Size

Stakeholder factors can significantly impact firm size outcomes. Research by Chang et al. (2021) indicated that the effect of ESG practices aimed at satisfying multiple stakeholders varies depending on the firm's size. Clarkson (1995) distinguished between primary and secondary stakeholders, noting that primary stakeholders have a greater influence on smaller enterprises than secondary stakeholders (Darnall et al., 2010; Preuss & Perschke, 2010; D'Souza et al., 2022). Empirical studies suggest that larger companies are better equipped to resist pressure from both internal and external stakeholders than smaller ones (Darnall et al., 2010; Seroka-Stolka & Fijorek, 2020). Darnall et al. (2010) hypothesized that stakeholder demand and environmental policy are differentially affected by firm size. In China, powerful stakeholders, aside from shareholders, have minimal impact on company environmental performance disclosure (Wang & Zhao, 2020). Xun (2013) notes that only government-directed corporate social responsibility initiatives enhance firm performance in China. Given China's recent emphasis on supporting small and medium-sized enterprises, key stakeholders play a crucial role in a company's success.

H2: The smaller the company, the more sensitive it is to the influence of stakeholders; the performance of Chinese firms is positively influenced by key stakeholders.

5. Research Design

5.1 Sample and Data

This study tests the research hypothesis of Chen and Xie (2022) by analysing data from A-share public firms in China between 2011 and 2021 to determine the impact of ESG variables on corporate performance. The China Stock Market & Accounting Research (CSMAR) database provides the financial data, while individual ratings of Huazheng, Hexun, and Bloomberg databases provide the ESG information. Bloomberg compiled both sets of rankings. The following methods were frequently used in this study to cleanse and organize data: to begin, know that commercial

Table 14.1 Variable Screening Procedure

Screening Criterion	*Rejection Sample*
Eliminate the financial sector	825
Elimination of ST enterprises	1,185
Exclude companies that have been listed for less than three years	1,398
Remove samples with missing key variables	3,600

Source: Table by authors

Note: This table presents the procedure for obtaining the final sample for testing.

enterprises are not part of the special treatment (ST) classification. Secondly, any publicly traded financial organizations were left out of consideration. Thirdly, we only looked at information from samples with a 1:1 gearing ratio. As a fourth factor, we did not include samples that are incomplete or otherwise invalid. Fifth, to lessen the weight of extreme data, we employed a tail decreasing technique called bilateral 1% tail shrinking for all continuous variables. The aforementioned methods were used to collect the raw unbalanced panel data for this study, which contains 31,242 observations from 4,366 unique companies. Table 14.1 summarizes the sample selection process.

5.2 *Variable Measurements*

5.2.1 Dependent Variable

Corporate performance, measured by Return on Assets (ROA), is used as the dependent variable in this study. Existing research typically analyzes both financial and operational performance of firms. Building on the approach of Shin et al. (2023) and considering the available data, this study uses the firm's net asset margin as a proxy for financial performance. In the robustness analysis section, we will further examine the results by replacing this measure of financial performance with an alternative metric.

5.2.2 Independent Variables

Scholars often rely on Huawei, Hexun, or Bloomberg's ESG evaluations of businesses, despite the fact that there is currently no agreement among academics on how to assess ESG ratings (Luo, 2022; He et al., 2022, 2023). In this study, we used the ESG rating from China Securities as our primary explanatory variable because their sample is larger than most. However, we also include the ESG ratings from other rating agencies in our robustness analysis to ensure our results hold up to scrutiny.

5.2.3 Control Variables

This study incorporates the findings of Jordan et al. (2016) to account for other firm-level control factors that may have an effect on organizational effectiveness.

Firm size (Size) is the natural logarithm of total assets, while cash flow from operating activities (Cash) is the ratio of net cash flow from operating activities to total assets, and fixed assets share (PPE) is the ratio of net fixed assets to total assets. A company's age is determined by taking the natural logarithm of its foundation year plus one, its progress is illustrated by the annual percentage change in per capita income, its position in the rankings is based on the percentage of shares held by the company's largest shareholder, and an extra point is added if the auditing firm is one of the "Big Four" accounting firms.

5.3 Model Specification

This work adopts the methodology of Schultz and Shive (2010) and implements the following econometric model to examine the relationship between corporate ESG practises and financial performance:

$$[\![ROA]\!]\_(i,t) = \alpha\_0 + \alpha\_1[\![ESG]\!]\_(i,t) + \sum Control + \sum IND + \sum YEAR + \varepsilon\_(i,t) \tag{1}$$

Here, the subscripts i and t denote the firm and year, respectively. $ROA_{i,t}$ denotes the operating performance of firm i in year t. $\sum Control$ is the set of control variables, including the relevant control variables mentioned in the previous section.$\sum IND$ and $\sum YEAR$ are industry and time fixed effects, respectively. $\varepsilon_{i,c,t}$ are random disturbance terms, which denote other factors that may affect firm performance but have not been controlled for in the empirical evidence of this study. The main focus here is on the regression coefficients of ESG variables α_1, and if α_1 is significantly positive, it indicates that a rise in ESG can improve the financial performance of firms, while the opposite indicates that a rise in ESG can reduce the financial performance of firms.

To estimate the impact of ESG on firm financial performance across firms of varying sizes, this study additionally takes into account the effect of firm size in the impact of ESG on firm financial performance, divides the sample into three groups according to firm size, and estimates model (1) again for the subdivided sample.

In addition, considering that ESG contains three components, *E*, *S*, and *G*, this study further splits ESG and estimates the effects of *E*, *S*, and *G* on corporate financial performance (CFP) separately to further explore the intrinsic mechanisms of ESG affecting corporate performance.

$$[\![ROA]\!]\_(i,t) = \beta\_0 + \beta\_1\, E\_(i,t) + \sum Control + \sum IND + \sum YEAR + \varepsilon\_(i,t) \tag{2}$$

$$[\![ROA]\!]\_(i,t) = \gamma\_0 + \gamma\_1\, S\_(i,t) + \sum Control + \sum IND + \sum YEAR + \varepsilon\_(i,t) \tag{3}$$

$$[ROA]\_(i,t) = \theta\_0 + \theta\_1\, G\_(i,t) + \sum Control + \sum IND + \sum YEAR + \varepsilon\_(i,t) \tag{4}$$

The other settings here are consistent with the econometric model (1) and focus on the regression coefficients of *E*, *S*, and *G*, respectively,β_1, γ_1, andθ_1, with all regressions controlling for industry fixed effects and time-fixed effects.

6. Empirical Results

6.1 Descriptive Statistics

Table 14.2 presents the descriptive statistics for the examined factors in the study. Observing the range of corporate performance, which spans from −0.292 to 0.194 and has a standard deviation of 0.065, it becomes evident that a significant disparity exists between the highest and lowest performing companies within China's publicly traded firms. The potential ESG scores for these organizations also exhibit a broad scope, with values varying from 6 to 1.25. The standard deviation of 1.014 highlights the considerable fluctuation in ESG scores, ranging from a maximum of 6 to a minimum of 1.25. Control variables' standard deviations are generally small, except for the notable deviation in company size. The descriptive statistics for the variables of interest in this research align with those found in other studies, thereby lending credibility to the obtained results.

Companies with better ESG ratings have a tendency to have comparatively stronger financial success, as seen in Table 14.3. At the 1% confidence level, the 0.253 association between ESG and business performance is statistically significant. Significantly negative correlation coefficients are found for gearing, fixed assets, intangible assets, and corporate performance among the control variables, while positive correlation coefficients are found for cash flow from operating activities, growth capacity, and whether or not the Big Four are audited.

Table 14.2 Descriptive Statistics

Variable	*Mean*	*p50*	*SD*	*Min*	*Max*	*N*
ROA	0.0364	0.0377	0.0650	−0.292	0.194	31242
ESG	4.109	4	1.014	1.250	6	31242
Size	22.15	21.96	1.288	19.83	26.19	31242
LEV	0.418	0.408	0.208	0.0518	0.904	31242
Cash	0.0453	0.0449	0.0693	−0.169	0.239	31242
PPE	0.207	0.173	0.158	0.0019	0.691	31242
Intang	0.0457	0.0331	0.0500	0	0.323	31242
Age	2.885	2.944	0.343	0.693	4.143	31242
Growth	0.173	0.109	0.408	−0.580	2.612	31242
Top1	0.342	0.320	0.148	0.0857	0.746	31242
Big4	0.0572	0	0.232	0	1	31242

Source: Table by authors.

Note: This table presents the descriptive statistics for each ROA variable.

Table 14.3 Correlation Coefficient Analysis of Variables

Variables	*ROA*	*ESG*	*Size*	*LEV*	*Cash*	*PPE*	*Intang*	*Age*	*Growth*	*Top1*	*Big4*
ROA	1.000										
ESG	0.253***	1.000									
Size	-0.002	0.192***	1.000								
LEV	-0.371***	-0.091***	0.512***	1.000							
Cash	0.374***	0.091***	0.077***	-0.162***	1.000						
PPE	-0.070***	-0.050***	0.108***	0.090***	0.230***	1.000					
Intang	-0.050***	-0.051***	0.027***	0.012**	0.066***	0.102***	1.000				
Age	-0.100***	-0.065***	0.178***	0.187***	0.028***	0.014**	0.006	1.000			
Growth	0.229***	0.008	0.043***	0.018***	0.022***	-0.071***	-0.010*	-0.049***	1.000		
Top1	0.145***	0.119***	0.193***	0.046***	0.096***	0.086***	0.014**	-0.100***	-0.001	1.000	
Big4	0.037***	0.105***	0.343***	0.103***	0.077***	0.040***	0.043***	0.022***	-0.011*	0.138***	1.000

Source: Table by authors.

Note: Values in brackets are *t* statistics, clustering values at the enterprise level; *, **, and *** are significant at the level of 10%, 5%, and 1%, respectively.
*** $p < 0.01$, ** $p < 0.05$, * $p < 0.1$.

Table 14.4 Multicollinearity

Variable	*VIF*	*1/VIF*
Size	1.74	0.5740
LEV	1.54	0.6511
Big4	1.15	0.8677
Cash	1.14	0.8743
ESG	1.12	0.8963
PPE	1.1	0.9088
Top1	1.08	0.9256
Age	1.08	0.9269
Intang	1.02	0.9831
Growth	1.01	0.9862
Mean VIF	1.2	

Source: Table by author.

Note: This table shows the corresponding estimation results.

To prevent the estimate bias introduced by cointegration in the regression estimation findings, this research further runs a multicollinearity test for each variable before doing the regression analysis. Table 14.4 displays the estimate findings; the VIF values for each variable are close to 1, with a mean of 1.2, indicating that there is no glaring multicollinearity issue among the variables used in this study.

6.2 Baseline Regression Results

According to the first column of Table 14.5, the regression coefficient of ESG is 0.0162 when just the most important explanatory factors are considered. At the 1% confidence level, this value is significantly different from 0. The control variables are given in the second column and industry- and year-fixed effects in the third and fourth columns, respectively. The results reveal that the regression coefficient of ESG is still significantly positive, albeit at a lower level, after controlling for all of the control variables and fixed effects. The estimate from the fourth column is used since the addition of the control variables and fixed effects greatly improves the model's goodness of fit.

The regression coefficient of ESG in the fourth column is 0.0093, which is statistically significant at the 1% level, showing that an increase in a company's ESG rating is associated to a 0.099% improvement in the company's performance. This study confirms the positive effect ESG has on the bottom lines of Chinese enterprises, as shown by Shin et al. (2023). According to the authors of this research, the importance of ESG and good corporate governance in inspiring confidence among investors is to blame. ESG is a comprehensive evaluation made by external agencies based on firms' environment, corporate governance, and social responsibility, which can reflect firms' current or future development potential, while the information asymmetry theory suggests that investors' concern about firms may be reduced or their worries about firms' operation may be increased due to the lack of information. Investors are more inclined to put their money into organizations with higher ratings because of the higher quality of their internal governance and

Table 14.5 Baseline Regression Results

	ROA	*ROA*	*ROA*	*ROA*
ESG	0.0162***	0.0094***	0.0095***	0.0093***
	(26.4489)	(19.9860)	(20.2067)	(19.8812)
Size		0.0064***	0.0065***	0.0074***
		(13.5327)	(13.3405)	(15.1343)
LEV		−0.1141***	−0.1155***	−0.1185***
		(−37.6119)	(−35.9335)	(−36.8046)
Cash		0.2874***	0.2844***	0.2953***
		(35.9437)	(35.8892)	(37.2801)
PPE		−0.0418***	−0.0568***	−0.0608***
		(−14.5757)	(−15.3504)	(−16.3696)
Intang		−0.0642***	−0.0901***	−0.0923***
		(−8.2624)	(−10.1430)	(−10.4659)
Age		−0.0058***	−0.0077***	0.0001
		(−4.6399)	(−6.1825)	(0.0897)
Growth		0.0339***	0.0338***	0.0327***
		(32.5550)	(32.4652)	(31.3406)
Top1		0.0435***	0.0411***	0.0387***
		(13.8918)	(13.3446)	(12.7096)
Big4		−0.0033*	−0.0028	-0.0035**
		(−1.7807)	(−1.5901)	(−2.0032)
Ind	No	No	Yes	Yes
Year	No	No	No	Yes
_cons	−0.0302***	−0.1014***	−0.1017***	−0.1261***
	(−11.2622)	(−10.5608)	(−7.7377)	(−9.3629)
N	31,242	31,242	31,242	31,242
Adj. R^2	0.064	0.362	0.381	0.390

Source: Table by author.

company growth plans. As a result, a company's goods become more competitive in the market, and the business as a whole benefits.

On the other hand, ESG also helps strengthen the internal corporate governance of companies, and companies with higher ESG ratings undoubtedly receive more attention from the market and the media, which makes it easier for companies with significant internal problems to have a negative impact, which leads to the attention generated by ESG to restrain inefficient investments and internal principal–agent behaviour, thus improving corporate performance by strengthening corporate governance and corporate performance. In addition, the signalling theory of ESG also helps firms raise funds at lower interest rates in the capital market, which helps firms implement market expansion strategies at lower costs and thus improve corporate performance.

6.3 ESG, Firm Size, and Firm Performance

According to the theoretical analysis shown above, the impact of ESG on corporate performance may differ depending on the size of the business. The sample is separated into three groups (small, medium, and large) based on company size, and Table 14.6 displays the associated regression estimate for each category.

At the 1% level of significance, the results demonstrate that the regression coefficients of ESG are 0.0123 for small samples, 0.0096 for medium samples, and 0.0061 for big samples. Although ESG has a large effect on firm performance at the individual level, the coefficients tend to decline as the dataset size increases. This study's authors suggest looking at it from two angles: firstly, the firm's competitiveness in the market and, secondly, the quality of its internal governance.

On the one hand, the reputation and market influence of small firms are relatively weak, so when small firms obtain higher ESG ratings, the positive effects can help them compensate for the lack of reputation and thus improve their performance. On the other hand, the talent and corporate governance of small enterprises are usually weaker than those of large enterprises, which suggests the organizational structure of small enterprises may have a lot of imperfections, and the positive effect of ESG will encourage enterprises to accelerate internal transformation and development, thus improving the performance of enterprises. Therefore, the positive effects of ESG are more evident in smaller firms, while the larger firms are able to stabilize their market share by virtue of their competitive advantages, and thus the positive effects of ESG are relatively weak.

Table 14.6 Results of Differentiating the Size of Enterprises

	Small Scale	*Medium size*	*Large Scale*
ESG	0.0123***	0.0094***	0.0061***
	(14.6615)	(12.1343)	(9.2640)
Size	0.0079***	0.0127***	0.0052***
	(4.0846)	(5.9734)	(7.2288)
LEV	−0.1076***	−0.1197***	−0.1337***
	(−18.6250)	(−24.6777)	(−26.6493)
Cash	0.2954***	0.3103***	0.2615***
	(23.0140)	(24.4037)	(20.4479)
PPE	−0.0757***	−0.0590***	−0.0514***
	(−10.9673)	(−9.5369)	(−9.6289)
Intang	−0.1118***	−0.0711***	−0.0750***
	(−5.9937)	(−4.6733)	(−6.9307)
Age	−0.0006	−0.0033	0.0024
	(−0.2839)	(−1.4606)	(1.0721)
Growth	0.0467***	0.0333***	0.0210***
	(18.9655)	(19.0907)	(16.7559)
Top1	0.0426***	0.0533***	0.0222***
	(7.5793)	(10.7443)	(5.4803)
Big4	0.0009	0.0032	−0.0020
	(0.1023)	(0.7777)	(−1.1484)
Ind	Yes	Yes	Yes
Year	Yes	Yes	Yes
_cons	−0.1617***	−0.2258***	−0.0549**
	(−3.8430)	(−4.7741)	(−2.3898)
N	10,606	10,449	10,187
Adj. R^2	0.401	0.380	0.448

Source: Table by author

6.4 Discussion on ESG Segmentation

Keeping in mind that ESG is threc-dimensional, this section will analyse *E*, *S*, and *G* separately to determine how they affect one another and a company's performance, with matching regression estimate findings shown in Table 14.7.

In Table 14.7, the first column displays the complete set of sample estimate findings. The environmental component of ESG currently has a very high negative effect coefficient on business results. This might be because environmental management often requires enterprises to spend some financial and material resources, but the return-on-investment cycle of this expenditure is rather late. Both the social responsibility and corporate governance regression coefficients are statistically significant positive, but the impact coefficient for the corporate governance dimension is larger, indicating that this ESG dimension has a more substantial positive effect

Table 14.7 Segmentation Dimensions of ESG

	Full Sample	*Small Scale*	*Medium Size*	*Large Scale*
E	−0.0007*	−0.0007	−0.0011	−0.0002
	−1.7752)	−0.8930)	(−1.3841)	(−0.3729)
S	0.0034***	0.0043***	0.0036***	0.0025***
	(12.2187)	(8.7201)	(7.5603)	(6.5647)
G	0.0069***	0.0091***	0.0072***	0.0040***
	(17.9021)	(12.9472)	(11.5900)	(7.1673)
Size	0.0076***	0.0086***	0.0131***	0.0053***
	(15.6536)	(4.4745)	(6.2099)	(7.2820)
LEV	−0.1125***	−0.0982***	−0.1137***	−0.1315***
	(−34.1890)	(−16.5528)	(−22.9342)	(−26.0203)
Cash	0.2927***	0.2916***	0.3059***	0.2610***
	(37.2444)	(23.0348)	(24.1966)	(20.4231)
PPE	−0.0598***	−0.0741***	−0.0567***	−0.0509***
	(−16.3187)	(−10.8959)	(−9.2231)	(−9.5544)
Intang	−0.0912***	−0.1120***	−0.0702***	−0.0741***
	(−10.5442)	(−6.0948)	(−4.7374)	(−6.9569)
Age	0.0007	−0.0002	−0.0031	0.0028
	(0.4728)	(-0.0825)	(−1.3632)	(1.2861)
Growth	0.0323***	0.0459***	0.0328***	0.0208***
	(31.2806)	(18.8698)	(19.0515)	(16.6910)
Top1	0.0365***	0.0391***	0.0505***	0.0220***
	(12.1944)	(7.1188)	(10.3449)	(5.4321)
Big4	−0.0042**	0.0008	0.0028	−0.0023
	(−2.3922)	(0.0980)	(0.6640)	(−1.3463)
Ind	Yes	Yes	Yes	Yes
Year	Yes	Yes	Yes	Yes
_cons	−0.1505***	−0.2003***	−0.2566***	−0.0660***
	(−11.1352)	(−4.7973)	(−5.4569)	(−2.8593)
N	31,242	10,606	10,449	10,187
Adj. R^2	0.395	0.408	0.386	0.449

Source: Table by author

Note: The table shows the how segmentation dimensions of ESG influence the different sizes for corporate.

on improving corporate performance than either social responsibility or environmental governance dimension.

The results of the subdivided dimensions of ESG are shown in columns two through four; at this point, they more closely match the estimation results of the full sample, in which only the regression coefficients of social responsibility and corporate governance are significantly positive across the board, with the effect being particularly pronounced for firms with a smaller asset base.

7. Mitigating Endogeneity Concerns

7.1 Instrumental Variables Method

Since organizations with superior corporate performance tend to draw the attention of key institutions and demonstrate stronger ESG rating performance, endogeneity difficulties, such as the issue of reverse causality, may affect the estimation results of this article. To improve the reliability of the estimation results presented here, we employ the 2SLS method to deal with the possible endogeneity problem in the model estimate. Using a notion from Breuer et al. (2018), the average ESG values of other businesses in the same location and the same year are employed as an instrumental variable in this research. The association between the instrumental variable and the explanatory variable can be explained by the fact that businesses and markets are highly comparable between locations that are close together geographically. A company's ESG practices and, by extension, its performance may be affected by the ESG practices of its competitors in the same industry; however, these effects are often indirect. In Table 14.8, the first column displays results from the initial estimate of the instrumental variable. In this case, the ESG ratings of competing businesses in the same sector have an effect on the company's own ESG rating, as indicated by the highly positive instrumental variable coefficient and the satisfaction of the criterion for correlation and exogeneity. As can be seen in the second column of Table 14.8, the regression coefficient of ESG remains quite positive even after controlling for endogeneity, suggesting that ESG continues to enhance company performance.

7.2 PSM Test

In addition, there is a possibility of endogeneity in this work due to sample selection bias. Systematic bias may also alter the findings of this article, as there may be significant discrepancies for business strategy formulation between organizations that are more inclined to control ESG and those with lower ESG ratings. In this study, we use the ESG rating to create three groups, with the highest ESG rating group serving as the experimental group and the lowest ESG rating group serving as the control group, both denoted by dummy variables equal to 1. We utilize this variable as the treatment variable in the logit regression and then use closest neighbour 1:1 matching to isolate the two sets of firms that are most similar to one another, before running the baseline regression on the resampled data. Table 14.9 displays the calculated model and its outcomes. The control variables are omitted

Table 14.8 Regression Results for Instrumental Variables

Variable	*ESG*	*ROA*
IV	0.5159*** (9.25)	
ESG		0.0185*** (3.97)
Size	0.2723*** (24.89)	0.0049*** (3.55)
LEV	−1.2970*** (−20.87)	−0.1064*** (−15.18)
Cash	0.6474*** (5.66)	0.2887*** (33.67)
PPE	−0.0072 (−0.08)	−0.0603*** (−15.94)
Intang	−0.3139 (−1.23)	−0.0891*** (−9.47)
Age	−0.1792*** (−5.10)	0.0020 (1.18)
Growth	−0.0150 (−1.05)	0.0328*** (31.72)
Top1	0.4343*** (5.70)	0.0346*** (9.25)
Big4	0.0703 (1.49)	−0.0042** (−2.27)
Ind	Yes	Yes
Year	Yes	Yes
Constant	−3.5481*** (−9.71)	−0.1125*** (−7.31)
Observations	31,242	31,242
R^2		0.376

Source: Table by author

from Table 14.9's first column, whereas they are included in the second. This study's estimate findings are robust, as shown by the fact that the regression coefficients of ESG are now considerably positive.

This study followed prior methodologies by using a dual-time and industry-fixed effect model for estimation; however, the estimation conclusions may be affected by endogeneity difficulties due to unaccounted for factors, such as some unobservable features at the firm level. The following section employs a regression with firm- and time-fixed effects for estimate; the outcomes are shown in Table 14.10. The regression coefficient of ESG is still quite positive after adjusting for potential confounding variables, suggesting the estimate findings reported here are robust.

8. Robustness Check

In addition, we will replace the measurements of crucial variables to see how well our estimates hold up. The first step is to do new measurements of the independent factors. By switching from ROA to ROE and Tobin Q, we remove the bias

Table 14.9 PSM Regression Results

	ROA	*ROA*
ESG	0.0117***	0.0090***
	(15.6880)	(15.9338)
Size		0.0061***
		(10.3301)
LEV		−0.1111***
		(−25.8935)
Cash		0.2947***
		(30.9760)
PPE		−0.0565***
		(−12.2939)
Intang		−0.1035***
		(−8.5037)
Age		0.0004
		(0.2240)
Growth		0.0317***
		(19.5608)
Top1		0.0363***
		(10.2374)
Big4		−0.0035*
		(−1.9422)
Ind	Yes	Yes
Year	Yes	Yes
_cons	−0.0166	−0.1076***
	(−0.9684)	(−6.1617)
N	14,250	14,250
Adj. R^2	0.100	0.394

Source: Table by author

associated with the firm's performance measure and present the corresponding regression estimation results in the first and second columns of Table 14.11. When controlling for a number of additional factors, statistical analysis reveals that the ESG regression coefficient is still positive.

Secondly, in order to eliminate estimation bias brought on by differences in ESG ratings between agencies, Bloomberg and Hexun's ESG ratings are used to stand in for the original explanatory variables in the benchmark regression used in this study (see the third and fourth columns of Table 14.11 for the corresponding estimation results). The coefficients of the primary explanatory variables maintain their positive signs and statistical significance, indicating the reliability of the estimate findings presented here.

9. Discussion

9.1 Relationship with Previous Literature

By altering the values of several central variables, we can assess the robustness of our estimates. The initial step is to review the values of the independent variable.

Table 14.10 Estimated Results of Replacement Fixed Effects

	ROA	*ROA*
ESG	0.0100***	0.0049***
	(14.1988)	(8.2357)
Size		0.0157***
		(11.9261)
LEV		−0.1760***
		(−33.3870)
Cash		0.1728***
		(21.7666)
PPE		−0.0607***
		(−8.9979)
Intang		−0.0869***
		(−5.2631)
Age		0.0130*
		(1.9261)
Growth		0.0298***
		(29.7497)
Top1		0.0694***
		(8.5031)
Big4		0.0044
		(1.3375)
Firm	Yes	Yes
Year	Yes	Yes
_cons	0.0168***	−0.2881***
	(5.5971)	(−9.0571)
N	31,242	31,242
Adj. R^2	0.058	0.278

Source: Table by author

Table 14.11 presents the results of the regression analyses performed after substituting the company's performance measure from ROA to return on equity (ROE) and Tobin's Q. After controlling for other factors, the results demonstrate that the ESG regression coefficient remains positive. Secondly, to eliminate estimation bias caused by differences in ESG ratings across agencies, Bloomberg and Hexun's ESG ratings are used as substitutes for the original explanatory variables in the benchmark regression (see the third and fourth columns of Table 14.11 for the corresponding estimation results). The coefficients of the primary explanatory variables retain their positive signs and statistical significance, indicating the reliability of the estimate findings.

9.2 *Theoretical Implications*

The findings suggest that significant stakeholders, particularly those supported by the government, are better positioned to positively influence company performance. This supports and extends stakeholder theory (Songling et al., 2018). Despite the potential increase in intra-firm agency conflicts (e.g., shareholders versus executives), this research corroborates the contributions of shareholder theory to

Table 14.11 Robustness Tests

	ROE	*TobinQ*	*ROA*	*ROA*
ESG	0.0185***	0.1364***		
	(18.9497)	(11.1745)		
ESG_PB			0.0140***	
			(5.0348)	
ESG_HX				0.0330***
				(41.6139)
Size	0.0195***	−0.3987***	0.0085***	-0.0000
	(17.0698)	(−20.6753)	(10.3579)	(-0.0943)
LEV	−0.1775***	−0.0358	−0.1379***	−0.0673***
	(−21.6697)	(−0.3796)	(−25.0159)	(−26.9440)
Cash	0.5184***	2.3823***	0.3385***	0.2069***
	(31.9969)	(12.6684)	(26.2110)	(32.1586)
PPE	−0.1198***	−0.5295***	−0.0683***	−0.0358***
	(−14.6099)	(−5.4616)	(−11.6296)	(−12.4017)
Intang	−0.1731***	0.3941	−0.0979***	−0.0519***
	(−8.8592)	(1.2179)	(−7.5288)	(−7.2259)
Age	0.0005	0.2113***	0.0013	−0.0011
	(0.1540)	(5.1656)	(0.5606)	(−1.0377)
Growth	0.0739***	0.1592***	0.0275***	0.0171***
	(31.0615)	(7.5114)	(16.5373)	(23.3086)
Top1	0.0748***	−0.3386***	0.0278***	0.0170***
	(11.6007)	(−3.8222)	(6.1966)	(7.0337)
Big4	−0.0060	0.3341***	−0.0053***	−0.0018
	(−1.4696)	(5.6697)	(−2.9441)	(−1.1894)
Ind	Yes	Yes	Yes	Yes
Year	Yes	Yes	Yes	Yes
_cons	−0.3818***	9.8096***	−0.1287***	−0.0325***
	(−13.2160)	(21.4989)	(−6.2759)	(−2.8675)
N	31,211	30,670	10,878	27,067
Adj. R^2	0.297	0.291	0.479	0.551

Source: Table by author

large-scale enterprises (Farndale et al., 2010). Moreover, our research highlights that ESG not only enhances firm performance but is particularly crucial for smaller businesses in implementing effective ESG practices.

9.3 Practical Implications

This study offers new insights for Chinese companies, especially small and medium-sized enterprises (SMEs). SMEs should leverage their agility in adapting and enhancing their ESG practices, thereby improving corporate performance and serving society more effectively with limited resources. Conversely, while large-scale firms possess relatively complex internal corporate governance structures and decision-making hierarchies, they can also benefit by focusing on the influence of key stakeholders on the firm. The composition structure of SMEs, characterized by a simple value chain and closer relationships with stakeholders, allows them to be more responsive and have a greater impact on the local community. This responsiveness enables SMEs to be more attuned to stakeholder concerns regarding ESG issues. Consequently, the development of communities can be significantly advanced through the growth of SMEs and their commitment to ESG principles. This study enriches the understanding of the impact of ESG on the corporate performance of companies of different sizes, offering valuable insights for corporate managers, investors, and policymakers involved in ESG strategy development and implementation.

10. Conclusion

This study utilizes stakeholder theory to examine the impact of ESG concerns on the financial health of enterprises of varied sizes. The analysis spans ESG and corporate performance from 2011 to 2022, also incorporating a review of the relevant literature on stakeholder theory. The empirical analysis employs data from the CSMAR database, encompassing all Chinese A-share listed enterprises from 2011 to 2021, along with ESG data from organizations such as China Securities, Hexun, and Bloomberg.

Despite the comprehensive dataset, the study's findings should be interpreted cautiously due to the lack of standardization in China's current ESG ratings and criteria. This inconsistency poses challenges to the reliability and comparability of ESG assessments. Additionally, the research does not account for the varying importance placed on the three components of ESG (environmental, social, and governance) across different sectors. For instance, the environmental sector might prioritize the *E* score more heavily than the *G* score, leading to sector-specific biases that are not addressed in this study due to the absence of comparable data.

Moreover, the study's scope is constrained by the lack of global data and perspective, limiting the generalizability of the findings. The current state of ESG development in China presents further limitations, as it may not fully capture the dynamics of ESG impacts observed in more mature markets. These constraints weaken the ability to draw broad conclusions and differentiate the specific influences of each ESG component across various sectors.

Despite these limitations, the research provides valuable insights into the role of ESG factors in influencing corporate performance, particularly in the context of Chinese enterprises. The findings contribute to the understanding of ESG impacts on firms of different sizes and offer implications for policymakers, investors, and corporate managers engaged in ESG initiatives. Future research should aim to address these limitations by incorporating standardized ESG ratings, sector-specific analyses, and broader international perspectives to enhance the robustness and applicability of the results.

References

Ali, W., Wilson, J., & Husnain, M. (2022). Determinants/motivations of corporate social responsibility disclosure in developing economies: A survey of the extant literature. *Sustainability*, *14*(6), 3474.

Bae, S. C., Chang, K., & Yi, H. C. (2018). Corporate social responsibility, credit rating, and private debt contracting: New evidence from syndicated loan market. *Review of Quantitative Finance and Accounting*, *50*, 261–299.

Baid, V., & Jayaraman, V. (2022). Amplifying and promoting the "S" in ESG investing: The case for social responsibility in supply chain financing. *Managerial Finance*, ahead-of-print.

Baraibar-Diez, E., & Odriozola, M. D. (2019). CSR committees and their effect on ESG performance in UK, France, Germany, and Spain. *Sustainability*, *11*(18), 5077.

Barnea, A., & Rubin, A. (2010). Corporate social responsibility as a conflict between shareholders. *Journal of Business Ethics*, *97*, 71–86.

Barnett, M. L. (2007). Stakeholder influence capacity and the variability of financial returns to corporate social responsibility. *Academy of Management Review*, *32*(3), 794–816.

Beaudoin, C. A. (2008). *Earnings management: The role of the agency problem and corporate social responsibility* [Doctoral dissertation, Drexel University].

Bissoondoyal-Bheenick, E., Brooks, R., & Do, H. X. (2023). ESG and firm performance: The role of size and media channels. *Economic Modelling*, *121*, 106203.

Boxer, B. (1989). China's environmental prospects. *Asian Survey*, *29*(7), 669–686.

Brooks, C., & Oikonomou, I. (2018). The effects of environmental, social and governance disclosures and performance on firm value: A review of the literature in accounting and finance. *The British Accounting Review*, *50*(1), 1–15.

Breuer, W., Müller, T., Rosenbach, D., & Salzmann, A. (2018). Corporate social responsibility, investor protection, and cost of equity: A cross-country comparison. *Journal of Banking & Finance*, *96*, 34–55.

Carroll, A. B. (2004). Managing ethically with global stakeholders: A present and future challenge. *Academy of Management Perspectives*, *18*(2), 114–120.

Chang, H. Y., Liang, L. W., & Liu, Y. L. (2021). Using environmental, social, governance (ESG) and financial indicators to measure bank cost efficiency in Asia. *Sustainability*, *13*(20), 11139.

Chava, S. (2014). Environmental externalities and cost of capital. *Management Science*, *60*(9), 2223–2247.

Chen, J., Huang, Q., Peng, H., & Zhong, H. (2010). *China corporate social responsibility research report*. Social Sciences Academic Press.

Chen, J., Huang, Q., Peng, H., & Zhong, H. (2015). *Research report on corporate social responsibility of China*. Springer.

Chen, Z., & Xie, G. (2022). ESG disclosure and financial performance: Moderating role of ESG investors. *International Review of Financial Analysis*, *83*, 102291.

Cini, A. C., & Ricci, C. (2018). CSR as a driver where ESG performance will ultimately matter. *Symphonya, Emerging Issues in Management*, *1*, 68–75.

Clarkson, M. E. (1995). A stakeholder framework for analyzing and evaluating: Corporate social performance. *Academy of Management Review*, *20*(1), 92–117.

Cornell, B. (2021). ESG preferences, risk and return. *European Financial Management*, *27*(1), 12–19.

Cornell, B., & Damodaran, A. (2020). *Valuing ESG: Doing good or sounding good?* NYU Stern School of Business.

Cornell, B., & Shapiro, A. C. (1987). Corporate stakeholders and corporate finance. *Financial Management*, 5–14.

Darnall, N., Henriques, I., & Sadorsky, P. (2010). Adopting proactive environmental strategy: The influence of stakeholders and firm size. *Journal of Management Studies*, *47*(6), 1072–1094.

Di Tommaso, C., & Thornton, J. (2020). Do ESG scores effect bank risk taking and value? Evidence from European banks. *Corporate Social Responsibility and Environmental Management*, *27*(5), 2286–2298.

Donaldson, T., & Preston, L. E. (1995). The stakeholder theory of the corporation: Concepts, evidence, and implications. *Academy of Management Review*, *20*(1), 65–91.

D'Souza, C., Ahmed, T., Khashru, M. A., Ahmed, R., Ratten, V., & Jayaratne, M. (2022). The complexity of stakeholder pressures and their influence on social and environmental responsibilities. *Journal of Cleaner Production*, *358*, 132038.

Farndale, E., Paauwe, J., & Boselie, P. (2010). An exploratory study of governance in the intra-firm human resources supply chain. *Human Resource Management, 49*(5), 849–868.

Freeman, R. E. (1994). The politics of stakeholder theory: Some future directions. *Business Ethics Quarterly*, 409–421.

Freeman, R. E. (2010). *Strategic management: A stakeholder approach.* Cambridge University Press.

Freeman, R. E., & Liedtka, J. (1991). Corporate social responsibility: A critical approach. *Business Horizons, 34*(4), 92–99.

Friede, G., Busch, T., & Bassen, A. (2015). ESG and financial performance: Aggregated evidence from more than 2000 empirical studies. *Journal of Sustainable Finance & Investment, 5*(4), 210–233.

Friedman, M. (1970). A Friedman doctrine: The social responsibility of business is to increase its profits. *The New York Times Magazine, 13*(1970), 32–33.

Friedman, A. L., & Miles, S. (2002). Developing stakeholder theory. *Journal of Management Studies, 39*(1), 1–21.

Giese, G., Lee, L. E., Melas, D., Nagy, Z., & Nishikawa, L. (2019). Foundations of ESG investing: How ESG affects equity valuation, risk, and performance. *The Journal of Portfolio Management, 45*(5), 69–83.

He, F., Ding, C., Yue, W., & Liu, G. (2023). ESG performance and corporate risk-taking: Evidence from China. *International Review of Financial Analysis, 87*, 102550.

He, F., Du, H., & Yu, B. (2022). Corporate ESG performance and manager misconduct: Evidence from China. *International Review of Financial Analysis, 82*, 102201.

He, G., Lu, Y., Mol, A. P., & Beckers, T. (2012). Changes and challenges: China's environmental management in transition. *Environmental Development, 3*, 25–38.

He, G., Zhang, L., Mol, A. P., Lu, Y., & Liu, J. (2013). Revising China's environmental law. *Science, 341*(6142), 133–133.

Henisz, W., Koller, T., & Nuttall, R. (2019). Five ways that ESG creates value. *McKinsey Quarterly, 4*, 1–12.

Huang, D. Z. (2021). Environmental, social and governance (ESG) activity and firm performance: A review and consolidation. *Accounting & Finance, 61*(1), 335–360.

Jang, G. Y., Kang, H. G., Lee, J. Y., & Bae, K. (2020). ESG scores and the credit market. *Sustainability, 12*(8), 3456.

Jordan, B. D., Kim, S., & Liu, M. H. (2016). Growth opportunities, short-term market pressure, and dual-class share structure. *Journal of Corporate Finance, 41*, 304–328.

Li, X., Yang, X., Wei, Q., & Zhang, B. (2019). Authoritarian environmentalism and environmental policy implementation in China. *Resources, Conservation and Recycling, 145*, 86–93.

Liang, H., & Renneboog, L. (2018). Is corporate social responsibility an agency problem? In *Research handbook of finance and sustainability* (pp. 54–71). Edward Elgar Publishing.

Luke, T. W. (2022). Investment and rapid climate change as biopolitics: Foucault and governance of the self and others through ESG. *Sustainability, 14*(22), 14974.

Luo, D. (2022). ESG, liquidity, and stock returns. *Journal of International Financial Markets, Institutions and Money, 78*, 101526.

Neville, B. A., Bell, S. J., & Mengüç, B. (2005). Corporate reputation, stakeholders and the social performance-financial performance relationship. *European Journal of Marketing, 39*(9–10), 1184–1198.

Nguyen, C. P. (2022). Tourism and gender (in) equality: Global evidence. *Tourism Management Perspectives, 41*, 100933.

Ning, L., Abbasi, K. R., Hussain, K., Alvarado, R., & Ramzan, M. (2023). Analyzing the role of green innovation and public-private partnerships in achieving sustainable development goals: A novel policy framework. *Environmental Science and Pollution Research*, 1–17.

Park, J. G., Park, K., Noh, H., & Kim, Y. G. (2023). Characterization of CSR, ESG, and corporate citizenship through a text mining-based review of literature. *Sustainability, 15*(5), 3892.

Parmar, B. L., Freeman, R. E., Harrison, J. S., Wicks, A. C., Purnell, L., & De Colle, S. (2010). Stakeholder theory: The state of the art. *Academy of Management Annals*, *4*(1), 403–445.

Pástor, Ľ., Stambaugh, R. F., & Taylor, L. A. (2021). Sustainable investing in equilibrium. *Journal of Financial Economics*, *142*(2), 550–571.

Phillips, R., Freeman, R. E., & Wicks, A. C. (2003). What stakeholder theory is not. *Business Ethics Quarterly*, *13*(4), 479–502.

Preuss, L., & Perschke, J. (2010). Slipstreaming the larger boats: Social responsibility in medium-sized businesses. *Journal of Business Ethics*, *92*, 531–551.

Rahman, M. J., & Wu, J. (2023). M&A activity and ESG performance: Evidence from China. *Managerial Finance*, *50*(1), 179–197.

Rahman, M. J., Wu, Q., & Zhu, H. (2024). Corporate social responsibility in times of social distancing: Evidence from China. *Business Ethics, the Environment & Responsibility*.

Rahman, M. J., Zhu, H., & Beiyi, S. (2023). Is COVID-19 a turning point? Evidence from CEOs' investment behavior and risk tolerance. *International Journal of Emerging Markets*.

Rahman, M. J., Zhu, H., & Chen, S. (2023). Does CSR reduce financial distress? Moderating effect of firm characteristics, auditor characteristics, and covid-19. *International Journal of Accounting & Information Management*, *31*(5), 756–784.

Rahman, M. J., Zhu, H., & Jiang, X. (2024). Family firms, client importance, and auditor reporting behavior: Evidence from China. *Meditari Accountancy Research*, *32*(2), 543–578.

Rodrigue, M., Magnan, M., & Boulianne, E. (2013). Stakeholders' influence on environmental strategy and performance indicators: A managerial perspective. *Management Accounting Research*, *24*(4), 301–316.

Scholtens, B., & Zhou, Y. (2008). Stakeholder relations and financial performance. *Sustainable Development*, *16*(3), 213–232.

Schultz, P., & Shive, S. (2010). Mispricing of dual-class shares: Profit opportunities, arbitrage, and trading. *Journal of Financial Economics*, *98*(3), 524–549.

Seroka-Stolka, O., & Fijorek, K. (2020). Enhancing corporate sustainable development: Proactive environmental strategy, stakeholder pressure and the moderating effect of firm size. *Business Strategy and the Environment*, *29*(6), 2338–2354.

Shah, S. Q. A., Lai, F. W., Shad, M. K., & Jan, A. A. (2022). Developing a green governance framework for the performance enhancement of the oil and gas industry. *Sustainability*, *14*(7), 3735.

Shin, J., Moon, J. J., & Kang, J. (2023). Where does ESG pay? The role of national culture in moderating the relationship between ESG performance and financial performance. *International Business Review*, *32*(3), 102071.

Songling, Y., Ishtiaq, M., Anwar, M., & Ahmed, H. (2018). The role of government support in sustainable competitive position and firm performance. *Sustainability*, *10*(10), 3495.

Van Beurden, P., & Gössling, T. (2008). The worth of values – a literature review on the relation between corporate social and financial performance. *Journal of Business Ethics*, *82*, 407–424.

Varvara, N., & Victoria, L. (2022). Do ESG factors influence investment attractiveness of the public companies? *Корпоративные финансы*, *16*(1), 38–64.

Wang, J. X., & Zhao, M. Z. (2020). Economic impacts of ISO 14001 certification in China and the moderating role of firm size and age. *Journal of Cleaner Production*, *274*, 123059.

Xun, J. (2013). Corporate social responsibility in China: A preferential stakeholder model and effects. *Business Strategy and the Environment*, *22*(7), 471–483.

Yang, L. (2014). The institutionalization of corporate social responsibility. *Journal of Legal Studies*, *5*, 131–158.

Zhang, B., Cao, C., Gu, J., & Liu, T. (2016). A new environmental protection law, many old problems? Challenges to environmental governance in China. *Journal of Environmental Law*, *28*(2), 325–335.

Zhang, L., He, G., Mol, A. P., & Zhu, X. (2013). Power politics in the revision of China's environmental protection law. *Environmental Politics*, *22*(6), 1029–1035.
Zhang, X., Zhao, X., & Qu, L. (2021). Do green policies catalyze green investment? Evidence from ESG investing developments in China. *Economics Letters*, *207*, 110028.
Zhang, Y. (2011, October). The analysis of shareholder theory and stakeholder theory. In *2011 fourth international conference on business intelligence and financial engineering* (pp. 90–92). IEEE.
Zhong, S., Hou, J., Li, J., & Gao, W. (2022). Exploring the relationship of ESG score and firm value using fsQCA method: Cases of the Chinese manufacturing enterprises. *Frontiers in Psychology*, *13*, 1019469.
Zhou, Z., He, D., & Li, Z. (2012). Institutional environment and corporate social responsibility performance: Empirical evidence from Chinese listed companies. *Chinese Soft Science*, *10*, 59–68.
Zhu, H., & Rahman, M. J. (2024). Ex-ante expected changes in ESG and future stock returns based on machine learning. *The British Accounting Review*, 101457.

15 ESG Disclosure as Advertisement of Corporate Bond Issue

Md Jahidur Rahman, Tarek Rana, Hongtao Zhu, and Xuxiaohui

1. Introduction

In contemporary business practices, environmental, social, and governance (ESG) disclosure has emerged as a crucial component of non-financial reporting for enterprises. This study investigates whether ESG disclosure can function as an advertising tool for corporate bond issuance, thereby generating positive impacts on corporate finance.

Building on the research of Hoepner et al. (2023), which examined the efficacy of ESG as a disclosure mechanism in bond issuance and its positive effects on corporate bonds, this study delves into the relationship between ESG disclosure and bond issuance within the Chinese market. The research aims to answer two primary questions: (1) do companies utilize ESG disclosure as a strategic tool to attract financing? (2) Do companies with higher financing needs prioritize ESG information disclosure more intensively (Hoepner et al., 2023)?

As an extension of prior studies, this research specifically examines the correlation between ESG disclosure and bond issuance among Chinese listed companies. The study focuses on the availability and scale of bond issuance across varying levels of ESG disclosure. By analysing these data, the study seeks to determine whether ESG disclosure attracts investors and influences corporate financing. The primary objectives are to assess (1) the impact of corporate ESG disclosure on the scale of bond issuance and (2) whether ESG disclosure by Chinese companies can serve as an effective advertisement, influencing investor preferences.

As awareness of corporate social responsibility (CSR) grows, investors increasingly consider ESG disclosures as a critical factor in their investment decisions. Corporate bonds, as a significant financing tool, play a vital role in corporate finance. Thus, exploring the impact of ESG accounting disclosure on corporate bond issuance is of substantial importance. This study aims to elucidate the relationship between investor preferences and ESG disclosure, encouraging Chinese companies to prioritize ESG information and integrate sustainable development into their strategic outlooks. Additionally, the study advocates for governmental emphasis on ESG disclosure and the establishment of comprehensive regulations.

The term ESG encompasses environmental, social, and governance factors, reflecting a company's commitment to CSR. Globally, ESG has become an essential

DOI: 10.4324/9781003488934-20

standard for corporate evaluation. Although ESG disclosure is voluntary (Ellili, 2022), numerous studies affirm its importance for investors seeking comprehensive information (Wen, 2022). Various countries and regions have implemented ESG standards for non-financial information disclosure.

Investors today look beyond financial metrics, seeking non-financial data to assess a company's overall stability and future prospects. ESG disclosure, encompassing environmental, social, and governance information, is integral to CSR. As social awareness of CSR increases, so does the importance of ESG disclosure in investment decisions. Given the significance of corporate bonds in financing, understanding the impact of ESG accounting disclosure on bond issuance is crucial.

This study explores the relationship between ESG disclosure and bond issuance among Chinese companies. The concept of ESG is not new in China. The Chinese government introduced "green finance" and "dual carbon" initiatives in 2016 and 2020, respectively (Hai et al., 2022; Cong et al., 2022). These initiatives encourage ESG disclosure, underscoring the government's commitment. The China Securities Regulatory Commission (CSRC) established unified ESG disclosure standards in 2021 (Yan et al., 2022), enhancing the credibility of ESG information. This credibility enables investors to evaluate companies' sustainability and investment potential effectively, making ESG disclosure a key consideration for Chinese investors. This research supports the feasibility of using ESG information as an advertising tool to attract investors.

According to De Jong and Rocco (2022), low ESG scores often lead to investor exit, while high ESG scores attract investors focused on both financial and non-financial information. Investor preferences can incentivize companies to adopt social responsibilities. This study investigates whether companies receive positive feedback from investors when disclosing ESG information, highlighting the significance of ESG as a strategic advertising tool.

The empirical analysis in this paper utilizes data from 3,567 Chinese listed companies from 2011 to 2021. The dependent variables are whether the company issues bonds and the scale of bond issuance. A regression model is employed to examine the impact of ESG disclosure on corporate bond issuance.

The analysis reveals a positive correlation between ESG disclosure and corporate financing costs. Specifically, greater ESG disclosure is associated with larger bond issuance scales and lower financing costs. This indicates that ESG disclosure can enhance investor trust and recognition, contributing to successful corporate financing. Additionally, ESG disclosure improves corporate reputation, further reducing financing costs.

While existing literature extensively covers ESG disclosures, this study's novelty lies in its specific focus on Chinese companies and the use of ESG disclosure as a strategic tool in bond issuance. Prior studies have discussed the attractiveness of ESG disclosure for financing (Hoepner et al., 2023), but research on its application in the Chinese bond market remains limited. Given the Chinese government's emphasis on ESG disclosure due to industrial transformation policies (Chen & Huo, 2022), this study fills a significant gap by examining ESG disclosure's role in the bond market.

Moreover, this study differentiates the impact of various ESG dimensions on bond issuance, providing a nuanced understanding of how environmental, social, and governance factors individually affect corporate finance. This approach offers valuable insights for companies to balance the benefits and drawbacks of ESG disclosure.

The study employs a regression model to analyse the impact of ESG accounting disclosure on corporate bond issuance. By exploring the role of ESG disclosure in corporate bond financing, the research aims to promote CSR awareness, encourage governmental and institutional improvements in ESG disclosure norms, and assist investors in making informed decisions.

The remainder of this paper is organized as follows: Section 2 defines key terms related to ESG, ESG disclosure, and bond issuance. Section 3 reviews theoretical research on the impact of ESG disclosure on bond issuance and investment. Section 4 presents the research hypotheses. Section 5 details the sample selection and data description. Section 6 discusses statistical and correlation analyses. Sections 7 and 8 address endogeneity and robustness tests. Finally, Section 9 concludes with a discussion of the research findings.

2. Background (ESG in China)

The principles of ESG disclosure originated in developed regions, notably Europe and the United States, around 2004 (Li et al., 2021). Although China's engagement with ESG practices began later, the country has made significant strides due to the heightened attention from both the government and society (Luo et al., 2023). Data from China's A-share market in 2020 reveals that 25.3% of companies disclosed ESG information, underscoring the growing importance placed on ESG disclosure by the Chinese government and enterprises (Ge et al., 2022). Several studies in China also investigates the relationship of environmental accounting and firm performance (Rahman & Wu, 2023; Rahman et al., 2023, 2024; Zhu & Rahman, 2024).

The Chinese government's support for high-quality production aligns with the principles of ESG, reflecting a commitment to transitioning towards a green and sustainable production model (Chen & Huo, 2022). This alignment has facilitated the implementation of ESG practices in China (Wang et al., 2023; Weber, 2014). As a socialist country, China's strong government support often serves as a critical driver for corporate development, setting a precedent for enterprises and investors alike.

ESG disclosure constitutes a vital element of CSR in China. As societal awareness of CSR grows, an increasing number of investors are considering corporate ESG disclosures and reputations as key factors in their investment decisions (Tan & Zhu, 2022). Given the significance of corporate bonds as a financing tool, understanding the impact of ESG accounting disclosure on bond issuance is crucial for corporate finance.

Despite the Chinese government's substantial emphasis on ESG development, several challenges persist. Due to the relatively recent introduction of ESG practices and the lack of comprehensive disclosure rules, ESG reporting in China remains inconsistent (Wen, 2022). Therefore, enhancing ESG disclosure policies and encouraging companies to provide comprehensive ESG information is advantageous for the overall development of Chinese enterprises.

3. Theoretical Background

Previous research on ESG disclosure and bond issuance posits that sustainable investment is increasingly valued, with high ESG scores associated with lower debt acquisition costs for firms (Aperies et al., 2022). This study investigates whether firms have sufficient incentive to enhance their ESG disclosure scores when seeking financing and whether ESG disclosure functions as a financing advertisement.

According to Hoepner et al. (2023), ESG disclosure aligns with observable and costly signaling theory. In the context of ESG, signalling theory emphasizes the importance of relevant information in business transactions (Carnini Pulino et al., 2022). Corporate ESG disclosure provides stakeholders with additional information, such as sustainability metrics, thereby reducing information asymmetry. The core concept of signalling theory involves the flow of relevant information from the sender to the receiver; in the case of ESG disclosure, this flow occurs from internal management to external stakeholders, fostering interaction (Carnini Pulino et al., 2022). By mitigating information asymmetry, ESG disclosure effectively signals CSR to investors, thereby attracting those interested in long-term sustainability and achieving the advertising effect of ESG disclosure.

The reduction of information asymmetry is a key benefit of ESG disclosure. Information asymmetry theory posits that improved internal information communication enhances trust levels (Balakrishnan & Koza, 1993), thereby facilitating the trust of external investors (Bartov & Bodnar, 1996). In this study, ESG disclosure signals to investors that the company is socially responsible and sustainable. Additionally, data analysis indicates that high ESG scores help reduce bond premiums, positively influencing investor perceptions (Hoang et al., 2023). Information asymmetry theory further suggests that the presence of non-public information can hinder a company's ability to build a good reputation among stakeholders (Billyray-Erdogan, 2022). By leveraging signalling and information asymmetry theories, this study explores the dual role of ESG disclosure in reducing information asymmetry and signalling corporate responsibility, ultimately enhancing investor trust and reducing financing costs.

4. Literature Review and Hypothesis Development

4.1 ESG Disclosure Affect Investor Choice

For companies, one of the primary motivations for ESG disclosure is the potential to reduce financing costs, thereby enhancing attractiveness to investors. According to research by Lavin and Montecinos-Pearce (2022), ESG disclosure significantly contributes to lowering financing costs. This reduction is largely due to the decreased information asymmetry between internal and external stakeholders, which increases investor trust. Additionally, companies with comprehensive ESG disclosures often demonstrate better solvency, making them more appealing to investors (Ellili, 2022). As previously discussed, ESG disclosure provides stakeholders with extensive information, thereby mitigating information asymmetry.

Moreover, ESG disclosure can enhance a company's reputation, which in turn reduces financing costs. A favourable corporate reputation is highly attractive to investors (Maaloul et al., 2023). By improving corporate reputation, ESG disclosure indirectly lowers financing costs. Cheng et al. (2023) found that controlling for various factors, ESG disclosure reveals the extent of corporate social responsibility to investors more effectively than other disclosures. In the context of China, the emergence of the sustainable development concept has heightened investor interest in companies' ESG performance (Tang, 2022), thereby attracting investors who prioritize sustainable development.

4.2 Disclosing ESG Can Become a Strategic Choice for Companies

As discussed, ESG disclosure can effectively aid companies in raising funds. A pertinent question is whether companies leverage ESG disclosure as an advertising method before issuing bonds. Research indicates that enhancing corporate reputation can lead to higher market valuations, serving as an intangible asset for both corporate and social value. Conversely, negative ESG-related news can lead to adverse investor valuations of stock prices (Wong & Zhang, 2022). Therefore, a high ESG disclosure score can convey positive investment signals to investors, aligning the company's value maximization goals with stakeholder interests, reducing information barriers, and creating competitive advantages (Frost et al., 2022).

Building on the work of Hoepner et al. (2023), ESG disclosure is seen as a determinant for attracting additional external capital. ESG disclosure not only helps companies avoid potential damages but also creates value (Li & Adriaens, 2023). Furthermore, it influences investor choices and effectively reduces financing costs. Therefore, disclosing ESG information before issuing bonds can be considered a strategic choice for companies. Based on this rationale, the following hypothesis is proposed:

H1: Firms are more likely to demonstrate higher levels of ESG disclosure when issuing bonds.

This hypothesis will be tested to determine if ESG disclosure indeed serves as a strategic tool for companies aiming to attract investors and reduce financing costs when issuing bonds. ESG disclosures, serving as a form of corporate advertising, can attract investors when companies prepare to issue bonds. Another critical question is whether high ESG disclosure scores can help companies expand their bond size and secure better financing. As previously discussed, ESG disclosure is an effective means of obtaining financing at a lower cost. According to Johnson et al. (2022), when ESG disclosures align with corporate values, investors are likely to maintain their support for the company over the long term. Empirical studies have further demonstrated that ESG has a positive impact on corporate financing expansion (Bai et al., 2022).

Theoretically, ESG disclosure exerts a positive information pricing effect on China's bond trading market (Zhang et al., 2022). ESG disclosures can attract more investors, thereby facilitating companies' efforts to scale up financing. Based on this rationale, the following hypothesis is proposed:

H2: Higher levels of ESG disclosure enable companies to increase the size of their bond issuance.

Thus, this study examines two strategic choices: whether corporate ESG disclosure influences bond issuance and whether it assists in scaling up bond issuance. These hypotheses will be tested to determine the effectiveness of ESG disclosure as a strategic tool in the bond market.

5. Research Design

5.1 Sample Selection and Data Description

The empirical analysis of this paper focuses on testing the impact of ESG on corporate debt issuance and the scale of corporate development, drawing on the research idea of Lian et al. (Cheng et al., 2023), and relevant data of Chinese. A-share listed companies from 2011 to 2021 are selected for analysis. For the raw data, the data are treated as follows here according to the conventional practice: (1) excluding special treatment (ST) enterprises, due to the large fluctuations in the financial status of ST enterprises; (2) excluding financial listed companies, which is due to the large differences between the financial data rules of financial listed companies and other enterprises; (3) excluding samples with missing key variables, which are not counted in the regression results, but will affect the descriptive statistics results; (4) excluding samples with less than three years of the listing period within the sample period; and (5) performing bilateral 1% tail-shrinking for all continuous variables. After the above processing, we finally obtain a total of 3,567 enterprises, containing 30,994 annual-firm dimensions of unbalanced panel data. The screening process of each variable is shown in Table 15.1.

5.2 Variable Definitions

5.2.1 Explained Variables

Corporate debt issuance, considering that corporate debt issuance includes not only whether to issue debt and the scale of debt issuance, i.e., but there is also an intensive margin and extensive margin of debt issuance, here this paper draws on the research idea of Cheng et al. (2023) to set whether the enterprise issues debt (Bond) and the scale of corporate debt issuance (Bond_value), where the scale of issuance is

Table 15.1 Variable Screening Process

Selection Criteria	*Culling the Sample*
Excluding the financial sector	825
Excluding ST companies	1,185
Excluding companies that have been listed for less than 3 years	1,398
Excluding samples with missing key variables	2,472

Source: Table by authors

Note: Table related to China A-Shares 2011–2021 variable screening process.

ten billion yuan, considering that ESG on corporate debt issuance behaviour. There may be a time lag, thus both whether the enterprise issues debt in the next period and the scale of the enterprise's debt issuance in the next period are used here to measure.

5.2.2 *Explanatory Variables*

ESG encompasses three aspects: environmental, social, and corporate governance and existing studies usually draw on agencies' ESG ratings or assess companies based on their actual performance related to the three aspects. Considering the relative objectivity of rating agencies, they are favoured by many scholars. For example, Jiang et al. (2023) and Cepni et al. (2023) adopted different agencies' ratings to measure companies' ESG levels. Combined with the availability of data, this study will take the ESG rating of Hwa Securities for measurement, which is due to the more comprehensive measurement sample of this institution and can more comprehensively assess the impact of ESG on corporate debt issuance. This study will adopt ESG ratings from Bloomberg and Hexun for replacement measures in the robustness analysis.

5.2.3 *Control Variables*

In order to accurately identify the impact of ESG on corporate debt issuance, here this study draws on (Hoepner et al., 2023) to control for other relevant factors that may affect corporate debt issuance. These include firm size (Size), measured by the natural logarithm of total assets; business gearing (Lev), measured by the ratio of total corporate liabilities to total assets; return on assets (ROA), measured by the ratio of net profit to total assets; cash flow from operating activities (Cash), measured by the ratio of net cash flow from operating activities to total assets; growth capacity (Growth), measured by the growth rate of revenue; Board, measured by the natural logarithm of the number of board members; Top10, measured by the shareholding ratio of the top 10 shareholders; Age, measured by the natural logarithm of the year of establishment + 1; Dual, measured by the natural logarithm of the number of board members when (Age), measured by using the year of establishment + 1 and taking the natural logarithm; Dual, which takes the value of 1 when the general manager and chairman of thc board are the same person, and 0 otherwise; Nature of ownership (SOE), which takes the value of 1 for state-owned enterprises and 0 for non-state-owned enterprises.

5.3 Model Construction

To test the impact of ESG on corporate debt issuance, here this paper draws on (Stellner et al., 2015) research and sets up the following econometric model for testing:

$$Bond_{i,t} = \alpha_0 + \alpha_1 ESG_{i,t} + \sum Control + \sum IND + \sum YEAR + \varepsilon_{i,t} \quad (1)$$

$$Bond\_value_{i,t} = \gamma_0 + \gamma_1 ESG_{i,t} + \sum Control + \sum IND + \sum YEAR + \varepsilon_{i,t} \quad (2)$$

Here:

Bond = Enterprise bonds are securities issued by enterprises in accordance with legal procedures in order to raise funds and promise to creditors to repay the principal and interest on a specified date;

i = enterprise;

t = year;

size = enterprise size, measured by the natural logarithm of total assets;

lev = corporate debt ratio, measured by the ratio of total corporate liabilities to total liabilities;

ROA = return on assets, the ratio of net profit to total assets;

Cash = cash flow from operating activities to total assets;

Growth = growth capacity, measured by the growth rate of revenue;

Board = measured by the natural logarithm of the number of board members;

Top10 = measured by the shareholding ratio of the top 10 shareholders;

Age = measured by the natural logarithm of the year of establishment + 1;

Dual = measured by the natural logarithm of the number of board members;

SOE = which takes the value of 1 for state-owned enterprises and 0 for non-state-owned enterprises;

$\sum Control$ = the set of control variables;

$\sum IND$ = industry effects;

$\sum YEAR$ = time-fixed effects.

Where subscripts i and t denote firm and year, respectively, and $\sum Control$ is the set of control variables, including the relevant control variables mentioned in the previous section. $\sum IND$ and $\sum YEAR$ re industry and time-fixed effects, respectively. $\varepsilon_{i,c,t}$ is the random disturbance term, which denotes other relevant factors that may affect firm debt issuance and debt issuance size. The focus here is on the regression coefficients of ESG α_1 and γ_1 which, if positive, indicate that ESG helps to increase the size of debt issuance and debt issuance. All regressions control for industry and time-fixed effect.

6. Analysis of Empirical Result

6.1 Descriptive Statistics and Correlation Analysis

Table 15.2 presents the results of the descriptive statistical distribution of the variables for the empirical analysis, where the mean value of the variable of whether to issue debt is 0.109, which indicates that the debt-issuing enterprises in the sample are relatively small, which may be related to the current financing results of the Chinese market, where banks have been used as the main source of financing for enterprises, which may lead to the tendency of most enterprises to meet their demand for credit funds through bank financing. The mean value of debt issuance size is 0.0395 and the maximum value is 13, which indicates that the overall debt issuance size of listed debt-issuing enterprises is relatively large due to the unit of tens of billions of yuan, which is related to the financing needs of enterprises. The mean value of the ESG rating is 4.101 and the standard deviation is 1.025, which indicates that the ESG of enterprises is relatively good, but the ESG varies widely among enterprises. The distribution of control variables is closer to that of existing studies, which can improve the reliability of the estimation results of this paper to a certain extent.

Table 15.3 presents the results of the correlation analysis of the variables for the empirical analysis of this paper. Among them, the correlation coefficient between two-tier equity structure and firm performance is 0.305 and significant at the 1% level, indicating that those firms that implement two-tier equity structure usually have higher performance. Among the control variables, firm size and age positively correlated with firm performance, while gearing is negatively correlated with firm performance. Cash flow from operating activities and growth capacity

Table 15.2 Descriptive Statistics

Variable	*Mean*	*p50*	*SD*	*Min*	*Max*	*N*
Bond	0.109	0	0.311	0	1	30994
Bond_value	0.0395	0	0.298	0	13	30994
ESG	4.101	4	1.025	1.250	6.250	30994
Size	22.20	22.02	1.303	19.83	26.19	30994
Lev	0.424	0.416	0.207	0.0518	0.899	30994
Roa	0.0401	0.0388	0.0656	−0.247	0.221	30994
Cash	0.0453	0.0448	0.0691	−0.164	0.239	30994
Growth	0.170	0.107	0.401	−0.568	2.499	30994
Board	2.124	2.197	0.199	1.609	2.708	30994
Top10	0.584	0.593	0.153	0.230	0.904	30994
Age	2.896	2.944	0.335	1.792	3.526	30994
Dual	0.284	0	0.451	0	1	30994
SOE	0.338	0	0.473	0	1	30994

Source: Table by authors

Note: Descriptive Statistics on Selected Variables in 2011–2021.

Table 15.3 Correlation Coefficient Analysis of Variables

Variable	*Bond*	*Bond_value*	*ESG*	*Size*	*Lev*	*ROA*	*Cash*	*Growth*	*Board*	*Top10*	*Age*	*Dual*	*SOE*
Bond	1												
Bond_value	0.304***	1											
ESG	0.124***	0.111***	1										
Size	0.428***	0.313***	0.218***	1									
Lev	0.280***	0.134***	−0.072***	0.507***	1								
ROA	−0.042***	−0.013**	0.249***	−0.009*	−0.381***	1							
Cash	−0.026***	0.021***	0.091***	0.079***	−0.160***	0.383***	1						
Growth	−0.012**	−0.009*	0.009	0.043***	0.019***	0.249***	0.021***	1					
Board	0.137***	0.097***	0.042***	0.260***	0.144***	0.014**	0.039***	−0.017***	1				
Top10	0.034***	0.107***	0.164***	0.128***	−0.104***	0.257***	0.125***	0.090***	0.023***	1			
Age	0.044***	0.035***	−0.055***	0.189***	0.190***	−0.120***	0.024***	−0.047***	0.037***	−0.211***	1		
Dual	−0.088***	−0.049***	−0.026***	−0.176***	−0.135***	0.048***	−0.016***	0.029***	−0.177***	0.036***	−0.106***	1	
SOE	0.190***	0.126***	0.091***	0.361***	0.282***	−0.095***	0.003	−0.068***	0.257***	−0.013**	0.176***	−0.296***	1

Source: Table by authors

Note: Analysis of variable correlation coefficients for selected data from 2011 to 2021.
*** $p < 0.01$, ** $p < 0.05$, * $p < 0.1$.

have insignificant correlation coefficients with firm performance. Overall, the correlation coefficients of all variables are low, which can prove the reliability of the estimation results of this paper to some extent.

Before conducting the regression analysis, it is necessary to conduct a VIF test for each variable, which can avoid the estimation bias caused by the problem of multicollinearity. The corresponding estimation results are shown in Table 15.4, where the mean value of VIF for each variable is 1.31, and the VIF of all variables is less than 2. This indicates that there is no significant cointegration problem among the variables in the empirical analysis of this paper, which helps to improve the reliability of the estimation results in the later paper.

6.2 Baseline Regression

Table 15.5 presents the results of the empirical analysis of this paper, in which the first and second columns include only the core explanatory variables, and the regression coefficients of ESG are 0.0404 and 0.0315 respectively, which are both significant at the 1% level, indicating that ESG helps to increase the probability of issuing debt and the size of debt issuance. The coefficients of ESG are still significantly positive at this time, and the goodness of fit of the model is significantly improved, so the third and fourth columns are chosen as the baseline regression estimation results in this paper.

For whether to issue debt, the regression coefficient of ESG is 0.0166 and is significant at the 1% level, indicating that a one percentage point increase in ESG increases the probability of a firm issuing debt by 0.0166 percentage points. As for the scale of development, the regression coefficient of ESG is 0.0129 and is also significant at the 1% level, indicating that for each percentage point increase in ESG, the scale of development of the firm will increase by 0.0129 percentage

Table 15.4 Multicollinearity Test

Variable	*VIF*	*1/VIF*
Size	1.75	0.5699
Lev	1.75	0.5703
ROA	1.61	0.6229
SOE	1.3	0.7698
Cash	1.2	0.8305
Top10	1.16	0.8616
ESG	1.16	0.8627
Age	1.13	0.8844
Board	1.12	0.8890
Dual	1.12	0.8945
Growth	1.1	0.9060
Mean VIF	1.31	

Source: Table by authors

Note: Multicollinearity test related variables

Table 15.5 Baseline Regression Results

	Bond	*Bond_value*	*Bond*	*Bond_value*
ESG	0.0404***	0.0315***	0.0166***	0.0129***
	(13.6355)	(8.2701)	(6.9377)	(4.9467)
Size			0.0923***	0.0640***
			(24.4254)	(10.0538)
Lev			0.0575***	−0.0526***
			(3.9460)	(−2.9391)
ROA			0.0554*	−0.1821***
			(1.8089)	(−4.7129)
Cash			−0.2112***	−0.0554***
			(−7.1990)	(−2.7213)
Growth			−0.0063	−0.0100***
			(−1.6196)	(−3.7583)
Board			0.0109	0.0170
			(0.7386)	(0.7652)
Top10			−0.0143	0.1153***
			(−0.7038)	(4.1183)
Age			−0.0028	−0.0024
			(−0.2832)	(−0.2336)
Dual			0.0045	0.0058*
			(0.9595)	(1.6922)
SOE			0.0008	−0.0014
			(0.1113)	(−0.1904)
Ind	Yes	Yes	Yes	Yes
Year	Yes	Yes	Yes	Yes
_cons	−0.0453*	−0.1162***	−1.9673***	−1.4850***
	(−1.7365)	(−7.1183)	(−22.5435)	(−.3397)
N	30994	30994	30994	30994
adj. R^2	0.114	0.109	0.233	0.165

Source: Table by authors

Note: Values in parentheses are *t*-statistics, clustering values at the firm level; *, **, and *** indicate significance at the 10%, 5%, and 1% levels, respectively, as in the latter table.

points. This is because companies with better ESG performance are usually better able to manage environmental and social risks and reduce operational risks, thus increasing investors' confidence and preference for their bonds. This makes these companies more likely to receive recognition and support from financing institutions, which in turn increases the probability and size of their debt issuance. In addition, actively focusing on and practicing ESG principles helps companies build a good reputation and brand image. Corporate performance in environmental protection, social responsibility, and good governance are valued by investors, consumers, and regulators. Companies with good ESG performance enjoy a higher reputation and credibility with the public and the market, which provides them with an advantage in their financing activities. Investors are more willing to invest and hold bonds from these companies, which increases the probability and size of corporate debt issuance.

6.3 Dimensional Analysis to Distinguish ESG

Further, considering that ESG contains three dimensions: environmental, social responsibility, and corporate governance, in order to identify the effect of different dimensions on corporate debt issuance, the regression results of the subdivided dimensions are further presented here, and the corresponding estimation results are shown in Table 15.6. The results in the first column of Table 15.6 show that the regression coefficients of social responsibility and corporate governance are significantly positive when to issue debt is the explanatory variable. For development size, again, only the regression coefficients of social responsibility and

Table 15.6 Segmentation Dimensions to Distinguish ESG

	Bond	*Bond_value*
E	−0.0003	0.0006
	(−0.1159)	(0.2134)
S	0.0047***	0.0030*
	(3.0927)	(1.7058)
G	0.0136***	0.0120***
	(7.6549)	(5.0341)
Size	0.0928***	0.0641***
	(24.6538)	(10.0430)
Lev	0.0689***	−0.0411**
	(4.6404)	(−2.2464)
ROA	0.0384	−0.1989***
	(1.2597)	(−4.9088)
Cash	−0.2116***	−0.0559***
	(−7.2273)	(−2.7337)
Growth	−0.0063	−0.0098***
	(−1.6211)	(−3.6533)
Board	0.0143	0.0206
	(0.9746)	(0.9353)
Top10	−0.0184	0.1110***
	(−0.9049)	(3.9712)
Age	−0.0023	−0.0020
	(−0.2268)	(−0.1907)
Dual	0.0038	0.0053
	(0.8103)	(1.5369)
SOE	−0.0025	−0.0050
	(−0.3348)	(−0.6610)
Ind	Yes	Yes
Year	Yes	Yes
_cons	−2.0261***	−1.5381***
	(−22.7623)	(−9.3678)
N	30994	30994
Adj. R^2	0.234	0.165

Source: Table by authors

Note: Multicollinearity test related variables, explain the correlation of E, S, G respectively corporate governance are significantly positive, and overall corporate governance has a stronger contribution to corporate debt issuance and debt issuance size, thus indicating that it is mainly social responsibility and corporate governance that have a positive effect on corporate debt issuance and debt issuance size in ESG.

7. Endogeneity Analysis

7.1 Heckman Analysis

The estimation results in this paper may have endogeneity analysis caused by sample selection bias, such as firms should first consider whether they issue debt and then consider the size of debt issuance. And the debt-issuing and non-debt-issuing firms may not be fully comparable with each other, here this paper draws on the research idea of (Gillan et al., 2021) and uses the Heckman two-step method for estimation. Firstly, the set is the variable of whether the firm issued debt or not and carry out logit model estimation with this variable as the explanatory variable to derive the inverse Mills ratio IMR, and then, incorporate the estimated IMR value into the benchmark regression, and the corresponding regression estimation results are shown in Table 15.7. First, set the variable whether the company issues bonds and use this variable as the explained variable to estimate the logit model to obtain the inverse Mills ratio IMR. The corresponding econometric model is shown in formula:

$$treat_{i,t} = \mu_0 + \mu_1 ESG_{i,t} + \sum Control + \sum IND + \sum YEAR + \varepsilon_{i,t} \quad (3)$$

Then, the estimated IMR value was incorporated into the baseline regression, and the corresponding regression estimation results are shown in Table 15.7.

$$Bond_{i,t} = \pi_0 + \pi_1 ESG_{i,t} + \pi_2 IMR_{i,t} + \sum Control + \sum IND + \sum YEAR + \varepsilon_{i,t} \quad (4)$$

$$Bond\_value_{i,t} = \tau_0 + \tau_1 ESG_{i,t} + \tau_2 IMR_{i,t} + \sum Control + \sum IND + \sum YEAR + \varepsilon_{i,t} \quad (5)$$

Here:

IMR = the inverse Mills ratio.

The first column of Table 15.7 is the estimation result of the first stage of Heckman, and the second and third columns are the estimation results of adding IMR. The results show that after using Hcekman to estimate, the coefficients of ESG on whether the company issues bonds and the scale of bond issuance are both significantly positive, which further shows that the estimation results of this paper are robust.

Table 15.7 Heckman Regression

	Treat	*Bond*	*Bond_value*
ESG		0.0130***	0.0079***
		(5.6665)	(3.2657)
Size	0.7410***	0.2628***	0.2994***
	(24.8016)	(18.3724)	(10.1923)
Lev	0.6854***	0.2326***	0.1882***
	(4.9497)	(12.7642)	(6.9562)
ROA	−0.6490**	−0.0893***	−0.3872***
	(−2.3465)	(−2.8187)	(−7.4996)
Cash	−0.8882***	−0.4206***	−0.3424***
	(−4.0234)	(−13.0672)	(−9.9932)
Growth	−0.0723***	−0.0178***	−0.0259***
	(−3.0236)	(−4.4198)	(−7.3884)
Board	0.0356	0.0223	0.0317
	(0.2793)	(1.5848)	(1.4878)
Top10	−1.4330***	−0.4110***	−0.4304***
	(−8.8358)	(−11.1125)	(−8.8242)
Age	−0.0310	−0.0086	−0.0106
	(−0.3142)	(−0.8913)	(−1.1933)
Dual	−0.1017**	−0.0285***	−0.0397***
	(−2.1362)	(−5.6216)	(−7.2044)
SOE	−0.1041*	−0.0215***	−0.0319***
	(−1.6673)	(−2.8936)	(−4.1790)
IMR		0.3567***	0.4931***
		(13.9968)	(9.4870)
Ind	30769	Yes	Yes
Year	30769	Yes	Yes
_cons	−15.1783***	−5.7350***	−6.6851***
	(−20.5419)	(−18.3721)	(−9.9813)
N	30769	30769	30769
Adj. R^2		0.262	0.225

Source: Table by authors

Note: The first column is the estimated result of Heckman, and the second and third columns are added to IMR.

7.2 PSM Analysis

In addition, to alleviate the endogeneity problem caused by sample selection, here, drawing on the idea of (Zhang et al., 2021) study, PSM is used for the analysis, and nearest neighbor 1:1 matching is conducted based on whether the firm issues debt as the treatment variable, and the baseline regression is conducted again based on the matched sample, and the corresponding estimation results are shown in Table 15.8. The results show that the regression coefficient of ESG remains significantly positive after sample matching using PSM, which in turn indicates that the estimation results of this paper are robust.

Table 15.8 PSM Regression

	Bond	*Bond_value*
ESG	0.0261***	0.0219***
	(6.2430)	(4.5355)
Size	0.1143***	0.1042***
	(19.0429)	(10.0155)
Lev	0.0518*	−0.0897**
	(1.8220)	(−2.4311)
ROA	0.2143***	−0.2926***
	(3.4624)	(−4.0159)
Cash	−0.3282***	−0.1059***
	(−5.9201)	(−2.7261)
Growth	0.0050	−0.0100*
	(0.6494)	(−2.1494)
Board	0.0286	0.0495
	(1.1305)	(1.2324)
Top10	−0.0526	0.1203***
	(−1.5455)	(2.8795)
Age	0.0013	−0.0102
	(0.0713)	(−0.5502)
Dual	0.0100	0.0091
	(1.0191)	(1.2818)
SOE	−0.0020	−0.0041
	(−0.1778)	(−0.3526)
Ind	Yes	Yes
Year	Yes	Yes
_cons	−2.4891***	−2.4584***
	(−18.3657)	(−9.3253)
N	15,553	15,553
Adj. R^2	0.192	0.194

Source: Table by authors

Note: the regression coefficient of ESG remains significantly positive after sample matching using PSM

7.3 Replacement of Fixed Effects

The previous estimation results in this paper control for industry and year dual fixed effects but consider the possible omitted variable bias due to unobservable factors at the individual firm level. To address this possible problem in model estimation, the individual and year dual fixed effects model is further estimated here, and the corresponding estimation results are shown in Table 15.9. The results show that the coefficients of the core explanatory variables remain significantly negative after replacing the individual and year dual fixed effects for estimation, thus indicating that unobservable factors at the individual level do not affect the findings of this paper.

8. Robustness Analysis

In order to further improve the reliability of the estimation results in this paper, robustness analysis will be conducted in the following three aspects. To avoid the

Table 15.9 Regression of Body Fixed Effects

	Bond	*Bond_value*
ESG	0.0118***	0.0116***
	(4.5110)	(3.4432)
Size	0.0510***	0.0069
	(9.1272)	(1.6213)
Lev	0.0250	0.0093
	(1.4807)	(0.9019)
ROA	0.1423***	0.0124
	(5.1771)	(0.8792)
Cash	-0.0963***	-0.0580***
	(-3.5841)	(-3.7888)
Growth	-0.0032	-0.0008
	(-0.9009)	(-0.4933)
Board	-0.0020	-0.0246
	(-0.1194)	(-0.9491)
Top10	0.0471	0.0939***
	(1.5846)	(3.7650)
Age	-0.1156***	-0.0485
	(-2.6650)	(-0.9458)
Dual	-0.0010	0.0040
	(-0.1886)	(1.0848)
SOE	0.0035	-0.0057
	(0.2279)	(-0.7393)
Firm	Yes	Yes
Year	Yes	Yes
_cons	-0.7610***	-0.0649
	(-4.9809)	(-0.4881)
N	30994	30994
Adj. R^2	0.017	0.009

Source: Table by authors

Note: Estimated using individual and year double fixed-effects models.

estimation bias caused by the variable measures, the explanatory variables are further replaced by whether the firm issues debt in the current period and the size of debt issuance in the current period and the corresponding estimation results are shown in the first and second columns of Table 15.10. The results show that the coefficient of ESG is still significantly positive after replacing the explanatory variables, which in turn indicates that the estimation results of this paper are robust.

Second, the measurement of the explanatory variables is replaced, considering that there are significant differences in the ESG rating systems of enterprises by different rating agencies, and thus the ESG ratings of different rating agencies may affect the estimation results of this paper. Here, Bloomberg and Hexun.com's ESG ratings of enterprises are further used to replace the explanatory variables, and the corresponding estimation results are shown in the third and fourth columns and the fifth and sixth columns of Table 15.10, respectively. The results show that the sign and significance of the coefficients of the core explanatory variables remain

Table 15.10 Substitution of Explanatory Variables

	Bond	*Bond_value*	*Bond*	*Bond_value*	*Bond*	*Bond_value*
ESG	0.0176***	1.0924***				
	(7.3671)	(5.0925)				
ESG_BP			0.1884***	0.2243***		
			(6.3810)	(5.3028)		
ESG_HX					0.0455***	0.0051**
					(11.9734)	(2.1764)
Size	0.0932***	5.8458***	0.1115***	0.1108***	0.0956***	0.0689***
	(25.0437)	(10.1749)	(15.5925)	(9.5162)	(24.1377)	(10.0368)
Lev	0.0935***	-4.7555***	0.0957***	-0.1239**	0.0554***	-0.0694***
	(6.5364)	(-2.8355)	(2.6252)	(-2.3411)	(3.4645)	(-3.4267)
ROA	-0.0250	-19.2901***	0.2239***	-0.2732***	-0.2740***	-0.2240***
	(-0.8056)	(-5.3036)	(2.8094)	(-2.9524)	(-5.1546)	(-4.3193)
Cash	-0.2025***	-6.3467***	-0.4443***	-0.1002*	-0.2044***	-0.0451**
	(-7.3202)	(-3.5211)	(-6.2909)	(-1.7364)	(-6.1436)	(-2.0693)
Growth	-0.0208***	-1.3882***	0.0140	-0.0068	-0.0111***	-0.0135***
	(-5.4317)	(-4.5614)	(1.4987)	(-1.0072)	(-2.5878)	(-4.5442)
Board	0.0097	1.0104	0.0229	0.0485	0.0081	0.0148
	(0.6554)	(0.5086)	(0.7179)	(0.9389)	(0.5086)	(0.6479)
Top10	-0.0475**	11.1612***	-0.1553***	0.1062*	-0.0179	0.1286***
	(-2.3707)	(4.6024)	(-3.5954)	(1.9372)	(-0.8273)	(4.5220)
Age	-0.0046	-0.5598	-0.0017	-0.0153	-0.0074	-0.0040
	(-0.4603)	(-0.5865)	(-0.0776)	(-0.6531)	(-0.7044)	(-0.3868)
Dual	0.0044	0.4592	0.0036	0.0056	0.0051	0.0082**
	(0.9552)	(1.5870)	(0.2883)	(0.5427)	(0.9952)	(2.2844)
SOE	-0.0101	-0.1079	-0.0039	0.0077	-0.0085	-0.0016
	(-1.3801)	(-0.1876)	(-0.2835)	(0.5421)	(-1.0722)	(-0.2478)
Ind	Yes	Yes	Yes	Yes	Yes	Yes
Year	Yes	Yes	Yes	Yes	Yes	Yes
_cons	-1.9739***	-1.3e+02***	-2.8441***	-3.1624***	-2.0660***	-1.5481***
	(-23.1675)	(-9.5122)	(-16.7671)	(-8.7895)	(-22.1629)	(-9.1887)
N	30994	30994	11315	11315	26738	26738
adj. R^2	0.230	0.163	0.256	0.218	0.237	0.176

Source: Table by author
Note: This table includes Substitution of explanatory variables in 2011–2021.

positive after replacing the ESG measure, which in turn indicates that the estimation results of this paper are robust.

9. Discussion

9.1 Relationship with Previous Literature

This study fills a notable gap in the literature by specifically examining the impact of ESG disclosure on corporate bond issuance in China. Prior research has not extensively explored this area, making our findings particularly valuable. Our results indicate that, similar to other regions, ESG disclosure by Chinese corporations can attract investors and facilitate bond issuance. For example, Hoepner et al. (2023)

analyzed 3,900 companies in the U.S. corporate bond market from 2009 to 2017, finding that ESG disclosures provided valuable investment signals to investors. Similarly, Hoang et al. (2022) documented a positive correlation between green bond issuance and ESG disclosure scores in Europe from 2016 to 2020. However, Requicha Ferreira (2022) highlighted that despite ESG's positive role in the bond market, ESG disclosure guidelines remain imperfect across various countries, and voluntary disclosures by companies often lack standardization (Xue, 2008). Our study confirms that ESG disclosure positively impacts bond issuance in China and underscores the need for improved ESG disclosure policies.

9.2 Theoretical Implications

The findings of this study provide robust support for information asymmetry and signaling theories. ESG disclosure, when used as an advertisement for bond issuance, effectively attracts financing by reducing information asymmetry. A high level of ESG disclosure can lower financing costs (Liu & Meng, 2022). Our results also demonstrate that the three dimensions of ESG (environmental, social, and governance) positively impact firms, supporting the idea that ESG disclosure fosters effective information exchange between internal and external stakeholders (Reber et al., 2022). This corroborates the benefit of ESG disclosure in garnering support from external stakeholders (Cheng et al., 2023). In line with signaling theory, comprehensive ESG information enables investors to trust the company and recognize its commitment to corporate social responsibility (Meng-Tao et al., 2023). Thus, our study illustrates the practical implications of ESG disclosure in financing and encourages firms to integrate ESG reporting into their financial statements, reinforcing the relevance of both information asymmetry and signalling theories.

9.3 Practical Implications

The positive impact of ESG disclosure on bond issuance observed in this study is consistent with findings from the US and European markets, confirming its applicability in China. Our research suggests that companies with superior ESG performance are better equipped to manage environmental and social risks, thereby attracting long-term investors. By analysing the distinct impacts of the three ESG dimensions, we conclude that corporate ESG disclosure, particularly regarding social responsibility and corporate governance, positively influences the scale of bond issuance. This study enriches the understanding of ESG disclosure's impact on bond issuance within the Chinese market and highlights its significance in corporate finance strategies. These practical implications underscore the necessity for companies to consider ESG disclosure not just as a regulatory requirement but as a strategic tool that can enhance their financial standing and market competitiveness. The study also suggests policymakers should continue to refine ESG disclosure guidelines to standardize practices and maximize their benefits for the corporate sector and the broader investment community.

10. Conclusion

This study investigates whether ESG disclosure can serve as an effective corporate financing advertisement, leading to improved financing outcomes. Based on our findings, we offer relevant recommendations to the government, enterprises, and investors. Our research demonstrates that ESG disclosure in China positively impacts bond issuance. The sample includes companies listed on China's A-shares from 2011 to 2021, resulting in a dataset of 3,567 companies with 30,994 unbalanced panel data entries.

Regression model tests confirm that ESG disclosure helps increase both corporate bond issuance and the scale of bond issuance. These findings contribute to understanding the relationship between ESG disclosure and bond issuance in several ways. Firstly, companies that issue bonds tend to have relatively high levels of ESG disclosure, indicating that firms seeking financing prioritize ESG practices to aid in their financing efforts. Secondly, greater ESG disclosure correlates with increased investor willingness to hold these bonds, suggesting that investors favour companies with strong ESG performance, thereby enhancing the firms' financing capabilities. Thirdly, among the three ESG dimensions – environmental, social, and governance – social responsibility and corporate governance have a particularly positive impact on corporate bond issuance and scale, highlighting the importance for companies to focus on these areas.

Despite the positive findings, this study acknowledges several limitations. Firstly, the analysis excludes samples with missing key variables, which, while not affecting regression results, could influence descriptive statistics. Secondly, the study period, from 2011 to 2021, may not fully capture long-term trends. Finally, the analysis is based solely on available data, without accounting for policy irregularities or the potential for financial fraud, which could affect the robustness of the results (He et al., 2022).

Based on the results, ESG disclosure has a positive effect in the bond market, offering guidance for the government, enterprises, and investors. The government should enhance the supervision of corporate ESG disclosures, improve disclosure standards, and ensure fairness in the bond market. Enterprises should prioritize ESG disclosure, embrace social responsibility, and incorporate sustainable development into their strategic goals. Investors should consider ESG information when making investment decisions, using a comprehensive set of factors to assess corporate prospects.

Despite the significant findings and contributions of this study, several limitations must be acknowledged. The study relies on data from 2011 to 2021, which may not fully capture long-term trends or the evolving nature of ESG practices. Additionally, the exclusion of samples with missing key variables might affect the overall representativeness of the dataset. The study focuses exclusively on Chinese companies listed on the A-shares market. While this provides valuable insights into the Chinese context, the findings may not be directly generalizable to companies in other regions or countries with different regulatory environments and market conditions. The analysis does not account for potential policy irregularities or changes in regulations that could impact ESG disclosures and their effects on bond issuance. Additionally, issues related to financial fraud and their influence on the results are not considered, which could affect the robustness of the findings (He et al., 2022). The study does not differentiate between the quality and depth of ESG disclosures. As a result, it treats all ESG disclosures as equal, potentially overlooking the varying impacts of comprehensive versus superficial disclosures. The analysis does not delve into sector-specific differences in ESG disclosure practices and their impact on bond issuance. Different industries may have distinct ESG priorities and regulatory pressures, which could influence the results.

To build on the findings of this study, future research could explore the following directions. Conducting longitudinal studies that extend beyond the 2011–2021 period could provide a more comprehensive understanding of the long-term impacts of ESG disclosure on corporate financing. Comparative studies involving companies from different countries and regions would help generalize the findings and identify contextual factors that influence the relationship between ESG disclosure and bond issuance. Future research should investigate the quality and comprehensiveness of ESG disclosures, assessing how detailed and meaningful disclosures impact investor behaviour and financing outcomes compared to more superficial reports. Examining the impact of specific policy changes and regulatory frameworks on ESG disclosure practices and their effectiveness in different contexts would provide valuable insights for policymakers and practitioners. Conducting sector-specific analyses could uncover how different industries respond to ESG disclosure requirements and how these responses impact bond issuance and investor perceptions. Exploring the role of technological advancements, such as blockchain and AI, in enhancing the transparency and reliability of ESG disclosures could offer new avenues for improving corporate reporting practices.

To this end, this chapter underscores the strategic importance of ESG disclosure in the corporate bond market. By demonstrating that ESG practices can attract investors and facilitate financing, it encourages stakeholders to adopt and enhance ESG disclosure practices for mutual benefit and sustainable development.

References

Aperies, N., Poutines, T., & Antonopoulos, A. (2022). ESG scores and cost of debt. *Energy Economics*, *112*, 106186.

Bai, X., Han, J., Ma, Y., & Zhang, W. (2022). ESG performance, institutional investors' preference and financing constraints: Empirical evidence from China. *Borsa Istanbul Review*, *22*, S157–S168.

Balakrishnan, S., & Koza, M. P. (1993). Information asymmetry, adverse selection and join ventures: Theory and evidence. *Journal of Economic Behavior & Organization*, *20*(1), 99–117.

Bartov, E., & Bodnar, G. M. (1996). Alternative accounting methods, information asymmetry and liquidity: Theory and evidence. *Accounting Review*, 397–418.

Billyray-Erdogan, S. (2022). Corporate ESG engagement and information asymmetry: The moderating role of country-level institutional differences. *Journal of Sustainable Finance & Investment, Istanbul Review*, 1–37.

Carnini Pulino, S., Ciaburri, M., Magnanelli, B. S., & Nasta, L. (2022). Does ESG disclosure influence firm performance? *Sustainability*, *14*(13), 7595.

Cepni, O., Demirer, R., Pham, L., & Rognone, L. (2023). Climate uncertainty and information transmissions across the conventional and ESG assets. *Journal of International Financial Markets, Institutions and Money*, *83*.

Chen, L., & Huo, C. (2022). The measurement and influencing factors of high-quality economic development in China. *Sustainability*, *14*(15), 9293.

Cheng, L. T., Sharma, P., & Broadstock, D. C. (2023). Interactive effects of brand reputation and ESG on green bond issues: A sustainable development perspective. *Business Strategy and the Environment*, *32*(1), 570–586.

Cong, Y., Zhu, C., Hou, Y., Tian, S., & Cai, X. (2022). Does ESG investment reduce carbon emissions in China? *Frontiers in Environmental Science*, *10*, 977049.

De Jong, M., & Rocco, S. (2022). ESG and impact investing. *Journal of Asset Management*, 1–3.

Ellili, N. O. D. (2022). Impact of ESG disclosure and financial reporting quality on investment efficiency. *Corporate Governance: The International Journal of Business in Society*, *22*.

Frost, T., Tsang, A., & Cao, H. (2022). *Environmental, social, and governance (ESG) disclosure: A literature review*. SSRN. https://ssrn.com/abstract=4270942

Ge, G., Xiao, X., Li, Z., & Dai, Q. (2022). Does ESG performance promote high-quality development of enterprises in China? The mediating role of innovation input. *Sustainability*, *14*(7), 3843.

Gillan, S. L., Koch, A., & Starks, L. T. (2021). Firms and social responsibility: A review of ESG and CSR research in corporate finance. *Journal of Corporate Finance*, *66*, 101889.

Hai, M., Fang, Z., & Li, Z. (2022). Does business group's conscious of social responsibility enhance its investment efficiency? Evidence from ESG disclosure of China's listed companies. *Sustainability*, *14*(8), 4817.

He, F., Du, H., & Yu, B. (2022). Corporate ESG performance and manager misconduct: Evidence from China. *International Review of Financial Analysis*, *82*, 102201.

Hoang, A. T., Varbanov, P. S., Nižetić, S., Sirohi, R., Pandey, A., Luque, R., & Ng, K. H. (2022). Perspective review on municipal solid waste-to-energy route: Characteristics, management strategy, and role in circular economy. *Journal of Cleaner Production*, *359*, 131897.

Hoang, T. H. V., Berrou, R., & Pham, L. (2023). *The impact of green bond issuance on firms' financial and ESG performance: Does the proportion of green bonds matter?* https://papers.ssrn.com/sol3/papers.cfm?abstract_id=4227810

Hoepner, A. G., Schiemann, F., Schneider, F., & Tietmeyer, R. (2023). *ESG disclosure as advertisement of corporate bond issuances*. https://papers.ssrn.com/sol3/papers.cfm?abstract_id=4336082

Jiang, Z., Xu, Y., Fang, M., Tang, Z., & Tao, C. (2023). How does the bond market price corporate ESG engagement? Evidence from China. *Economic Analysis and Policy*, *78*, 1406–1423.

Johnson, J. A., Theis, J. C., Vitalis, A., & Young, D. (2022). Your emissions or mine? Examining how emissions management strategies, ESG performance, and targets impact investor perceptions. *Journal of Sustainable Finance & Investment*, 1–19.

Lavin, J. F., & Montecinos-Pearce, A. A. (2022). Heterogeneous firms and benefits of ESG disclosure: Cost of debt financing in an emerging market. *Sustainability*, *14*(23), 15760.

Li, D., & Adriaens, P. (2023). *Deconstructing the impact of ESG ratings on US corporate bond credit spreads: Evidence of information channeling?* SSRN 4330619. https://www.researchgate.net/publication/367984874_Deconstructing_the_Impact_of_ESG_Ratings_on_Us_Corporate_Bond_Credit_Spreads_Evidence_of_Information_Channeling

Li, T. T., Wang, K., Sueyoshi, T., & Wang, D. D. (2021). ESG: Research progress and future prospects. *Sustainability*, *13*(21), 11663.

Liu, L., & Meng, Z. (2022, September). Research on the impact of ESG evaluation on financing cost of bond issuers. *Bond Monthly*. https://papers.ssrn.com/sol3/papers.cfm?abstract_id=4257371

Luo, C., Wei, D., & He, F. (2023). Corporate ESG performance and trade credit financing – evidence from China. I*nternational Review of Economics & Finance*, *85*, 337–351.

Maaloul, A., Zéghal, D., Ben Amar, W., & Mansour, S. (2023). The effect of environmental, social, and governance (ESG) performance and disclosure on cost of debt: The mediating effect of corporate reputation. *Corporate Reputation Review*, 26(1), 1–18.

Meng-Tao, C., Da-Peng, Y., Wei-Qi, Z., & Qi-Jun, W. (2023). How does ESG disclosure improve stock liquidity for enterprises – empirical evidence from China. *Environmental Impact Assessment Review*, *98*, 106926.

Rahman, M. J., & Wu, J. (2023). M&A activity and ESG performance: Evidence from China. *Managerial Finance*, *50*(1), 179–197.

Rahman, M. J., Wu, Q., & Zhu, H. (2024). Corporate social responsibility in times of social distancing: Evidence from China. *Business Ethics, the Environment & Responsibility.*

Rahman, M. J., Zhu, H., & Chen, S. (2023). Does CSR reduce financial distress? Moderating effect of firm characteristics, auditor characteristics, and covid-19. *International Journal of Accounting & Information Management*, *31*(5), 756–784.

Reber, B., Gold, A., & Gold, S. (2022). ESG disclosure and idiosyncratic risk in initial public offerings. *Journal of Business Ethics*, *179*(3), 867–886.

Requicha Ferreira, M. (2022). The new ESG bond markets. In *The Palgrave handbook of ESG and corporate governance* (pp. 149–165). Springer International Publishing.

Stellner, C., Klein, C., & Zwergel, B. (2015). Corporate social responsibility and Eurozone corporate bonds: The moderating role of country sustainability. *Journal of Banking & Finance*, *59*, 538–549.

Tan, Y., & Zhu, Z. (2022). The effect of ESG rating events on corporate green innovation in China: The mediating role of financial constraints and managers' environmental awareness. *Technology in Society*, *68*, 101906.

Tang, H. (2022). ESG performance, investors' heterogeneous beliefs, and cost of equity capital in China. *Frontiers in Environmental Science*, *10*, 992559.

Wang, L., Fan, X., & Zhuang, H. (2023). ESG disclosure facilitator: How do the multiple large shareholders affect firms' ESG disclosure? Evidence from China. *Frontiers in Environmental Science*, *11*.

Weber, O. (2014). Environmental, social and governance reporting in China. *Business Strategy and the Environment*, *23*(5), 303–317.

Wen, S. (2022). Construction and research of China's ESG information disclosure system. *Management*, *10*(6), 377–382.

Wong, J. B., & Zhang, Q. (2022). Stock market reactions to adverse ESG disclosure via media channels. *The British Accounting Review*, *54*(1), 101045.

Xue, W. (2008). Voluntary disclosure behavior and strategy in Chinese listed companies. *Journal of Modern Accounting and Auditing*, *4*(4), 36.

Yan, Y., Cheng, Q., Huang, M., Lin, Q., & Lin, W. (2022). Government environmental regulation and corporate ESG performance: Evidence from natural resource accountability audits in China. *International Journal of Environmental Research and Public Health*, *20*(1), 447.

Zhang, C., Gao, L., Wang, W., Hao, D., & Wang, Q. (2024). ESG ratings, monetary policy uncertainty, and bond issuance premium. *Environmental Science and Pollution Research*, 31(7), 10071–10085.

Zhang, R., Li, Y., & Liu, Y. (2021). Green bond issuance and corporate cost of capital. *Pacific-Basin Finance Journal*, *69*, 101626.

Zhu, H., & Rahman, M. J. (2024). Ex-ante expected changes in ESG and future stock returns based on machine learning. *The British Accounting Review*, 101457.

16 The Impact of Banks as Large Creditors on ESG Performance

Md Jahidur Rahman, Tongshu Cen, Tarek Rana, and Hongtao Zhu

1. Introduction

Building upon prior literature (Chang et al., 2021; Danielson & Scott, 2004; Del Giudice & Rigamonti, 2020; He et al., 2021; Tang, 2022), ample evidence indicates the association between environmental, social, and governance (ESG) performance and various corporate outcomes, including financial performance, audit quality, ownership structure, and innovation. Additionally, existing research has explored firms' bank loan degrees in other contexts. Identifying factors that influence ESG performance is crucial for companies aiming to enhance their overall performance, with a firm's bank credit exposure (BCE) potentially being one such factor. However, the specific relationship between a firm's BCE and its ESG performance, particularly within the context of China, requires further investigation. Thus, this study explores whether firms exhibit high or low ESG performance when faced with varying degrees of BCE, focusing on the Chinese corporate landscape.

This research is motivated by several factors. Firstly, the integration of ESG elements into corporate processes has become increasingly essential due to businesses' growing interest in demonstrating their contributions to sustainability, social responsibility, and ethical business conduct (Chang et al., 2021; Del Giudice & Rigamonti, 2020; Friede et al., 2015; Gerard, 2019; He et al., 2021; Tang, 2022). ESG performance has emerged as a critical component in evaluating a firm's overall performance and sustainability, reflecting corporate strategy, stakeholder views, investment decisions, and long-term economic viability (Amel-Zadeh & Serafeim, 2017; Tang, 2022). This underscores the global focus on sustainable finance and responsible investing, highlighting the importance for investors, stakeholders, and society to emphasize corporate performance in terms of sustainable and ethical behaviour. To maintain a competitive edge and meet stakeholder expectations, firms must focus on potentially relevant factors that can influence ESG performance, demonstrating their commitment to sustainable development and high ethical standards (Van Duuren et al., 2015; Lokuwaduge & Heenetigala, 2016). As a significant financial factor, bank credit exposure may impact firms' ESG performance, and investigating this link can provide valuable insights into the interaction between financial factors and sustainability practices.

DOI: 10.4324/9781003488934-21

Secondly, ESG factors are closely connected with risk management, presenting both risks and opportunities for companies' long-term viability. Companies operate in an evolving business environment characterized by growing social and environmental issues, which are now considered critical drivers of long-term success, reputation accumulation, and value creation (Herbohn et al., 2017; Lokuwaduge & Heenetigala, 2016). ESG risks, such as climate-related risks, social issues, and governance problems, pose significant threats to companies, potentially harming supply chains, assets, and reputation, leading to financial losses and legal consequences (Giese et al., 2019). Conversely, ESG factors also present opportunities for companies to enhance resilience, competitiveness, and investor appeal. For example, energy efficiency and emission reduction efforts can yield cost savings and operational efficiency; strong employee welfare and community engagement can attract talent and improve productivity; and robust governance practices can enhance decision-making and stakeholder relationships, contributing to long-term value creation (Korinth & Lueg, 2022). By evaluating the relationship between bank credit exposure and ESG performance, companies can better manage ESG risks and integrate sustainability into their risk management strategies, increasing their resilience to ESG-related risks, improving financial stability, and mitigating potential negative effects on reputation and competitiveness.

Thirdly, this study is motivated by the evolving regulatory landscape and the increasing demand for transparency in ESG reporting. Governments and regulators worldwide are recognizing the significance of ESG factors in evaluating a company's sustainability and its impact on the environment and society, leading to the implementation of stricter guidelines and disclosure frameworks (Singhania & Saini, 2021). In China, the strategy for green and sustainable development has prompted authorities and regulators to intensify environmental supervision of businesses, emphasizing green governance and environmental legislation. The government is establishing a stringent regulatory environment with new regulations and reporting frameworks to standardize ESG disclosures (Wang & Sun, 2022; Yan et al., 2022). Consequently, companies are under greater pressure to improve their ESG performance and provide credible information to regulators, investors, and other stakeholders, demonstrating compliance with legal frameworks and maintaining their reputation (Van Duuren et al., 2015). Non-compliance with regulatory requirements can result in reputational damage, loss of investor trust, and potential legal and financial consequences. A company's BCE, reflecting its reliance on external financing, can impact its ability to comply with ESG regulations and meet required reporting standards (Wang & Sun, 2022; Yoon et al., 2021). By understanding the connection between a company's BCE and ESG performance, businesses can evaluate the effect of their financing choices on their compliance efforts, ensuring alignment with regulatory requirements and maintaining stakeholder trust.

This study provides an empirical investigation into the relationship between BCE and ESG performance within the context of Chinese listed firms. Data for this analysis were sourced from the Shanghai and Shenzhen stock markets, covering the period from 2012 to 2022. The dataset utilized for this study is the China Stock

Market & Accounting Research (CSMAR) database. ESG performance is proxied by the ESG rating scores issued by Shanghai Huazheng Index Information Service Limited Corporation. To address potential endogeneity concerns, we employ the two-stage least squares (2SLS) regression model, propensity score matching (PSM), and a fixed-effect model, as validated by Hausman tests. The findings reveal a significant and positive correlation between a company's BCE and its ESG performance, suggesting that firms with higher BCE tend to exhibit superior ESG performance. These results remain consistent and reliable across various endogeneity and robustness tests.

This study makes several contributions to both academic literature and practical applications. Firstly, it offers empirical evidence regarding the association between BCE and ESG performance, thus filling a significant gap in the existing literature. By examining how reliance on external financing impacts ESG performance, the study provides insights into the financial indicators that influence companies' sustainability initiatives. This enhanced understanding can help firms align their financial strategies with sustainability goals, thereby improving risk management procedures and financial stability in the face of ESG-related risks.

Secondly, the findings offer valuable insights for banks and financial institutions. By incorporating ESG considerations into their lending decisions, banks can develop more robust risk management frameworks that account for ESG variables. This integration enhances their ability to identify potential risks and opportunities related to sustainability, supporting the development of responsible lending practices. Consequently, banks can align their financing activities with the increasing demand for sustainable investments, fostering an environmentally and socially responsible banking sector.

Thirdly, the study's results have implications for the establishment of robust ESG reporting frameworks. By investigating the connection between BCE and ESG performance, the study aids businesses in improving compliance efforts and aligning reporting procedures with legal requirements. This promotes consistent and comparable ESG disclosures, enhancing transparency in corporate sustainability reporting.

From a theoretical perspective, this study contributes to agency theory and stakeholder theory by highlighting the alignment of corporate actions with stakeholder expectations and reducing conflicts of interest. It also advances institutional theory by examining the influence of external factors on a company's sustainability practices. The findings underscore the role of external financing in driving sustainable initiatives and the impact of stakeholders and regulatory institutions on a company's commitment to ESG performance. Practically, the study provides companies with insights into integrating financial factors (BCE) and ESG factors in strategic decision-making. By focusing on BCE and its impact on ESG, companies can emphasize stakeholder engagement, risk management, and resilience, thereby enhancing their long-term sustainability.

The subsequent sections of this chapter are structured as follows. Section 2 outlines the theoretical frameworks employed in this study. Section 3 conducts a literature review and elaborates on the development of hypotheses. Section 4 describes the research design, encompassing the methodology, sample, and model. Section 5 presents the empirical results. Section 6 presents the endogeneity test. Section 7 presents the robustness test. Section 8 provides a thorough discussion of the results, and finally, Section 9 concludes the study.

2. Theoretical Framework

The theoretical framework for this study encompasses three main perspectives: agency theory, stakeholder theory, and institutional theory (Herold, 2018).

Agency theory posits that conflicts of interest arise due to goal divergence and information asymmetry between a company's management (agents) and its shareholders (principals) or other stakeholders (Eisenhardt, 1989). In the context of this study, agency theory helps explain the potential conflicts between a company's external financing activities (BCE) and its sustainability efforts (ESG performance). Shareholders typically prioritize profit maximization, while managers may allocate firm resources to ESG activities for personal benefits or to enhance their reputation (Lee & Isa, 2020). High levels of external financing can enable a company to engage more actively in ESG practices due to increased financial capacity. However, significant external financing also exerts pressure to prioritize short-term financial goals, such as repaying bank loans, potentially leading to the avoidance or rejection of ESG practices (Tarmuji et al., 2016; Dawar, 2014). Thus, agency theory suggests that companies may face challenges in balancing financial obligations with sustainability objectives, highlighting the potential conflicts between BCE and ESG performance.

Stakeholder theory proposes that organizations should consider the interests of various stakeholders beyond shareholders, including employees, customers, suppliers, communities, and the environment (Donaldson & Preston, 1995). Companies must actively engage with stakeholders to create value and address their concerns, as stakeholders significantly influence the company's reputation, financial performance, and long-term viability (Argandoña, 2011). In examining the connection between BCE and ESG performance, it is crucial to consider the interests and expectations of all stakeholders, including bank lenders. Organizations need to strike a balance between the interests of multiple stakeholders and pursue sustainable and responsible business practices to maintain stakeholder trust and support.

Institutional theory emphasizes that companies should adhere to institutional standards and rules to gain legitimacy and acceptance within their social and economic environments (Zucker, 1987). Regulatory requirements for ESG reporting compel companies to incorporate ESG considerations into their decision-making processes to meet these standards and maintain legitimacy (Wang & Sun, 2022; Yan et al., 2022). This theoretical perspective provides insight into the institutional pressures that businesses face in managing financial commitments while integrating ESG factors. Understanding these pressures can guide both practice and research into how companies navigate the demands of external financing and sustainability. Thus, the theoretical framework of this study integrates agency theory, stakeholder theory, and institutional theory to provide a comprehensive understanding of the dynamics between BCE and ESG performance. These perspectives highlight the conflicts, stakeholder engagements, and institutional pressures that companies must manage to align their financial strategies with sustainability goals.

3. Literature Review and Hypothesis Development

3.1 Firm's BCE and ESG Performance

Our research is connected to two key streams of literature. The first stream focuses on public firms' BCE (including relevant factors such as financial leverage and trade credit) and its impact on financial performance. The second stream examines firms' ESG performance and the various factors influencing it. We primarily reviewed literature pertinent to both these aspects to align with the research question in this study and to situate our work within the existing body of literature on each component.

For public firms, financing activities are crucial. Companies often rely on external sources of finance to sustain operations and achieve long-term financial objectives. External financing includes bank loans, bonds, and equity investments (Huberman, 1984; Inderst & Müller, 2003). This study focuses specifically on bank loans, with the intensity of bank loans representing a firm's BCE. Previous research has investigated the impact of BCE on a company's financial conditions (Bondt & Thaler, 1985; Danielson & Scott, 2004; Dawar, 2014; Geng et al., 2015; Habermann & Fischer, 2021). Findings from these studies indicate that increased BCE has both positive and negative impacts. Several studies in China also investigates the relationship between environmental accounting and firm performance (Rahman & Wu, 2023; Rahman, Wu, et al., 2024; Rahman et al., 2023; Zhu & Rahman, 2024).

Positively, companies with higher BCE can secure more funding for investment, working capital, and expansion, leading to improved profitability, growth, and market value (Huberman, 1984; Inderst & Müller, 2003; Marco, 1992). However, excessive reliance on bank loans can also pose risks. Companies with higher BCE may face substantial repayment obligations, be subject to stricter loan covenants, and be more vulnerable to economic downturns. High levels of debt can restrict a company's ability to respond to market changes or investment opportunities (He & Hu, 2016; Huberman, 1984; Inderst & Müller, 2003).

In addition to BCE, the ESG factor has garnered significant attention due to its importance in assessing sustainability and responsible business practices. Companies with robust ESG performance can achieve a competitive edge and higher corporate reputation than their peers (Amel-Zadeh & Serafeim, 2017). In China, the regulatory environment imposes stringent guidelines and disclosure requirements related to ESG factors, compelling companies to adhere to specific rules and reporting formats. Effective communication of ESG performance to stakeholders is thus essential (Herold, 2018; Wang & Sun, 2022).

Previous studies have identified several factors affecting ESG performance, including financial performance, board structure, audit quality, and corporate governance (Del Giudice & Rigamonti, 2020; Friede et al., 2015; Giese et al., 2019).

Additionally, the literature has explored the relationship between ESG performance and financing activities. For example, Chang et al. (2018) found that stronger environmental performance can reduce the cost of capital and lower leverage ratios. He et al. (2021) noted that banks tend to provide lower loan sizes to companies with ESG incidents. However, much of this research has focused on US firms rather than Chinese-listed firms (Habermann & Fischer, 2021; He et al., 2021). Thus, whether a firm's BCE positively or negatively impacts its ESG performance remains an empirical question requiring further exploration.

Drawing on the aforementioned literature, our study addresses the reverse causality of a firm's BCE and ESG performance. We control for additional factors influencing ESG performance to isolate the effect of a firm's BCE. By establishing the causality of the effects of BCE on ESG performance, we provide further evidence that banks' lending activities play a crucial role in promoting sustainable economic practices. This study contributes to the literature by offering empirical insights into the relationship between BCE and ESG performance, particularly within the context of Chinese listed firms, and underscores the political function of bank lending in fostering a sustainable economy.

3.2 Trade-Off between BCE and ESG Performance

This study investigates whether a firm's BCE has a favourable or unfavourable effect on its ESG performance. Drawing on agency theory and considering the role of stakeholders, it is evident that conflicts of interest can arise among different stakeholders within an organization (Dawar, 2014). Agency theory predicts that companies reliant on bank funding may face pressure to prioritize short-term financial aims over long-term sustainability goals. This suggests that firms might choose to meet bank loan repayment obligations rather than adhere to ESG requirements when balancing BCE and ESG performance.

Empirical literature supports the notion that managers may prioritize immediate financial objectives over long-term sustainability goals when companies are under the pressure of bank borrowing. This prioritization is necessary to fulfil financial commitments to lenders and maintain financial stability (Bassey, 2017; Herbohn et al., 2017). Consequently, businesses with higher levels of debt are likely to allocate fewer resources to ESG initiatives. Additionally, companies operating with higher credit risk and financial constraints typically encounter greater difficulties in allocating resources towards ESG operations (Anderson, 1960; Kaminker & Stewart, 2012). Therefore, the trade-off between a firm's BCE and ESG performance becomes more pronounced.

To this end, we argue that companies with higher levels of BCE will face pressure to repay financing funds, leading to a trade-off between short-term financial objectives and long-term sustainable development objectives. Firms may opt to use available funds to repay bank loans rather than invest in ESG initiatives. Based on theoretical and empirical insights, we establish the following hypothesis:

H1: Firms with higher levels of BCE will exhibit lower levels of ESG performance than firms with lower levels of BCE.

3.3 Leveraging Financing Relationships for Enhanced ESG Performance

Contrary to the previous assumption that a firm's BCE negatively impacts ESG performance, another perspective integrates stakeholder theory and institutional theory to propose an alternative hypothesis. Stakeholder theory emphasizes that organizations must consider the interests of all parties, including consumers, employees, communities, and shareholders (Herold, 2018; Lee & Isa, 2020). Within this context, banks, as crucial creditors, also represent essential stakeholders whose interests must be considered. According to Habermann and Fischer (2021), companies that excel in ESG factors are less likely to face bankruptcy. Additionally, He et al. (2021) found that companies with higher ESG performance can secure lower bank loan interest rates. This implies that banks may require companies to meet specific ESG criteria as a condition for providing loans. Consequently, firms with significant BCE may be more motivated to invest in ESG initiatives to meet the expectations and requirements of their stakeholders.

Empirical studies support a positive correlation between a firm's BCE and its ESG performance. For example, companies with higher levels of debt often exhibit superior environmental performance, indicating potential alignment between financial leverage and sustainability efforts (Jebe, 2019; Nega & Diala-Nettles, 2018).

From the perspective of institutional theory, companies operate within a broader institutional context that includes societal norms, industry standards, and regulatory frameworks (Herold, 2018). ESG factors have gained significant attention due to increased regulations and investor demands for transparency and sustainability (Lokuwaduge & Heenetigala, 2016; Singhania & Saini, 2021). Consequently, companies with higher BCE may experience greater institutional pressures from creditors and adopt ESG practices to comply with socially and environmentally responsible standards, thereby reducing their exposure to regulatory and reputational risks. Thus, we argue that firms with higher BCE will encounter increased pressure from stakeholders and regulatory institutions, driving them to enhance their ESG practices to maintain credibility and reputation. Companies may leverage their financing relationships to bolster their sustainability efforts. Based on these theoretical and empirical insights, we establish the following hypothesis:

H2: Companies with higher BCE will exhibit higher levels of ESG performance than companies with lower BCE.

4. Research Design

4.1 Sample and Data

To conduct analysis, our study focuses on Chinese listed firms in the Shanghai and Shenzhen stock markets. These markets serve as a representative of the major Chinese stock exchanges and provide comprehensive coverage of listed firms (Adcock et al., 2023). We utilize ESG rating data from the Huazheng database, audit types, and other financial information from the CSMAR database. These data were gathered from 2012 to 2022. Our initial dataset consists of 59,521 firm-year observations from 5,528 enterprises. However, data processing is necessary to guarantee the validity of our sample. To confirm the validity of our analysis, we first exclude the missing data for the dependent, independent, and control variables. Then, we exclude financial and insurance institutions due to the potential differences in the economic significance of the accounting numbers used in this study between financial, insurance, and non-financial firms, as well as the unique regulation of utility companies (Ho et al., 2001). Moreover, we exclude special treatment (ST) companies. ST companies refer to firms have received special treatment due to continuous years of financial deficits (Geng et al., 2015). To maintain the consistency of our sample, we treat ST companies as companies in financial crisis. Also, to lessen the possible impact of outliers, we employ a winsorized method on all continuous variables at the top and bottom 1 percentile of values. Finally, there are 37,694 firm-year observations in our sample. Table 16.1 provides a summary of the sample selection process, presenting an overview of the initial sample size and selections due to the exclusion criteria and winsorization.

4.2 *Variable Measurements*

4.2.1 Dependent Variable

The dependent variable is the ESG rating score issued by Shanghai Huazheng Index Information Service Limited Corporation, a reputable ESG rating institution in China, following Chang et al. (2021). This ESG rating score encompasses the evaluation of ESG performance of Chinese listed firms (Tang, 2022). Based on Huazheng's unique assessment system, each company is given a numerical rating score, reflecting its overall ESG performance compared to the industry peers. The ESG rating levels for corporations are categorized into nine grades: AAA, AA, A, BBB, BB, B, CCC, CC, and C. Using the method of converting qualitative categories into quantitative values, these numerical rating scores are represented as dummy variables, with assigned numerical values of 9, 8, 7, 6, 5, 4, 3, 2, and 1, respectively.

Table 16.1 Sample Selection

Sample Selection Criterion	*No. of Companies*	*No. of Firm-Year Observations*
Total number	5,528	59,521
Less: missing sample data	2,492	17,207
Less: companies in the financial industry	138	1,972
Less: companies in the insurance industry	7	82
Less: companies in the public utility industries	91	1,022
Less: ST companies	107	1,544
Equal to = final sample	2,693	37,694

Source: Table by authors

Note: This table presents the process of selecting sample for testing the relationship between BCE and ESG.

The selection of the ESG rating score from Huazheng as a dependent variable is driven by the significance of understanding the impact of banks as large creditors on the ESG performance of companies in China. Therefore, by examining the relationship between BCE and ESG rating scores, we aim to assess whether companies with significant borrowing from banks demonstrate higher ESG performance than those with lower credit exposure.

4.2.2 Independent Variables

Bank Credit Exposure: The independent variable is BCE, which represents the level of a firm's borrowing from banks. We chose the number of total loans as a proxy for BCE. In accordance with previous literature (He & Hu, 2016), we used the logarithm of the total loan amount (Loan Size) to capture the BCE. Specifically, we extracted relevant data on the total amount of credit extended by banks to the company during the specified year from financial statements and financial databases and calculated it in natural logarithm form as a measure of BCE. We considered BCE as a continuous variable that represents the financial dependence of the company on the bank. A high value of BCE indicates that banks are large creditors to the company. More precisely, high BCE represents an important level of indebtedness to banks and potential financial implications.

4.2.3 Control Variables

This study employs several control variables to consider additional variables that can affect the relationship between BCE and ESG performance, These control variables can isolate the specific effects of our independent variable of interest. Following Habermann and Fischer (2021), we consider several financial-level proxies for a firm's credit risk that can potentially influence ESG performance. The financial statements variables include *Leverage* (total liabilities divided by total assets), *Profitability* (income after tax divided by average total assets), *Firm Size* (natural logarithm of total assets), and *liquidity* (the ratio of cash and short-term assets to total assets). Firms with high corporate governance are more possible to reveal better ESG performance and accountability (Lavin & Montecinos-Pearce, 2021). Therefore, we add a firm-level control variable including *Corporate Governance* (the proportion of independent directors: the number of independent directors divided by the number of directors). Moreover, a firm's financial health and the financial resources available can also have the potential influence on ESG initiatives. Hence, following Yoon et al. (2021), we selected two financial-level control variables including *Interest Expense Ratio* (interest expenses divided by total operating revenue) and *Tax Burden* (tax and surcharges divided by total operating revenue). Additionally, investment intensity is the proportion of capital expenditures to sales or assets of a company. It demonstrates the company's extent of spending on long-term assets and shows a determination of sustainable business practices and ESG-related investments (Gerard, 2019). Thus, we used the *Investment Intensity* (ratio in total investments of the reporting period) as a control variable as well.

Besides, the bank loan ratio indirectly indicates the reliance of a company on bank loans as a source of funding, which can reflect the level of interaction and influence of banks on a firm's operations and ESG performance (Danielson & Scott, 2004). Various bank loan ratios even imply various operating performances of companies. Some organizations rely heavily on bank loans to fund their operations or investment ventures. Therefore, we include the *Bank Loan Ratio* (ratio of borrowing money from banks) as a control variable to differentiate firms having loan-funded activities. This differentiation can help isolate the specific effect of such loan-funded activities on ESG performance.

Furthermore, following literature (Del & Rigamonti, 2020), the accuracy and dependability of financial reporting can influence ESG performance. The accuracy and dependability of financial reporting will be affected by different auditor types due to differences between auditors' expertise, resource, or independence. Therefore, we included *Audit Type* (an indicator that assumes a value of 1 if a company's audit is performed by one of the Big Four auditing firms: Deloitte, PricewaterhouseCoopers (PwC), Ernst & Young (EY), and KPMG, and otherwise 0 as a control variable. This helps isolate the specific effect of auditing practices on ESG performance. Finally, we also included *Industry* (industry-specific fixed effect) and *Year* (year-specific fixed effect) in our empirical models to control for variations across industries or over time.

4.3 Model Specification

To test our above hypothesis and check whether BCE is related to ESG performance, we followed and combined the previous literature (He et al., 2022; Del & Rigamonti, 2020; Habermann & Fischer, 2021), estimating the following fixed-effect regression model:

$$\begin{aligned} ESGP = {} & \beta_0 + \beta_1 BCE + \beta_2 Leverage + \beta_3 ROA + \beta_4 LnSize \\ & + \beta_5 Liquidity + \beta_6 CG + \beta_7 IERatio + \beta_8 TaxBurden \\ & + \beta_9 BLRatio + \beta_{10} InvIntensity + \beta_{11} Auditor\ Type \\ & + Industry - Specific\ Fixed\ effect + Year\ Fixed\ effect + \varepsilon \end{aligned} \tag{1}$$

Here:

ESGP	=	ESG performance, a dummy variable ranging from 1 to 9, Corresponding to C, CC, CCC, B, BB, BBB, A, AA, and AAA, respectively.
BCE	=	bank credit exposure, natural logarithm of the firm's total amount loan
Leverage	=	leverage measured as total debt divided by total assets
ROA	=	return on assets (earnings divided by average total assets)
LnSize	=	natural logarithm of the firm's total assets
Liquidity	=	liquidity measured by calculating the ratio of cash and short-term assets to total assets

CG = corporate governance measured as the proportion of independent directors (the number of independent directors/the number of directors)
IE Ratio = interest expense ratio (interest expenses divided by total operating revenue)
Tax Burden = tax burden measured as tax and surcharges divided by total operating revenue
BL Ratio = bank loan ratio, the proportion of bank loans in the firms' total liabilities, indicating their reliance on bank financing
Inv Intensity = investment intensity measured by the ratio in total investments of the reporting period
Auditor type = auditor type, an indicator that assumes a value of 1 if a company's audit is performed by one of the Big Four auditing firms, and otherwise 0
Industry = industry-specific fixed effect
Year = year-specific fixed effect (2012–2022)

5. Empirical Results

5.1 Descriptive Statistics

Table 16.2 displays the descriptive statistics of the entire sample. It demonstrates that the majority of variables have a low standard deviation, while the variable Inv Intensity stands out among the others, exhibiting a higher level of variability. The sampled organizations' average ESG score is 2.706, which represents a moderate degree of overall ESG performance. The average logarithmic value of the total loan balance is 20.04, indicating a moderate level of loan exposure among the observed entities. Leverage has a large difference between the maximum (191.7)

Table 16.2 Descriptive Statistics

Variable	*N*	*Mean*	*SD*	*Min*	*Max*
ESG	37694	2.706	2.082	0	8
BCE	37694	20.04	2.135	8.870	27.04
Leverage	37694	0.473	1.389	−0.684	191.7
LnSize	37694	22.41	1.447	13.96	29.33
ROA	37694	0.0456	2.746	−30.69	442.3
BL Ratio	37694	0.145	0.267	−9.9	54.51
Inv Intensity	37694	89.79	26.98	0	100
PE Ratio	37694	3.824	1.099	−1.879	12.95
CG	37694	21.11	1.526	12.71	28.78
Tax Burden	37694	0.919	2.597	−8.652	14.39
Auditor Type	37694	0.009	0.097	0	1

Source: Table by authors

Note: This table presents the summary statistics for the sample for the years 2012–2022.

and minimum (−0.684) values, which points to a high degree of instability and wide variance in leverage ratios across the sampled enterprises. The mean auditor type is approximately 0, demonstrating that the majority of firms choose a certain type of auditors rather than Big4 auditors, and these companies' auditing procedures need to be improved.

Before conducting the baseline regression analysis, in this study we carried out the Pearson correlation matrix on all variables, and Table 16.3 demonstrates the correlation coefficient of the relevant variables. From the test results, BCE is significantly and positively correlated with ESG; therefore, hypothesis H2 has been initially verified. Additionally, the correlation coefficients for all other combinations of variables in the model are small with each other, indicating that there is no possibility of serious co-linearity problem between the explanatory variables.

5.2 Baseline Regression Results

This study aims to examine the association between BCE and ESG. In order to examine the impact of variables of interest such as BCE on the dependent variable ESG, this study adopts the time-fixed effect model to test. The specific equation is as follows:

$$\mathrm{Y}_{\mathrm{it}} = \beta_0 + \beta_i \mathrm{X}_{\mathrm{it}} + \gamma_i \mathrm{Z}_{\mathrm{it}} + \theta_i + \varepsilon_{\mathrm{it}} \tag{2}$$

Here, *Yit* represents the ESG held by the ith individual at time *t*; *β0* represents the intercept term of the regression model; *Xit* is the core explanatory variable of BCE; *βi* is the estimated parameter: a positive value indicates that BCE has a significant facilitation on ESG and a negative value indicates BCE has a significant suppression on ESG; and *Zit* represents the control variables, including Leverage, ROA, LnSize, BL Ratio, Inv Intensity, Tax Burden, Corporate Governance, IE ratio, and Auditor Type. To avoid heteroscedasticity, we process these several data in natural logarithm form including PE ratio, Tax Burden, Corporate Governance, and IE Ratio. *θi* represents the time-fixed effects, and *εit* represents the residual term of the estimation model.

Table 16.4 displays the results of logistic regression analysis for ESG performance. Column 1 presents the regression results of single explanatory variables on the dependent variables without considering any control variable. Column 2 demonstrates the regression results of explanatory variables on the dependent variables after adding control variables.

Column 1 displays that the coefficient of BCE is statistically significant and positive (coefficient = 0.0719, *t*-stat = 0.0042), suggesting that the higher BCE is likely to promote the company's ESG performance.

Regarding column 2, the regression result of the explanatory variable BCE are similar to those in the first column: the coefficient of the BCE remains positive and is significant at the 1% confidence level. However, the absolute value of the coefficient reduces to 0.0382 with 0.0059 *t*-stat. It is possible that adding control

Table 16.3 Pairwise Correlations

Variable	*ESG*	*BCE*	*Leverage*	*LnSize*	*ROA*	*PE Ratio*	*BL Ratio*	*Inv Intensity*	*Liquidity*	*IE Ratio*	*CG*	*Tax Burden*	*Auditor Type*
ESG	1.000												
BCE	0.094**	1.000											
Leverage	−0.003*	0.008	1.000										
LnSize	0.029	0.021*	0.002***	1.000									
ROA	0.004**	0.003	0.095	−0.040	1.000								
PE Ratio	−0.001*	0.005***	0.718**	0.005	−0.037	1.000							
BL Ratio	0.022**	0.006**	0.004*	0.003	−0.002**	−0.005	1.000						
Inv Intensity	−0.058*	0.021*	0.004***	0.007	0.002***	0.002**	0.007	1.000					
Liquidity	−0.058***	0.000	−0.008	0.021	0.003	−0.005	0.006	0.021**	1.000				
IE Ratio	−0.035**	−0.044*	−0.009*	−0.028	−0.006	−0.006	-0.006	0.009	0.044	1.000			
CG	0.042*	0.001**	0.075	0.930	−0.034	0.076	0.004	0.006	0.001	−0.027	1.000		
Tax Burden	−0.111**	−0.621*	0.052**	0.524*	−0.015***	0.048**	0.000**	0.027**	0.621	0.019	0.559	1.000	
Auditor Type	0.054***	0.011**	0.012*	−0.001*	−0.001*	0.011**	0.011	0.036**	0.011**	−0.002**	−0.003*	−0.006*	1.000

Source: Table by authors

Note: This table presents the Pearson's correlations. Standard errors in parentheses.* $p < 0.1$, ** $p < 0.05$, *** $p < 0.01$.

Table 16.4 Baseline Regression Results

Variable	*Coeff. (t-stat)* *ESG*	*Coeff. (t-stat)* *ESG*
BCE	0.0719***	0.0382***
	(0.0042)	(0.0059)
Leverage		−0.0154
		(0.0402)
LnSize		0.6782***
		(0.0198)
ROA		0.0053**
		(0.0023)
PE Ratio		−0.0280***
		(0.0101)
CR		−0.6214***
		(0.0201)
Tax Burden		−0.0419***
		(0.0065)
BL Ratio		0.1581**
		(0.0693)
Inv Intensity		−0.0018***
		(0.0004)
IE Ratio		0.0646*
		(0.0392)
Auditor Type		0.2080**
		(0.1231)
Constant	0.1255	0.2260
	(0.0889)	(0.2170)
Industry	Yes	Yes
Year	Yes	Yes
N	37,694	37,694
Adj. *R2*	0.1284	0.1162

Source: Table by authors

Notes: This table presents the results of testing the effects of BCE on ESG with baseline models. Standard errors in parentheses.

* $p < 0.1$, ** $p < 0.05$, *** $p < 0.01$.

variables can capture some of the variances in the dependent variable to reduce the unique impact of the independent variable on the dependent variable.

Moreover, the coefficient of Leverage shows negative (coefficient = −0.0154, *t*-stat = 0.0402) but not significant, indicating that the Leverage variable does not exhibit a significant influence on the firm's ESG performance. The coefficient of LnSize is statistically significant and positive (coefficient = 0.6782, *t*-stat = 0.0198), suggesting that the bigger firm size has a positive influence on its ESG performance. Additionally, the coefficient of PE Ratio (coefficient = −0.0280, *t*-stat = 0.0101), corporate governance (coefficient = −0.6214, *t*-stat = 0.0201), and tax burden (coefficient = −0.0419, *t*-stat = 0.0065) are significantly negative, suggesting that the higher PE ratio, higher level of corporate governance, and the higher tax burden will restrain the firm's ESG performance. Besides, the coefficient of investment intensity is statistically significant and negative (coefficient = −0.0018, *t*-stat = 0.0004) at the 1% confidence level, while the coefficient of bank loan ratio has a significant positive (coefficient = 0.1581, *t*-stat = 0.0693) effect on firm's ESG performance at the 5% confidence level. This indicates that lower investment intensity and higher bank loan ratio will lead companies to face greater operational risks, resulting in lower ESG performance for companies. It also implies that the sample companies as a whole demonstrate a tendency to be risk-averse and balance business risks by optimizing the levels of investment intensity and bank loan ratio, which significantly affects the ESG performance of the organization.

6. Mitigating Endogeneity Concerns

6.1 2SLS Test

Endogeneity arises when there is an omitted variable that can have a simultaneous connection between the independent variable (BCE) and the dependent variable (ESG performance), leading to biased and unreliable estimates (Bassey Edem, 2017; Chang et al., 2018; He & Hu, 2016). To solve this problem, the 2SLS method can be employed to mitigate endogeneity concerns in this research. We employed the following models to estimate the selection of BCE:

$$\mathrm{BCE} = \beta_0 + \beta_1 * \textbf{Financial Market Conditions} + \varepsilon_1 \quad (3)$$

$$\mathrm{ESGP} = \beta_0 + \beta_1 PBCE_{i,t+1} + \sum \beta_i Controls + \sum \beta_k Year + \sum \beta_k\ Industry + \varepsilon_2 \quad (4)$$

Here, BCE is bank credit exposure measured as the natural logarithm form of the company's total amount of loan; ESGP is ESG performance, a dummy variable ranging from 1 to 9 for C, CC, CCC, B, BB, BBB, A, AA, and AAA, respectively; $\mathrm{PBCE}_{i,t+1}$ is the predicted value of BCE; control variables include Leverage, LnSize, ROA, PE Ratio, CR, Tax Burden, BL Ratio, Inv Intensity, IE Ratio, and Auditor Type.

For this method, there is an instrumental variable. To be more specific, we chose financial market conditions (measured as P/E ratio) as an instrumental variable to estimate the endogenous variable. Following the previous literature, the requirements of an ideal instrumental variable are as follows (Wooldridge, 2023; DeMaris, 2014; Cahan et al., 2021). Firstly, the variable should be directly relevant to the independent variable. Secondly, it can only affect the dependent variable by affecting the independent variable. Thirdly, it is uncorrelated with other unmeasured variables and error terms of the model. Therefore, we include financial market conditions as an instrumental variable, which directly influences the firm's BCE and can only affect ESG performance by acting on BCE (Pagano, 1993). Moreover, in order to assess the financial market conditions, the P/E ratio can be an indicator which reflects investor sentiment, market expectations, and risk appetite. A higher

P/E ratio may indicate positive market sentiment and better financial market conditions (Thaler et al., 2001). In the model, $PBCE_{i,t+1}$ is the predicted value of BCE in lagged one-period, which accounts for time lag effects. Following previous literature (Habermann & Fischer, 2021), there may be a delayed response between variables. Hence, we incorporate lagged one-period variables to better capture these time lag effects and reduce the potential for endogeneity to accurately assess the influence of the independent variables on the dependent variable.

6.1.1 First-Stage Results

In Table 16.5, Column 1 demonstrates the outcomes of the first stage regression in the 2SLS method for the instrumental variable. The coefficient on *FMC* (exogenous

Table 16.5 Mitigating Endogeneity Concerns with the 2SLS Method

Variable	*First Stage*	*Second Stage*
	Coeff. (*t*-stat)	Coeff. (*t*-stat)
Dependent variable	BCE	ESG
FMC	0.320***	
	(0.033)	
BCE		0.0498***
		(0.0071)
Leverage	−0.008	−0.0437
	(0.039)	(0.0560)
LnSize	0.034***	0.6922***
	(0.002)	(0.0660)
ROA	−1.212***	0.0052**
	(0.065)	(0.0021)
CG	0.065***	−0.6524***
	(0.004)	(0.0776)
Tax Burden	−0.994***	−0.0253*
	(0.030)	(0.0138)
BL Ratio	0.225***	0.1487
	(0.022)	(0.1006)
Inv Intensity	0.202***	−0.0015***
	(0.020)	(0.0003)
IE Ratio	0.118***	0.0856
	(0.012)	(0.0550)
Constant	1.153***	1.5551***
	(206)	(0.4178)
Industry	Yes	Yes
Year	Yes	Yes
N	37,694	37,694
Adj. R^2	0.754	0.562

Source: Table by authors

Notes: This table presents the results of testing the effects of BCE on ESG with 2SLS models. Standard errors in parentheses.

* $p < 0.1$, ** $p < 0.05$, *** $p < 0.01$.

instrument) is significantly positive (coefficient = 0.320, *t*-stat = 0.033). This significantly positive coefficient reflects a significantly positive association between FMC and BCE. It implies that the change in financial market conditions can directly act on the level of the firm's BCE.

6.1.2 Second-Stage Results

In Table 16.5, Column 2 demonstrates the outcomes of the second stage regression in the 2SLS method, focusing on the association between BCE and ESG performance. The coefficient of BCE is significantly positive (coefficient = 0.0498, *t*-stat = 0.0071) at the 1% confidence level. This indicates that BCE still significantly contributes to promoting the company's ESG performance: the higher BCE level will lead to higher ESG performance.

6.2 PSM Test

To further mitigate endogeneity concerns and consider that there are outliers in the used data and the existing problem of heteroscedasticity in the benchmark model. We also adopt propensity score matching to conduct empirical analysis again and improve the estimation accuracy.

Table 16.6 shows the propensity score matching method. We use the median of variable BCE as a criterion for classifying the control group and experimental group, which can isolate the causal effect of BCE on the ESG. The regression coefficient of variable BCE is positive (coefficient = 0.3440, *t*-stat = 0.0365) and statistically significant at the 1% confidence level. This indicates a significantly positive association between a firm's BCE and a firm's ESG performance, implying that firms with higher bank credit exposure tend to exhibit better ESG performance.

Therefore, the findings suggest a causal link between BCE and the bank's ESG performance. The results demonstrate that BCE has a significant positive impact on the bank's ESG performance, indicating a cause-and-effect relationship between these two variables. By PSM test, we confirm that the observed relationship between BCE and the bank's ESG is not driven by omitted variables or reverse causality.

6.3 Fixed-Effect Model (Based on Hausman Tests)

To further mitigate endogeneity concerns, we follow previous literature (Rahman et al., 2023; Rahman, Zhu, et al., 2024) and use Hausman tests to determine the most appropriate model between the fixed effects model and random effects model. The two models' differences are as follows: whether the error term is correlated with the independent variables (Borenstein et al., 2010). We conduct the Hausmann test method to determine whether the error terms are correlated with the independent variables, thus clarifying the association between the error terms and the dependent variable.

Table 16.6 Mitigating Endogeneity Concerns with the PSM Test

Variable	*Coeff. (t-stat)* *ESG*
BCE	0.3430***
	(0.0365)
Leverage	−0.083**
	(0.006)
LnSize	0.184***
	(0.019)
ROA	4.269**
	(0.623)
PE Ratio	−1.27***
	(0.313)
CG	−0.043*
	(0.041)
Tax Burden	0.384**
	(0.281)
Bank Loan Ratio	−0.079**
	(0.211)
Inv Intensity	0.200**
	(0.189)
IE Ratio	−0.208*
	(0.116)
Constant	−0.276**
	(0.046)
Year	Yes
Industry	Yes
N	37,694
Adj. R^2	0.316

Source: Table by authors

Notes: This table presents the results of testing the effects of BCE on ESG with the PSM test. Standard errors in parentheses.
* $p < 0.1$, ** $p < 0.05$, *** $p < 0.01$.

The hypotheses tested in the Hausman test are as follows:

H0 (null hypothesis): The appropriate model is the random effects model.
H1 (alternative hypothesis): The appropriate model is the fixed effects model.

According to Table 16.7, the *p*-value is 0.0000, which is lower than the conventional significance level of 0.05. Therefore, the null hypothesis is not valid, suggesting that the random effects model is not appropriate for the analysis. It also indicates that the alternative hypothesis is true, and we should choose more suitable fixed effects model to build the panel model.

7. Robustness Check

7.1 Alternative Measure of BCE

To test the robustness of the above empirical findings, this study first re-estimates the correlation by replacing the measures of the explanatory variables. We employ

Table 16.7 Hausman Tests

Test Summary	*Chi² Statistic*	*Chi-Stl.d.f*	*Prob*
Random effect model	191.88	8	0.0000

Table 16.8 Robustness Test: Alternative Measure of BCE

Variable	*Coeff. (t-stat)* *ESG*	*Coeff. (t-stat)* *ESG*
BCE	0.0418*** (0.0044)	0.0123** (0.0049)
Leverage		0.1071*** (0.0297)
LnSize		0.6542*** (0.0207)
ROA		0.0039 (0.0035)
PE Ratio		−0.0239** (0.0104)
CG		−0.5854*** (0.0207)
Tax Burden		−0.0607*** (0.0054)
BL Ratio		0.0337 (0.0258)
Inv Intensity		−0.0019*** (0.0004)
IE Ratio		−0.0999*** (0.0310)
Year	Yes	Yes
Industry	Yes	Yes
Constant	0.6552*** (0.0915)	0.5527** (0.2336)
N	37,694	37,694
Adj. R^2	0.1418	0.1149

Source: Table by authors

Notes: This table presents the results of testing the effects of BCE on ESG with baseline models. Standard errors in parentheses.
* $p < 0.1$, ** $p < 0.05$, *** $p < 0.01$.

the natural logarithm form of the credit loan amount to replace the total loan amount as a measure of BCE on the explanatory variable. Table 16.8 shows the influence of the new indicator of BCE (LnCL) on ESG, where columns 1 and 2 display the regression outcomes of the robustness test using the replaced explanatory variables. Column 1 reveals that the correlation coefficient of BCE in the first column is significant and positive (coefficient = 0.0418, *t*-stat = 0.0044) at the 1% confidence level. Similarly, column 2 also shows a significant positive correlation (coefficient = 0.0123, *t*-stat = 0.0049) at the 5% confidence interval level. The findings demonstrate that the impact of BCE on ESG remains statistically significant and positive, which aligns with the previous regression results. Moreover, all of the correlation coefficients of the control variables are at the 1%-10% confidence interval level, which is steady. Hence, we replace the measurement indicator of the independent variable, and the results after replacing provide evidence of the robustness of the analysis.

7.2 Alternative Measure of ESG

Additionally, we also use an alternative measure in the dependent variable ESG. Instead of directly using each company's annual ESG data, we measure the yearly ESG score by summing the quarterly scores and dividing by the number of quarters. Table 16.9 demonstrates the regression results of the robustness test after replacing the dependent variables. The correlation coefficient of BCE in column 1 is statistically significant positive (coefficient = 0.0719, *t*-stat = 0.0042) at the 1% confidence level, and column 2 also demonstrates a significantly positive correlation (coefficient = 0.0622, *t*-stat = 0.0059) at the 1% confidence interval level. These results align with the previous regression findings and confirm the robustness of the study. Furthermore, the correlation coefficients of the control variables remain stable and statistically significant with the range of 1%–10% confidence interval level. Thus, through the substitution of measurement indicators for the dependent variable, we confirm the reliability and consistency of the analysis.

7.3 State-Owned Enterprises vs. Non-State-Owned Enterprises

Besides, we use the enterprise property as a selection criterion to divide firms into state-owned enterprise (SOE) and non-SOE, then compare the effect of a firm's bank credit exposure on ESG performance. Column 1 shows the full sample number is 37,694. Among them, there are 8,357 firms that are SOEs, which are presented in column 2, and in column 3, 29,337 firms are non-SOEs. Table 16.10 demonstrates the regression results in three conditions: column 1 presents the entire sample, encompassing both SOEs and non- SOEs in the same regression model, and we find a significant and positive correlation (coefficient = 0.0382, *t*-stat = 0.0059), which is similar with previous outcomes; column 2 represents the SOE and the coefficient is positive (coefficient = 0.0366, *t*-stat = 0.0060); column 3 represents the non-SOE and the correlation relationship is significantly positive (coefficient = 0.0318, *t*-stat = 0.0084). Moreover, they are all significant at the 1% confidence level.

Table 16.9 Robustness Test: Alternative Measure of ESG

Variable	*Coeff. (t-stat)* *ESG*	*Coeff. (t-stat)* *ESG*
BCE	0.0719***	0.0622***
	(0.0042)	(0.0059)
Leverage		−0.0134
		(0.0402)
LnSize		0.6169***
		(0.0198)
ROA		0.1495**
		(0.0023)
PE Ratio		−0.0280***
		(0.0101)
CG		−0.6276***
		(0.0201)
Tax Burden		−0.1532***
		(0.0065)
BL Ratio		0.1135**
		(0.0693)
Inv Intensity		−0.0724***
		(0.0004)
IE Ratio		0.0652*
		(0.0392)
Year	Yes	Yes
Industry	Yes	Yes Yes
Constant	0.1255	0.1768
	(0.0889)	(0.2170)
N	37,694	37,694
Adj. *R2*	0.1284	0.1272

Source: Table by authors

Notes: This table presents the results of testing the effects of BCE on ESG with baseline models.Standard errors in parentheses.

* $p < 0.1$, ** $p < 0.05$, *** $p < 0.01$.

The results imply that both SOEs and non-SOEs show a significant positive influence of a company's BCE on its ESG performance. This finding aligns with previous results. However, the different nature of the enterprises introduce some variation in the regression coefficients. Specifically, the impact of BCE on ESG is larger for SOEs compared to SOEs. This difference can be attributed that SOEs may enjoy more advantages like having greater access to resources and support from the government, which allows them to implement ESG initiatives more effectively compared to non-SOEs. Overall, regardless of the nature of the enterprise, a firm's BCE indeed has a significant and positive effect on a firm's ESG performance. Hence, this observation further reinforces the reliability of the analysis.

Table 16.10 Robustness Test: Heterogeneity Regression Result (SOE vs. Non-SOE)

Variable	*Full Sample* *ESG*	*SOE* *ESG*	*Non-SOE* *ESG*
BCE	0.0382*** (0.0059)	0.0366*** (0.0060)	0.0318*** (0.0084)
Leverage	−0.0154 (0.0402)	−0.0806 (0.0569)	0.0436 (0.1640)
LnSize	0.6782*** (0.0198)	0.6776*** (0.0200)	−0.0106** (0.0287)
ROA	0.0053** (0.0023)	0.0052** (0.0023)	−0.0183 (0.0474)
PE Ratio	−0.0280*** (0.0101)	−0.0284*** (0.0101)	−0.0096** (0.0143)
CG	−0.6214*** (0.0201)	−0.6255*** (0.0202)	0.1061*** (0.0278)
Tax Burden	−0.0419*** (0.0065)	−0.0430*** (0.0065)	−0.0429*** (0.0091)
BL Ratio	0.1581** (0.0693)	0.1555** (0.0697)	-0.0164 (0.1017)
Inv Intensity	−0.0018*** (0.0004)	−0.0018*** (0.0004)	−0.0017*** (0.0005)
IE Ratio	0.0646* (0.0392)	0.1600*** (0.0595)	0.1293 (0.1637)
Year	Yes	Yes	
Industry	Yes	Yes	
Constant	0.2080** (0.1231)	−0.4555*** (0.0798)	−1.6181*** (0.3190)
N	37,694	8,357	29,337
Adj. R^2	0.1162	0.1451	0.1254

Source: Table by authors

Notes: The regression results of SOE firms and Non-SOE firms in China. The regression results of tests on the effect of firm nature on ESG and full samples.Standard errors in parentheses.

* $p < 0.1$, ** $p < 0.05$, *** $p < 0.01$.

7.4 Big Four vs. Non-Big Four

Furthermore, we divide firms into two categories by examining whether the company's auditor type is big four accounting firms, and then compare the influence of the company's bank credit exposure on its ESG performance. Column 1 presents the total sample size of 37,694 firms, among which there are 8,357 firms audited by Big Four accounting firms in column 2, and 29,337 firms are categorized as non-Big Four in column 3. Table 16.11 shows the regression results under three conditions: column 1 includes both big Four and non-Big Four in the same regression model, demonstrating a significant and positive correlation (coefficient = 0.0382, *t*-stat = 0.0059), consistent with previous findings. Column 2 focuses on Big Four companies, indicating a positive correlation (coefficient = 0.0379, *t*-stat = 0.0088), and column 3 with non-Big Four companies also reveals a significantly

Table 16.11 Robustness Test: Heterogeneity Regression Result (Big Four vs. Non-Big Four)

Variable	*Full Sample* *ESG*	*Big Four* *ESG*	*Non-Big Four* *ESG*
BCE	0.0382*** (0.0059)	0.0379*** (0.0088)	0.1053*** (0.0093)
Leverage	−0.0154 (0.0402)	0.0668 (0.1717)	0.0821 (0.0944)
LnSize	0.6782*** (0.0198)	−0.0293 (0.0298)	−0.0386 (0.0237)
ROA	0.0053** (0.0023)	−0.0261 (0.0496)	−0.0028 (0.0460)
PE Ratio	−0.0280*** (0.0101)	−0.0042 (0.0150)	−0.0198 (0.0122)
CG	-0.6214*** (0.0201)	0.1386*** (0.0287)	0.1043*** (0.0230)
Tax Burden	−0.0419*** (0.0065)	−0.0514*** (0.0094)	−0.0027 (0.0090)
BL Ratio	0.1581** (0.0693)	−0.0236 (0.1064)	0.0835 (0.0887)
Inv Intensity	−0.0018*** (0.0004)	−0.0022*** (0.0006)	−0.0020*** (0.0005)
IE Ratio	0.0646* (0.0392)	0.1638 (0.1713)	0.0154 (0.0817)
Year	Yes	Yes	Yes
Industry	Yes	Yes	Yes
Constant	0.2080** (0.1231)	1.2797*** (0.3276)	1.7323*** (0.2639)
N	37,694	9,541	28,153
Adj. R^2	0.1162	0.0315	0.1429

Source: Table by authors

Notes: The regression results of Big Four firms and non-Big Four firms in China. The regression results of tests on the effect of firm nature on ESG and full samples. Standard errors in parentheses.

* $p < 0.1$, ** $p < 0.05$, *** $p < 0.01$.

positive relationship (coefficient = 0.1053, *t*-stat = 0.0093). Moreover, all coefficients are statistically significant at the 1% confidence level.

These findings imply that both Big Four companies and non-Big Four companies exhibit a significant positive effect of a company's BCE on its ESG performance, which is similar to previous findings. However, the influence of a company's BCE on its ESG is more pronounced in Big Four companies compared to non-Big Four companies. This variation can be explained by the active participation of Big Four accounting firms in the development of ESG reporting frameworks and standards, which gives them a deep understanding of evolving regulatory requirements and industry best practices related to ESG reporting. Therefore, companies audited by Big Four firms may receive better guidance and support in meeting ESG reporting standards and disclosing their ESG

Table 16.12 Multicollinearity Test

Variable	*VIF*	*1/VIF*
Credit Loan	1.40	0.715
Leverage	2.29	0.437
LnSize	7.60	0.131
ROA	1.01	0.990
IE Ratio	2.30	0.434
Bank Loan Ratio	1.01	0.990
Inv Intensity	1.01	0.993
Total Loan	1.02	0.984
PE Ratio	1.01	0.990
Corporate Governance	8.09	0.123
Tax Burden	2.26	0.442
Auditor Type	1.02	0.982
Mean VIF	2.37	

performance. However, regardless of the firm's auditor type, BCE has remained a significant and positive impact on ESG performance. Hence, this observation further proves the credibility of the analysis.

7.5 Multicollinearity Test

Table 16.12 represents the variance inflation factor (VIF) information and 1/VIF (the tolerance level) to verify multicollinearity. If the maximum VIF is less than 10, the model is deemed to be free from multicollinearity concerns (Gao et al., 2020). The results in Table 16.12 suggest that each VIF value is less than 10, with the maximum VIF at 7.60 and the average VIF at 2.37. Thus, this suggests that there is no multicollinearity issue in the model and the results are reliable.

8. Discussion

8.1 Relationship with Previous Literature

This study investigates the impact of a company's BCE on ESG performance. Our findings indicate that companies with higher BCE exhibit higher levels of ESG performance. To the best of our knowledge, no prior studies have examined whether a firm's BCE positively or negatively influences ESG performance in Chinese listed firms. These finding challenges traditional expectations that higher BCE negatively affects ESG performance. For instance, previous studies have suggested that external financing negatively impacts ESG performance, arguing that companies dependent on external financing may prioritize short-term financial goals over long-term sustainability objectives (Inderst & Müller, 2003; Jebe, 2019; Kaminker & Stewart, 2012). However, our research offers a new perspective, positing that companies can leverage their bank financing connections to enhance their commitment to sustainable practices.

To some extent, our findings align with literature that recognizes the potential benefits of financial leverage and sustainable business practices. Financial leverage can provide businesses with the resources and incentives needed to invest in ESG projects, thereby improving overall sustainability performance (Rahman et al., 2021; He et al., 2021; Nega & Diala-Nettles, 2018). Additionally, banks, as creditors and stakeholders, along with regulatory institutions, can exert pressure on enterprises with higher BCE to demonstrate a stronger commitment to ESG practices (Habermann & Fischer, 2021; Herold, 2018; Lokuwaduge & Heenetigala, 2016; Singhania & Saini, 2021). Consequently, companies with higher BCE may invest resources in sustainable development to maintain access to financing and mitigate potential risks.

The findings build upon and extend previous literature by offering valuable insights into the association between a company's BCE and ESG performance. While prior studies have suggested a negative association between these variables, our study challenges conventional expectations by combining theoretical frameworks and presenting empirical evidence supporting a potential positive correlation between BCE and ESG performance. These findings imply that companies can leverage their financial relationships to enhance sustainability efforts, and banks as creditors can influence sustainable economic development. This broadens our understanding of the correlation between bank funding and sustainability, offering practical advice for businesses and regulatory institutions seeking to enhance sustainable development.

8.2 Theoretical Implications

Our finding that companies with higher BCE exhibit higher levels of ESG performance has several theoretical implications.

This finding challenges the traditional assumption that BCE negatively impacts ESG performance. Prior studies have focused on potential conflicts between financial goals and sustainability objectives, suggesting that reliance on external financing leads companies to prioritize short-term financial goals over long-term sustainability objectives (Inderst & Müller, 2003; Jebe, 2019; Kaminker & Stewart, 2012). Our research reveals that companies with BCE may be encouraged to prioritize sustainable practices due to pressure from banks and regulatory institutions.

According to agency and stakeholder theories, conflicts of interest can arise due to differing aims and information asymmetry (Lee & Isa, 2020). Our findings suggest that companies with a higher BCE may align their actions with the expectations of lenders and other stakeholders, demonstrating a commitment to ESG aspects to enhance their reputation and attract investors. This alignment can be motivated by the need to minimize potential financial risks and preserve access to financing. Thus, our study offers insights into how external financing affects a company's commitment to sustainable practices, providing a way to reduce agency concerns.

Institutional theory posits that organizations must conform to the rules and standards of their institutional environment to gain legitimacy (Zucker, 1987). Our findings advance understanding of how institutional influences from external sources, such as creditors, can impact a company's sustainability practices. By integrating financing strategies and ESG performance, we contribute to the literature on institutional theory.

Our findings suggest that firms can improve their ESG performance by adjusting their external financing strategies. This provides credibility to the argument that stakeholders, particularly lenders and regulatory institutions, can influence a company's sustainability initiatives, prompting businesses to strategically allocate resources to sustainable practices to meet stakeholder expectations.

8.3 Practical Implications

The present findings have significant implications for companies, banks, investors, and regulators. These implications can guide decision-making and actions in promoting sustainable practices in the following ways. Companies, should understand and take advantage of the beneficial effects of bank credit exposure on ESG performance by integrating ESG considerations into decision-making, developing comprehensive ESG reporting systems, and aligning sustainability goals with stakeholder expectations. Lenders can incorporate ESG considerations into their lending criteria, investigate ESG indicators, and develop sustainable finance products to stimulate companies to improve their ESG performance. Investors should consider ESG performance when choosing investments, interact with companies to encourage more advancements, and demand transparency in ESG disclosures. Regulators, should consider the positive association between bank credit exposure and ESG performance in regulations, promote standardized ESG reporting frameworks, and collaborate with financial institutions to develop guidelines for incorporating ESG factors into lending practices. Additionally, our findings show that in the context of China, firms with higher BCE will exhibit higher ESG performance. These findings not only inform the above practitioners but also policymakers. Besides, the results based on Chinese listed companies may also be applicable to other developing countries possessing similar political, economic, and legal backgrounds to China. These practical implications emphasize the significance of integrating ESG performance into business strategies, decision-making, and reporting, as well as the role of stakeholders in promoting and rewarding companies' sustainable practices. This finding may prove useful for companies, lenders, investors, and regulatory bodies to develop sustainable business practices and create positive environmental, social, and governance outcomes.

9. Conclusion

This study examined whether firms with higher BCE have higher ESG performance or lower ESG performance. We analyse a sample dataset consisting of firm-year observations from the Huazheng database and the CSMAR database. The dataset covers the period from 2012 to 2022 and includes information from 26,934 observations of 2,693 Chinese listed companies in the Shanghai and Shenzhen stock markets. The fixed-effect model is used to analyse how a firm's BCE affects its ESG performance, and we also use several endogeneity tests and robustness tests to secure the credibility of the results. The findings demonstrate a positive relationship between the firm's BCE and ESG performance. Firms with higher BCE will exhibit higher ESG performance compared with firms with lower BCE.

The findings makes numerous contributions to the literature on a firm's bank credit exposure and ESG performance. Firstly, this study combines the two research streams by investigating the potential impact of a company's BCE on ESG performance. Secondly, based on our current understanding and available information, no prior study has examined the relationship of a company's BCE on ESG performance in China. Thirdly, this study also focuses on the specific effect of two classification firms in the robustness tests, the first classification is stated-own enterprise and non-stated-own enterprise, considering whether SOE with higher BCE will exhibit higher or lower ESG performance compared with non-SOE. The second classification is Big Four and non-Big Four, considering whether Big Four with higher BCE will exhibit higher or lower ESG performance in contrast to non-Big Four.

We also recognize several limitations in our analysis. Firstly, this study is based on the background of China, we use data from CSMAR and Chinese-listed companies in the Shanghai and Shenzhen stock markets. China is a developing country, and its political, economic, and legal background may differ from other countries or regions. Therefore, the findings may not directly apply to other countries or regions. Future research endeavours may focus on addressing these limitations to enhance the generalizability of the study's findings by considering other data from both different background countries or regions like developed countries and emerging economies, considering cross-country studies and specific industry studies, conditions permitting.

Second, we use alternative proxies as a measure of firms' BCE. Although we use multiple indirect indicators like total loan amounts (logarithm form) and credit loan amounts (logarithm form), this cannot be a comprehensive indicator to measure firms' BCE. They cannot sufficiently explain firms' BCE. Also, the additional noise may not be processed well due to limited available data. To some extent, these limitations may weaken our inference. Hence, in future research, we will take more proxy indicators to comprehensively measure the firms' BCE and process more relevant control variables to reduce the influence of extraneous noise during the research.

Finally, this study focuses on the direct association between a company's BCE and ESG performance, lacking consideration for mediating factors that can influence the relationship between them. For instance, varying levels of environmental, social, and governance concerns across industries, as well as firm-specific factors like size, ownership structure, and financial health, can influence this relationship (Borenstein et al., 2010; Marco, 1992). Future research is recommended to investigate the moderating impacts of industry and firm-specific factors on the correlation between BCE and ESG performance. This will clarify the conditions that strengthen or weaken this relationship.

References

Adcock, C., Ye, C., Yin, S., & Zhang, D. (2023). Are Chinese B-shares dead? An analysis of price limits on AB-shares on the Shanghai and Shenzhen stock exchanges. *International Review of Economics & Finance*, *85*(85), 306–315.

Amel-Zadeh, A., & Serafeim, G. (2017). Why and how investors use ESG information: Evidence from a global survey. *SSRN Electronic Journal*, *74*(3).

Anderson, R. B. (1960). Financial policies for sustainable growth. *The Journal of Finance*, *15*(2), 127.

Argandoña, A. (2011). Stakeholder theory and value creation. *SSRN Electronic Journal*. https://papers.ssrn.com/sol3/papers.cfm?abstract_id=1947317

Bassey Edem, D. (2017). Liquidity management and performance of deposit money banks in Nigeria (1986–2011): An investigation. *International Journal of Economics, Finance and Management Sciences*, *5*(3), 146.

Bondt, W. F. M. D., & Thaler, R. (1985). Does the stock market overreact? *The Journal of Finance*, *40*(3), 793.

Borenstein, M., Hedges, L. V., Higgins, J. P. T., & Rothstein, H. R. (2010). A basic introduction to fixed-effect and random-effects models for meta-analysis. *Research Synthesis Methods*, *1*(2), 97–111.

Cahan, S., Lam, B. M., Li, L. Z., & Rahman, M. J. (2021). Information environment and stock price synchronicity: Evidence from auditor characteristics. *International Journal of Auditing*, *25*(2).

Chang, K., Cheng, X., Wang, Y., Liu, Q., & Hu, J. (2021). The impacts of ESG performance and digital finance on corporate financing efficiency in China. *Applied Economics Letters*, *30*(4), 1–8.

Chang, X., Fu, K., Li, T., Tam, L., & Wong, G. (2018). Corporate environmental liabilities and capital structure. *SSRN Electronic Journal*. https://papers.ssrn.com/sol3/papers.cfm?abstract_id=3200991

Danielson, M. G., & Scott, J. A. (2004). Bank loan availability and trade credit demand. *The Financial Review*, *39*(4), 579–600.

Dawar, V. (2014). Agency theory, capital structure and firm performance: Some Indian evidence. *Managerial Finance*, *40*(12), 1190–1206.

DeMaris, A. (2014). Combating unmeasured confounding in cross-sectional studies: Evaluating instrumental-variable and Heckman selection models. *Psychological Methods*, *19*(3), 380.

Del Giudice, A., & Rigamonti, S. (2020). Does audit improve the quality of ESG scores? Evidence from corporate misconduct. *Sustainability*, *12*(14), 5670.

Donaldson, T., & Preston, L. E. (1995). The stakeholder theory of the corporation: Concepts, evidence, and implications. *The Academy of Management Review*, *20*(1), 65–91.

Eisenhardt, K. M. (1989). Agency theory: An assessment and review. *The Academy of Management Review*, *14*(1), 57–74.

Friede, G., Busch, T., & Bassen, A. (2015). ESG and financial performance: Aggregated evidence from more than 2000 empirical studies. *Journal of Sustainable Finance & Investment*, *5*(4), 210–233.

Gao, R., Huang, S., & Wang, R. (2020). Data analytics and audit quality. *SSRN Electronic Journal*. https://papers.ssrn.com/sol3/papers.cfm?abstract_id=3928355

Geng, R., Bose, I., & Chen, X. (2015). Prediction of financial distress: An empirical study of listed Chinese companies using data mining. *European Journal of Operational Research*, *241*(1), 236–247.

Gerard, B. (2019). ESG and socially responsible investment: A critical review. *Beta*, *33*(1), 61–83.

Giese, G., Lee, L.-E., Melas, D., Nagy, Z., & Nishikawa, L. (2019). Foundations of ESG investing: How ESG affects equity valuation, risk, and performance. *The Journal of Portfolio Management*, *45*(5), 69–83.

Habermann, F., & Fischer, F. B. (2021). Corporate social performance and the likelihood of bankruptcy: Evidence from a period of economic upswing. *Journal of Business Ethics*, *182*(1).

He, F., Du, H., & Yu, B. (2022). Corporate ESG performance and manager misconduct: Evidence from China. *International Review of Financial Analysis*, *82*, 102201.

He, R., Chen, X., Chen, C., Zhai, J., & Cui, L. (2021). Environmental, social, and governance incidents and bank loan contracts. *Sustainability*, *13*(4), 1885. https://doi.org/10.3390/su13041885

He, W., & Hu, M. (Rong). (2016). Religion and bank loan terms. *Journal of Banking & Finance*, *64*(64), 205–215.

Herbohn, K., Gao, R., & Clarkson, P. (2017). Evidence on whether banks consider carbon risk in their lending decisions. *Journal of Business Ethics*, *158*(1), 155–175.

Herold, D. (2018). Demystifying the link between institutional theory and stakeholder theory in sustainability reporting. *Economics, Management and Sustainability*, *3*(2), 6–19.

Ho, S., Jiang, L. J., & Kim, J. H. (2001). Shareholdings by financial institutions, information asymmetry and the intertemporal return-earnings relation in Japan. *Asia-Pacific Financial Markets*, *8*(2), 119–135.

Huberman, G. (1984). External financing and liquidity. *The Journal of Finance*, *39*(3), 895–908.

Inderst, R., & Müller, H. M. (2003). Internal versus external financing: An optimal contracting approach*. *The Journal of Finance*, *58*(3), 1033–1062.

Jebe, R. (2019). The convergence of financial and ESG materiality: Taking sustainability mainstream. *SSRN Electronic Journal*. https://doi.org/10.2139/ssrn.3730792

Kaminker, C., & Stewart, F. (2012). *The role of institutional investors in financing clean energy*. OECD Working Papers on Finance, Insurance and Private Pensions No. 23. OECD.

Korinth, F., & Lueg, R. (2022). Corporate sustainability and risk management – the U-shaped relationships of disaggregated ESG rating scores and risk in the German capital market. *Sustainability*, *14*(9), 5735.

Lavin, J. F., & Montecinos-Pearce, A. A. (2021). ESG disclosure in an emerging market: An empirical analysis of the influence of board characteristics and ownership structure. *Sustainability*, *13*(19), 10498.

Lee, S. P., & Isa, M. (2020). Environmental, social and governance (ESG) practices and performance in Shariah firms: Agency or stakeholder theory? *Asian Academy of Management Journal of Accounting and Finance*, *16*(1), 1–34.

Lokuwaduge, C. S. D. S., & Heenetigala, K. (2016). Integrating environmental, social and governance (ESG) disclosure for a sustainable development: An Australian study. *Business Strategy and the Environment*, *26*(4), 438–450.

Marco, P. (1992). Financial markets and growth: An overview. *European Economic Review*, *37*(2–3), 613–622.

Nega, F., Dr., & Diala-Nettles, I., Dr. (2018). Examining financial performance, firm size, leverage and corporate social responsibility. *International Journal of Computer Applications Technology and Research*, *7*(2), 78–85.

Pagano, M. (1993). Financial markets and growth: An overview. *European Economic Review*, *37*(2–3), 613–622.

Rahman, M. J., Jia, L., & Sultana, R. (2021). Business strategy and systematic risk: Evidence from China. *Journal of Corporate Accounting & Finance*, *32*(4), 99–117.

Rahman, M. J., & Wu, J. (2023). M&A activity and ESG performance: Evidence from China. *Managerial Finance*, *50*(1), 179–197.

Rahman, M. J., Wu, Q., & Zhu, H. (2024). Corporate social responsibility in times of social distancing: Evidence from China. *Business Ethics, the Environment & Responsibility*.

Rahman, M. J., Zhu, H., & Chen, S. (2023). Does CSR reduce financial distress? Moderating effect of firm characteristics, auditor characteristics, and covid-19. *International Journal of Accounting & Information Management*, *31*(5), 756–784.

Rahman, M. J., Zhu, H., & Jiang, X. (2024). Family firms, client importance, and auditor reporting behavior: Evidence from China. *Meditari Accountancy Research, 32*(2), 543–578.
Singhania, M., & Saini, N. (2021). Quantification of ESG regulations: A cross-country benchmarking analysis. *Vision: The Journal of Business Perspective, 26*(2), https://doi.org/10.1177/09722629211054173
Tang, H. (2022). The effect of ESG performance on corporate innovation in China: The mediating role of financial constraints and agency cost. *Sustainability, 14*(7), 3769.
Tarmuji, I., Maelah, R., & Tarmuji, N. H. (2016). The impact of environmental, social and governance practices (ESG) on economic performance: Evidence from ESG score. *International Journal of Trade, Economics and Finance, 7*(3), 67–74.
Thaler, J. S., Stout, M. J., Karban, R., & Duffey, S. S. (2001). Jasmonate-mediated induced plant resistance affects a community of herbivores. *Ecological Entomology, 26*(3), 312–324.
Van Duuren, E., Plantinga, A., & Scholtens, B. (2015). ESG integration and the investment management process: Fundamental investing reinvented. *Journal of Business Ethics, 138*(3), 525–533.
Wang, F., & Sun, Z. (2022). Does the environmental regulation intensity and ESG performance have a substitution effect on the impact of enterprise green innovation: Evidence from China. *International Journal of Environmental Research and Public Health, 19*(14), 8558.
Wooldridge, J. M. (2023). Simple approaches to nonlinear difference-in-differences with panel data. *The Econometrics Journal, 26*(3), C31–C66.
Yan, Y., Cheng, Q., Huang, M., Lin, Q., & Lin, W. (2022). Government environmental regulation and corporate ESG performance: Evidence from natural resource accountability audits in China. *International Journal of Environmental Research and Public Health, 20*(1), 447.
Yoon, B., Lee, J.-H., & Cho, J.-H. (2021). The effect of ESG performance on tax avoidance – evidence from Korea. *Sustainability, 13*(12), 6729.
Zhu, H., & Rahman, M. J. (2024). Ex-ante expected changes in ESG and future stock returns based on machine learning. *The British Accounting Review*, 101457.
Zucker, L. G. (1987). Institutional theories of organization. *Annual Review of Sociology, 13*(1), 443–464.

17 Integrating ESG Accounting with Performance Measurement, Risk Management, and Climate Change

Tarek Rana, Md Jahidur Rahman, and Peter Öhman

1. Introduction

The integration of environmental, social, and governance (ESG) accounting with performance measurement, risk management, and climate change has emerged as a pivotal area of interest within accounting research. This integration addresses the increasing demand for comprehensive corporate reporting that transcends traditional financial metrics, incorporating non-financial dimensions that reflect a company's sustainability and ethical impact. The evolving landscape of corporate accountability necessitates a robust understanding of how ESG factors influence and are influenced by performance metrics, risk management frameworks, and climate-related considerations.

The need for integrating ESG considerations into corporate strategies is underscored by the growing body of evidence linking ESG performance with financial outcomes. Eccles et al. (2014) demonstrated that companies with high sustainability standards outperform their peers in financial markets. This finding aligns with the broader trend of investors incorporating ESG criteria into their investment decisions, thereby exerting pressure on companies to enhance their ESG disclosures and performance. The role of accounting in this context is crucial, as it provides the necessary frameworks and standards for consistent and comparable ESG reporting (Bebbington et al., 2014).

Performance measurement systems have traditionally focused on financial indicators such as revenue, profit margins, and return on investment. However, the integration of ESG metrics into these systems reflects a more comprehensive approach to assessing corporate performance. Adams and McNicholas (2007) argued that incorporating ESG factors into performance measurement not only provides a more holistic view of a company's impact but also drives behaviour change towards sustainable practices. This shift is evident in the adoption of sustainability balanced scorecards and other integrated reporting tools that align financial and non-financial performance indicators (Gond et al., 2012).

Risk management is another critical area where ESG integration plays a significant role. ESG-related risks, such as those associated with climate change, labour practices, and corporate governance, can have profound implications for a company's operational and financial stability. Khan et al. (2016) highlighted the

DOI: 10.4324/9781003488934-22

materiality of ESG factors, noting that companies that effectively manage these risks tend to experience lower costs of capital and better financial performance. This underscores the importance of incorporating ESG considerations into risk management frameworks to enhance corporate resilience and mitigate potential adverse impacts.

Climate change, as a central element of the environmental dimension of ESG, presents both risks and opportunities for businesses. The Paris Agreement and subsequent regulatory developments have intensified the focus on reducing greenhouse gas emissions and transitioning to a low-carbon economy (IPCC, 2018). Companies are increasingly required to disclose their climate-related risks and strategies, as evidenced by the recommendations of the Task Force on Climate-related Financial Disclosures (TCFD, 2017). These disclosures are crucial for investors and other stakeholders to assess a company's exposure to climate risks and its preparedness for the transition to a sustainable future (Financial Stability Board, 2017).

The empirical link between ESG performance and financial performance has been extensively studied, with mixed results depending on the context and methodologies employed. Friede et al. (2015) conducted a comprehensive meta-analysis of over 2,000 empirical studies, finding a generally positive relationship between ESG and financial performance. This relationship suggests that companies that prioritize ESG factors may enjoy competitive advantages such as enhanced reputation, operational efficiencies, and access to capital. However, the strength and direction of this relationship can vary based on industry, geographic region, and specific ESG dimensions (Clark et al., 2015).

The role of accounting in promoting the integration of ESG factors into corporate practices cannot be overstated. Accounting standards and frameworks, such as those developed by the Global Reporting Initiative (GRI) and the Sustainability Accounting Standards Board (SASB), provide the necessary guidelines for ESG reporting (GRI, 2020; SASB, 2018). These frameworks facilitate the disclosure of relevant ESG information, enabling stakeholders to make informed decisions and hold companies accountable for their sustainability practices. Moreover, the ongoing efforts to harmonize global ESG reporting standards, such as the initiative by the International Financial Reporting Standards (IFRS) Foundation to establish a sustainability standards board, highlight the importance of consistent and comparable ESG reporting (IFRS, 2020).

The integration of ESG accounting with performance measurement and risk management also has significant implications for corporate governance. Effective governance structures that incorporate ESG considerations can enhance accountability and transparency, fostering trust among stakeholders (Eccles & Youmans, 2015). Boards of directors play a critical role in overseeing ESG integration, ensuring that the company's strategies align with its sustainability goals and risk management frameworks (Lins et al., 2017). Furthermore, linking executive compensation to ESG performance metrics can incentivize management to prioritize sustainable practices, aligning their interests with long-term value creation (Edmans et al., 2009).

Despite the advancements in integrating ESG accounting with performance measurement, risk management, and climate change, several challenges remain. One major challenge is the lack of standardized metrics and methodologies for measuring and reporting ESG performance. The diversity of ESG reporting frameworks and the absence of a unified standard complicate the comparability of ESG data across companies and industries (Hahn & Kühnen, 2013). Addressing this challenge requires collaboration among standard-setting bodies, regulators, and industry stakeholders to develop harmonized reporting standards.

Another challenge is the need for robust data and analytical tools to assess ESG performance and risks accurately. The availability and quality of ESG data vary significantly, posing challenges for investors and other stakeholders in making informed decisions (Cheng et al., 2014). Advances in technology, such as big data analytics and artificial intelligence, hold promise for improving the collection, analysis, and reporting of ESG data, enabling more accurate and timely assessments (Deloitte, 2020).

Moreover, the dynamic nature of ESG risks, particularly climate-related risks, necessitates continuous monitoring and adaptation of risk management processes. Climate change presents long-term and evolving risks that require forward-looking approaches to risk management (Linnenluecke et al., 2012). Scenario analysis and stress testing are essential tools for assessing the potential impacts of climate change on business operations and financial performance, allowing companies to develop resilient strategies (TCFD, 2017). Thus, the integration of ESG accounting with performance measurement, risk management, and climate change represents a transformative shift in corporate reporting and strategy. The increasing recognition of the financial and strategic importance of ESG factors underscores the need for comprehensive and consistent reporting frameworks that enable stakeholders to assess corporate performance holistically. Despite the challenges, advancements in technology, regulatory initiatives, and collaborative efforts among stakeholders hold promise for overcoming these obstacles. As companies continue to integrate ESG considerations into their performance measurement and risk management processes, they can enhance their resilience, create long-term value, and contribute to sustainable development.

2. Background

The integration of ESG accounting with performance measurement, risk management, and climate change has garnered significant scholarly attention in recent years. This comprehensive review synthesizes the current state of research within these intersecting domains, drawing from accounting literature to elucidate the complex dynamics at play.

The emergence of ESG accounting as a critical component of corporate reporting reflects an increasing awareness of the broader impacts of business activities. ESG accounting encompasses the disclosure of non-financial information related to ESG factors, aimed at providing stakeholders with a holistic view of a company's performance and sustainability practices (KPMG, 2020). The integration of ESG factors into performance measurement systems has become essential as stakeholders demand greater transparency and accountability from corporations.

Performance measurement, traditionally focused on financial metrics, is evolving to include ESG indicators, reflecting a shift towards more comprehensive assessments of corporate performance. Eccles et al. (2014) highlight the importance of integrating ESG metrics into performance measurement frameworks to align corporate strategies with sustainable development goals. This integration not only enhances the relevance of performance assessments but also drives corporate behaviour towards long-term value creation.

The linkage between ESG accounting and risk management is pivotal, given the increasing recognition of ESG-related risks. These risks, encompassing ESG dimensions, can significantly impact a company's financial performance and operational stability (Khan et al., 2016). Incorporating ESG factors into risk management processes allows companies to identify and mitigate potential risks, thereby enhancing their resilience and sustainability. For instance, environmental risks related to climate change, such as regulatory changes and physical impacts, can pose substantial threats to business operations and financial stability (Bebbington & Larrinaga, 2014).

Climate change, as a critical aspect of the environmental dimension of ESG, presents multifaceted risks and opportunities for businesses. The Paris Agreement and subsequent regulatory frameworks have intensified the pressure on companies to reduce their carbon footprints and transition towards more sustainable practices (IPCC, 2018). Integrating climate-related metrics into ESG accounting and performance measurement systems enables companies to track their progress in mitigating climate risks and capitalizing on opportunities arising from the transition to a low-carbon economy (TCFD, 2017). The TCFD has provided a robust framework for companies to disclose climate-related financial risks, emphasizing the need for transparent and comparable reporting (TCFD, 2017).

Empirical studies underscore the financial implications of integrating ESG factors into corporate strategies. Friede et al. (2015) conducted a meta-analysis of over 2,000 empirical studies and found a positive correlation between ESG performance and financial performance. This relationship underscores the strategic importance of ESG integration, as companies that effectively manage ESG risks and opportunities tend to exhibit superior financial performance. Similarly, Flammer (2015) demonstrated that corporate initiatives aimed at improving environmental performance led to enhanced financial outcomes, reinforcing the business case for integrating ESG considerations into corporate strategies.

The role of accounting in facilitating the integration of ESG factors into performance measurement and risk management is crucial. Accounting standards and frameworks, such as the GRI and the SASB, provide guidelines for ESG reporting, promoting consistency and comparability (GRI, 2020; SASB, 2018). These frameworks enable companies to disclose relevant ESG information, which can be integrated into performance measurement systems and used for risk management purposes. Moreover, the IFRS Foundation's initiative to establish a sustainability standards board signifies a significant step towards global harmonization of ESG reporting (IFRS, 2020).

The integration of ESG accounting with performance measurement and risk management also aligns with broader corporate governance principles. Effective governance structures that incorporate ESG considerations enhance accountability and transparency, fostering trust among stakeholders (Eccles & Youmans, 2015). Boards of directors play a crucial role in overseeing ESG integration, ensuring that ESG risks and opportunities are adequately addressed within the corporate strategy (Lins et al., 2017). Furthermore, linking executive compensation to ESG performance metrics can incentivize management to prioritize sustainable practices, aligning their interests with long-term value creation (Edmans et al., 2009).

Despite the growing recognition of the importance of integrating ESG accounting with performance measurement, risk management, and climate change, several challenges persist. One significant challenge is the lack of standardized metrics and methodologies for measuring and reporting ESG performance. The diversity of ESG reporting frameworks and the absence of a unified standard complicate the comparability of ESG data across companies and industries (Hahn & Kühnen, 2013). Addressing this challenge requires collaboration among standard-setting bodies, regulators, and industry stakeholders to develop harmonized reporting standards.

Another challenge is the need for robust data and analytical tools to assess ESG performance and risks accurately. The availability and quality of ESG data vary significantly, posing challenges for investors and other stakeholders in making informed decisions (Cheng et al., 2014). Advances in technology, such as big data analytics and artificial intelligence, hold promise for improving the collection, analysis, and reporting of ESG data, enabling more accurate and timely assessments (Deloitte, 2020).

Moreover, the dynamic nature of ESG risks, particularly climate-related risks, necessitates continuous monitoring and adaptation of risk management processes. Climate change presents long-term and evolving risks that require forward-looking approaches to risk management (Linnenluecke et al., 2012). Scenario analysis and stress testing are essential tools for assessing the potential impacts of climate change on business operations and financial performance, allowing companies to develop resilient strategies (TCFD, 2017).

The integration of ESG accounting with performance measurement, risk management, and climate change also has implications for regulatory and policy frameworks. Governments and regulatory bodies play a critical role in promoting ESG integration through the establishment of regulatory requirements and incentives (UNPRI, 2018). Policy initiatives, such as mandatory ESG disclosures and carbon pricing mechanisms, can drive corporate behaviour towards sustainability and enhance the accountability of businesses in addressing ESG issues (OECD, 2019).

To this end, the integration of ESG accounting with performance measurement, risk management, and climate change represents a transformative shift in corporate reporting and strategy. The increasing recognition of the financial and strategic importance of ESG factors underscores the need for comprehensive and consistent reporting frameworks that enable stakeholders to assess corporate performance holistically. Despite the challenges, advancements in technology, regulatory initiatives, and collaborative efforts among stakeholders hold promise for overcoming these obstacles. As companies continue to integrate ESG considerations into their performance measurement and risk management processes, they can enhance their resilience, create long-term value, and contribute to sustainable development.

3. Emerging Themes

3.1 ESG Accounting and Risk Management

Risk management in the corporate sector involves identifying, assessing, and mitigating risks associated with ESG factors. Corporations face various risks, including financial, operational, reputational, legal, and strategic risks related to their ESG activities. Effective risk management is essential to ensure that companies can achieve their sustainability goals and deliver value to their stakeholders while minimizing potential negative outcomes. This involves identifying potential ESG risks that might arise from corporate policies, programmes, or operations. Such risks include regulatory compliance, stakeholder satisfaction, or operational efficiency.

Once ESG risks are identified, they need to be assessed in terms of their potential impact and likelihood of occurring. This assists companies in prioritizing their risk management efforts and allocating resources effectively. It involves implementing strategies to reduce the likelihood of risks occurring or minimizing their impact if they do occur. For instance, companies might implement compliance monitoring processes, develop contingency plans, or implement internal controls. After implementing risk mitigation strategies, it is important to use management control systems (MCS) to monitor the effectiveness of these strategies and to detect any new risks that might arise. This enables companies to adjust their risk management strategies as needed.

The need for a scientific foundation for corporate risk management is emphasized, arguing that a rigorous and evidence-based approach is essential for effective ESG risk management. Companies should adopt a systematic approach to ESG risk management involving the development of risk management policies and procedures, establishing risk management teams, and using risk management tools and techniques. The importance of risk management in the corporate sector is also highlighted by the work of various scholars who argue that risk management enables companies to identify, assess, and manage ESG risks effectively while enhancing transparency and accountability in decision-making processes. This is particularly relevant in today's heightened public scrutiny.

Risk management should be an integral part of the governance process, involving a systematic and structured approach to identifying and managing ESG risks. Effective ESG risk management requires a holistic approach involving identifying potential risks, assessing their likelihood and potential impact, and developing and implementing strategies to mitigate or manage them. Empirical evidence highlights the benefits of a proactive and strategic approach to ESG risk management, suggesting that effective risk management can improve organizational performance, enhance stakeholder trust, and reduce reputational risk.

Recent global events, notably the COVID-19 pandemic, have intensified the interest in understanding risks and risk management practices. Today's supply chains are more dynamic, complex, and international, and inevitably more susceptible to the risk of failure in times of global disruption. Contemporary corporations operate in an environment where global events such as trade disputes, political relations, and natural disasters are more frequent. During the COVID-19 pandemic, companies across various industries experienced severe disruption of supply chains in many essential areas, including food, agriculture, education, health, and medical products. Geopolitical uncertainties highlight the importance of further research into technology, management control, and supply chain risks.

Thus, risk management in the corporate sector is essential to ensure that organizations can achieve their goals and effectively deliver value to their stakeholders while minimizing the potential for dysfunctional outcomes. This involves identifying, assessing, and mitigating risks through risk management strategies and contingency planning, and communicating effectively with stakeholders about the risks involved. This leads to examining how effectively companies understand, assess, manage, and govern risks in their supply chains and how emerging technologies, such as data analytics, can enhance MCS. This applies particularly to the operation of cultural and technical controls, enabling risk management of overall supply chain operations.

This chapter, therefore, discusses the benefits and challenges of using MCS for supply chain risk management in the corporate sector, aiming to develop a framework that integrates MCS and resilience for supply chain risk management. This involves analysing chapters of this book, focusing on how companies can use MCS and resilience as a framework for supply chain risk management. In addition, it proposes how companies can embed integrated MCS and risk management in their governance and accountability practices and how emerging technologies can play a role in this. Furthermore, it explores how technology-enabled MCS can be used to manage such risks. Ultimately, this chapter identifies emerging themes and offers future research directions.

3.2 ESG Accounting, MCS, and Supply Chain Management

This theme focuses on the role of MCS in managing supply chain risks within the context of ESG accounting. Supply chain risk management refers to identifying, assessing, and mitigating risks in a supply chain network, encompassing risks associated with sourcing raw materials, manufacturing products, transporting goods, and delivering products or services to customers. Effective supply chain risk management ensures that companies can maintain operations and deliver products or services to their customers even when disruptions occur. The corporate sector increasingly relies on complex and dynamic supply chains to deliver goods and services, making them vulnerable to a range of risks that can impact their ability to operate effectively. The COVID-19 pandemic has highlighted the critical need for effective risk management in supply chains, particularly in sectors such as healthcare, where shortages of essential supplies had significant impacts on service delivery. This underscores the importance of integrating supply chain risk management into ESG accounting practices.

MCS play an important role in identifying and managing risks in the corporate sector. They are designed to assist managers in making informed decisions based on information about the risks involved in their operations and to ensure that these risks are appropriately monitored and managed. In the context of supply chain management, MCS can help companies identify and manage risks that arise from their relationships with suppliers, customers, and other stakeholders. Prior studies have identified crucial MCS components essential to ensuring supply chains' operational performance during crises, including risk management, collaboration, communication, and performance measurement. Effective MCS can ensure the resilience of supply chains during crises, and companies must invest in these mechanisms to respond effectively to future disruptions. This includes managing risks related to quality, delivery, pricing, and geopolitical, economic, and social factors.

One way that MCS can help manage supply chain risks is by providing real-time information about the status of the supply chain. For instance, a system that tracks inventory levels and delivery times can alert managers to potential disruptions before they occur. Similarly, a system that monitors supplier performance can help identify potential quality issues before they become problematic. Information technology (IT) systems provide real-time visibility into the supply chain, enabling managers to identify and respond to potential risks quickly. In this case, an online dashboard that tracks inventory levels, order volumes, and delivery times can help managers quickly identify potential supply chain disruptions and take proactive measures to mitigate them.

While there is a burgeoning literature in the private sector on risk management and its interrelatedness with MCS practices, our knowledge of MCS practices for supply chain risk management in the corporate sector is still developing. Prior research highlights how particular moral ideals have provided a rationale for risk-related reforms while also critically engaging with policy initiatives aimed at transforming risk management. Comparative analyses of the adoption of risk management structures across different contexts and the prescription of practices that can ensure effective risk management have been explored. Effective supply chain risk management is essential for the success of companies, and it should be integrated into the overall supply chain management process, involving a structured and systematic approach to identifying and managing risks.

Effective risk management requires a collaborative approach involving the engagement of stakeholders across the supply chain. A proactive and strategic approach to supply chain risk management involves identifying potential risks, assessing their likelihood and potential impact, and developing and implementing strategies to mitigate or manage these risks. Various tools and techniques, including risk mapping, scenario planning, and supplier risk assessments, are essential for effective supply chain risk management. Empirical evidence highlights the benefits of a proactive and strategic approach, suggesting that effective supply chain risk management can improve supply chain performance, enhance stakeholder trust, and reduce reputational risk.

The COVID-19 pandemic has highlighted the importance of crisis scenario planning in the corporate sector. The pandemic caused unprecedented disruption to operations, forcing companies to adapt to new working conditions and changing demands rapidly. In response, many companies have likely engaged in crisis scenario planning designed to stress test their ability to manage disruptions and evaluate the impact of current threats identified in risk assessments. The pandemic has also highlighted the importance of risk assessments, with many organizations identifying the risks associated with global crises in their risk assessments prior to the outbreak. However, there is an inadequate understanding of corporate processes to identify, assess, and manage supply chain risk and how MCS may be implicated in these processes.

There is a need for further research to explore the role of data analytics in enhancing MCS for supply chain risk management. Data analytics can provide valuable insights into supply chain performance and risk factors, enabling companies to make more informed decisions. By leveraging data analytics, companies can enhance their ability to identify and manage supply chain risks more effectively, improve supply chain resilience, and enhance overall performance and accountability.

Supply chain risk management is a critical aspect of ESG accounting, as it ensures that companies can maintain operations and deliver products or services to their customers even in the face of disruptions. MCS play a crucial role in managing supply chain risks by providing real-time information, enabling proactive risk management, and facilitating collaboration across the supply chain. The COVID-19 pandemic has underscored the importance of effective supply chain risk management and crisis scenario planning. By integrating data analytics into MCS, companies can enhance their ability to manage supply chain risks, improve resilience, and achieve their sustainability goals. Future research should focus on the implications of MCS in supply chain risk management, exploring how emerging technologies can enhance risk management practices and contribute to the overall effectiveness of ESG accounting.

3.3 Climate Change Risk Management in the Context of ESG Accounting

Climate change presents significant challenges for risk management as its effects can be both pervasive and unpredictable, impacting ecosystems, biodiversity, and human well-being. In the corporate sector, climate change risk management has become increasingly important as the impacts of global warming intensify and the need for effective action becomes more urgent. However, the COVID-19 pandemic has created additional challenges for climate change risk management, as companies struggle to balance the need for climate action with the immediate demands of the pandemic. Both COVID-19 and climate change are global crises that significantly impact human health and well-being, with COVID-19 causing widespread illness and economic disruption, while climate change leads to extreme weather events, rising sea levels, and biodiversity loss. While fundamentally different, these issues can be managed more effectively through the integration of ESG accounting and MCS.

One key role of MCS in managing climate change risks is to enable companies to identify and assess these risks comprehensively. Effective risk identification and assessment require a holistic approach that includes the identification of climate change risks, assessment of their potential impacts, and development of strategies to mitigate them. MCS provide a framework for risk identification and assessment, along with tools for data analysis and modelling. Effective monitoring and reporting are also critical roles of MCS in managing climate change risks. This requires the development of appropriate performance metrics and the implementation of controls to ensure the accuracy and reliability of financial and non-financial data.

MCS help companies identify and assess climate change risks by providing a structured approach to risk identification and assessment. This includes tools for data analysis and modelling that allow companies to evaluate the potential impacts of climate change risks on their operations and develop strategies to mitigate these risks. Effective monitoring and reporting are also essential components of MCS, enabling companies to track their performance in managing climate change risks and ensure the accuracy and reliability of their data.

MCS facilitate the development of performance metrics and reporting frameworks that help companies monitor and report on their climate change risks. By implementing controls to ensure data accuracy and reliability, companies can enhance their ability to manage climate change risks effectively and demonstrate their commitment to sustainability.

Climate change presents a range of risks to companies, including physical risks, such as damage to infrastructure from extreme weather events, and transition risks, such as changes in policies and regulations that affect corporate performance. Climate change is a complex and dynamic phenomenon that is difficult to predict, involving multiple interconnected factors such as temperature changes, rising sea levels, and extreme weather events. These factors interact in complex ways, and their timing and effects are difficult to predict with certainty. As a result, a high degree of uncertainty is associated with climate change risk management, making it challenging to plan and prepare for potential risks.

Climate change risk management requires a long-term perspective, as its effects may not be felt for decades. This can make it difficult for companies to prioritize climate change risks over more immediate concerns. Furthermore, global climate change risks can have cascading effects across multiple sectors and geographic regions, making it difficult to isolate and systematically manage individual risks. These challenges are compounded by access to reliable data and information, which may be limited or incomplete in some regions or sectors.

Climate change risk management is influenced by political and social factors such as competing priorities, multiple and sometimes conflicting stakeholder interests, and institutional barriers. These factors can complicate efforts to address climate change risks in a coordinated and effective manner. Addressing these challenges requires a coordinated and collaborative effort across sectors, and a commitment to ongoing monitoring and adaptation in the face of changing climate conditions. Companies able to manage climate change risks effectively will be better positioned to achieve long-term sustainability and resilience in the face of a rapidly changing climate.

Managing climate change risk in the corporate context involves adopting strategic approaches that consider available resources and competing priorities. This may involve conducting thorough risk assessments to identify the most significant climate change risks facing the company and then prioritizing risk management activities based on their impact and feasibility. Companies may also need to seek alternative sources of funding and support for climate change risk management activities, such as leveraging partnerships with private sector actors or seeking grants and other forms of external funding.

Collaborating with researchers, community organizations, and private sector actors is crucial for effective climate change risk management. Sharing information and expertise can help companies identify emerging risks and develop more effective risk management strategies. Engaging in partnerships can also provide access to additional resources and support for climate change risk management activities.

Climate change risk management can often be politically charged, with differing opinions and priorities among stakeholders. This can create challenges for companies in developing and implementing effective risk management strategies. Companies may need to communicate openly and transparently with stakeholders to build support for climate change risk management activities. Educating stakeholders about the potential risks and impacts of climate change and working to identify common ground and shared goals can guide risk management efforts.

Climate change risk management is a critical component of ESG accounting, as it enables companies to identify, assess, and manage the risks associated with climate change. MCS play a crucial role in facilitating effective climate change risk management by providing frameworks for risk identification, assessment, monitoring, and reporting. Despite the significant challenges posed by climate change, including uncertainty, political and social factors, and the need for specialized knowledge, companies can enhance their ability to manage these risks through strategic approaches, collaboration, and capacity building. By integrating climate change risk management into their ESG accounting practices, companies can achieve greater resilience and sustainability, contributing to long-term value creation and the well-being of stakeholders. Future research should continue to explore the role of MCS in climate change risk management and develop innovative strategies to address the complex and dynamic nature of climate change risks.

4. Research Propositions

4.1 ESG Accounting and Risk Management

Effective risk management is crucial for navigating the complexities of integrating ESG factors into corporate strategies. ESG-related risks, including regulatory changes, environmental impacts, and social issues, can have significant implications for corporate performance and sustainability. This section examines how companies can incorporate ESG considerations into their risk management frameworks.

4.1.1 Identifying ESG-Related Risks

The first step in integrating ESG into risk management is identifying the specific ESG-related risks that a company faces. These risks can be categorized into environmental, social, and governance risks. Environmental risks might include climate change, resource scarcity, and pollution. Social risks could involve labour practices, human rights, and community relations. Governance risks might encompass regulatory compliance, ethical conduct, and corporate governance practices.

4.1.2 Risk Management Strategies for ESG Integration

Once the ESG-related risks are identified, companies can implement various risk management strategies to mitigate these risks. Scenario analysis, stress testing, and risk mapping are effective tools for assessing the potential impacts of ESG risks. These tools enable companies to anticipate and prepare for different risk scenarios, enhancing their resilience to ESG-related disruptions.

4.1.3 Role of MCS in ESG Risk Management

MCS play a critical role in monitoring and managing ESG risks by providing a structured framework for tracking risk indicators, implementing risk mitigation measures, and ensuring compliance with ESG standards. By integrating MCS with ESG accounting, companies can create a comprehensive risk management system that addresses both financial and non-financial risks.

4.1.4 Case Studies of Effective ESG Risk Management

Several companies have successfully integrated ESG into their risk management frameworks. For instance, multinational corporations like Unilever and Nestlé have implemented comprehensive ESG risk management strategies that include robust environmental and social impact assessments. These companies have demonstrated that proactive ESG risk management can enhance corporate resilience and contribute to long-term value creation.

4.2 ESG Accounting and Performance Measurement

The integration of ESG factors into performance measurement systems is pivotal for providing a holistic view of corporate performance. Traditional financial metrics alone are insufficient to capture the multifaceted impacts of corporate activities on the environment and society. By incorporating ESG metrics, companies can better align their strategies with sustainable development goals and demonstrate their commitment to long-term value creation.

4.2.1 Role of Key Performance Indicators in ESG Measurement

Key performance indicators (KPIs) are essential tools for measuring and managing corporate performance. In the context of ESG accounting, KPIs provide quantitative measures that reflect a company's ESG performance. Effective ESG KPIs should be relevant, measurable, and aligned with the company's strategic objectives.

4.2.2 Examples of Effective ESG Metrics

Leading companies have adopted various ESG metrics to track their performance. For instance, environmental KPIs may include metrics such as greenhouse gas emissions, energy consumption, and water usage. Social KPIs might encompass metrics related to employee diversity, labour practices, and community engagement. Governance KPIs could include board diversity, executive compensation, and compliance with regulatory standards.

4.2.3 Challenges in Integrating ESG Metrics

Despite the benefits of integrating ESG metrics, companies face several challenges. Data availability and reliability are significant obstacles, as ESG data are often fragmented and inconsistent. Additionally, there is a lack of standardized methodologies for measuring ESG performance, which complicates benchmarking and comparison across companies and industries.

4.2.4 Solutions for Overcoming Integration Challenges

To overcome these challenges, companies should invest in robust data management systems and adopt standardized reporting frameworks such as GRI and SASB. Collaboration with industry peers and stakeholders can also facilitate the development of best practices and enhance the comparability of ESG data.

4.3 ESG in the Context of Global Crises

It is also important to delve into the role of ESG accounting in addressing global crises such as climate change, economic disruptions, and pandemics. These crises underscore the need for robust ESG accounting systems that can capture the long-term impacts of corporate activities on the environment and society. This section discusses how companies can use ESG accounting to enhance their crisis preparedness and response capabilities.

4.3.1 Climate Change and ESG Accounting

Climate change poses significant risks to businesses, including physical risks from extreme weather events and transitional risks from regulatory changes and market shifts. ESG accounting can help companies assess and manage these risks by providing a comprehensive framework for measuring and reporting their environmental impact.

4.3.2 Economic Disruptions and ESG Resilience

Economic disruptions, such as financial crises and trade wars, can have profound effects on corporate performance. ESG accounting enables companies to identify and manage the social and governance risks associated with economic disruptions, such as workforce management, supply chain resilience, and regulatory compliance.

4.3.3 Pandemics and ESG Preparedness

The COVID-19 pandemic has highlighted the importance of ESG preparedness in ensuring business continuity and resilience. Companies with strong ESG practices have been better able to navigate the challenges posed by the pandemic, including protecting employee health and safety, maintaining supply chain integrity, and supporting communities. ESG accounting provides a framework for tracking these efforts and demonstrating corporate responsibility.

4.3.4 Case Studies of ESG in Crisis Management

The importance of case studies of companies that have effectively used ESG accounting to manage global crises should not be forgotten. For instance, during the pandemic, companies like Johnson & Johnson and Microsoft leveraged their ESG frameworks to enhance their crisis response efforts. These companies prioritized employee welfare, community support, and sustainable operations, demonstrating the value of ESG accounting in crisis management.

4.4. Climate Change Risk Management Knowledge and Expertise

Climate change risk management requires specialized knowledge and expertise, including knowledge of climate science, risk assessment methodologies, and risk management strategies. In smaller or less well-funded companies, this may be aggravated by inadequate funding, training, and staffing capacity. These challenges are further complicated by the rapid and ongoing emergence of new research and practices in this field, making it difficult for companies to keep up with developments and incorporate them into risk management strategies.

4.4.1 Building Capacity and Collaboration

Staff training, expertise capacity building, and collaboration with external partners such as academic institutions, industry associations, and non-governmental organizations are essential for effective climate change risk management. Companies may need to invest in building their internal capacity to manage climate change risks and seek out opportunities for collaboration with external partners to enhance their risk management strategies.

4.4.2 Long-Term Strategic Prioritization

The long-term perspective required for managing climate change risks poses particular political and strategic prioritization challenges for companies that conventionally operate within shorter time horizons. Companies may be pressured to prioritize more immediate concerns, such as addressing a current public health crisis or responding to a natural disaster, leaving little funding for longer-term climate change risk management activities. To address these challenges, companies must adopt a strategic approach that balances immediate and long-term priorities, ensuring that climate change risk management remains a key focus.

5. Mapping Future Research Directions

The chapter concludes with a discussion of future research directions aimed at enhancing the integration of ESG accounting with performance measurement and risk management. Key areas for future research include the following.

5.1 Developing Standardized ESG Metrics

Research is needed to develop standardized ESG metrics that can be universally applied across industries. Standardization will enhance the comparability of ESG disclosures and provide a clearer picture of corporate sustainability. Future research should focus on creating universally accepted metrics for environmental impact, social responsibility, and governance practices.

5.2 Exploring the Role of Technology in ESG Accounting

Emerging technologies, such as big data analytics and blockchain, have the potential to revolutionize ESG accounting. Future research should explore how these technologies can be leveraged to enhance the accuracy, reliability, and transparency of ESG reporting. This includes investigating the use of artificial intelligence for predictive analytics and blockchain for secure and transparent data sharing.

5.3 Assessing the Impact of ESG Integration on Financial Performance

While there is growing evidence of the positive impact of ESG practices on financial performance, more research is needed to quantify this relationship. Future studies should examine how integrating ESG factors into corporate strategies can drive financial performance and create long-term value. This includes analysing the impact of ESG integration on stock prices, profitability, and risk mitigation.

5.4 Understanding the Role of Stakeholders in ESG Accounting

Stakeholder groups play a critical role in shaping corporate ESG practices. Future research should explore how stakeholder engagement can be enhanced to promote more effective ESG accounting. This includes investigating the influence of stakeholder pressure on corporate ESG disclosures and the role of shareholder activism in driving ESG improvements.

5.5 Integrating ESG Accounting with Corporate Governance

Corporate governance plays a crucial role in ensuring the effective integration of ESG factors into business strategies. Future research should examine how governance structures, such as board composition and executive compensation, influence ESG performance. This includes exploring the impact of diverse and independent boards on ESG decision-making and the role of performance-based incentives in promoting ESG goals.

5.6 Investigating the Long-Term Impacts of ESG Practices

Future research should focus on the long-term impacts of ESG practices on corporate performance and sustainability. This includes longitudinal studies that track the evolution of ESG practices and their effects over time. Such research can provide valuable insights into the sustainability and resilience of companies that prioritize ESG factors.

5.7 Enhancing ESG Reporting and Transparency

Transparency is a key component of effective ESG accounting. Future research should investigate ways to enhance the transparency and credibility of ESG disclosures. This includes exploring best practices for ESG reporting, such as third-party verification and integrated reporting, and assessing the impact of transparent reporting on stakeholder trust and corporate reputation.

5.8 ESG Accounting in Emerging Markets

Emerging markets present unique challenges and opportunities for ESG accounting. Future research should examine the adoption and implementation of ESG accounting practices in emerging markets, considering factors such as regulatory environments, cultural differences, and economic conditions. This includes exploring the role of ESG accounting in driving sustainable development in these markets.

5.9 Standardization of ESG Metrics for Climate Risk

Future research should focus on developing standardized ESG metrics specifically tailored to climate risk management. While general ESG metrics exist, there is a need for specific indicators that accurately capture the nuances of climate-related risks. Research can explore the creation of universally accepted climate risk metrics that can be integrated into existing ESG frameworks, enhancing comparability and reliability of climate-related disclosures across industries and regions.

5.10 Integration of Advanced Technologies in ESG Accounting

Exploring the role of advanced technologies such as big data analytics, artificial intelligence, and blockchain in enhancing ESG accounting for climate risk management presents a rich area for future research. Studies can investigate how these technologies can improve data accuracy, provide real-time monitoring, and facilitate transparent reporting of climate risks. Research could also focus on developing predictive models that use AI to forecast potential climate-related impacts on business operations and financial performance.

5.11 Impact of ESG Integration on Corporate Financial Performance

There is growing evidence suggesting that robust ESG practices, including climate risk management, positively impact financial performance. Future research should aim to quantify this relationship more precisely. Longitudinal studies that track companies over time can provide insights into how integrating climate risk management into ESG accounting affects profitability, stock performance, and overall financial health.

5.12 Role of Corporate Governance in Climate Risk Management

Investigating how different governance structures influence the effectiveness of climate risk management within ESG frameworks is a crucial area for future research. Studies could examine the role of board diversity, executive compensation tied to climate performance, and the presence of dedicated sustainability committees in enhancing corporate responses to climate risks. This research can help identify governance practices that support better climate risk management outcomes.

5.13 Stakeholder Engagement and Climate Risk Disclosure

Research should explore how companies can effectively engage stakeholders, including investors, regulators, consumers, and the public, in their climate risk management efforts. Studies could investigate the impact of stakeholder pressure on the quality and transparency of climate risk disclosures. Additionally, research can assess how enhanced stakeholder engagement can drive corporate action towards better climate risk management and sustainability practices.

5.14 Climate Risk Management in Emerging Markets

Emerging markets face unique challenges and opportunities in climate risk management. Future research should focus on understanding how companies in these regions are integrating climate risk into their ESG accounting practices. This includes exploring the regulatory landscape, cultural factors, and economic conditions that influence climate risk management in emerging markets. Comparative studies can provide insights into best practices and areas for improvement.

5.15 Long-Term Impacts of Climate Risk Management Practices

Longitudinal research is needed to understand the long-term impacts of effective climate risk management practices on corporate sustainability and resilience.

Studies can track companies that have implemented robust climate risk management strategies to evaluate their performance over extended periods. This research can provide valuable insights into the sustainability benefits and potential financial gains of proactive climate risk management.

5.16 Enhancing Climate Risk Reporting Frameworks

Current ESG reporting frameworks often lack detailed guidance on climate risk management. Future research should aim to enhance these frameworks by providing specific guidelines and best practices for reporting climate risks. This includes developing detailed disclosure requirements and methodologies for assessing and reporting on climate-related risks and opportunities.

5.17 Climate Risk Scenario Analysis and Stress Testing

Research can focus on developing and refining methods for climate risk scenario analysis and stress testing within ESG accounting. This involves creating robust models that simulate various climate scenarios and their potential impacts on business operations. Studies can also explore how companies can integrate these scenarios into their strategic planning and risk management processes.

5.18 Policy Implications and Regulatory Frameworks

Future research should examine the role of policy and regulatory frameworks in shaping corporate climate risk management practices. This includes analysing the effectiveness of existing regulations, identifying gaps, and proposing new policies that can enhance corporate transparency and accountability in climate risk management. Research can also explore the implications of different regulatory approaches on corporate behaviour and market dynamics.

6. Discussion

This chapter contributes to the development of theoretical frameworks that integrate ESG factors into performance measurement and risk management systems. By building on the foundational work of Adams and McNicholas (2007), who argued for the inclusion of sustainability metrics in performance measurement systems, this research advances the discourse by providing a comprehensive framework that aligns ESG metrics with traditional financial indicators. This alignment not only enhances the relevance of performance assessments but also promotes a holistic view of corporate success that incorporates sustainable practices (Eccles et al., 2014).

The chapter contributes to the theoretical refinement of risk management by incorporating ESG considerations into risk assessment frameworks. Building on the work of Khan et al. (2016), which highlighted the materiality of ESG factors, this research extends the understanding of how ESG risks, such as climate change and governance issues, can be systematically integrated into corporate risk management strategies. This contribution is crucial for developing more resilient corporate structures that can anticipate and mitigate ESG-related risks, thereby enhancing long-term sustainability and stability (Linnenluecke et al., 2012).

Another incremental contribution is the exploration of the intersection between ESG integration and corporate governance. Eccles and Youmans (2015) emphasized the importance of effective governance structures in enhancing accountability and transparency. This chapter expands on their work by proposing mechanisms such as linking executive compensation to ESG performance metrics and incorporating ESG considerations into board responsibilities. These theoretical insights contribute to a more nuanced understanding of how governance structures can be designed to promote sustainable business practices and long-term value creation (Lins et al., 2017).

This chapter also contributes to the literature on the standardization of ESG accounting practices. Hahn and Kühnen (2013) identified the lack of standardized metrics as a significant challenge in ESG reporting. By proposing specific guidelines and methodologies for ESG disclosures, this chapter addresses this gap and provides a foundation for developing harmonized reporting standards. This contribution is vital for enhancing the comparability and reliability of ESG data, which are essential for investors and other stakeholders to make informed decisions (GRI, 2020; SASB, 2018).

The chapter also explores the role of advanced technologies such as big data analytics and artificial intelligence in enhancing ESG accounting practices. Building on the insights from Deloitte (2020), this research investigated how these technologies can improve data accuracy, provide real-time monitoring, and facilitate transparent reporting. This contribution is particularly relevant in the context of dynamic ESG risks, where timely and accurate data are crucial for effective decision-making and risk management (Cheng et al., 2014).

The integration of ESG factors into performance measurement and risk management is a relatively nascent field within accounting research. This chapter provided a theoretical contribution by enhancing the understanding of how ESG factors can be systematically incorporated into traditional accounting frameworks. Adams and McNicholas (2007) highlighted the potential for ESG factors to drive behaviour change towards sustainable practices when integrated into performance measurement systems. By building on these foundations, this study provides a comprehensive framework that aligns ESG metrics with financial performance indicators, thus broadening the theoretical understanding of corporate performance evaluation beyond traditional financial metrics.

This chapter contributes to the theoretical development of risk management by integrating ESG factors into risk assessment frameworks. Khan et al. (2016) underscore the materiality of ESG factors and their impact on corporate financial performance. The theoretical framework proposed in this chapter extends this understanding by incorporating ESG risks such as climate change, labour practices, and corporate governance into risk management processes. This integration helps in formulating more robust risk management strategies that are focused not only on financial risks but also on ESG-related vulnerabilities, thus providing a more holistic approach to corporate risk management.

Another theoretical contribution is the exploration of the impact of ESG integration on corporate governance structures. Eccles and Youmans (2015) emphasized the role of effective governance structures in enhancing accountability and transparency. This chapter extends their work by proposing that integrating ESG considerations into corporate governance can enhance stakeholder trust and corporate transparency. By linking executive compensation to ESG performance metrics, as suggested by Edmans et al. (2009), this chapter provides a theoretical basis for aligning management incentives with long-term sustainable value creation.

One significant policy contribution is the development of a framework for regulatory standardization of ESG disclosures. The lack of standardized metrics and methodologies for measuring and reporting ESG performance is a major challenge identified in the literature (Hahn & Kühnen, 2013). The chapter addresses this gap by proposing standardized guidelines for ESG reporting, which can be adopted by regulatory bodies to enhance the comparability and reliability of ESG data across companies and industries. This contribution is critical for policymakers aiming to develop coherent regulatory frameworks that promote consistent and transparent ESG reporting practices.

This chapter also provides policy contributions by offering detailed guidelines for climate-related financial disclosures. The recommendations of the TCFD (2017) highlight the need for transparent and comparable climate-related reporting. By building on these guidelines, specific disclosure requirements and methodologies for assessing and reporting climate risks are proposed. These policy recommendations are essential for regulators seeking to mandate climate-related disclosures and ensure that companies adequately disclose their exposure to climate risks and their strategies for managing these risks.

From a practical standpoint, this chapter offers actionable strategies for companies to implement ESG integration into their performance measurement and risk management systems. By adopting sustainability balanced scorecards and integrated reporting tools, companies can align their financial and non-financial performance indicators, as suggested by Gond et al. (2012). These practical guidelines provide a roadmap for managers to incorporate ESG factors into their strategic decision-making processes, thereby enhancing their ability to achieve long-term sustainability goals.

Practical tools for ESG risk assessment and management are also highlighted. Scenario analysis, stress testing, and risk mapping are identified as effective tools for assessing the potential impacts of ESG risks (Khan et al., 2016). By providing detailed methodologies for using these tools, this chapter equips managers with the necessary resources to anticipate and prepare for ESG-related disruptions. These practical contributions are vital for enhancing corporate resilience and ensuring that companies can navigate the complexities of integrating ESG factors into their risk management frameworks.

7. Conclusion

This chapter underscores the importance of integrating ESG accounting with performance measurement and risk management. By doing so, companies can better navigate the complexities of the contemporary business environment and align their strategies with sustainable development goals. The proposed future research directions aim to advance the field of ESG accounting and provide actionable insights for companies seeking to enhance their ESG practices. Through robust ESG accounting systems, companies can achieve greater transparency, accountability, and long-term sustainability.

The integration of ESG accounting into corporate strategies is not just a regulatory requirement but a strategic imperative for ensuring long-term corporate resilience and sustainability. As global challenges such as climate change, economic disruptions, and pandemics become more prevalent, the need for comprehensive and effective ESG accounting systems will only grow. By investing in robust ESG accounting practices and continuous improvement, companies can not only enhance their performance and risk management but also contribute to a more sustainable and equitable global economy.

References

Adams, C. A., & McNicholas, P. (2007). Making a difference: Sustainability reporting, accountability and organisational change. *Accounting, Auditing & Accountability Journal*, *20*(3), 382–402.

Bebbington, J., & Larrinaga, C. (2014). Accounting and sustainable development: An exploration. *Accounting, Organizations and Society*, *39*(6), 395–413.

Bebbington, J., Unerman, J., & O'Dwyer, B. (2014). *Sustainability accounting and accountability*. Routledge.

Cheng, B., Ioannou, I., & Serafeim, G. (2014). Corporate social responsibility and access to finance. *Strategic Management Journal*, *35*(1), 1–23.

Clark, G. L., Feiner, A., & Viehs, M. (2015). *From the stockholder to the stakeholder: How sustainability can drive financial outperformance*. University of Oxford and Arabesque Partners.

Deloitte. (2020). *Technology and ESG: Enhancing decision-making and disclosure*. https://www2.deloitte.com/global/en/pages/risk/articles/technology-and-esg.html

Eccles, R. G., Ioannou, I., & Serafeim, G. (2014). The impact of corporate sustainability on organizational processes and performance. *Management Science*, *60*(11), 2835–2857.

Eccles, R. G., & Youmans, T. (2015). Materiality in corporate governance: The statement of significant audiences and materiality. *Journal of Applied Corporate Finance*, *27*(2), 39–46.

Edmans, A., Gabaix, X., & Landier, A. (2009). A multiplicastive model of optimal CEO incentives in market equilibrium. *Review of Financial Studies*, *22*(12), 4881–4917.

Financial Stability Board (FSB). (2017). *Recommendations of the task force on climate-related financial disclosures*. www.fsb-tcfd.org/recommendations/

Flammer, C. (2015). Does corporate social responsibility lead to superior financial performance? A regression discontinuity approach. *Management Science*, *61*(11), 2549–2568.

Friede, G., Busch, T., & Bassen, A. (2015). ESG and financial performance: Aggregated evidence from more than 2000 empirical studies. *Journal of Sustainable Finance & Investment*, *5*(4), 210–233.

Global Reporting Initiative (GRI). (2020). *GRI standards*. www.globalreporting.org/standards

Gond, J. P., Grubnic, S., Herzig, C., & Moon, J. (2012). Configuring management control systems: Theorizing the integration of strategy, sustainability, and financial control. *Management Accounting Research*, *23*(3), 205–223.

Hahn, R., & Kühnen, M. (2013). Determinants of sustainability reporting: A review of results, trends, theory, and opportunities in an expanding field of research. *Journal of Cleaner Production*, *59*, 5–21.

Intergovernmental Panel on Climate Change (IPCC). (2018). *Global warming of 1.5°C*. www.ipcc.ch/sr15

International Financial Reporting Standards (IFRS). (2020). *Consultation paper on sustainability reporting*. www.ifrs.org/projects/work-plan/sustainability-reporting

Khan, M., Serafeim, G., & Yoon, A. (2016). Corporate sustainability: First evidence on materiality. *The Accounting Review*, *91*(6), 1697–1724.

KPMG. (2020). *The time has come: The KPMG survey of sustainability reporting*. https://home.kpmg/xx/en/home/insights/2020/11/the-time-has-come-survey-of-sustainability-reporting.html

Linnenluecke, M. K., Griffiths, A., & Winn, M. I. (2012). Extreme weather events and the critical importance of anticipatory adaptation and organizational resilience in responding to impacts. *Business Strategy and the Environment*, *21*(1), 17–32.

Lins, K. V., Servaes, H., & Tamayo, A. (2017). Social capital, trust, and firm performance: The value of corporate social responsibility during the financial crisis. *The Journal of Finance*, *72*(4), 1785–1824.

Organisation for Economic Co-operation and Development (OECD). (2019). *Business and finance outlook 2019: Strengthening trust in business*. www.oecd.org/finance/business-and-finance-outlook

Sustainability Accounting Standards Board (SASB). (2018). *SASB standards*. www.sasb.org/standards

TaskForce on Climate-related Financial Disclosures (TCFD). (2017). *Recommendations of the taskforce on climate-related financial disclosures*. www.fsb-tcfd.org/recommendations

United Nations Principles for Responsible Investment (UNPRI). (2018). *Fiduciary duty in the 21st century: Final report*. www.unpri.org/fiduciary-duty-in-the-21st-century

Index

Note: Page numbers in **bold** indicate tables in the text

For Product Safety Concerns and Information please contact our EU representative GPSR@taylorandfrancis.com
Taylor & Francis Verlag GmbH, Kaufingerstraße 24, 80331 München, Germany

www.ingramcontent.com/pod-product-compliance
Ingram Content Group UK Ltd.
Pitfield, Milton Keynes, MK11 3LW, UK
UKHW020156200926
475702UK00016B/2729
9781032786766